JOHN HENRY NEWMAN

GARLAND REFERENCE LIBRARY
OF SOCIAL SCIENCE
(VOL. 239)

JOHN HENRY NEWMAN
An Annotated Bibliography of His Tract and Pamphlet Collection

James David Earnest
Gerard Tracey

GARLAND PUBLISHING, INC. • NEW YORK & LONDON
1984

Library of Congress Cataloging in Publication Data
Earnest, James David, 1947—
John Henry Newman : an annotated bibliography of his
tract and pamphlet collection.

(Garland reference library of social science ;
vol. 239)
Includes index.
1. Theology—Bibliography—Catalogs. 2. Newman,
John Henry, 1801–1890—Library—Catalogs. 3. Oratory
of St. Philip Neri (Birmingham, West Midlands, England)
—Catalogs. I. Tracey, Gerard, 1954—   . II. Title.
III. Series: Garland reference library of social science ;
v. 239.
Z7755.E27 1984 [BR118]   016.2   84-48069
ISBN 0-8240-8958-8 (alk. paper)

Printed on acid-free, 250-year-life paper
Manufactured in the United States of America

IN MEMORY OF
FATHER CHARLES STEPHEN DESSAIN
OF THE BIRMINGHAM ORATORY

CONTENTS

INTRODUCTION

Besides being a prolific writer, John Henry Newman was a persistent collector of books. Throughout his long life he continued to collect books, and the final result, at the Birmingham Oratory, was a fine library of about 17,500 items. Among these are many rare books of great bibliographical interest. But for pure historical interest nothing in the library rivals the small corner containing Newman's extensive tract and pamphlet collection. Like the rest of the library, the tracts were amassed throughout the course of Newman's life, but unlike the working folios of the theological scholar or the valuable incunabula presented as tokens of esteem to the aged Cardinal, the tracts come straight from Newman's battles as a controversialist and party leader. They are the sermons and speeches, broadsides and critiques of friends and enemies in the Oxford Movement and the various controversies of Newman's Catholic years. Newman's collection is also important because of the occasional annotations to be found in various items. The annotations frequently reveal his immediate critical responses to various doctrinal, religious, or political issues.

It may be helpful to look at the form in which the collection was built up before pointing out some of the particularly interesting types of material to be found in it. The collection consists of seven differently designated sets of bound volumes and an additional group of unbound items. Of greatest interest is the seventy-volume set which Newman labeled "Tracts" and which he collected during his years in the Church of England. The items in the first volume were bought by Newman while an undergraduate; the contents of the majority of the volumes come from the years of the Oxford Movement; and among the final volumes there are some items dating from his early Catholic years, suggesting that he had a large batch that was not bound up until the library reached its final home at Edgbaston in 1852–53.

Contemporary with this set are thirty duodecimo volumes designated "Sermons and Tracts." They mostly consist of sermons
and liturgical or catechetical works, but there is a fair sprinkling
of controversial material. Also contemporary with the Tractarian
Movement are fifteen volumes of "Treatises." These contain
fewer and lengthier items, usually concerned with specifically
theological problems, and include many of E. B. Pusey's charac-
teristically weighty tracts. The provenance of the seven volumes
entitled "Political Pamphlets" is a mystery. They contain a series
of extremely interesting pamphlets on topical questions, mostly
from the first fifteen years of the nineteenth century, and were
certainly not collected by Newman himself. They were probably
presented to him much later, though there is no indication of
who the donor was.

During the years 1853–65, twelve volumes were bound up
and labeled "Pamphlets." They contain works on a great variety
of subjects, including many on educational, social, and ecclesiastical questions. A further twenty-five volumes of "Collections"
contain items from controversies on religious questions and also
a good deal on political and social matters, mostly from the
1860s and 1870s. During 1869–71, Newman collected together
twelve volumes of pamphlets, labeled "Concilio Vaticano," concerning the First Vatican Council and the definition of papal
infallibility. Finally there is a collection of unbound pamphlets,
mostly from the decade of Newman's cardinalate, which is now
housed in box files in the separate Newman Research Library at
the Birmingham Oratory. The tracts from the Catholic period
have to be assessed carefully, as they contain some items collected
by Newman's fellow Oratorians. However, there are usually clear
indications as to their provenance, and, in any case, they were all
available to Newman.

For all practical purposes, the contents of Newman's collection of tracts and pamphlets have previously been available only
to scholars working at the Birmingham Oratory. Yet Newman
read many of these materials more fiercely than some better
known books, and the collection helps to throw light upon all the
varied controversies and issues that shaped Newman's life and
writings. Tracts were the immediate tool of controversy in Newman's day. Points that were later elaborated in polished treatises

or in courses of sermons were first hammered out in quickly printed pamphlets. There is no better example of how the medium was used for instant reply or defense than Newman's *Letter to Faussett* of 1838. Godfrey Faussett preached his anti-Tractarian sermon on *The Revival of Popery* on May 20, 1838, but delayed the publication of the sermon until just before the end of the university term so that there would be no time for a defense to be written, published, and circulated. Newman, however, found out the main points of the sermon from someone who had been present, started writing a reply on June 18, worked at it all through the night of June 21, and took it to the printer on the following morning. The pamphlet was published on June 25, only one or two days after Faussett's own.

As well as throwing light on controversies, the collection contains works that had a great influence upon Newman's opinions, particularly in the earlier volumes. For instance, among the very first items to be bound up was Newman's copy of Edward Hawkins's *Dissertation upon Unauthoritative Tradition,* which was so important in pointing him towards one of the central doctrinal positions of the Oxford Movement, as Newman relates in the first pages of the *Apologia pro Vita Sua.* Also important, though not so widely recognized, was Hawkins's *Systematic Preaching Recommended* of 1825, the principles of which Newman took up in his first years as a preacher. The strength of Newman's Evangelicalism in 1822 can be seen by examining his copies of the controversy between H. H. Norris and James Scholefield over the Bible Society: the pencil marks show the young Newman's sympathies were not with the High Churchman. The early volumes also contain some pieces of lighter reading, such as the first edition of Byron's *Manfred,* which Newman bought while at Trinity College.

However, the chief interest of the collection undoubtedly lies in the Tractarian material. There are some uncommon documents from the beginning of the Movement, such as the two different sets of *Remarks on Suggestions for an Association of Friends of the Church* from the end of 1833, a pamphlet that was printed but never published. As the Movement progressed, Newman kept extensive and comprehensive sets of pamphlets concerning the main controversies in which the Tractarians were involved, such as those over the admission of dissenters to Oxford and over the appointment of R. D. Hampden as Regius Professor of Divinity. There are eight volumes of pamphlets concerning *Tract 90,* for and against, and the various Bishops' *Charges* condemning it. Other disputes that aroused considerable attention were those over Pusey's 1843 sermon on the Eucharist, W. G. Ward's degradation in 1845, and the proposed censure of *Tract 90* in the same year.

Here and there it is possible to gain a clearer insight into the particular positions and views which the Tractarians were most determined to oppose. "Theological liberalism" was a great enemy as far as Newman was concerned. One of the first statements from the emerging liberal school was Richard Whately's pamphlet on the *Omission of Creeds* of 1831. Just before the outbreak of the Oxford Movement, while preaching at the English Ambassador's Chapel in Naples, during his Mediterranean tour, Newman warned: "Most necessary is this rule of shunning all who speak against the doctrine of Christ. . . ." And he took this pamphlet as a particular example. Liberalism was of course also at the heart of the Hampden controversy. Newman's famous pamphlet of *Elucidations* defined the points that he found deficient in Hampden's teaching. Invaluable further light can be gained, however, from the copious annotations in Newman's copy of Hampden's separately printed pamphlet introduction to the second edition of his Bampton Lectures. The notes were undoubtedly made in preparation for the review article that Newman was intending to write for the *British Critic* of October 1837 but which was given up after the editors' mistaken insertion of one on the same work in the preceding issue. As the Oxford Movement progressed, the Liberals turned their controversial guns on the Tractarians in works such as Baden Powell's *Tradition Unveiled.*

Another important group of critics of the Movement were the Evangelicals, and Newman collected copies of many of their animadversions. At first they had been cautiously sympathetic, but events drew them into open opposition. Keble's sermon on *Primitive Tradition* of 1836 was one of the first Tractarian works to receive strong condemnation from them. The notes in Newman's copy of William Wilson's reply to Keble suggest that he took their criticism seriously at first, though he soon took them more lightly. The publication of Froude's *Remains* and of Isaac Williams' *Tract 80* on reserve brought more vehement criticism, and from then on they remained in fierce opposition to the Tractarians. These controversies are amply represented in the collection.

The Tractarians were not just concerned with theological issues. State interference in ecclesiastical affairs had been the spark which set off the Movement in 1833, and the Tractarians continued to take a leading part in the debates over the various attempts at Church reform which the government undertook in the 1830s. The recommendations of the Ecclesiastical Commission were one of the chief points of attention, particularly concerning the reform of Church rates, cathedral chapters, and the distribution of dioceses. All these questions prompted a crowd of pamphlets protesting against arbitrary government handling of Church matters. On a more positive note, the Tractarians, like the Evangelicals, were concerned with the urgent need for the provision of more churches and more clergymen to cope with the religious needs of an expanding population. They were keen supporters of bodies such as the Church Building Society and the Additional Curates Fund. Quite a number of pamphlets are devoted to such Church needs as well as to the needs of the colonial Church.

The Oxford Movement gives a unity to the volumes of pamphlets from Newman's Anglican years, but there is no similar theme to the material from the Catholic period, and the items cover a far more wide-ranging and miscellaneous number of topics. The obvious issues affecting the Catholic Church, such as the reestablishment of the hierarchy (and the consequent no-popery scare) and the temporal power of the Pope, are well represented. There are likewise many pamphlets concerning educational matters—not surprising, considering Newman's involvement. The divergence between ultramontane and more liberal theological views in the Church constantly reappears, especially concerning the question of papal infallibility.

In the series of "Pamphlets" there is a great deal of material on educational questions, chiefly collected at the time of Newman's Dublin University scheme. The constitution of the Catholic University of Louvain was taken as a model for Dublin, and

Newman carefully collected copies of Louvain statutes, syllabuses, and examination papers. Together with these he obtained the discourses and various addresses of Mgr. de Ram, the famous Rector who was doing so much to re-establish and develop Louvain. Newman acquired various other works on educational ideas, such as J.-J. Gaume's *Le Ver Rongeur,* which advocated the exclusion of secular classics from education, a policy Newman was critical of, as his annotations show. The contemporary debate about the reform of the University of Oxford is represented, as well as the controversies over college and university reform from the time of Newman's residence. Likewise dating from Newman's Oxford years are pamphlets dealing with the question of national education and the role of the Church of England in it. In the earlier volumes are various specimens of liberal educational thinking, such as Brougham's Glasgow *Discourse* of 1825 and the *Discourse of the Objects, Advantages, and Pleasures of Science,* which Newman vigorously opposed, notably in the first of his *Oxford University Sermons* in 1826, in "The Tamworth Reading Room," and later in Discourse II of *The Idea of a University.*

Examples of the tension between liberal Catholics and those of the dominant ultramontane party become more frequent in Newman's series of "Collections." The opposition between the two parties can be seen hardening in the various disputes over the *Rambler,* starting with that over Döllinger's "Paternity of Jansenism" article of 1858. The infallibility of the Pope was the main issue, and three years before the definition there was an important exchange of pamphlets on the subject between the ultramontane W. G. Ward and Newman's fellow Oratorian Ignatius Ryder. The copies preserved in the collection are all the more valuable because of the annotation and scoring made by both Newman and Ryder.

The series devoted to the Vatican Council, which Newman put together, contains uncommon works by leading council figures such as the inopportunists Dupanloup and Kenrick and the Jesuit theologian Kleutgen. Four years later another debate arose over the issue, started by Gladstone's pamphlet on *The Vatican Decrees* and culminating in Newman's own *Letter to the Duke of Norfolk.* Again it is most valuable to have Newman's own copies at hand, with his on-the-spot observations in the margin and the little notes he made in Gladstone's *Vaticanism* to use in writing his own *Postscript.*

The aim of this bibliography is to make the collection known and available to students of Newman everywhere. Annotation has been held to a minimum, but all significant features of each item are identified. Informational notes, whether on the background of items or on their place in Newman's writings, have been provided on the assumption that users of this bibliography will have a reasonable knowledge of Newman's career and of the nineteenth century in general. The diversity of the collection, however, testifies to the complexity of the age, and the annotation will seem more or less complete according to one's familiarity with the various issues represented.

In the bibliographical entries, all titles are cited in full. Authors' names are supplied in full whenever possible. Thus, names are not necessarily as they appear on the title page of each item. There are naturally many entries in which initials of given names have been expanded. Likewise, the names of clergy have been silently supplied when the title page has given only the ecclesiastical title. Whenever possible, the authors of anonymous and pseudonymous works have been identified. For anonymous works, the author's name appears in square brackets. For pseudonymous works, the bracketed name is followed by the pseudonym. For works published under only the author's initials, the remainder of the name is supplied in brackets. In cases where identification of authors has been only tentative, the name of the probable author is mentioned in the annotation; and these items have been included in the lists of "Works by Unidentified Authors" that follow each year's listing of works by known authors.

In some cases, Newman himself has identified on the title pages the authors of anonymous works. The authors of certain other anonymous items have indicated their authorship in inscriptions. The authorship of other anonymous items has been established using the *Dictionary of National Biography,* the *Dictionary of American Biography,* the *British Museum General Catalogue of Printed Books,* the *National Union Catalogue,* and the *Catalogue général des livres imprimés de la Bibliothèque Nationale.* Likewise useful were the *Bibliography of the English Province of the Society of*

Jesus, 1773–1953 by Edmund F. Sutcliffe, S. J. (Roehampton and London: Manresa Press, 1957) and *Modern English Biography* by Frederic Boase (Truro: Netherton and Worth, 1892–1921).

Titles have been cited in full. The date of publication has determined the location of each item in the bibliography. When the date of publication has been indicated elsewhere than on the title page, it appears in square brackets. If the date of publication has been supplied through external information, the entry will indicate that no date is given, but the item will be included among the other works from that year. If the dating of an item is tentative, the entry will contain the "D?" symbol.

Each item's location in Newman's tract and pamphlet collection at the Birmingham Oratory is given according to volume and number within the various sets of tracts and pamphlets. The labels of the bound sets (and their abbreviations in this bibliography) are as follows: "Tracts" (T), "Sermons and Tracts" (ST), "Treatises" (Tre), "Political Pamphlets" (PP), "Pamphlets" (P), "Collections" (C), and "Concilio Vaticano" (CV). The unbound pamphlets Newman owned, which are now in the Newman Research Library, are abbreviated "NL."

Scholars wishing further information on Newman's tract and pamphlet collection should address inquiries to The Librarian and Archivist, Birmingham Oratory, Edgbaston, Birmingham B16 8UE, England.

This bibliography is in part a tribute to the late Father Charles Stephen Dessain, Librarian and Archivist of the Birmingham Oratory, who knew the contents of Newman's tract and pamphlet collection so well that he needed no bibliography. It was Father Dessain who first encouraged this undertaking. The authors are grateful for many reasons to countless people in Birmingham, in particular Philip Higgins, Mr. and Mrs. Frank Higgins, Mr. and Mrs. David Tracey, and of course the Fathers of the Birmingham Oratory. We are likewise grateful to Mr. and Mrs. Jim Scott and the members of the Oratory Parish Social Club, and to the amiable and efficient staff at the Plough and Harrow Hotel, for their support. Very special thanks are due to Angela Smith Franklin and Kenneth Franklin, and to their friends. The assiduous, conscientious research assistance of Desirée LaOrange was valuable beyond measure; and the careful work of Jamie Helton, who typed the bibliography, will be evident to its users. Grants for research and manuscript preparation have been provided by the Committee on Institutional Studies and Research of Murray State University, Murray, Kentucky.

SYMBOLS AND ABBREVIATIONS

Unless otherwise indicated, references are to volumes in the uniform edition of Newman's works.

D?   Date uncertain

I.   Inscribed

M.   Marginalia

M*.   Extensive marginalia

S.   Scoring

S*.   Extensive scoring

Apo.   *Apologia pro Vita Sua,* ed. Martin J. Svaglic (Oxford: Clarendon Press, 1967)

Ari.   *The Arians of the Fourth Century*

Blehl   Vincent Ferrer Blehl, *John Henry Newman: A Bibliographical Catalogue of His Writings* (Charlottesville: University Press of Virginia, 1978)

Call.   *Callista: A Tale of the Third Century*

Dev.   *An Essay on the Development of Christian Doctrine*

G.A.   *An Essay in Aid of a Grammar of Assent*

Idea   *The Idea of a University,* ed. Ian T. Ker (Oxford: Clarendon Press, 1976)

Jfc.   *Lectures on the Doctrine of Justification*

K.C.   *Correspondence of John Henry Newman with John Keble and Others, 1839–45* (London: Longmans, Green, 1917)

L.D.   *The Letters and Diaries of John Henry Newman,* ed. C. S. Dessain et al., London and Oxford, 1961– (in progress)

L.G.   *Loss and Gain: The Story of a Convert*

Moz.   *Letters and Correspondence of John Henry Newman,* ed. Anne Mozley, 2 vols., 2nd ed. (London: Longmans, 1891)

U.S.   *Fifteen Sermons Preached before the University of Oxford*

JOHN HENRY NEWMAN

1815 AND BEFORE

1. Baillie, Joanna. The family legend: a tragedy; with prologue by Walter Scott. Edinburgh: James Ballantyne, 1810. PP6.10.

2. [Barnes, Thomas.] Parliamentary portraits; or sketches of the public character of some of the most distinguished speakers of the House of Commons. London: Baldwin, Cradock, and Joy, 1815. PP1.2.

3. [Bentley, Thomas Richard.] A Near Observer, pseud. The Battle of Waterloo, containing the series of accounts published by authority, British and foreign, with circumstantial details, previous, during, and after the battle, from a variety of authentic and original sources, with relative official documents, forming an historical record of the operations in the campaign of the Netherlands; to which is added an alphabetical list of the officers killed and wounded, from 15th to 26th June, 1815, and the total loss of each regiment, with an enumeration of the Waterloo honours and privileges, conferred upon the men and officers, and lists of regiments, &c. entitled thereto; illustrated by a panoramic sketch of the field of battle, and a plan of the position and movements, with those of Prussians, traced. 5th ed. London: J. Booth, 1815. PP5.6.

4. Birch, John Francis. Memoir on the national defence. 2nd ed. London: J. Stockdale, 1808. PP4.3.

5. [Brougham, Henry Peter.] An inquiry into the state of the nation, at the commencement of the present administration. 6th ed. London: Longman, Hurst, Rees and Orme, 1806. PP4.7. Scoring, not N's.

6. Burgess, Thomas, ed. Excerpta ex Chrysostomi Libro de sacerdotio: graece et latine. London: I. et I. B. Nichols, 1815. ST2.2.

7. [Copleston, Edward.] A reply to the calumnies of the Edinburgh Review against Oxford, containing an account of studies pursued in that university. Oxford: J. Cooke, 1810. PP7.2.

8. [Copleston, Edward.] A second reply to the Edinburgh Review, by the author of A Reply to the Calumnies of That Review against Oxford. Oxford: J. Cooke, 1810. PP7.3. Marginalia, not N's.

9. [Copleston, Edward.] A third reply to the Edinburgh Review, by the author of A Reply to the Calumnies of That Review against Oxford. Oxford: J. Cooke, 1811. PP7.4.

10. Douglas, Thomas, Earl of Selkirk. A letter addressed to John Cartwright, Esq., chairman of the Committee at the Crown and Anchor; on the subject of parliamentary reform. London:

1

Constable, Hunter, Park and Hunter, 1809. PP3.8. Scoring and marginalia, not N's.

11.   Drummond, Henry Home. Observations, suggested by the strictures of the Edinburgh Review upon Oxford; and by the two replies containing some account of the late changes in that university. Edinburgh: James Ballantyne, 1810. PP7.5.

12.   [Dundonald, Thomas Cochrane.] The trial of Lord Cochrane and others, for a conspiracy; tried in the Court of King's Bench, Guildhall, London; before Lord Ellenborough; June 8th and 9th, 1814; with the pleadings of counsel on both sides; Lord Cochrane's motion for a new trial; Lord Ellenborough's reply; and the sentence of the court; embellished with a portrait. London: Coxhead, n.d. PP6.11.

13.   Erskine, Thomas. A letter by Thomas Lord Erskine, to "an elector of Westminster," author of "A Reply to the Short Defence of the Whigs." London: James Ridgway, 1814. PP2.5.

14.   Eugène de Savoie, Prince. Mémoires du Prince Eugène de Savoie; écrits par lui-même; seconde réimpression conforme à l'édition de Weymar (1809). London: L. Deconchy, 1811. PP5.7.

15.   Eustace, John Chetwode. Answer to the charge delivered by the Lord Bishop of Lincoln to the clergy of that diocese, at the triennial visitation in the year 1812. London: J. Mawman, 1813. NL79.29.

16.   [Evans, Robert Harding.] Publicola, pseud. Six letters of Publicola, on the liberty of the subject, and the privileges of the House of Commons; originally published in the Times; and now collected and illustrated with notes and additional proofs, by the author. London: T. Collins, 1810. PP4.1.

17.   Fraser, Robert. A letter to the Right Hon. Charles Abbot, Speaker of the House of Commons, containing an enquiry into the most effectual means of the improvement of the coasts and western isles of Scotland, and the extension of the fisheries; with a letter from Dr. Anderson to the author, on the same subject. London: W. Bulmer and Co., 1803. PP3.2. Scoring, not N's.

18.   Giraud, P. F. F. J. Campagne de Paris en 1814, précédée d'un coup-d'œil sur celle de 1813, ou précis historique et impartial des événemens [sic], depuis l'invasion de la France, par les armées étrangères, jusques à la capitulation de Paris, la déchéance et l'abdication de Buonaparte, inclusivement; suivie de l'exposé de principaux traits de son caractère, et des causes de son élévation; rédigée sur des documens [sic] authentiques, et d'après les renseignemens [sic] recueillis de plusieurs témoins; accompagnée d'une carte pour l'intelligence des mouvemens [sic] des armées, dressée et gravée avec soin. 3rd ed. Paris: A. Eymery, 1814. PP5.4.

19.   [Glover, Richard.] Memoirs of a celebrated literary and political character, from the resignation of Sir Robert Walpole, in 1742, to the establishment of Lord Chathams' second administration, in 1757; containing strictures on some of the most distinguished men of that time. London: T. Bensley, 1813.

PP2.2.

20. [Gregory, James.] Lucubrations on the epigram. Edinburgh: James Ballantyne, 1808. PP3.7. Title-page is headed "Dr. Gregory."

21. Grey, Charles, Earl. Speech of Charles, Earl Grey, on the state of the nation; in the House of Lords, on Friday, June 14th, 1810, taken in shorthand by Mr. Power. 2nd ed. London: James Ridgway, 1810. PP6.6. Marginalia, not N's.

22. [Hawker, Peter.] Journal of a regimental officer during the recent campaign in Portugal and Spain under Lord Viscount Wellington, with a correct plan of the Battle of Talavera. London: J. Johnson, 1810. PP5.5.

23. [Huskisson, William.] Orders in council; or, an examination of the justice, legality, and policy of the new system of commercial regulation, with an appendix of state papers, statutes, and authorities. 2nd ed. London: Longman, Hurst, Rees, and Orme, 1808. PP4.4. Scoring and marginalia, not N's.

24. Huskisson, William. The question concerning the depreciation of our currency stated and examined. 2nd ed. London: John Murray, 1810. PP6.3.

25. Leckie, Gould Francis. An historical survey of the foreign affairs of Great Britain, with a view to explain the causes of the disasters of the late and present wars. London: J. Bell, 1808. PP3.4. Scoring and marginalia, not N's.

26. Leckie, Gould Francis. State of the foreign affairs of Great Britain, for the year 1809. London: C. Chapple, 1809. PP3.6.

27. Malthus, Thomas Robert. The grounds of an opinion on the policy of restricting the importation of foreign corn; intended as an appendix to "Observations on the Corn Laws." London: John Murray, 1815. PP7.9.

28. Malthus, Thomas Robert. An inquiry into the nature and progress of rent, and the principles by which it is regulated. London: John Murray, 1815. PP7.10.

29. [Martin, Samuel.] Britannicus, pseud. Present state of the British Constitution, historically illustrated. London: Longman, Hurst, Rees, and Orme, 1807. PP3.1.

30. The Monthly Register, December, 1807. PP6.2. The conclusion of an article on slavery.

31. Peel, Robert, Daniel O'Connell, Charles Saxton, and George Lidwill. A genuine collection of all the original documents and correspondence which have appeared in the public papers, respecting the affair between the Right Honourable Robert Peel, and Daniel O'Connell, Esq: and between Sir Charles Saxton, Bart. and George Lidwill, Esq. Dublin: Bernard Dowling, 1815. PP6.8.

32. The Political Review, 2, No. 2 (Dec. 1807). PP6.1.

33. Priestley, Joseph. The present state of Europe compared with antient prophecies; a sermon, preached at the Gravel Pit meeting in Hackney, Feb. 28, 1794, being the day appointed for

a general fast; with a preface, containing the reasons for the author's leaving England. 4th ed. London: J. Johnson, 1794. PP7.1.

34. Ricardo, David. The high price of bullion, a proof of the depreciation of bank notes. 2nd ed. London: John Murray, 1810. PP6.4.

35. Ricardo, David. Reply to Mr. Bosanquet's practical observations on the report of the Bullion Committee. London: John Murray, 1811. PP6.5.

36. Romilly, Samuel. Observations on the criminal law of England, as it relates to capital punishments, and on the mode in which it is administered. London: J. M'Creery, 1810. PP3.3.

37. Rose, George. The speech of the Right Hon. George Rose, in the House of Commons, on the 5th of May 1814, on the subject of the Corn Laws. London: T. Cadell and W. Davies, 1814. PP2.1.

38. [Sabatier, Jean Joseph.] Observations sur les dépenses et les recettes à venir de la France et sur les finances. N.l., n.p., n.d. PP5.1. Advertisement for 39.

39. Sabatier, Jean Joseph. Observations sur les dépenses et les recettes à venir de la France, et sur les finances. Paris: Bacot, n.d. PP5.2.

40. Scott, Thomas. Essays on the most important subjects in religion. 7th ed. London: L. B. Seeley, 1814. ST3.2. M*. Marginalia with biblical and patristic references.

41. Vince, Samuel. The credibility of the Scripture miracles vindicated, in answer to Mr. Hume; in two discourses preached before the University of Cambridge; second edition, corrected; to which are added notes and remarks upon Mr. Hume's principles and reasoning. Cambridge: R. Watts, 1809. T3.1. M. S. Vince was a mathematician and astronomer. See L.D., I, 249.

42. [Wilkins, M. J.] Scaevola, pseud. Letters of Scaevola, on the dismissal of His Majesty's late ministers; part I. 2nd ed. London: J. Ridgway, 1807. PP4.5.

43. [Wilkins, M. J.] Scaevola, pseud. Letters of Scaevola, on the dismissal of His Majesty's late ministers; part II. London: J. Ridgway, 1807. PP4.6.

44. Windham, William. Speech of the Rt. Hon. William Windham, in the House of Commons, May 26th, 1809, on Mr. Curwen's Bill, "for better securing the independence and purity of Parliament, by preventing the procuring or obtaining of seats by corrupt practices." London: J. Budd, 1810. PP6.7.

WORKS BY UNIDENTIFIED AUTHORS

45. Anon. Historical sketches of politics and public men, for the year 1812. London: Longman, Hurst, Rees, Orme, and Brown, 1813. PP1.4.

46. Anon. An historical survey of the affairs of Great Britain; part II. N.l., n.p., n.d. PP3.5. D? Scoring, not N's.

47.   Anon. In philosophia, quae moralis dicitur, tractanda,
       quaenam sit praecipue Aristotelicae disciplinae virtus?
       Dissertatio latina Cancellarii Praemio dignata et in Theatro
       Oxoniensi habita, die Jun. VII, 1815. N.l., n.p., n.d.
       PP7.6.

48.   Anon. Remarks on the injustice and impolicy of our late
       attack upon Denmark. London: Mathews and Leigh, 1807. PP4.2.

49.   Anon. Statements and arguments relative to the exclusive pre-
       ference of D. as candidates for F., and to their vacating
       their D. upon the completion of the 24th year of their age.
       Bath: Meyler and Son, 1814. PP7.8.

50.   S., C. H., pseud. Essai sur le système militaire de Bonaparte,
       suivi d'une courte notice sur la Révolution Française, et le
       couronnement de Sa Majesté Corse; par C. H. S., officier-
       d'état-major moscovite. London: R. Juigné, 1810. PP5.3.

                                1816

51.   Prinsep, Charles Robert. A letter to the Earl of Liverpool,
       on the cause of the present distresses of the country, and
       the efficacy of reducing the standard of our silver currency
       towards their relief. London: Ridgway and Sons, 1816. PP1.1.

52.   Western, Charles Robert. The speech of Charles C. Western,
       Esq. M.P., on moving that the House should resolve itself into
       committee of the whole House to take into consideration the
       distressed state of the agriculture of the United Kingdom,
       March 7, 1816. London: Budd and Calkin, n.d. PP7.11.

WORKS BY UNIDENTIFIED AUTHORS

53.   Anon. Ireland not England: or, a letter to Lord Castlereagh
       on the subject of Irish affairs. London: C. Richards, 1816.
       PP6.9.

54.   Anon. A letter from a rector to his curate, on the subject of
       the Bible Society. London: J. Hatchard, 1816. PP7.7.

55.   The Author of "A Few Pages on the Book of Job," pseud. At-
       tempt at a new mode of metaphysical enquiry, illustrated as
       here employed upon perception. Oxford: J. Parker, 1816.
       PP6.12. Marginalia, not N's.

56.   An Hereditary Planter, pseud. Observations upon the oligarchy,
       or committee of soi-disant saints, in a letter to the Right
       Honorable Viscount Sidmouth, Secretary of State. London:
       Edmund Lloyd, 1816. PP6.13.

                                1817

57.   Brougham, Henry Peter. The speech of Henry Brougham, Esq.
       M.P., in the House of Commons, March 13, 1817, on the state

of the nation. London: Ridgways, 1817. PP6.14.

58. Davison, John. Considerations on the Poor Laws. Oxford: J. Parker, 1817. PP1.3.

59. Gordon, George, Lord Byron. Manfred, a dramatic poem. London: John Murray, 1817. T1.9. 1st ed.

1818

60. Canning, George. The speech (so much the subject of interest and animadversion) of the Right Honourable George Canning, in the House of Commons, on the 11th of March, 1818, upon the third reading of the Indemnity Bill (reported by a hearer) with a preface and notes. London: Hatchard, 1818. PP2.8.

61. Payne, John Howard. Brutus; or, the fall of Tarquin: an historical tragedy, in five acts, by John Howard Payne; first presented at the Theatre Royal, Drury-Lane, on Thursday evening, December 3, 1818. 4th ed. London: T. Rodwell, 1818. T1.10.

1819

62. Burgess, Thomas. English reformation and papal schism; or, the grand schism of the sixteenth century, in this country, shewn to have been the separation of the Roman Catholics from the Church of England and Ireland; in a letter to the Right Honourable Lord Kenyon, on Mr. Wix's plan of union between the Churches of England and of Rome; to which is added a postscript, in answer to Dr. Milner's postscript. London: Rivingtons, 1819. C8.6. Probably acquired by N in the 1860s. Scoring on p. 46.

63. [Copleston, Edward.] One of His Constituents, pseud. A letter to the Right Hon. Robert Peel, M.P. for the University of Oxford, on the pernicious effects of a variable standard of value, especially as it regards the condition of the lower orders and the Poor Laws, by one of his constituents. Oxford: John Murray, 1819. PP2.4.

64. [Copleston, Edward.] One of His Constituents, pseud. A second letter to the Right Hon. Robert Peel, M.P. for the University of Oxford, on the causes of the increase of pauperism, and on the Poor Laws. Oxford: John Murray, 1819. PP2.3.

65. Copleston, Edward. A sermon, preached at the anniversary of the Devon and Exeter Hospital, August 25, 1818. 2nd ed. Oxford: W. Baxter, 1819. T2.1. Signature dated 1829.

66. Dennis, Jonas. Gravamina Ecclesiæ: a statement of the numerous and increasing oppressions of the Church, comprising a review of various parliamentary proceedings connected with ecclesiastical concerns; the substance of a speech addressed to the clergy of the Diocese of Exeter, in the Episcopal

Consistorial Court of the Church of Saint Peter of Exeter, at a second election of representatives of the clergy of the said Diocese in convocation, on Friday, March 19, 1819; to which is subjoined, a plan for establishing a summary adjudication of ecclesiastical suits. Exeter: T. Flindell, 1819. ST10.1.

67. Erskine, Thomas. A short defence of the Whigs, against the imputations attempted to be cast upon them during the late election for Westminster. 2nd ed. London: James Ridgway, 1819. PP2.7.

68. Hawkins, Edward. A dissertation upon the use and importance of unauthoritative tradition, as an introduction to the Christian doctrines; including the substance of a sermon, preached before the University of Oxford, May 31, 1818, upon 2 Thess. ii. 15. Oxford: W. Baxter, 1819. T2.2. I.

69. Plunket, William Conyngham. The substance of the speech of the Right Honourable W. C. Plunket, in the House of Commons, on Tuesday the 23rd of November, 1819. 2nd ed. Manchester: Bancks, 1819. T1.1. Signature: "John Henry Newman May 15th 1820." A speech made at the debate over repressive measures which were to lead to the Six Acts. Plunket lost favor of his supporters (Brougham, Grey, etc.) by this turn with Grenville back to the Tories.

WORKS BY UNIDENTIFIED AUTHORS

70. Anon. The Vampyre; a tale. London: Sherwood, Neely, and Jones, 1819. T1.7. Attributed to Byron by the anonymous editor. Also contains "Extract of a Letter, Containing an Account of Lord Byron's residence in the Island of Mitylene," which is a vindication of Byron's character.

71. An Elector of Westminster, pseud. Reply to Lord Erskine. London: W. Hone, 1819. PP2.6.

1820

72. Canning, George. Speech of the Rt. Hon. George Canning, de- livered at the Liverpool dinner, given in celebration of his re-election, March 18, 1820. 4th ed. London: Cox and Baylis, 1820. T1.4. Signature: "John Henry Newman April 3rd 1820."

73. Canning, George. Substance of the speech of the Right Hon. George Canning in the House of Commons, on Wednesday, November 24, 1819, on the address to the Throne, upon the opening of the session of Parliament. 2nd ed. London: John Murray, 1820. T1.3. Signature: "John Henry Newman May 15th 1820." Speech in the debate leading to Six Acts. See 69, 74.

74. Grenville, Richard Brydges-Chandos, Duke of Buckingham. Sub- stance of the speech of the Right Hon. Lord Grenville, in the House of Lords, November 30, 1819, on the Marquis of Landsdowne's motion that a select committee be appointed to inquire into the state of the country, and more particularly into the distresses and discontents prevalent in the

manufacturing districts, and the execution of the laws with
respect to the numerous meetings which have taken place. 4th
ed. London: John Murray, 1820. T1.2. Speech made during
Lansdowne's motion on the state of the country; noted for its
gloominess and urge for repressive measures. Cf. Canning on
the same subject, 73. The issue had drawn Grenville back
with the Tory party. See the speech of Plunket, Grenville's
supporter: 69.

1821

75. Gordon, George, Lord Byron. Letter to **********, on the Rev.
W. L. Bowles' strictures on the life and writings of Pope.
London: John Murray, 1821. T1.8. The Letter was written to
Byron's friend John Murray, the publisher. Bowles' had brought
out an edition of Pope in 1807 with some censuring of Pope;
Campbell had been the first to answer him; then, late in the
day, Byron contributed this pamphlet.

76. [Whately, Richard.] Historic doubts relative to Napoleon
Buonaparte. 2nd ed. London: J. Hatchard, 1821. T3.2. M.
See L.D., I, 248.

1822

77. Copleston, Edward. Remarks upon the objections made to certain passages in the Enquiry Concerning Necessity and Predestination. London: John Murray, 1822. T2.3. Copleston's
Enquiry into the Doctrines of Necessity and Predestination
was published in 1821.

78. Glen, John. A treatise on the Sabbath; or, illustrations of
the origin, obligation, change, proper observance, and spiritual advantages of that holy day. Edinburgh: Oliver & Boyd,
1822. ST4.2. Marginal comment by N on p. 32: "when we say
we owe our religion to Luther and Calvin, we by no means imply that it was then first promulgated to the world."

79. The Lady's Magazine; or, Mirror of the Belles-Lettres, Fashions, Fine Arts, Music, Drama, &c., N.S.3, No. 10 (31 Oct.
1822), 513-76. T1.6. Includes poetry by Bernard Barton and
a review of John Lewis Burckhardt's Travels in Syria and the
Holy Land (1822).

80. Marsh, Edward Garrard. A sermon in aid of the Church Missionary Society preached at Hampstead Chapel on Sunday, the sixth
day of October, in the year of Our Lord 1822. London: F. C.
and J. Rivington, 1822. T3.3.

81. Norris, Henry Handley. A respectful letter to the Earl of
Liverpool, K. G., First Lord of His Majesty's Treasury, &c.
&c. &c., occasioned by the speech imputed to his Lordship at
the Isle of Thanet Bible Society meeting, October XVII,
M.DCCC.XXI. London: F. C. & J. Rivington, 1822. T2.7.

M*. A High Church accusation that the Bible Society was working against the Established Church. Cf. 83.

82. Sandford, Daniel K. A letter to the Reverend Peter Elmsley,
A.M., in answer to the appeal made to Professor Sandford, as
umpire between the University of Oxford and the Edinburgh Review. Oxford: Munday and Slatter, 1822. T7.2. A reply to
86.

83. Scholefield, James. A second letter to the Right Hon. the
Earl of Liverpool, K.G., First Lord of His Majesty's Treasury,
&c. &c. in reply to that from the Rev. H. H. Norris, A.M., on
the subject of the British and Foreign Bible Society. London:
L. B. Seeley, 1822. T2.8. M. A reply to 81. Cf. 89.

84. Silver, Thomas. A lecture on the study of Anglo-Saxon; read
before the Vice-Chancellor, and printed at his request. Oxford: W. Baxter, 1822. T2.6. I.

WORKS BY UNIDENTIFIED AUTHORS

85. A Graduate, pseud. A letter to the author of "An Appeal to
the Heads of the University of Oxford" upon compulsory attendance at Communion, by a graduate. Oxford: W. Baxter, 1822.
T2.5. M. Signature dated 1823. Marginalia and many queries.

86. A Member of a Close College, pseud. A letter to Daniel K.
Sandford, Esq., Professor of Greek in the University of Glasgow, in answer to the strictures of The Edinburgh Review on
the open colleges of Oxford, by a member of a close college.
Oxford: W. Baxter, 1822. T7.1. Cf. 82.

87. An Undergraduate, pseud. An appeal to the Heads of the University of Oxford, by an undergraduate. London: Sherwood, Neely,
and Jones, 1822. T2.4. S. A protest against compelling
students to receive the Sacrament. Cf. 85.

1823

88. The British Review, and London Critical Journal, 23, No. 41
(Aug. 1823), i-162. T4.5.

89. [Norris, Henry Handley.] A vindication of A Respectful
Letter to the Earl of Liverpool, &c., re-establishing in all
the material particulars the facts which have been impugned,
by the author of the said letter. London: C. &. J. Rivington,
1823. T2.9. M. A reply to 83 in defense of 81.

90. Welchman, Edward. The Thirty-Nine Articles of the Church of
England, illustrated with notes, and confirmed by texts of the
Holy Scripture, and testimonies of the primitive Fathers, together with references to the passages in several authors,
which more largely explain the doctrine contained in the said
articles. London: C. and J. Rivington, 1823. Tre5.3.

1824

91. The British Review, and London Critical Journal, 22, No. 44
     (May 1824), 1-167. T5.1. M. On the inside front cover of
     this volume of tracts N calls attention to his review of John
     M. Duncan's Travels through Part of the United States and Cana-
     da in 1818 and 1819, 2 vols. (London: Hurst, 1823).

92. Butler, Joseph. The analogy of religion, natural and revealed,
     to the constitution and course of nature; to which are added
     two brief dissertations. Glasgow: Chalmers and Collins, 1824.
     ST2.1. S*. M*. "With an introductory essay, by the Rev.
     Daniel Wilson . . . ." Some marginalia obliterated in binding.

93. Gleig, George Robert. Some observations on the constitution
     and tendency of the Church Missionary Society. 2nd ed. Lon-
     don: Longman, Hurst, Rees, Orme, Brown, and Green, 1824.
     T4.1. M. Cf. 97.

94. Henderson, Ebenezer. An appeal to the members of the British
     and Foreign Bible Society, on the subject of the Turkish New
     Testament printed at Paris, in 1819, containing a view of its
     history, an exposure of its errors, and palpable proofs of the
     necessity of its suppression. London: B. J. Holdsworth, 1824.
     T3.4. Cf. 95.

95. Lee, Samuel. Remarks on Dr. Henderson's Appeal to the Bible
     Society, on the subject of the Turkish New Testament printed
     at Paris, in 1819; to which is added an appendix, containing
     certain documents on the character of that version. Cambridge:
     J. Smith, 1824. T3.5. A reply to 94.

96. Rickards, Samuel. The good of the many designed in the af-
     flictions of a few; a sermon preached in the Parish Church of
     Ulcombe, in the County of Kent, at the funeral of Elizabeth
     Biggs, who died in the ninety-eighth year of her age, and had
     been confined entirely to her bed for the last eight years.
     London: John Hatchard and Son, 1824. T4.3. Duplicate copy:
     T6.1.

97. Rickards, Samuel. A Letter to Sir E. Knatchbull, Bart., Mem-
     ber of Parliament for the County of Kent, in reply to a let-
     ter, &c., by the Rev. G. R. Gleig, A.M., rector of Ivy Church,
     perpetual curate of Ash, and domestic chaplain to the Right
     Hon. the Earl of Dunmore. London: J. Hatchard, 1824. T4.2.
     A reply to 93.

98. Rose, Hugh James. Letter to the Lord Bishop of London, in re-
     ply to Mr. Pusey's work on the causes of rationalism in Ger-
     many: comprising some observations on confessions of faith,
     and their advantages. London: C. J. G. & F. Rivington, 1824.
     Tre5.1. M*. See 134 and 174.

1825

99. Blomfield, Charles James. A letter to Charles Butler, Esq.,
     of Lincoln's Inn, in vindication of English Protestants from
     his attack upon their sincerity in the "Book of the Roman

Catholic Church" by C. J. Blomfield, Bishop of Chester; third
edition; to which is added a postscript in reply to Mr. Butler's Letter to the author. 3rd ed. London: R. Clay, 1825.
T3.6. Cf. 101.

100. Brougham, Henry Peter. Inaugural discourse of Henry Brougham,
Esq., M.P., on being installed Lord Rector of the University
of Glasgow, Wednesday, April 6, 1825. Glasgow: University
Press, 1825. T7.3.

101. Butler, Charles. A letter to the Right Reverend C. J. Blomfield, D.D., Bishop of Chester; from Charles Butler, Esq., in
vindication of a passage in his "Book of the Roman Catholic
Church," censured in a letter addressed to him by His Lordship.
3rd ed. London: John Murray, 1825. T3.7. A reply to 99.

102. Church Missionary Society. An invitation to assist the attempts of the Church Missionary Society, for the conversion
of the heathen: addressed, by the committee of the Society,
to the inhabitants of the United Empire, more especially to
those of them who are members of the Established Church. London: Richard Watts, 1825. ST24.1.

103. Cooper, Edward. A letter to the editor of the British Review,
occasioned by his remarks on "The Crisis," in the number for
May, 1825. London: T. Cadell, 1825. ST1.1. Cf. N's review
of Cooper's The Crisis (London: Cadell, 1825) in 106.

104. Hawkins, Edward. Systematic preaching recommended, in a sermon, preached June 4, 1825, in the Church of St. Mary the Virgin, Oxford, at the visitation of the Venerable the Archdeacon. Oxford: W. Baxter, 1825. T3.8. I.

105. Mullens, John. Address to the congregation of Streatham Chapel, Surrey. London: Gold and Walton, 1825. T4.4. I.

106. Quarterly Theological Review, 2, No. 3 (June 1825), 1-276.
T5.2. On the inside front cover of this volume N calls atten-
tion to his review of Edward Cooper, The Crisis, on pp. 33-44.
See L.D., I, 223; XXV, 263. Cf. 103.

                                1826

107. Brock, Thomas. An affectionate address to the members of the
Church of England, in which the most popular arguments for
separation are considered and refuted. Guernsey: T. Dumaresq,
1826. ST1.5.

108. Comyn, Henry. Lectures on Regeneration, infant baptism, and
the lawful modes of its administration; delivered at Boldre
and Brockenhurst, Hants., 1817. Falmouth: J. Philp, n.d.
T6.4.

109. Hall, Robert. A short statement of the reasons for Christian,
in opposition to party Communion. London: Hamilton, Adams,
1826. T6.2. M. S. Deals with baptism and the Eucharist.

110. H[awkins], E[dward]. A manual for Christians after

Confirmation. N.l., n.p., n.d. ST1.2. I.

111. [Whately, Richard.] An Episcopalian, pseud. Letters on the
Church, by an Episcopalian. London: Longman, Rees, Orme,
Brown, and Green, 1826. Tre2.1. For the influence of this
work on the development of Newman's understanding of the Church
as a substantive and independent body, see Apo., pp. 24-25.
His late criticisms of it can be found in Diff., I, 203-15.
Newman also had an independently bound copy, kept in his
library, with scoring and some marginalia. There was a later
debate about the authorship: see L.D., XXIV, 217-19.

1827

112. Blanco White, Joseph. A letter to Protestants converted from
Romanism. Oxford: W. Baxter, 1827. T8.2. I. S. M.

113. James, William. A sermon preached in the chapel of Lambeth
Palace on Whit-Sunday, June III., M.DCCC.XXVII. at the con-
secration of the Right Reverend John Thomas, Lord Bishop of
Calcutta. London: Bagster and Thoms, 1827. T6.5. I. The
Bishop of Calcutta was J. T. James. Duplicate copy: T51.1.

114. London, University of. Statement by the Council of the University of London, explanatory of the nature and objects of
the institution. London: Richard Taylor, 1827. T7.4.

115. London, University of. University of London: proprietors of
shares. [London: S. Holdsworth] n.d. T7.5. A list.

116. M'Neile, Hugh. A sermon preached in the parish Church of St.
Antholin, Watling Street, on Monday, March 19, 1827, for the
benefit of the City Missionary Society; with an appendix containing the first report of the Committee, a list of subscribers, etc. London: City Missionary Society, 1827. T6.6.

117. Marsh, Edward Garrard. A sermon on behalf of the Spanish
refugees, preached in Hampstead Chapel, Hampstead, on Sunday,
January 14, 1827. London: Bagster and Thoms, 1827. T6.7.

118. Maxwell, John Maxwell-Parry, Lord Farnham. The substance of
a speech delivered by the Rt. Hon. Lord Farnham, at a meeting
held in Cavan, on Friday, January 26, 1827, for the purpose of
promoting the Reformation in Ireland. Dublin: Richard Moore
Tims, 1827. T8.1. I. Given to N by Joseph Blanco White. N
has noted at end: "N.B. April 28. 3000 already converted
in different parts of Ireland."

119. Phillpotts, Henry. A short letter to the Right Honourable
George Canning, &c. &c. &c. on the present position of the
Roman Catholic question. London: John Murray, 1827. T8.4.

120. Senior, Nassau William. An introductory lecture on political
economy, delivered before the University of Oxford, on the 6th
of December, 1826. London: J. Mawman, 1827. T7.8.

121. Society for the Diffusion of Useful Knowledge. A discourse of
the objects, advantages, and pleasures of science. London:

Baldwin, Craddock, and Joy, 1827. T7.6. S. M.

122. Society for the Diffusion of Useful Knowledge. Society for
the Diffusion of Useful Knowledge. London: William Clowes,
n.d. T7.7. The initial prospectus for the SDUK.

123. Thelwall, Algernon Sydney. An important enquiry; with some
directions what should follow it; chiefly extracted from the
works of Howe. London: James Nisbet, 1827. ST30.1. An
Evangelical tract by the "Missionary to the Jews" at Amsterdam.
Contains excerpts from the works of John Howe (1630-1705).

WORK BY UNIDENTIFIED AUTHOR

124. Anon. The admission of Catholics into the legislature inconsistent with constitutional principles, and of advantage to
none but the priesthood. London: J. Hatchard and Son, 1827.
T8.3.

1828

125. Bingham, William Augustus Alexander. A summary statement of
facts, and copies of certain letters connected with the case
of Mr. Bingham, gentleman commoner of St. Mary Hall. Oxford:
n.p., "printed exclusively for the use of his friends, but
not published," 1828. ST14.6. Bingham's denial that he had
fought in a duel with Duke Yonge, Jr., of Oriel College.

126. Burton, Walter Henry. Dialogues on the first principles of
the Newtonian system. Oxford: University Press, 1828. T7.16.

127. Butt, Thomas. A sermon preached in the Parish Church of Newport, in the County of Salop, at the triennial visitation of
the Lord Bishop of Lichfield and Coventry, August 12, 1828.
London: John Hatchard and Son, 1828. T11.23. I.

128. Hull, William Winstanley. An inquiry concerning the means and
expedience of proposing and making any changes in the canons,
articles, or liturgy, or in any of the laws affecting the interests of the Church of England. Oxford: J. Parker, 1828.
Tre1.4.

129. Inglis, Robert Harry. On the Roman Catholic question; sub-
stance of two speeches delivered in the House of Commons, on
May 10, 1825, and May 9, 1828. London: R. Gilbert, 1828.
Tre2.3.

130. Le Bas, Charles Webb. Considerations on miracles; containing
the substance of an article in the British Critic, on Mr. Pen-
rose's Treatise on the Evidence of the Scripture Miracles;
with additions. London: John Murray, 1828. ST3.1. The article appeared in B.C., 1 (Jan. 1827).

131. McCaul, John. Remarks, explanatory and illustrative, on the
Terentian metres, with a sketch of the history, etc. of
ancient comedy. Dublin: Richard Milliken, 1828. C7.12. M.
See L.D., XXII, 105.

132. Mills, William. The belief of the Jewish people and of the
      most eminent Gentile philosophers, more especially of Plato
      and Aristotle, in a future state, briefly considered; includ-
      ing an examination into some of the leading principles contain-
      ed in Bishop Warburton's Divine Legation of Moses; in a dis-
      course preached beofre the University of Oxford at St. Mary's,
      March 30, 1828; with notes and an appendix. Oxford: J. Parker,
      1828. Trell.l.

133. Oxford, University of. Questions at the mathematical examina-
      tion, Oxford, Easter Term, 1828. N.l., n.p., 1828. T7.12.

134. Pusey, Edward Bouverie. An historical enquiry into the prob-
      able causes of the rationalist character lately predominant
      in the theology of Germany; to which is prefixed, a letter
      from Professor Sack, upon the Rev. H. J. Rose's discourses on
      German Protestantism; translated from the German. London:
      C. & J. Rivington, 1828. Tre4.l. S. M. Reply to Rose's
      Discourses on the State of the Protestant Religion in Germany
      (Cambridge, 1825). See L.D., II, 71; and for N's view of the
      work's obscurity, II, 76.

135. Tyler, James Endell. A sermon preached in the Chapel of Lam-
      beth Palace, on Sunday, January XIII, M.DCCC.XXVIII, at the
      consecration of the Right Reverend Edward Lord Bishop of
      Llandaff. London: C. and J. Rivington, 1828. T56.1. The
      Bishop of Llandaff was Edward Copleston.

136. Vansittart, Nicholas, Lord Bexley. Address to the freeholders
      of the County of Kent. London: C. and J. Rivington, 1828.
      T8.6. Against Catholic Emancipation.

137. Woodward, Robert. The causes and pretences for separation
      from the established religion, candidly considered: and the
      doctrines, worship, and government of our Church, vindicated
      from the objection of dissenters. 4th ed. Gloucester: W.
      Verrinder, 1828. NL27.20.

WORKS BY UNIDENTIFIED AUTHORS

138. A., J. Two letters to William Wilberforce, Esq. London: W.
      Stevenson, 1828. T8.5. I. "Not published for Sale."
      Against Catholic Emancipation.

                                1829

139. Arnold, Thomas. The Christian duty of granting the claims of
      the Roman Catholics; with a postscript in answer to the letters
      of the Rev. G. S. Faber, printed in the St. James's Chronicle.
      Oxford: W. Baxter, 1829. T8.10. M.

140. Copleston, Edward. Speech of the Bishop of Llandaff, in the
      House of Lords, on Tuesday, the 7th of April, 1829, in the
      debate on the Roman Catholic Relief Bill. London: Proprie-
      tors of "The Mirror of Parliament," n.d. ST1.3.

141. Davison, John. Considerations on the justice and wisdom of

conciliatory measures towards Ireland; addressed to the electors of the University of Oxford. Oxford: W. Baxter, 1829. T8.8. Cautions against the effects in Ireland of Catholic Emancipation. Cf. 144.

142. Grenville, Richard Brydges-Chandos, Duke of Buckingham. Oxford and Locke. London: John Murray, 1829. T7.9.

143. [Gurney, Joseph John.] One of His Fellow Citizens, pseud. Some account of John Stratford, who was executed after the last assizes for the city of Norwich for the crime of murder. Norwich: S. Wilkin, 1829. ST30.11.

144. Hull, William Winstanley. A statement of some reasons for continuing to Protestants the whole legislature of Great Britain and Ireland: in reply to the Considerations of the Reverend John Davison, B.D. late Fellow of Oriel College, Oxford. London: C. and J. Rivington, 1829. T58.2. Against Catholic emancipation: a reply to 141.

145. [London Association in Aid of the Moravian Missions.] Brief narrative of the origin and progress of the Church of the United Brethren; (commonly called Moravians,) and of its recognition by the Church and government of England. [London: Marshall,] n.d. T59.17. D?

146. [London Association in Aid of the Moravian Missions.] Sketch of the history of the Church and missions of the United Brethren, commonly called Moravians. [London: F. Marshall, 1829.] T59.18.

147. Merewether, Francis. A letter to the Rev. W. Holme, B.D., Rector of Loughbrough: on the comparative merits of a shop for the publications of the Society for Promoting Christian Knowledge; and of the General Baptist Depository: both open in that town. Ashby de la Zouch: W. Hextall, 1829. T22.1.

148. Miller, John. Truth's resting place amid the strife of tongues; a sermon preached before the University of Oxford, on Sunday, May 18, 1828, being the Sunday after Ascension Day. Oxford: W. Baxter, 1829. T6.8.

149. Oxford and Oxfordshire Auxiliary Bible Society. The sixteenth report of the Oxford and Oxfordshire Auxiliary Bible Society; with a list of subscribers and benefactors for the year preceding; published by order of the meeting, held on June 17, 1829. Oxford: T. Bartlett, 1829. NL28.28.

150. Oxford, University of. An authentic copy of the poll, for a member to serve in the present Parliament for the University of Oxford, in the room of the Right Hon. Robert Peel, D.C.L. of Ch. Ch. resigned; taken on Thursday the 26th, Friday the 27th, and Saturday the 28th of February, MDCCCXXIX; candidates: the Right Hon. Robert Peel, D.C.L. of Ch. Ch.; Sir Robert Harry Inglis, Bart., D.C.L. of Ch. Ch.; by the authority of the Vice-Chancellor. Oxford: Clarendon Press, 1829. T8.12.

151. Short, Thomas Vowler. A letter addressed to the Very Reverend the Dean of Christ Church on the state of the public examinations in the University of Oxford. 1822; rpt. Oxford: J.

Parker, 1829. T67.1. Duplicate copy: T7.13.

152. Todd, Henry John, ed. Faith and Justification: two discourses
    by the Most Reverend Dr. John Sharp, formerly Lord Archbishop
    of York; and the late Owen Manning, B.D., Prebendary of Lin-
    coln, &c.; with a preface, noticing objections made by the pre-
    sent Archdeacon of Ely to a public declaration of these doc-
    trines at the beginning of the Reformation in England; and with
    an appendix of notes from the writings of many of our most dis-
    tinguished divines. London: C. J. G. & F. Rivington, 1829.
    Tre6.3.

153. Whately, Richard. No title page. N.l., n.p., n.d. T7.10.
    This pamphlet is a reprint of part of the Preface of Whately's
    Elements of Logic. The anonymous editor has prefaced the re-
    print with brief remarks indicating that he disagrees with
    Whately's assertion that logic is a requirement of the Exami-
    nation Statute. Cf. 156.

154. Wilson, Daniel. A letter to the editor of the Christian Ob-
    server, on the Bill for the Relief of Catholic Disabilities.
    [London: G. Wilson,] n.d. T8.11. The letter, dated March 23,
    1829, favors Catholic Emancipation.

155. Yonge, James. The religious improvement of sickness; a ser-
    mon, addressed to invalids and their friends; visiting
    Torquay. Torquay: Edward Cockrem, 1829. ST27.1.

WORKS BY UNIDENTIFIED AUTHORS

156. Anon. A few remarks suggested by the reprinting of part of the
    preface to Dr. Whately's Elements of Logic. T7.11. A reply
    to 153.

157. Anon. A short view of the Catholic question. London: W.
    Baxter, 1829. T8.7. I.

158. The Author of "Natural History of Enthusiasm," pseud. New
    model of Christian missions to Popish, Mahometan, & pagan
    nations explained, in four letters to a friend, by the author
    of "Natural History of Enthusiasm." London, 1829. T6.3.
    A plan for ecumenical missionary undertakings.

159. A Ch[rist] Ch[urch] Master of Arts, pseud. A letter to Sir
    Robert Harry Inglis, Bart., one of the representatives of the
    University of Oxford in Parliament, from one of his constit-
    uents. Oxford: The Journal Office, 1829. T58.1. Opposes
    Inglis's stand on Catholic Emancipation, which the author
    favors.

160. A Resident Member of the University, pseud. A letter to a
    country clergyman on his "Serious Appeal to the Bible," from
    a resident member of the University. Oxford: W. Baxter, 1829.
    T8.9. Favors Catholic Emancipation.

1830

161. Blomfield, Charles James. A letter on the present neglect of

the Lord's Day addressed to the inhabitants of London and Westminster. London: B. Fellowes, 1830. T6.13.

162. Brougham, Henry Peter. The country without a government; or,
plain questions upon the unhappy state of the present administration. 3rd ed. London: James Ridgway, 1830. T9.2. A criticism of the Duke of Wellington.

163. Brougham, Henry Peter. The result of the general election; or,
what has the Duke of Wellington gained by dissolution? 3rd ed.
London: James Ridgway, 1830. T9.1. A criticism of the Duke
of Wellington.

164. Elrington, Thomas. A review of the correspondence between the
Earl of Mountcashell and the Bishop of Ferns; together with
the letters, and a report of Lord Mountcashell's speech at the
meeting held in Cork on September 5th, 1829. Dublin: Richard
Milliken and Son, 1830. Tre2.2. M. S. See L.D., II, 246.

165. Faussett, Godfrey. Jewish history vindicated from the unscriptural view of it displayed in the History of the Jews, forming
a portion of the Family Library, in a sermon preached before
the University of Oxford, at St. Mary's, Feb. 28, 1830. 2nd
ed. Oxford: J. Parker, 1830. T6.11. I. A reply to Henry
Hart Milman's A History of the Jews (1829). Cf. L.D., II, 160,
299; Idea, pp. 85-86.

166. Forster, Charles. A vindication of The Theory of Mahometanism
Unveiled against the strictures of a writer in No. XIII. of
the British Critic and Quarterly Theological Review; in a
letter to the Rev. Hugh James Rose, B.D., Christian advocate
in the University of Cambridge. [London: A.& E. Spottiswoode,]
1830. T6.9. "Not published." A reply to a review of
Forster's The Theory of Mahometanism Unveiled (London, 1829).

167. Hawkins, Edward. Christianity not the religiion either of the
Bible only, or of the Church; a sermon, preached at Maldon,
July 28, 1830, at the primary visitation of Charles James,
Lord Bishop of London. Oxford: W. Baxter, 1830. T6.15.

168. Hinds, Samuel. The three temples of the one true God contrasted. Oxford: W. Baxter, 1830. Tre13.6.

169. Kinsey, William Morgan. On the distinction of classes into
rich and poor; a sermon on the present times, by the Rev. W.
M. Kinsey, B.D., Fellow of Trinity College Oxford, and lec-
turer of St. Nicholas, delivered in the parish church of
St. Helen, Abingdon, before the Mayor and Corporation, on
Sunday, December 5th, 1830, and published at their desire.
Abingdon: C. Evans, n.d. T6.14. I.

170. Law, George Henry. Remarks on the present distresses of the
poor. Wells: B. Backhouse, n.d. T9.3.

171. Mason, James Austin. Sermon on the divine authority of the
Catholic Church, and its essential properties, delivered
at the Catholic Chapel of St. Peter's, Cobridge, June 20th,
1830. Birmingham: R. P. Stone, n.d. NL23.12.

172. [Newman, John Henry.] Suggestions respectfully offered to
certain resident clergyman of the University, in behalf of

the Church Missionary Society, by a Master of Arts. Oxford: n.p., 1830. T6.10. Now **V.M.**, II, 2-10. See **L.D.**, II, 192-94, 198.

173. Poliziano, Angelo. Congiura de' pazzi, descritta in latino da messer Agnolo Poliziano e volgarizzata da G. I. M. col testo a fronte; agguiuntovi la vita del Poliziano ed una breve prefazione del traduttore, e le note di Giovanni Adimari dei Marchesi Bombe tolte dall'edizione fatta dal medesimo in Napoli nell'anno 1769. Livorno: Glauco Masi, 1830. ST12.1. Inscribed by Ignazio Lamba[rdi?] and dated "Malta, Valletta, dì 6 Febbrajo 1833."

174. Pusey, Edward Bouverie. An historical enquiry into the causes of the rationalist character lately predominant in the theology of Germany; part II, containing an explanation of the views misconceived by Mr. Rose, and further illustrations. London: C. J. G. & F. Rivington, 1830. Tre4.2. Part I had been criticized by Rose in 98. Pusey would seem to have consulted N a good deal about this second part: see **L.D.**, II, 155.

175. [Ryder], H[enry]. To the parents, guardians, masters and mistresses of young persons who are of a suitable age to be confirmed in the Diocese of Lichfield and Coventry. [Birmingham: T. Knott,] n.d. ST30.6. D?

176. Saunders, Augustus Page. Observations on the different opinions held as to the changes proposed in the Examination Statute, with the view principally to encourage the study of mathematics in the University, and a plan of examination respectfully submitted to the committee now appointed to frame the new Statute, as well as to the Members of Convocation generally. Oxford: Henry Cooke, 1830. T7.14. I.

177. Swan, William. Letters on missions, by William Swan, missionary in Siberia; with an introductory preface by William Orme, foreign secretary to the London Missionary Society. London: Westley and Davis, 1830. ST4.1.

178. Whately, Richard. Thoughts on the Sabbath; being an additional note appended to the second edition of "Essays on Some of the Difficulties in the Writings of St. Paul, & in Other Parts of the New Testament." London: B. Fellowes, 1830. T6.12.

WORKS BY UNIDENTIFIED AUTHORS

179. Anon. Considerations respecting the most effectual means of encouraging mathematics in Oxford. Oxford: J. L. Wheeler, 1830. T7.15.

180. Anon. Why are you a Dissenter? Or a conversation on the principles of the Church of England and Dissent. [Stroud: W. A. Baylis,] n.d. ST30.2. D? An evangelical Dissenting tract.

181. Anon. Why have you become a Baptist? Or a conversation between a Pædobaptist and a Baptist. N.l., n.p., n.d. ST30.3. D? Against infant baptism.

182. A Lay Member of Magdalen College, Cambridge, pseud. An apostolical catechism, or a brief summary of the arguments in
support of the Established Church; particularly adapted for
the confirmation of orthodox principles in the minds of young
persons. London: C. J. G. & F. Rivington, 1830. ST1.4.

183. A Minister of the Church of England, pseud. An essay towards
a proposal for Catholick Communion, wherein above sixty of the
principal controverted points, which have hitherto divided
Christendom, being call'd over, 'tis examined how many of them
may, and ought to be laid aside, and how few remain to be
accommodated for the effecting a general peace. 1704; rpt.
London: James Whittaker, 1830. ST19.1.

1831

184. Barberi, Dominic. The lamentation of England, or the prayer
of the prophet Jeremiah, applied to the same. Leicester: A.
Cockshaw, 1831. ST17.2. Anon. translation by Ambrose
Phillips de Lisle.

185. British and Foreign Bible Society. Extracts from the correspondence, and other documents, of the Provisional Committee,
formed at 32, Sackville-Street, London, 20th May, 1831, "for
the purpose of uniting in such measures as may induce the
British and Foreign Bible Society to re-consider the decision
of the late Anniversary General Meeting, and to bring about a
separation, in point of membership, from those who do not ac-
knowledge the scriptural doctrine of the Holy Trinity." N.l.,
n.p., 1831. T66.1.

186. [Brougham, Henry Peter.] Friendly advice, most respectfully
submitted to the Lords, on the Reform Bill. London: J. Ridgway, 1831. T9.5. Cf. 205.

187. Brougham, Henry Peter. Speech of the Right Honourable Lord
Brougham, Lord High Chancellor of England, on the second
reading of the Reform Bill, delivered in the House of Lords
on the memorable night of Friday, the 7th October, 1831. London: James Cochrane, 1831. T9.7. Obliterated inscription.
Cf. 207.

188. Gemmellaro, Carlo. Relazione dei fenomeni del nuovo vulcano
sorto dal mare fra la costa di Sicilia e l'isola di
Pantelleria nel mese di luglio 1831; letta nella gran sala
della R. Università degli Studii in Catania il dì 28 agosto
1831. Catania: Torchi della Regia Università, 1831. T37.1.

189. George IV, King. A Letter from the King to his people. 23rd
ed. London: William Sams, 1831. T1.5. An explanation of his
marital difficulties.

190. Girdlestone, Charles. The Church Catechism, broken into more
questions and answers. Oxford: W. Baxter, 1831. ST1.7.

191. Hawkins, Edward. A sermon, upon the way of salvation, preached in the Chapel of Oriel College, Oxford, February 27, 1831.
Oxford: W. Baxter, 1831. T6.16. I. M. Two marginal queries

regarding Justification.

192. Ken, Thomas. Three hymns, for morning, evening, and midnight.
     Hymnoi Treis: ēgoun, heōthinos te kai hesperinos kai
     mesonūktios. Oxford, n.p., 1831. ST1.17. I. A bi-lingual
     edition by an anonymous translator. Duplicate copy: ST5.1.

193. Kinsey, William Morgan. A sermon: the public advantages of
     social combinations, founded on Christian principles, con-
     sidered in an address to the members of the Benevolent Friends'
     Societies, Cheltenham. [Cheltenham: Harper,] 1831. ST1.9. I.

194. Neate, Charles. A statement of the arguments against reform,
     brought forward in the late debates; with the answers that
     were given to them by the speakers themselves; by the speakers
     on the other side; or by the other speakers on the same side.
     London: James Ridgway, 1831. T9.9.

195. Oxford, University of. Mathematical and physical questions at
     the general examination, Oxford, Easter Term, 1831. N.1.,
     n.p., 1831. T7.17.

196. Pilkington, George. The unknown tongues discovered to be
     English, Spanish and Latin; and the Rev. Edw. Irving proved to
     be erroneous in attributing their utterance to the influence
     of the Holy Spirit; also a private arrangement in his closet,
     previous to a prayer meeting and consultation in the vestry,
     to which the writer was invited by Mr. Irving, because he be-
     lieved him to be in "the Spirit," and prayed that he might re-
     ceive the gift of interpretation; various interesting collo-
     quies between the writer and Mr. Irving and his followers; and
     observations which manifestly show that they are all under a
     delusion. 2nd ed. London: Field & Bull, 1831. T6.17. I.

197. Privy Council. Papers relative to the disease called cholera
     spasmodica in India, now prevailing in the north of Europe;
     with extracts of letters, reports and communications received
     from the Continent. London: Winchester and Varnham, 1831.
     T6.21. Scoring, and the remark: "N. B. Flannel for Little-
     more."

198. Ryder, Dudley, Earl of Harrowby. Substance of the speech of
     the Right Honourable Earl of Harrowby, in the House of Lords,
     October 4th, 1831: on the motion, that the Reform Bill should
     be read a second time. London: Roake & Varty, 1831. T9.10.
     I.

199. Silver, Thomas. The coronation service or consecration of the
     Anglo-Saxon kings, as it illustrates the origin of the consti-
     tution. Oxford: W. Baxter, 1831. T10.1.

200. Stephens, William. A treatise on the nature and constitution
     of the Christian Church: wherein are set forth the form of its
     government the extent of its powers, and the limits of our
     obedience. New York: Protestant Episcopal Tract Society, 1831.
     ST15.1. Tract No. 45.

201. Whately, Richard. An essay on the omission of creeds, litur-
     gies and codes of ecclesiastical canons, in the New Testament.
     London: B. Fellowes, 1831. T11.8.

202. [Whately, Richard.] A Country Pastor, pseud. Village conversation in hard times; revised and prepared for publication under the inspection of a country pastor, author of An Address to His Parishioners, etc. London: B. Fellowes, 1831. ST1.8.

WORKS BY UNIDENTIFIED AUTHORS

203. Anon. An answer, to the question, "Is it permitted me to leave one Gospel ministry for another Gospel ministry?" In five letters to a friend. Guernsey: T. J. Mauger, 1831. ST1.6. The author is possibly Thomas Brock.

204. Anon. The new constitution. 6th ed. London: Roake & Varty, n.d. ST1.12. Against the proposed Reform Bill.

205. Anon. Observations on a pamphlet falsely attributed to a great person; entitled "Friendly Advice to the Lords on the Reform Bill." London: John Murray, 1831. T9.6. Cf. 186.

206. Anon. The real character and tendency of the proposed reform. 4th ed. London: Roake & Varty, n.d. ST1.11. Against the proposed Reform Bill.

207. Anon. Reply to a pamphlet, entitled Speech of the Right Hon. Lord Brougham, Lord High Chancellor of England, on Friday, October 7, 1831. London: J. Hatchard and Son, 1831. T9.8. A criticism of Brougham; a reply to 187.

208. A Country Parson, pseud. Ten letters on reform, by a country parson. Birmingham: H. C. Langbridge, 1831. ST1.13. I. Favors the proposed Reform Bill.

209. A Country Parson, pseud. Ten letters on the election of a member of Parliament, by a country parson. Oxford: W. Baxter, 1831. ST1.15.

210. A Country Parson, pseud. Ten more letters on reform, by a country parson. Oxford: W. Baxter, 1831. ST1.14.

211. A Member of a Country Congregation, pseud. A letter addressed to a friend, on occasion of the removal of their pastor, with some remarks on systematic theology, &c. Oxford: n.p., 1831. T37.2. The "letter" is headed "Ryde, Jan. 20, 1831."

1832

212. Benson, Christopher. Duty of contending for the faith; a sermon preached in the Temple Church, on Sunday the 22nd of January, 1832. N.l., Baldwin and Cradock, 1832. T58.4. Duplicate copy: T6.18.

213. Burton, Edward. Sermon preached before the University of Oxford on the 21st of March, 1832, being the day appointed for a General Humiliation. 2nd ed. Oxford: S. Collingwood, 1832. T6.20. A commentary on the cholera epidemic.

214. Cox, Robert. The liturgy revised; or the importance and beneficial effects of an authorized abridgment and careful revision

of the various services of the Established Church; to which is
prefixed an address to the bishops on the subject of ecclesiastical discipline. London: Hatchard & Son, 1832. ST1.10.
Advocates, among other things, eliminating the Creeds in favor
of "a sort of abridgement of our own Articles."

215. Douglas, James. The prospects of Britain. 3rd ed. Edinburgh:
Adam Black, 1832. T9.13.

216. Hey, William. The authority of a threefold ministry in the
Church; bishops, priests, and deacons, proved from the New
Testament. 2nd ed. London: J. G. & F. Rivington, 1832.
ST31.6. A publication of the Society for Promoting Christian
Knowledge.

217. House of Commons. Evidence given by Apsley Pellatt, Esq., a
member of the Common Council in the City of London: Messrs.
George and McKechney, agents of the Sabbath Protection Society,
various retail traders, namely--bakers, butchers, fishmongers,
&c. &c. and persons connected with the public markets, before
the Select Committee of the House of Commons on the Observance
of the Lord's Day; ordered by the House of Commons to be
printed August 6, 1832. [London: Ellerton & Henderson,] 1832.
T10.3. A publication of the Society for Promoting the Observance of the Lord's Day.

218. House of Commons. Evidence given by the Lord Bishop of London
and Dr. Farre before the Select Committee of the House of Commons on the Observance of the Lord's Day; ordered by the House
of Commons to be printed August 6, 1832. [London: Ellerton &
Henderson,] n.d. T10.4. A publication of the Society for
Promoting the Observance of the Lord's Day. The Bishop of
London was C. J. Blomfield.

219. House of Commons. Report from the Select Committee of the
House of Commons on the Observance of the Lord's Day; ordered
by the House of Commons to be printed August 6, 1832. [London:
Ellerton & Henderson,] 1832. T10.2. A publication of the
Society for Promoting the Observance of the Lord's Day.

220. Hull, William Winstanley. Thoughts on Church reform. London:
B. Fellowes, 1832, T58.3.

221. Merewether, Francis. An appeal to the nobility and gentry of
the county of Leicester, in behalf of the Church of England;
dedicated by permission to the Duke of Rutland. Ashby de la
Zouch: W. Hextall, 1832. T22.2.

222. [Palmer, William (of Magdalen College, Oxford.)] A Member of
the Church of God at Oxford, pseud. A hard nut to crack, or a
word in season for Mr. Bulteel, by a member of the Church of
God at Oxford. 2nd ed. Oxford: W. Baxter, 1832. ST1.16.
Henry B. Bulteel had been deprived of his curacy by the Bishop
of Oxford in August 1832 and was engaged in free-lance healing.

223. Patrick, Simon. Bishop Patrick's Persuasive to a Cheerful
Trust in God; a consolatory discourse, in these times of
trouble and danger, London, M.DCLXV. 1655; rpt. London: J.
G. & F. Rivington, 1832. NL25.16. Society for Promoting
Christian Knowledge Tract No. 429.

224. Pelham Clinton, Henry Pelham Fiennes, Duke of Newcastle. An
     address to all classes and conditions of Englishmen. London:
     T. and W. Boone, 1832. T9.12.

225. Pusey, Edward Bouverie. A sermon preached at the consecration
     of Grove Church on Tuesday, August 14, 1832. Oxford: S. Col-
     lingwood, 1832. T51.3. I. Duplicate copy: T11.1.

226. Rogers, John. Remarks on the principles adopted by Bishop
     Lowth in correcting the text of the Hebrew Bible. Oxford: S.
     Collingwood, 1832. ST6.1. Rogers was rector of Mawnan, Corn-
     wall. N dined with him there two days before sailing on his
     Mediterranean journey in 1832; see L.D., III, 128.

227. Scrope, George Julius Duncombe Poulett. Extracts of letters
     from poor persons who emigrated last year to Canada and the
     United States, printed for the information of the labouring
     poor, and their friends in this country. 2nd ed. London:
     James Ridgway, 1832. T9.4.

228. Walsh, John. The present balance of parties in the state. 3rd
     ed. London: John Murray, 1832. T9.11. M.

229. Whately, Richard. The evidence of His Grace the Archbishop of
     Dublin, as taken before the Select Committee of the House of
     Lords, appointed to inquire into the collection and payment
     of tithes in Ireland and the state of the laws relating
     hitherto. London: B. Fellowes, 1832. T8.13.

WORKS BY UNIDENTIFIED AUTHORS

230. Anon. A few words after the Fast Day. Peterborough: G. K.
     Clifton, 1832. T11.3. S.

231. Anon. The godly discipline of the Church, requiring that all
     baptisms be performed before the congregation, and that only
     communicants be sponsors, simply explained and enforced in an
     address from a clergyman to his parishioners. Salisbury:
     W. B. Brodie, 1832. ST7.9.

232. Anon. A hymn. N.l., n.p., n.d. T6.19. Possibly by a
     Tractarian classical scholar.

233. Anon. "The single talent well employed;" or, the history of
     Ruth Clark, for thirty years a servant of the late Rev. Henry
     Venn, vicar of Huddersfield and Yelling, and author of the
     "Complete Duty of Man," &c. &c. 7th ed. London: J. Hatchard
     and Son, 1832. ST7.1. "She died in May 1807, aged sixty-six,
     and was buried in the same grave with her late much honoured
     and beloved master" (p. 22).

234. A Clergyman of the Established Church, pseud. The infliction
     of the sword of God upon our land, betokening actual wrath and
     future judgement; a sermon delivered on the National Fast Day,
     before a numerous congregation in a country town, by a clergy-
     man of the Established Church. London: Longman, Rees, Orme,
     Brown, Green, and Longman, 1832. T11.2. S.

1833

235. [Church of England.] Morning Prayer. N.1., n.p., n.d. ST30.5.
     D? Contains the Psalms for Morning and Evening Prayer, phrased
     for singing.

236. Clerke, Charles Carr. A charge delivered to the clergy of the
     Archdeaconry of Oxford, at the visitation held June 1833. Ox-
     ford: S. Collingwood, 1833. T11.5.

237. England, John. Explanation of the construction, furniture and
     ornaments of a church, of the vestments of the clergy, and of
     the nature and ceremonies of the Mass. Rome: Francis Doublie,
     1833. ST12.2. Dated in N's hand, "March 29" [1833], on title-
     page.

238. Froude, Richard Hurrell. National education considered, in a
     sermon preached in the Cathedral Church, at Exeter, on Thurs-
     day the 31st day of October, 1833. Totnes: Samuel Hannaford,
     1833. T26.2.

239. Girdlestone, Charles. Church rates lawful, but not always ex-
     pedient: a sermon, on I Cor. 9, 11, 12, preached at St. Mary's,
     Bilston, October 6, 1833, at a collection towards defraying
     expences usually paid out of the Church Rate. London: J. G. &
     F. Rivington, 1833. T13.14.

240. Goode, Francis. The better covenant practically considered
     from Hebrews VIII. 6, 10-12; with a supplement on Philippians
     II. 12, 13; to which are added notes on the Sinai covenant,
     general redemption, the sympathy of Christ, &c. &c. London:
     J. Hatchard and Son, 1833. Tre7.2. S.

241. Gordon, Mr. Speeches delivered by Mr. Gordon at the Conserva-
     tive meeting, held at the George the Fourth Inn, Nottingham,
     on Tuesday evening, 13th Dec 1832, and by Colonel Wood, at the
     Shire Hall, Brecon, upon his being elected, for the ninth time,
     to represent the county. Lutterworth: E. Bottrill, 1833. ST
     30.4. Tory speeches against Roman Catholic emancipation and
     reform and on other minor political issues.

242. Hawkins, Edward. Discourses upon some of the principal objects
     and uses of the historical scriptures of the Old Testament,
     preached before the University of Oxford. Oxford: J. H. Park-
     er, 1833. Tre8.2.

243. Keble, John. National apostasy considered in a sermon preached
     in St. Mary's, Oxford, before His Majesty's Judges of Assize,
     on Sunday, July 14, 1833. Oxford: Parker, 1833. T26.1. I.
     Signed: "J. H. Newman. Oriel College."

244. New York Protestant Episcopal Tract Society. Candid hints
     concerning the Protestant Episcopal Church. New York: New
     York Protestant Episcopal Tract Society, 1833. ST27.2.

245. Onderdonk, Henry Ustick. The rule of faith; a charge to the
     clergy of the Protestant Episcopal Church in the Commonwealth
     of Pennsylvania; delivered in St. James' Church, Pennsylvania,
     May 22, 1833, at the opening of the convention. Philadelphia:

n.p., 1833. T20.23.

246. Perceval, Arthur Philip. A clergyman's defence of himself, for refusing to use the Office for the Burial of the Dead over one who destroyed himself, notwithstanding the coroner's verdict of mental derangement. London: J. G. & F. Rivington, 1833. ST8.2. Perceval originally sent this copy to R. H. Froude on 26 June 1833, inscribed: "Dear Sir, As my name is joined with yours in the remains of the R. C. you will perhaps take an interest in my defence of my conduct in a matter of official anxiety." See Froude's letter to N in L.D., IV, 17.

247. Powell, Baden. Revelation and science: the substance of a discourse, delivered before the University of Oxford, at St. Mary's, March VIII, MDCCCXXIX; with some additional remarks, occasioned by the publication of the Bampton Lectures for 1833, and other recent works. Oxford: J. H. Parker, 1833. T11.9. A response to Nolan's Bampton Lectures.

248. Pusey, Edward Bouverie. Remarks on the prospective and past benefits of cathedral institutions, in the promotion of sound religious knowledge and of clerical education. London: Roake & Varty, 1833. Tre3.1.

249. Pusey, Edward Bouverie. Remarks on the prospective and past benefits of cathedral institutions, in the promotion of sound religious knowledge, occasioned by Lord Henley's plan for their abolition. London: Roake & Varty, 1833. T68.1. A response to A Plan of Church Reform (1832), by Robert Henley Eden, second Baron Henley. See L.D., III, 126-28.

250. Rose, Hugh James. The Churchman's duty and comfort in the present times; a sermon preached at Ipswich, before the Suffolk Society, for the relief of the widows and orphans of the clergy, on July 18, 1833. Ipswich: [R. Deck], 1833. T12.1.

251. Sinclair, John. Dissertations vindicating the Church of England, with regard to some essential points of polity and doctrine. London: J. G. and F. Rivington, 1833. Tre9.1.

252. Trench, Francis. Remarks on the advantages of loan funds for the benefit of the poor and the industrious, with directions for their establishment. 2nd ed. London: James Ridgway, 1833. T10.5.

253. Whately, Richard. A speech in the House of Lords, August 1, 1833, on a bill for the removal of certain disabilities from His Majesty's subjects of the Jewish persuasion, with additional remarks on some of the objections urged against that measure; also, a petition to the House of Lords from the clergy of the Diocese of Kildare, relative to Church reform, with observations made on the occasion of presenting it, August 7, 1833. London: B. Fellowes, 1833. T22.3. I.

254. Wix, Edward. A retrospect of the operations of the Society for the Propagation of the Gospel in North America; a sermon preached Sunday, March 31, MDCCCXXXIII, at St. John's Church, Newfoundland. 2nd ed. St. John's, Newfoundland: J. M'Coubrey, 1833. T11.4.

WORKS BY UNIDENTIFIED AUTHORS

255. Anon. The donkey-driver; a tale. London: J. Hatchard &
Son, 1833. ST8.1.

256. Anon. Remarks on "Suggestions for an Association of Friends
of the Church." [Oxford: King,] n.d. T26.5. Inscription:
"Nov. 30. 1833. (The First Edition; which was not issued.)"
See Moz., I, 429-32, and II, 5-8.

257. Anon. Remarks on "Suggestions for an Association of Friends
of the Church." [2nd ed.] [Oxford: King,] n.d. T26.6. Inscription: "Dec. 2. 1833. (The second Edition, which was not
issued.)" Cf. 256.

258. [A Layman of the United Church, pseud.] An invitation to the
Lord's Supper; given in a paraphrase of passages selected from
the Old and New Testament, the Book of Common Prayer, and the
Communion Service, according to the use of the United Church
of England and Ireland; with references to the texts. London:
J. Hatchard, 1833. ST31.13.

1834

259. Benson, Christopher. A certain and sufficient maintenance,
the right of Christ's ministers, a sermon preached in the
Temple Church on Sunday, January 19th, 1834. London: Baldwin
and Cradock, 1834. T15.14.

260. Blanco White, Joseph. An answer to some friendly remarks on
"The Law of Anti-religious Libel Reconsidered," in a letter
to a Christian minister; with an appendix, on the true meaning
of an epigram of Martial, supposed to relate to the Christian
martyrs. Dublin: Richard Milliken and Son, 1834. Trel.2. A
sequel to Trel.1.

261. Blanco White, Joseph. The law of anti-religious libel reconsidered, in a letter to the editor of the Christian Examiner,
in answer to an article of that periodical against a pamphlet,
entitled "Considerations, &c." by John Search. Dublin: Richard
Milliken and Son, 1834. Trel.1. Signed: "John H. Newman
March 30, 1835."

262. Burton, Edward. Thoughts on the separation of Church and
state. London: Roake & Varty, 1834. T24.1. M.

263. Church of England, Diocese of Gloucester. At a general
meeting of the clergy of the Diocese of Gloucester, held in
pursuance of an advertisment by the Archdeacon, in the
Cathedral Library, in the City of Gloucester, on Tuesday, the
14th instant. Gloucester: Jew and Bryant, 1834. T26.4. Inscription: "Please, return this. J.H.N." On the back of the
pamphlet is part of a note from James Bliss along with the
address. Comprised of resolutions, an address, a petition, a
report and documents.

264. Cooper, Charles Purton. Substance of the speech of Charles

Purton Cooper Esq. as counsel for the Rev. Charles Wellbeloved, in the suit of the Attorney General versus Shore, instituted in the High Court of Chancery, respecting Lady Hewley's foundations, Wednesday, 2d July, 1834. 2nd ed. London: R. Hunter, 1834. T16.19.

265. Dalby, William. The real question at issue between the opponents and the supporters of a bill now before the House of Commons, and entitled, "A Bill to Remove Certain Disabilities Which Prevent Some Classes of His Majesty's Subjects from Resorting to the Universities of England, and Proceeding to Degrees Therein." London: J. G. & F. Rivington, 1834. T16.16.

266. Eden, Robert Henley, Lord Henley. A plan for a new arrangement and increase in number of the dioceses of England and Wales. London: Roake & Varty, 1834. T15.4.

267. Faussett, Godfrey. The alliance of Church and state explained and vindicated in a sermon preached before the University of Oxford at St. Mary's, on Sunday, June 8, 1834. Oxford: J. H. Parker, 1834. T11.14.

268. Greswell, William. A popular view of the correspondency between the Mosaic ritual and the facts and doctrines of the Christian religion in nine discourses. Oxford: J. G. and F. Rivington, 1834. Tre8.1.

269. Hampden, Renn Dickson. Observations on religious dissent. Oxford: S. Collingwood, 1834. T17.18.

270. Hampden, Renn Dickson. Observations on religious dissent with particular reference to the use of religious tests in the university. 2nd ed. Oxford: B. Fellowes, 1834. T17.19. On the verso of the title-page Newman copied out his letter to Hampden of 28 Nov. 1834 (printed in <u>Moz</u>., II, 69) and also copied Hampden's reply.

271. Hook, Walter Farquhar. On the Church and the establishment; two plain sermons. London: John Turrill, 1834. T58.5. Defends the Established Church.

272. [Horne, George.] A Member of Convocation, pseud. A letter to the Right Hon. the Lord North, Chancellor of the University of Oxford, concerning subscription to the Thirty-Nine Articles, and particularly the undergraduate subscription in the university, by a member of Convocation, (generally supposed to be George Horne, D.D., the learned President of Magdalen College), with a preface and notes by the editor. Oxford: J. Parker, 1834. T17.9.

273. Hughes, Henry. The annual pastoral letter, addressed to the inhabitants of Great-Linford, Bucks., and intended for general parochial distribution. London: J. G. and F. Rivington, 1834. ST7.2. I.

274. Inglis, Robert Harry. The universities and the dissenters; substance of a speech delivered in the House of Commons, on Wednesday, 26th March, 1834, in reference to a petition from certain members of the Senate of the University of Cambridge. London: J. Hatchard & Son, 1834. T16.10.

275. Jebb, John. Heavenly conversation: a sermon preached in the Cathedral Church of St. Mary, Limerick, on Sunday, January 19. 1834. London: R. Spottiswoode, 1834. T11.12.

276. Maitland, Samuel Roffey. A letter to the Rev. Hugh James Rose, B.D., chaplain to His Grace the Archbishop of Canterbury; with strictures on Milner's Church History. London: J. G. & F. Rivington, 1834. T12.7. Cf. 485.

277. Moberly, George. A few remarks on the proposed admission of dissenters into the University of Oxford. Oxford: J. H. Parker, 1834. T16.15.

278. Pearson, George. The character and tendency of the principles and opinions of infidel and deistical writers considered with reference to the doctrines and evidences of revealed religion; being the Christian Advocate's publication for the year 1834. Cambridge: John Smith, 1834. Tre8.3. Makes appreciative references to <u>Ari</u>.

279. Pearson, George. The danger of abrogating the religious tests and subscriptions which are at present required from persons proceeding to degrees in the universities, considered, in a letter to His Royal Highness the Duke of Gloucester, K.G., Chancellor of the University of Cambridge. Cambridge: J.& J.J. Deighton, 1834. T16.8.

280. [Perceval, Arthur Philip.] The Churchman's manual; or, questions on the Church; on Protestant and Romish dissenters; and Socinians. Oxford: S. Collingwood, 1834. ST8.3. See <u>L.D.</u>, IV, 40-41.

281. [Perceval, Arthur Philip.] A Late Fellow of All Souls College, Oxford, pseud. A letter to the members of both houses of Parliament, on the dissenters' petitions, and on Church grievances; by a late fellow of All Souls College, Oxford. London: J. G. & F. Rivington, 1834. T15.6. I.

282. Perceval, Arthur Philip. The necessity of episcopal ordination in order to a valid administration of the word and sacraments, shewn to be the doctrine of the Church of England: in a letter to the Right Rev. Charles-Richard, Bishop of Winchester, Prelate of the Order of the Garter. London: J. G. & F. Rivington, 1834. T26.10. I.

283. Perceval, Arthur Philip. Observations on the proposed alterations, and present system, of the Society for Promoting Christian Knowledge, with suggestions for its improvement. London: J. G. & F. Rivington, 1834. ST8.4. I.

284. Phillpotts, Henry. Speech of Henry, Lord Bishop of Exeter, on occasion of a petition from certain members of the Senate of Cambridge, presented to the House of Lords, on Monday, April 21, 1834. London: John Murray, 1834. T16.11.

285. Powell, Baden. A letter to the editor of the British Critic, and Quarterly Theological Review; occasioned by an article in the number of that journal for April 1834. Oxford, 1834. T11.10.

286. Powell, Baden. On the achromatism of the eye. Oxford:

Ashmolean Society, 1834. T10.12.

287. Rogers, John. The scriptural character of the doctrines and services of the Church of England; a sermon preached in the Parish Church of Mawnan, on Sunday, June VIII, MDCCCXXXIV. London: J. G. & F. Rivington, 1834. T11.13. I.

288. Rose, Henry John. The law of Moses viewed in connexion with the history and character of the Jews, with a defence of the book of Joshua against Professor Leo of Berlin: being the Hulsean Lectures for 1833; to which is added, an appendix containing remarks on the arrangement of the historical scriptures adopted by Gesenius, De Wette, and others. Cambridge: J. G. & F. Rivington, 1834. Tre5.2.

289. Rose, Hugh James. Christians, the light of the world: a sermon, preached at Chelmsford, on Friday, July 25, 1834, at the visitation of the Right Hon. and Right Rev. the Lord Bishop of London. London: J. G. & F. Rivington, 1834. T12.3.

290. Rose, Hugh James. The duty of maintaining the truth: a sermon preached before the University of Cambridge, on Sunday, May 18, 1834. Cambridge: J. Deighton and Rivington, 1834. T12.2.

291. Rose, Hugh James. The study of Church history recommended: being the Terminal Divinity Lecture delivered in Bishop Cosins' Library, April XV, MDCCCXXXIV, before the Right Rev. the Dean, the Chapter, and the University of Durham. London: J. G. & F. Rivington, 1834. T12.4. Signed: "John H. Newman. Second Lecture." See 365.

292. Selwyn, William. Extracts from the college examinations in divinity for the last four years, with a letter to the lecturers and examiners in the several colleges. Cambridge: J. & J. J. Deighton, 1834. T16.3.

293. Sewell, William. The attack upon the University of Oxford, in a letter to Earl Grey. 2nd ed. London: James Bohn, 1834. T16.14. I.

294. Sewell, William. A second letter to a dissenter on the opposition of the University of Oxford to the charter of the London College. Oxford: D. A. Talboys, 1834. T16.12.

295. Sewell, William. Thoughts on subscription, in a letter to a member of Convocation. Oxford: D. A. Talboys, 1834. T17.5. I.

296. Sewell, William. Two sermons on the enforcement of attendance upon daily worship, preached in the chapel of Exeter College, Oxford; to which is annexed a letter to the Right Hon. E. G. Stanley, one of His Majesty's principal Secretaries of State. London: James Bohn, 1834. T16.13. I.

297. Snow, Thomas. The Church, in England, the pillar and ground of the truth; her episcopacy and orders scriptural; the substance of two sermons, preached at Richmond Church, January 1834. London: James Nisbet, n.d. T32.1.

298. Stephenson, J. A. The sword unsheathed; the polity of the

Church of England, the polity enforced by St. Paul, Romans
XIII. 1-8. London: L. B. Seeley, 1834. T26.3.

299. Thirlwall, Connop. A letter to the Rev. Thomas Turton, D.D.
on the admission of dissenters to academical degrees. Cambridge: J. & J. J. Deighton, 1834. T16.2. A reply to 301.

300. Thirlwall, Connop. A second letter to the Rev. Thomas Turton,
containing a vindication of some passages in a former letter,
on the admission of dissenters to academical degrees. Cambridge: J. & J. J. Deighton, 1834. T16.5. A sequel to 299.

301. Turton, Thomas. Thoughts on the admission of persons without
regard to their religious opinions to certain degrees in the
universities of England. Cambridge: John W. Parker, 1834.
T16.1. Cf. 299.

302. Whately, Richard. Address to the Clergy of the Dioceses of
Dublin and Glandelough, on the conclusion of the confirmation,
1834. Dublin: Richard Milliken and Son, 1834. T11.7. I.

303. Whately, Richard. A charge delivered at the primary visitation
of the clergy of the Dioceses of Dublin and Glandelagh. Dublin: Richard Milliken and Son, 1834. T11.6. I. On Church
reform.

304. Whewell, William. Additional remarks on some parts of Mr.
Thirlwall's two letters on the admission of dissenters to
academical degrees. Cambridge: J. & J. J. Deighton, 1834.
T16.6. A sequel to 299 and a reply to 305 and 300.

305. Whewell, William. Remarks on some parts of Mr. Thirlwall's
letter on the admission of dissenters to academical degrees.
Cambridge: J. & J. J. Deighton, 1834. T16.4. A reply to 299.

306. Wilson, William. Thoughts on some points connected with the
present state of the Society for Promoting Christian Knowledge;
in a letter to a friend. London: L. B. Seeley and Sons, 1834.
T10.6. I.

307. Wordsworth, Christopher. On the admission of dissenters to
graduate in the University of Cambridge: a letter to the Right
Hon. Viscount Althorp, M.P., Chancellor of the Exchequer, &c.
Cambridge: J. & J. J. Deighton, 1834. T16.7.

WORKS BY UNIDENTIFIED AUTHORS

308. Anon. ed. Attempt of King James the Second to force a dissent-
er upon Magdalen College, Oxford, April, 1687. (Compiled from
Howell's State Trials, and other sources.) Oxford: J. H.
Parker, 1834. T16.17. I.

309. Anon. Evening Conversations. N.l., n.p., n.d. T26.11. D?
Contains miscellaneous essays on various religious subjects.

310. Anon. The exclusive power of the episcopally ordained clergy
to administer the Word and the sacraments, and consequently
the divine authority of the episcopacy, discussed in a letter
to a friend. Cambridge: T. Stevenson, 1834. T26.9.

311. Anon. Meaning of the answer "I Do" in the Confirmation

Service. [Oxford: King,] n.d. Tll.ll. D?

312. Anon. Ode for the Encænia at Oxford, June 11, 1834, in honour
of his Grace, Arthur, Duke of Wellington, Chancellor of the
University. Oxford: n.p., 1834. Tl6.9.

313. Anon. An urgent plea for an immediate revision of the Articles
and Homilies of the United Church of England and Ireland;
grounded upon the inconsistencies of those formularies, and
the present state of these realms; most humbly addressed to
the King, the Parliament, and the numerous supporters of our
religious institutions; with a note on a recent decision of
the Society for Promoting Christian Knowledge, and on academic
tests. London: Hamilton and Adams, 1834. Tl5.l.

314. K., H. Gava fluvius; carmen latinum alcaicum. Oxford: n.p.,
1834. ST5.2.

315. A Lay Member of the University of Oxford, pseud. Hints toward
forming a correct opinion on the question of altering the
liturgy; by a lay member of the University of Oxford. London:
J. G. & F. Rivington, 1834. Tl5.2. I.

316. An Undergraduate, pseud. The state of the Church considered,
her apostolicity vindicated, and the evils of schism exposed;
a letter addressed to the Rev. J. Newman, M.A. Fellow of Oriel
College; by an undergraduate. Oxford: Talboys, 1834. T26.8.
I.

1835

317. Blanco White, Joseph. Observations on heresy and orthodoxy.
London: J. Mardon, 1835. Trel.3. For Newman's reaction to
this "most miserable book," which appeared at the time of
Blanco White's adoption of Unitarianism, see L.D., V, 118-21.

318. [Bowden, John William.] A Non-Resident Layman, pseud. A
religious reason, against substituting a declaration of conformity to the Church, for the subscription to the Articles
required at matriculation in the university; suggested to his
brother members of Convocation, by a non-resident layman.
Oxford: J. H. Parker, 1835. Tl7.15. Duplicate copy: C4.7.

319. British Society for Promoting the Religious Principles of the
Reformation. N.l., n.p., n.d. Tl4.2. A prospectus of the
Society, which was founded in 1827.

320. Burgess, Thomas. A letter to the Right Honourable Lord Viscount Melbourne, on the idolatry and apostasy of the Church
of Rome; in proof that the doctrines of the Church of Rome are
not fundamentally the same with those of the Church of England.
Salisbury: J. Hearn, 1835. Tl4.l. Burgess was Bishop of
Salisbury.

321. Carter, C. C. Hymns for children on the Lord's Prayer, and
scripture subjects. London: Bradbury and Evans, 1835. ST21.1.

322. Chalmers, Thomas. Remarks on the right exercise of Church

patronage, extracted, by permission of the author, from "The Christian and Civil Economy of Large Towns." [Glasgow: W. Collins,] n.d. T13.4. D? Anon. ed.

323. Chase, Philander. Appeal, by Bishop Chase, in behalf of a Protestant Episcopal Theological Seminary for the Diocese of Illinois. London: Richard Watts, 1835. T10.8.

324. [Christie, John Frederick.] The views of our Reformers as bearing on religious dissent. Oxford: J. H. Parker, 1835. C4.10. Against Observations on Religious Dissent, by R. D. Hampden. Duplicate copy: T17.23.

325. Connelly, Pierce. A letter and a farewell sermon, with notes. Natchez: Stanton and Besançon, 1835. NL19.17. Incomplete copy.

326. Copleston, Edward. Speech of the Bishop of Llandaff, on the Earl of Radnor's motion for returns from the Universities of Oxford and Cambridge, on the subject of oaths; in the House of Lords, on Friday, the 6th of March, 1835. London: The "Mirror of Parliament," n.d. ST7.3.

327. Cotton, Henry. Fiat justitia; a letter to the Right Hon. Sir H. Hardinge, on the present circumstances of the Established Church in Ireland. Dublin: Richard M. Tims, 1835. T14.5.

328. Dealtry, William. A charge delivered in the autumn of 1834, at the visitation in Hampshire. London: J. Hatchard and Son, 1835. T15.13. I.

329. Denison, Edward. A review of the state of the question respecting the admission of dissenters to the universities; new edition, corrected and enlarged. London: John Cochran, 1835. T17.1. I.

330. Doane, George Washington. The missionary bishop: the sermon at the consecration of the Right Reverend Jackson Kemper, D.D., Missionary Bishop for Missouri and Indiana; in St. Peter's Church, Philadelphia, September 25, 1835. Burlington, N.J.: J. L. Powell, 1835. T54.6.

331. Dodsworth, William. A sermon, preached in Margaret Chapel, St. Marylebone, in behalf of the All Souls and Trinity Districts National Schools. London: James Nisbet, 1835. ST31.7. S*. A Tory sermon.

332. Dowling, John Goulter. A letter to the Rev. S. R. Maitland, on the opinions of the Paulicians. London: J. G. & F. Rivington, 1835. T12.9.

333. Dymond, Jonathan. Oaths: their moral character and effects. 3rd ed. London: Edward Couchman, 1835. ST7.4. Tract Association of the Society of Friends, No. 53.

334. [Faussett, Godfrey.] [Quinquagenarius, pseud.] A few plain reasons for retaining our subscription to the Articles at matriculation, in preference to the subjoined declaration, which it is proposed to substitute. N.l., n.p., n.d. T17.12. Signed at end, "Quinquagenarius. Oxford, April 9, 1835." A slightly later edition, signed "by a Bachelor of Divinity": C4.6.

335. Fitz-Gerald, William Robert. The burning of Moscow: a prize
     poem, recited in the Theatre, Oxford, July 1, MDCCCXXXV. Ox-
     ford: D. A. Talboys, 1835. NL21.7. I.

336. Girdlestone, Charles. An exposition of the Book of Revelation,
     (being part of a commentary on the New Testament,) with an
     introduction and notes, a list of symbols, and tabular arrange-
     ment. London: J. G. & F. Rivington, 1835. T10.10. I.

337. Hampden, Renn Dickson. A postscript to observations on reli-
     gious dissent with particular reference to the use of religious
     tests in the university. London: B. Fellowes, 1835. T17.20.

338. [Harrison, Benjamin.] Latitudinarianism in Oxford in 1690; a
     page from the life of Bishop Bull. Oxford: n.p., 1835. T17.22

339. [Harrison, Benjamin.] A Resident Member of Convocation, pseud.
     1835 and 1772: the present attack on subscription compared with
     the last, in a letter to "A Resident Member of Convocation,"
     occasioned by some remarks in his "Letter to the Earl of Rad-
     nor"; by a resident member of Convocation. Oxford: J. H.
     Parker, 1835. C4.5. Against R. D. Hampden. Cf. 340, 363.
     Duplicate copy: T17.16.

340. [Hawkins, Edward.] A Resident Member of Convocation, pseud. A
     letter to the Earl of Radnor upon the oaths, dispensations, and
     subscription to the XXXIX Articles at the University of Oxford.
     Oxford: J. H. Parker, 1835. T17.2. Inscribed: "John H. New-
     man," and pencilled over "resident member," "the Provost of
     Oriel." Cf. 364, 339.

341. Hill, Rowland. Enthusiasm detected: a dialogue. London: J. G.
     and F. Rivington, 1835. ST7.5.

342. Hook, Walter Farquhar. Private prayers. N.1., n.p., 1835.
     ST8.11. "Private Impression." A gift from Hook to N. In-
     cludes "Devotions for the Ancient Hours of Prayer."

343. Jager, Jean Nicolas, abbé. Le célibat ecclésiastique,
     considéré dans ses rapports religieux et politiques. Paris:
     Gaume Frères, 1835. T25.4.

344. Jarvis, Samuel Farmar. A sermon preached in Christ Church,
     Hartford, before the Church Scholarship Society, Wed. eve.
     August 5th, 1835, and by request, at an adjourned meeting of
     the Society, in Christ Church, Middletown, before the annual
     convention of the Protestant Episcopal Church in the Diocese of
     Connecticut, Wed. eve. October 14th, 1835. Hartford: n.p.,
     1835. T21.3.

345. Kempthorne, John. The Church's self-regulating privilege, a
     national safeguard in respect of real Church-reform; or,
     reasons for reviving convocations, or restoring provincial and
     diocesan synods. London: J. Hatchard and Son, 1835. Tre12.1.
     S. M*. See L.D., V, 126. Newman may have written a critical
     notice of this for the British Magazine.

346. Kinsey, William Morgan. The jubilee of the Bible; or, three
     hundredth anniversary of Coverdale's translation of the whole
     Bible into English: "Printed a sermon preached at St. John's

Church, Cheltenham, in the yeare of Our Lorde MDXXXV and fynished the fourth daye of October." London: J. and S. Rivington, 1835. T11.19.

347. Law, James Thomas. An address, delivered at the first anniversary meeting of the Birmingham School of Medicine and Surgery. Birmingham: Richard Davies, 1835. T23.7.

348. Liguori, Alphonsus. The true spouse of Jesus Christ, or the nun sanctified by the virtues of her state. Dublin: John Coyne, 1835. ST17.1. "Translated from the Italian, by a Catholic clergyman."

349. MacDonnell, Eneas. The Roman Catholic Oath considered by Eneas MacDonnell, Esq., barrister at law, agent to the Roman Catholics of Ireland, from November, 1824, till the passing of the "Act for the Relief of His Majesty's Roman Catholic Subjects," in April, 1829. London: Edward Churton, 1835. T14.4.

350. Maitland, Samuel Roffey. A letter to the Rev. John King, M.A., incumbent of Christ's Church, Hull; occasioned by his pamphlet entitled, "Maitland Not Authorized to Censure Milner." London: J. G. & F. Rivington, 1835. T12.10. I.

351. Maitland, Samuel Roffey. A second letter to the Rev. Hugh James Rose, B.D., Chaplain to His Grace the Archbishop of Canterbury; containing notes on Milner's History of the Church in the Fourth Century. London: J. G. & F. Rivington, 1835. T12.8. The sequel to 276.

352. Manning, Henry Edward. The English Church: its succession, and witness for Christ; a sermon, preached in the Cathedral Church, July 7, 1835, at the visitation of the Ven. the Archdeacon of Chichester. London: J. G. & F. Rivington, 1835. T32.2.

353. [Marriott, Charles.] Meaning of subscription. N.1., n.p., n.d. T17.17. Dated at end: "Oxford, May 18, 1835."

354. [Maurice, Frederick Denison.] Rusticus, pseud. Subscription no bondage, or the practical advantages afforded by the Thirty-Nine Articles as guides in all the branches of academical education; with an introductory letter on the declaration which it is proposed to substitute for subscription to the Articles at matriculation. Oxford: J. H. Parker, 1835. C4.1. N has supplied author's name. Scorings on pp. 38, 39, 42, and 43: the relationship between theology and Aristotle's Ethics, and the connection between education and moral practice. Duplicate copy: T17.14.

355. Moberly, George. Things indifferent; a sermon on I Corinthians X.23; preached at St. Mary's, Oxford, on Sunday evening, Feb. 8, 1835. Oxford: J. H. Parker, 1835. T11.15.

356. Newman, John Henry. The restoration of suffragan bishops recommended, as a means of effecting a more equal distribution of episcopal duties, as contemplated by His Majesty's recent Ecclesiastical Commission. London: J. G. & F. Rivington, 1835. T15.5. Now V.M., II, 41-84. Duplicate copy: NL:D4.6.5.

357. Newton, Thomas. Beware of Popery: read, mark, and understand the following testimony of Holy Scripture, against the anti-christian Church of Rome. Birmingham: Charles Hammond, 1835. T35.3. Extracts from Thomas Newton's Dissertations on the Prophecies (1754, 1758). Duplicate copy: T14.3.

358. Norris, Henry Handley. Neutrality in time of danger to the Church, an abandonment of the faith, and very short-sighted worldly policy: an admonition to the members of the Church of England, delivered in a sermon at South Hackney Church, on Sunday, April 5th, 1835. London: J. G. & F. Rivington, 1835. T11.16.

359. Oakeley, Frederick. A letter to His Grace the Duke of Wellington, Chancellor of the University of Oxford, upon the principle and tendency of a bill now before Parliament, entitled, "A Bill for Abolishing Subscription to Articles of Religion in Certain Cases." Oxford: J. H. Parker, 1835. T17.7. I. 2nd ed., inscribed: T17.8.

360. [Pusey, Edward Bouverie.] Churches in London; the voluntary system; past and present exertions of the Church, and present needs. Oxford: J. H. Parker, n.d. T58.7. Rpt. of The British Magazine, 8 (Nov. 1835), 581-90; with an appendix.

361. P[usey], E[dward] B[ouverie]. Fasting; (to the Editor of the British Magazine). N.l., n.p., n.d. T58.6. Reprint of Pusey's reply to "Clericus" in The British Magazine, 7 (1 May 1835), 524-32. Duplicate copy: T26.7.

362. [Pusey, Edward Bouverie.] A second edition of the questions respectfully addressed to members of Convocation on the subjoined declaration, which is proposed as a substitute for the subscription to the Thirty-Nine Articles at matriculation, with some additional queries suggested by the foregoing ones. Oxford: n.p., n.d. T17.3. Cf. 376. 2nd ed. of 363.

363. [Pusey, Edward Bouverie.] A Bachelor of Divinity, pseud. Subscription to the Thirty-Nine Articles: questions respectfully addressed to members of Convocation on the declaration proposed as a substitute for the subscription to the Thirty-Nine Articles, by a Bachelor of Divinity, with answers by a resident member of Convocation, and brief notes upon those answers by the Bachelor of Divinity. Oxford: J. H. Parker, 1835. T17.4. Cf. 340, 362, 339. Duplicate copy: T17.13.

364. Rogers, John. A sermon preached in Exeter Cathedral at the anniversary of the Devon and Exeter National Schools, July 28th, 1835. Falmouth: J. Trathan, 1835. T11.18. I.

365. Rose, Hugh James. An apology for the study of Divinity: being the Terminal Divinity Lecture delivered in Bishop Cosins's Library, before the Bishop, the Dean and Chapter, & the University of Durham, in MDCCCXXXIV. 2nd ed., rev. London: J. G. & F. Rivington, 1835. T12.5. N has noted on the title-page: "First Lecture. These two Lectures are misplaced." That is, this pamphlet should have been bound in before 291.

366. Rose, Hugh James. Concio ad clerum provinciae cantuariensis,

in Aede Paulina habita, XXo. die Febr. MDCCCXXXV, jussu reverendissimi. London: J. G. & F. Rivington, 1835. T12.6. I.

367. Sanderson, Robert. De juramenti obligatione, Prael. iii.18. N.l., n.p., n.d. ST7.10. An extract, "Cas. 16," on oaths, from his legal lectures of 1646, which were first published in 1670.

368. Sewell, William. Postscript to thoughts on subscription. Oxford: D. A. Talboys, 1835. T17.6. Inscribed: "The Revd. J. Tackley[?]. With the kind regards of WS."

369. Silver, Thomas. A memorial to His Majesty's Government on the danger of intermeddling with the Church rates. Oxford: J. H. Parker, 1835. T13.15.

370. [Sinclair, John.] Essay on Church patronage; or, a brief inquiry, on the ground of scripture and antiquity, into the people's right of choosing their own minister. Edinburgh: William Blackwood & Sons, 1835. T13.5. Inscription: "From the Author." Also, in similar handwriting, on flyleaf: "the Revd. John Sinclair, MA. Pemb. Coll. Oxford. Minister of St. Paul's Episcopal Church, Edinburgh and author of 'Dissertations vindicating the Church of England.' George Street, Edinburgh."

371. Smith, John Pye. The Protestant dissent further vindicated on the grounds of Holy Scripture, the moral obligations of men, and the liberties of Britons; in a rejoinder to the Rev. Samuel Lee upon that gentleman's second letter to the author, repeating his former charges. London: Jackson and Walford, 1835. T15.12. A sequel to 372.

372. Smith, John Pye. The Protestant dissent vindicated from the charge of being "unscriptural and unjustifiable," in a letter to the Rev. Samuel Lee, D.D. &c., in reply to that gentleman's letter to the author entitled, "Dissent Unscriptural and Unjustifiable." London: Jackson and Walford, 1835. T15.11.

373. Warter, John Wood. A sermon preached on the re-opening of Patching Church, July XII, MDCCCXXXV. London: J. G. & F. Rivington, 1835. T11.17.

374. Waymouth, Henry. To the Right Honourable Charles, Baron Glenelg, His Majesty's Principal Secretary of State for the Colonial Department: the memorial of the Anti-Slavery and Abolition Societies of the United Kingdom. [London:] n.p., n.d. T10.7. D?

375. Westmacott, Richard. A letter on government encouragement of the higher classes of art; addressed to Edward J. Stanley, Esq., M. P., Secretary to the Treasury. [London:] Blackburn, 1835. T10.13.

376. [Wilberforce, Henry William.] A Clerical Member of Convocation, pseud. The foundation of the faith assailed in Oxford: a letter to His Grace the Archbishop of Canterbury, &c. &c. &c. visitor of the university, with particular reference to the changes in its constitution, now under consideration; by a clerical member of Convocation. London: n.p., 1835. T17.21.

An appendix reprints 362. A criticism of 269.

377. Willis, William Downes. Suggestions for the regulation of
Church patronage, preferment, etc. in a letter to His Grace
the Archbishop of Canterbury. London: Rivingtons, 1835.
T13.6. I.

378. Wilson, Robert Francis. A farewell sermon; preached at Bocking
Church, Essex, on Sunday, November 1, 1835. N.1., n.p., 1835.
T32.3.

379. The World. Commemoration dinner at the Freemason's Hall,
Wednesday, June 18, 1828, His Royal Highness the Duke of Sussex
in the chair, William Smith Esq. M.P. Deputy Chairman, William
Smith, chairman of the United Committee for Conducting the
Application to Parliament; extracted from "The World" Newspaper
of June 19th, 1828. West Hackney: n.p., 1835. T15.10. I. A
list of those present at the dinner and an account with extracts from speeches.

WORKS BY UNIDENTIFIED AUTHORS

380. Anon. An appeal to patrons on their solemn responsibility before God and man for the religious exercise of their sacred
trust. London: Ellerton, 1835. T13.3.

381. Anon. A claim for relief on behalf of the Church of England,
at the hands of His Majesty's ministers. London: n.p., 1835.
T15.7. No inscription but addressed and posted to Newman. The
author is probably A. P. Perceval.

382. Anon. The evidence for infant baptism; being the substance of
a sermon, by the author of "Notitiæ Ludæ," "A New Hebrew Con-
cordance," (now in the course of publication) &c. London:
Jackson and Walford, 1835. T10.11. The author was the "pastor" of the Cannon Street Chapel, Louth.

383. Anon. Lines on attempts to diffuse Popery. Oxford: W. Baxter,
1835. ST30.10. An anti-Catholic poem.

384. Anon. On national property, and on the prospects of the present administration and of their successors. 3rd ed. London:
B. Fellowes, 1835. T13.2.

385. Anon. ed. Pamphlets in defence of the Oxford usage of subscription to the XXXIX Articles at matriculation. Oxford:
J. H. Parker, 1835. C4.9. Incomplete copy. Contains the
anonymous preface, postscript, and table of contents only. Included in the collection were reprints of 354, 339, 318,
324, as well as the following: "Self-Protection; the Case
of the Articles," by Clericus; "Thoughts on Subscription, in
a Letter to a Member of Convocation," by William Sewell;
"Questions Addressed to Members of Convocation . . . ," by
E. B. Pusey; "Meaning of Subscription"; "A Letter to the Right
Hon. the Lord North, Concerning Subscription to the XXXIX
Articles . . . , by a Member of Convocation [1772], with a
Preface and Notes by the Editor"; "Extracts from a Collection
of Papers Published in Oxford in 1772 on the Subject of Sub-
scription to the XXXIX Articles . . . , with a Preface by the
Editor"; "The Foundation of the Faith Assailed in Oxford: A

Letter to His Grace the Archbishop of Canterbury . . . , by a
Resident Member of Convocation"; "The Views of Our Reformers
as Bearing on Religious Dissent"; and "Latitudinarianism in
Oxford in 1690, a Page from the Life of Bishop Bull." Duplicate copy: T17.24.

386. Anon. ed. Undergraduate subscription: extracts from a collection of papers published in Oxford in 1772 on the subject of
subscription to the XXXIX Articles, required from young persons
at their matriculation; with a preface by the editor. To which
is added, the debate in the House of Commons upon Sir William
Meredith's motion on the same subject, Feb, 1773. Oxford: W.
Baxter, 1835. T17.10. I.

387. Anon. The universities and the dissenters. London: James
Fraser, 1835. T16.20.

388. A Churchman, pseud. On the expected dissolution of Parliament:
an address to the members of the Church of England, entitled
to vote for members of Parliament. London: J. G. & F. Rivington, 1835. ST8.5. An anti-Catholic pamphlet protesting
against the Maynooth Grant.

389. A Churchman, pseud. Practical hints on Church reform. London:
James Fraser, 1835. T13.7. Inscription: "Revd. <u>William</u> <u>Dods-</u>
<u>worth</u> M.A. Minister of Margaret Chapel, St. Marylebone."

390. A Country Clergyman, pseud. Reasons for preferring a simple
declaration, to the present method of exacting signature to
the Thirty-Nine Articles at matriculation, in the University
of Oxford; in a letter from a country clergyman to his friend.
Speenhamland: n.p., 1835. T17.11.

391. A Graduate of the University of Oxford, pseud. An appeal to
the wisdom and piety of our ancestors; as affecting the ex-
pediency of Church reform; by a graduate of the University of
Oxford. London: Hamilton, Adams, 1835. T15.3.

392. L., M. F. Cottage theologians. Oxford: W. Baxter, 1835.
ST8.9. A tract against enthusiasm and dissent, in the form
of an imaginary dialogue.

1836

393. Anderson, James Stuart Murray. The people of God called upon
to build His house of prayer: a sermon, preached at St.
Peter's Church, Colchester, May XI, MDCCCXXXVI; on the occasion of laying the foundation stone of the new church to be
erected in the Parish of St. Botolph, Colchester. London:
J. G. & F. Rivington, 1836. T11.21. I.

394. Bethell, Christopher. A general view of the doctrine of regeneration in baptism. 2nd ed. London: J. G. & F. Rivington,
1836. Tre7.1. M. S.

395. Boyd, George. "The old paths," or the apostolic Church.
Philadelphia: Jesper Harding, 1836. ST16.1.

396. Boyd, George. A pastoral letter addressed to the members of St. John's Church, in the Northern Liberties, Philadelphia, on the subject of abolishing the system of pew rents, and making their place of worship free. Philadelphia: Wm. Stavely, 1836. T54.1. Sent to N.

397. British Magazine. Churches in London; the voluntary system; past and present exertions of the Church, and present needs; reprinted from the British Magazine for November, 1835. Oxford: n.p., n.d. T13.8.

398. Butt, Thomas. A sermon preached in St. Mary's Church, Stafford, at the primary visitation of the Lord Bishop of Lichfield and Coventry, September 11, MDCCCXXXVI. London: J. G. & F. Rivington, 1836. T11.24 I.

399. Cameron, Charles Richard. Does Dr. Hampden's inaugural lecture imply any change of his theological principles? A letter from the Rev. C. R. Cameron, M.A. of Christchurch, to a resident member of Convocation. Oxford: J. H. Parker, 1836. T18.10.

400. Cary, Henry. The Apostolical Succession in the Church of England briefly deduced, in answer to certain popular objections. Reading: R. & J. Snare, 1836. T26.12. I. Duplicate copy: NL:D4.6.4.

401. [Chandler, John.] A Non-Resident M.A., pseud. A non-resident M.A.'s self-vindication for attending to support the vote of censure on Dr. Hampden's writings. Oxford: W. Baxter, 1836. T18.13. Duplicate copy: NL80.10.

402. Chichester, Diocese of. The address of the clergy of the Archdeaconry of Chichester, to His Grace the Archbishop of Canterbury. N.l., n.p., n.d. T58.16. Protesting against usurpation of power by the Ecclesiastical Commission. This is only a draft proposal submitted to the Archdeaconry for their approval. Duplicate copy: C4.8.

403. Churton, Edward. The Church of England a witness and keeper of the Catholic tradition; a sermon preached at the visitation of the Venerable Charles Thorp, D.D., Archdeacon of Durham, July 18, 1836. Durham: F. Humble, 1836. T32.5.

404. Churton, Edward. A letter to an Edinburgh reviewer, on the case of the Oxford Malignants and Dr. Hampden. London: J. G. & F. Rivington, 1836. T18.21. I. Cf. 458.

405. [Dickinson, Charles.] Pastoral epistle from His Holiness the Pope to some members of the University of Oxford; faithfully translated from the original Latin; (a burlesque). 3rd ed. London: Fellowes, 1836. T18.7. See 444.

406. Dodsworth, William. A sermon, occasioned by the appeal of the Lord Bishop of London for the building of additional churches in the metropolis. London: James Burns, 1836. T13.11.

407. Edinburgh Academy. Prize list; Public Exhibition Day of the Edinburgh Academy, Friday, 29th July, 1836. Edinburgh: Adam and Charles Black, 1836. T68.2.

408.   Faber, George Stanley. An account of Mr. Husenbeth's professed
       refutation of the argument of The Difficulties of Romanism, on
       the entirely new principle of a refusal to meet it. London:
       William Crofts, 1836. T14.7.

409.   Glover, Frederick A. Popish sham-bishops: what be they? Dor-
       chester: Simonds and Sydenham, 1836. ST8.15.

410.   Hampden, Renn Dickson. Inaugural lecture read before the Uni-
       versity of Oxford in the Divinity School on Thursday, March
       17th, 1836. London: B. Fellowes, 1836. T18.9.

411.   [Hampden, Renn Dickson.] Statements of Christian doctrine ex-
       tracted from the published writings of R. D. Hampden, D.D.,
       Regius Professor of Divinity in the University of Oxford. 2nd
       ed. London: B. Fellowes, 1836. T18.5.

412.   Hook, Walter Farquhar. The Catholic clergy of Ireland: their
       cause defended, in a sermon, preached in the parish church of
       Buckingham, on Thursday, January VII, MDCCCXXXVI. London:
       J. G. & F. Rivington, 1836. T14.6.

413.   Hull, William Winstanley. Remarks intended to shew how far
       Dr. Hampden may have been misunderstood and misrepresented
       during the present controversy at Oxford. London: B. Fellowes,
       1836. T18.19.

414.   Irons, William Josiah. On the whole doctrine of final causes;
       a dissertation in three parts, with an introductory chapter
       on the character of modern deism. London: J. G. & F. Riving-
       ton, 1836. Trell.2.

415.   Jager, Jean Nicolas, abbé. Controverse: A M. N....., ministre
       anglican et membre de l'Université d'Oxford; septième lettre:
       dogmes fondamentaux. Paris: L. D. De Lossy, n.d. T25.2.
       From the <u>Moniteur de la Religion</u>. Cf. 416. See Louis Allen,
       <u>John Henry Newman and the Abbé Jager: A Controversy on Scrip-</u>
       <u>ture and Tradition (1834-1836)</u> (London: Oxford Univ. Press,
       1975), pp. 184-85.

416.   Jager, Jean Nicolas, abbé. Controverse: A M. N....., ministre
       anglican et membre de l'Université d'Oxford; suite de la 7e
       lettre: dogmes fondamentaux. Paris: L. D. De Lossy, n.d.
       T25.3. From the <u>Moniteur de la Religion</u>. A sequel to 415.

417.   Jager, Jean Nicolas, abbé. Le Protestantisme aux prises avec
       la doctrine catholique, ou controverses avec plusieurs minis-
       tres anglicans, membres de l'Université d'Oxford; tome
       premier. Paris: Debécourt, 1836. T25.1.

418.   James, William. The co-operation of religion and the law: and
       the Christian's use of the law of the land: two sermons,
       preached at the Assizes in the County of Surrey. London: J. G.
       & F. Rivington, 1836. T11.20.

419.   Kinsey, William Morgan. A sermon in behalf of the Cheltenham
       National and Sunday Schools; preached in St. John's Church,
       Cheltenham, on Sunday morning, April 24, 1836. Cheltenham:
       J. J. Hadley, n.d. ST30.9. I.

420.   Lancaster, Thomas William. Strictures on a late publication

of Dr. Hampden. Oxford: J. Vincent, 1836. T18.4. I.

421. Laurence, Robert French. Remarks on the Hampden controversy addressed principally to members of Convocation. Oxford: D. A. Talboys, 1836. T18.20.

422. [Lorimer, John Gordon?] The Church establishment defended from the strictures of a Congregationalist. London: J. G. & F. Rivington, 1836. ST8.7. By the author of 423. Contains an excerpt from the sermon of a Mr. Harris, a Congregationalist minister, entitled The Divine Establishment (London: Westley and Davis, 1835), to which this tract is an answer.

423. [Lorimer, John Gordon?] The voluntary principle tried by the scriptures of the New Testament. London: J. G. and F. Rivington, 1836. ST8.6. A tract against Dissenters as schismatics, by the author of 422.

424. Loughborough and Ashby Protestant Tract Society. The first annual report of the proceedings of the committee of the Loughborough and Ashby Protestant Tract Society. Ashby-de-la-Zouch: W. Hextall, 1836. ST8.10.

425. Maitland, Samuel Roffey. Remarks on that part of the Rev. J. King's pamphlet entitled "Maitland Not Authorized to Censure Milner," which relates to the Waldenses, including a reply to the Rev. G. S. Faber's supplement entitled "Reinerius and Maitland." London: J. G. & F. Rivington, 1836. T12.11.

426. Melmoth, William, the elder. Rejected passages from Melmoth's Great Importance of a Christian Life Considered: intended as a companion to the Christian Knowledge Society's new edition, as a manual of reference for its members. West Hackney: G. Masters, 1836. ST8.16. Great Importance was first published in 1711. Duplicate copy: ST27.3.

427. Merewether, Francis. Popery, a new religion, compared with that of Christ and His Apostles; a sermon, &c. 3rd ed. N.l., Loughborough and Ashby Protestant Tract Society, 1836. ST8.14.

428. Miller, Charles. A sermon, preached in Harlow Church, to a country congregation, relative to the observance of Holy Thursday or Ascension-Day, on Sunday, the 24th of May, 1835. ST28.12. Bishop's Stortford, Herts.: T. Bradfield, 1836.

429. Miller, John. A Christian guide for plain people. New York: Protestant Episcopal Tract Society, n.d. ST15.4. Tract No. 108. Miller was of Worcester College, Oxford, and participated in the Tractarian Movement.

430. Miller, John. Conspectus of the Hampden case at Oxford, in a letter to a friend; addressed particularly to the consideration of clerical non-resident members of Convocation. London: J. G. & F. Rivington, 1836. T18.14.

431. Newman, Francis William. Essay towards a grammar of the Berber language. N.l., n.p., 1836. T38.11. Offprint from the West of England Journal of Science and Literature, 1, No. 5 (Jan. 1836), 1-24. Duplicate copy: T10.14.

432. [Newman, John Henry.] Elucidations of Dr. Hampden's theological statements. Oxford: J. H. Parker, 1836. T18.1.

433. Newman, John Henry. Make ventures for Christ's sake; a sermon. Oxford: J. H. Parker, 1836. T13.10. Later republished as "The Venture of Faith."

434. Oakeley, Frederick. A sermon preached at the general ordination of the Honourable and Right Reverend Richard, Lord Bishop of Oxford, in the Cathedral of Christ Church, Oxford, on Trinity Sunday, May 29, 1836. Oxford: J. H. Parker, 1836. T11.22.

435. Ogilvie, Charles A. The apostolical origin of the three orders of the Christian ministry: a sermon, preached on the occasion of the triennial visitation of the Lord Bishop of Exeter, held at Liskeard, on Tuesday, the twentieth day of September, A. D. MDCCCXXXVI. Devonport: G. W. Hearle, 1836. T32.6.

436. Patteson, Thomas. The apostolical Church of Christ and the bond of union between the clergy and laity: a sermon, preached at the visitation of the Venerable the Archdeacon of Sarum, held at Devizes, July 8, 1836, by the Venerable the Archdeacon of Wilts. London: J. G. & F. Rivington, 1836. T32.4.

437. Perceval, Arthur Philip. Reasons for withdrawing the clergy remonstrance. London: J. Leslie, 1836. T15.9.

438. [Perceval, Arthur Philip.] A Civilian, pseud. Remarks upon the bill for Church Discipline, now before Parliament; by a civilian. London: J. Leslie, 1836. T15.8.

439. Phillpotts, Henry. Charge delivered to the clergy of the Diocese of Exeter, by the Right Reverend Henry, Lord Bishop of Exeter, at his triennial visitation in the months of August, September, and October, 1836. London: John Murray, 1836. T34.1.

440. Powell, Baden. Remarks on a letter from the Rev. H. A. Woodgate to Viscount Melbourne, relative to the appointment of Dr. Hampden. Oxford: D. A. Talboys, 1836. T18.17. A reply to 452.

441. Pusey, Edward Bouverie, ed. Dr. Hampden's past and present statements compared. Oxford: J. H. Parker, 1836. T18.11.

442. Pusey, Edward Bouverie, ed. Dr. Hampden's past and present statements compared. 2nd ed. Oxford: J. H. Parker, 1836. T18.12. I.

443. [Pusey, Edward Bouverie.] A Resident Member of Convocation, pseud. Dr. Hampden's theological statements and the Thirty-Nine Articles compared; by a resident member of Convocation; with a preface and propositions extracted from his works. Oxford: J. H. Parker, 1836. I. T18.2.

444. Pusey, Edward Bouverie. An earnest remonstrance to the author of the "Pope's Pastoral Letter to Certain Members of the University of Oxford:" with a postscript, noticing the Edinburgh Review, and other pamphlets, and an appendix on Apostolical Succession. London: J. G. & F. Rivington, 1836. T26.13. I. A reply to 405.

445. Stanley, Edward. A few observations on religion and education in Ireland. 3rd ed. London: J. Ridgway and Sons, 1836. T14.9.

446. Stewart, James Haldane. The new year; concert for prayer on the first Monday of the year, for the outpouring of the Holy Spirit; an invitation. London: L. and G. Seeley, 1836. ST30.8.

447. Thomas, Vaughan, et al. Requisition to the Rev. the Vice-Chancellor. Oxford: [Baxter,] 1836. T60.1. No title-page. Signed: "John H. Newman." This is the address, dated 22 Mar. 1836, sent by members of the Corpus Committee to the Vice-Chancellor censuring Hampden, printed together with the requisition to the Vice-Chancellor and the statute which was promulgated. The address is signed by the Committee: Vaughan Thomas, Pusey, Newman, John Hill, William Sewell, and Edward Greswell. Duplicate copy: T18.15.

448. Thomas, Vaughan, ed. The universal profitableness of Scripture for doctrine asserted, and the allegations of the sixth Article maintained, in a collection of translations from the Fathers and of abridgements of treatises by Spanheim, Turretin, Bp. Smalridge, and the Rev. John Cumming, shewing the divine nature and authority of Scripture-consequences for teaching the truths of the Gospel, and specially for the defence and establishment of them against the gainsayer and heretic. Oxford: W. Baxter, 1836. Tre10.1.

449. [Todd, James Henthorn.] Sanctissimi Domini Nostri Gregorii Papæ XVI.; epistola ad archiepiscopos et episcopos Hiberniæ, a letter of our most Holy Father, by divine Providence, Pope Gregory XVI., to the archbishops and bishops of Ireland; translated from the original Latin, and now first published. N.l., n.p., n.d. T14.11. The title-page of the "1st ed." of 450.

450. [Todd, James Henthorn.] A second edition of a pamphlet lately published under the title of A Letter of Our Most Holy Father by Divine Providence, Pope Gregory XVI., to the archbishops and bishops of Ireland; with an explanatory introduction by the author. Dublin: Milliken and Son, 1836. T14.10.

451. Wiseman, Nicholas. Letters to John Poynder, Esq., upon his work entitled "Popery in Alliance with Heathenism." London: Joseph Booker, 1836. T14.8.

452. Woodgate, Henry Arthur. A letter to Viscount Melbourne, on the recent appointment to the office of Regius Professor of Divinity, in the University of Oxford. London: J. G. & F. Rivington, 1836. T18.16. I. Cf. 440, 453.

WORKS BY UNIDENTIFIED AUTHORS

453. Anon. An elucidation of Mr. Woodgate's pamphlet, in a letter to a friend. London: B. Fellowes, 1836. T18.18. A reply to 452. Contains an advertisement of various Hampden pamphlets published by B. Fellowes.

454. Anon. Justice to the Church of England. London: J. Hatchard, n.d. T22.5.

455. Anon. A sermon for the Enfield Highway National School,
      preached in St. James's Chapel, Enfield Highway, July 23, 1837.
      N.l., n.p., n.d. T32.7.

456. Anon. ed. Specimens of the theological teaching of certain
      members of the Corpus Committee at Oxford. London: B. Fel-
      lowes, 1836. T18.6. For members of the Corpus Committee, see
      447.

457. Anon. State of the parties in Oxford; from the public prints;
      with an appendix containing some letters relative to the per-
      secution of the Regius Professor of Divinity. London: B. Fel-
      lowes, 1836. T18.23. A pamphlet on the Hampden controversy.

458. Anon. Strictures on an article in the Edinburgh Review; en-
      titled, "The Oxford Malignants and Dr. Hampden," with some ob-
      servations on the present state of the Hampden Controversy; by
      a member of Convocation. Oxford: J. Vincent, 1836. T18.22.
      A reply to Thomas Arnold's article in Edinburgh Review, 63
      (April 1836), 225-39. The author is possibly Vaughan Thomas.

459. A Clergyman, pseud. Remarks upon the system of lay-teaching
      as proposed by the Church Pastoral Aid Society, in its seventh
      regulation. London: John Hatchard, 1836. T22.6.

460. Clericus Anglicanus, pseud. Ecclesiastical legislation; three
      letters to His Grace the Lord Archbishop of Canterbury; on
      Church property, episcopacy, cathedrals, and the clergy.
      London: L. and G. Seeley, 1836. T13.1.

461. A Lay Member of the University of Oxford, pseud. Facts and
      feelings, relative to the necessity of church building through-
      out England, and the means of forming an association for the
      collection and distribution of funds to this end, by a lay
      member of the University of Oxford. Oxford: J. H. Parker,
      1836. T13.9.

462. A Member of the University, pseud. A tract for the times, in
      reply to the Oxford tracts, on scriptural views of Holy Bap-
      tism; with an appendix, containing a few observations on the
      chapter on efficacy of baptism, in "The Church of England a
      Protester against Romanism and Dissent," by William Dodsworth,
      M.A., by a member of the University. London: James Nisbet and
      Co., 1836. T26.14.

463. A Member of the University of Oxford, pseud., and Jortin
      Redivivus, pseud. A letter to His Grace the Archbishop of
      Canterbury, explanatory of the proceedings at Oxford, on the
      appointment of the present Regius Professor of Divinity; by a
      member of the University of Oxford; third edition: with a
      letter to the Corpus Committee, by Jortin Redivivus. 3rd ed.
      London: B. Fellowes, 1836. T18.8.

464. A Resident Member of Convocation, pseud. The propositions
      attributed to Dr. Hampden by Professor Pusey compared with the
      text of the Bampton Lectures; in a series of parallels; by a
      resident member of Convocation. London: B. Fellowes, 1836.
      T18.3.

1837

465. Barlow, Henry Clark. A dissertation on the causes and effects
      of disease, considered in reference to the moral constitution
      of man. Edinburgh: Adam and Charles Black, 1837. T38.3.

466. Blakesley, Joseph Williams. Thoughts on the recommendations
      of the Ecclesiastical Commission: particularly in reference to
      their probable influence on the state of the universities; in
      a letter to William Ewart Gladstone, Esq. M.P. London: J. G. &
      F. Rivington, 1837. T24.11.

467. Butt, Thomas. Observations on primitive tradition and its
      connexion with evangelical truth; with particular reference
      to and examination of Professor Keble's visitation sermon,
      preached at Winchester, September 27, 1836. London: H. G.
      Bohn, 1837. T26.17. A reply to 462.

468. Clement, Saint. The apostolical Fathers: Clement, Bishop of
      Rome: Epistle to the Corinthians. Burlington, N.J.: J. L.
      Powell, 1837. T20.1.

469. Close, Francis. Thoughts upon the scriptural authority for
      the duty of fasting; suited to the season of Lent. London:
      Hatchard and Son, 1837. ST7.6.

470. Craufurd, Charles Henry. The law of the mind and the law of
      the members; a sermon preached before the University of Ox-
      ford on St. Peter's Day, 1837, with notes and an appendix,
      wherein the existence of an innate moral faculty is maintained,
      and some observations are offered on Mr. Woodgate's late ser-
      mon. Oxford: D. A. Talboys, 1837. T38.2. A response to
      511.

471. Crosthwaite, John Clarke. Order and mission: a limited com-
      mission essential to the sacred ministry; a sermon, preached
      at the ordination held by the Lord Bishop of Kildare, on the
      Feast of Saint Michael and All Angels, M.DCCC.XXXVII. Dub-
      lin: Milliken and Son, 1837. T32.10.

472. [Dallas, Alexander Robert Charles, ed.] A Popish political
      catechism; or, a view of the principles of the synagogue of
      Antichrist concerning the power of kings: taken out of their
      most approved writers; reprinted from an old tract. London:
      James Nisbet, 1837. ST10.2. "The following is an exact re-
      print of a [late seventeenth- or early eighteenth-century]
      Tract which is preserved in a volume of 'Pamphlets mostly re-
      lating to Dissenters,' in Oriel College Library."

473. Doane, George Washington. The Apostolical Commission, the
      missionary charter of the Church: the sermon at the ordina-
      tion of Mr. Joseph Wolff, in Trinity Church, Newark, September
      26, 1837. Burlington, N.J.: J. L. Powell, 1837. T20.10.

474. Doane, George Washington. The Gospel in the church: the ser-
      mon before the annual convention of the Diocese of Massachu-
      setts, in Christ Church, Boston, Wednesday, June 20, 1832.
      Burlington, N.J.: Missionary Press, 1837. T54.7.

475. Golightly, Charles Portales. Look at home, or short and easy method with the Roman Catholics. Oxford: J. H. Parker, 1837. T14.13.

476. Hampden, Renn Dickson. Introduction to the second edition of the Bampton Lectures, of the year 1832. London: B. Fellowes, 1837. T39.1. M*.

477. Hobart, John Henry. The Churchman; the principles of the Churchman stated and explained, in distinction from the corruptions of the Church of Rome, and from the errors of certain Protestant sects, in a third charge, delivered to the clergy of the Protestant Episcopal Church in the State of Connecticut, at the opening of the convention of said Church, in Trinity Church, New Haven, June, 1818; and subsequently to the clergy of said Church in the State of New York, in St. Peter's Church, Albany, October, 1819. New York: Protestant Episcopal Tract Society, 1837. ST15.2.

478. Hook, Walter Farquhar. A farewell sermon, preached in Trinity Church, Coventry, June IV, MDCCCXXXVII, being the second Sunday after Trinity. London: J. G. & F. Rivington, 1837. T32.9. I.

479. Hook, Walter, Farquhar. Questions and answers on Confirmation. 3rd ed. London: J. G. & F. Rivington, 1837. ST30.7.

480. Hook, Walter Farquhar. Scriptural principles as applicable to religious societies. Leeds: R. Perring, n.d. ST8.13. "Private Impression." Published in 1837 or after, when Hook was vicar of Leeds. D?.

481. Irons, William Josiah. The perpetuity of the Church; a sermon preached at St. Mary's, Newington, Surrey. London: J. G. & F. Rivington, 1837. T11.25.

482. Jarvis, Samuel Farmar. Christian unity necessary for the conversion of the world: a sermon, preached in St. Thomas's Church, New York, Sunday evening, June 26, 1836, before the bishops, clergy, and laity, constituting the Board of Missions of the Protestant Episcopal Church in the United States of America. New York: William Osborn, 1837. T21.8.

483. King, surgeon of Chelmsford. Speech of a dissenter on Church-rates. London: R. Clay, 1837. ST7.8. "The Report of this Speech is taken from the Standard, without alteration." The speech was made on 18 Jan. 1837, in favor of Dissenters' paying Church-rates.

484. Library and Reading Room, Darby Street, Rosemary Lane (London). Catalogue of Books, belonging to the Library and Reading Room, Darby Street, Rosemary Lane. [London: Samuel Bentley,] 1837. T10.15. I.

485. Maitland, Samuel Roffey. An enquiry into the grounds on which the prophetic period of Daniel and St. John, has been supposed to consist of 1260 years. 2nd ed. London: J. G. & F. Rivington, 1837. T12.13. I.

486. Maitland, Samuel Roffey. A review of Fox the martyrologist's History of the Waldenses. London: Rivington, 1837. C13.17.

A hostile review of the new 1836 edition of Fox's work.

487. Maitland, Samuel Roffey. Six letters on Fox's Acts and Monuments, addressed to the editor of the British Magazine and reprinted from that work with notes and additions. London: J. G. & F. Rivington, 1837. T12.12. I.

488. Merewether, Francis. A letter to the Rev. Dr. Pusey, the Rev. Vaughan Thomas, the Rev. John Henry Newman, and the Rev. John Keble, on certain recent and contemplated theological publications at Oxford. Ashby de la Zouch: W. Hextall, 1837. T26.18. I.

489. Metropolis Churches Fund. First report of the Metropolis Churches Fund, June 23, 1837. London: n.p., 1837. T13.12.

490. Newman, John Henry. Make ventures for Christ's sake; a sermon. New York: Doolittle & Vermilye, 1837. ST10.5. "First American Edition." See Blehl A51b. First published in England in 1836, it was later published as "The Ventures of Faith," P.S., IV, 295-306.

491. Oakeley, Frederick. Remarks upon Aristotelian and Platonic ethics, as a branch of the studies pursued in the University of Oxford. Oxford: J. H. Parker, 1837. T14.14.

492. Perceval, Arthur Philip. The origin of Church-rates, with remarks on the proposal of His Majesty's Government. London: J. G. & F. Rivington, 1837. T13.16. I.

493. Polycarp, St., and St. Ignatius. The apostolical Fathers: Polycarp and Ignatius. Burlington, N.J.: J. L. Powell, 1837. T20.2.

494. Pratt, John B. Fidelity to the truth, and love for all men; a sermon, preached in St. James's Chapel, Cruden, on the 8th Sunday after Trinity, 1837, being the 16th day of July, and Sunday after the funeral of the Rev. Alexander Cock, established minister of the parish for upwards of fifty-nine years. Aberdeen: A. Brown, 1837. T32.11.

495. Pratt, John B. Scottish episcopacy and Scottish Episcopalians; three sermons preached in St. James's Episcopal Chapel, Cruden, on the 22d and 23d Sundays after Trinity, 1837; at which season a collection is annually made in aid of a fund for keeping the chapel in repair. Aberdeen: A. Brown, 1838. T32.12. I.

496. Protestant Episcopal Church in the United States of America, Board of Missions. Missions in the Church; the spirit of missions; edited for the Board of Missions of the Protestant Episcopal Church in the United States of America; Volume I, for 1836, J. L. Powell, at the Missionary Press, Burlington, New Jersey; Volume II, for 1837, New York, published for the Board of Missions, by Swords, Stanford & Co., with postscript. T20.9.

497. Pusey, Edward Bouverie. Patience and confidence the strength of the Church; a sermon preached on the fifth of November before the University of Oxford, at St. Mary's, and now published at the wish of many of its members. Oxford: J. H.

Parker, 1837. T27.1. I. Cf. 625. Duplicate copy: Tre13.1.

498. Ramsay, E. B. The Church considered as the "pillar and ground of the truth"; a sermon, preached in the Episcopal Chapel of St. John the Evangelist, Edinburgh, on Sunday October 8, 1837, at the consecration of the Rev. M. Russell, LL.D., as Bishop of Glasgow, and of the Rev. D. Moir, M.A., as Bishop Assistant of Brechin, in the Scottish Episcopal Church. Edinburgh: Robert Grant and Son, 1837. T32.13. I.

499. Rogers, John. A brief statement of the origin, the regulations, and the proceedings, of the Board of Governors of Queen Anne's Bounty, for the augmentation of small livings; with suggestions for the more efficient application of the revenues placed at their disposal to the spiritual benefit of populous and laborious parishes; addressed to His Grace, the Archbishop of Canterbury. 2nd ed. Falmouth: J. Trathan, 1837. ST6.2. I.

500. [Roman Catholic Church.] Order for the benediction of churches, as used in the Catholick Church. Loughborough: Samuel Lee, 1837. ST26.1.

501. St. Mary's Hall, Burlington, N.J. An appeal to parents for female education on Christian principles; with a prospectus of St. Mary's Hall, Green Bank, Burlington, New Jersey. Burlington: J. L. Powell, 1837. T20.3.

502. Sewell, William. An inaugural lecture delivered in the Clarendon, May 25th, 1836. Oxford: D. A. Talboys, 1837. T14.15. I.

503. Society for Promoting the Employment of Additional Curates in Populous Places. London: n.p., 1837. T13.13. Prospectus with list of subscribers.

504. Todd, James Henthorn. The restoration of the kingdom to Israel; a sermon, preached in the chapel of the Molyneux Asylum, Dublin, on Sunday, October 29, 1837. Dublin: Milliken and Son, 1837. T11.26.

505. Vaughan, Charles John, and Philip Freeman. Prolusiones academicæ præmiis annuis dignatæ et in curia Cantabrigiensi recitatæ comitiis maximis A.D. M.DCC.XXXVII. Cambridge: J. William Parker, n.d. T68.3. Annotation, not by N.

506. Ward, William. Memorial of the Bishop of Sodor and Man, to His Majesty's commissioners appointed to consider the state of the Established Church with reference to ecclesiastical duties and revenues. Colchester: John Taylor, 1837. ST31.8. Opposing the proposed suppression of the Diocese of Sodor and Man.

507. Williams, J., ed. The old religion: a treatise, wherein is laid down the true state of the difference between the Reformed and Roman Church; and the blame of this schism is cast upon the authors: serving for the vindication of our innocence--for the settling of wavering minds--for a preservative against Popish insinuations; by Jos. Hall, B. of Exon.; anno 1633; the following reprint of the above work, (with some abbreviations, and a dedication, with a short account of

the Bishop's life) is now offered to the public by the Rev. J.
Williams, Prebendary of Wells, Vicar of Merston Magna, Somer-
set, and formerly Fellow of Oriel College, Oxford. Bath: H. E.
Carrington, 1837. T14.12.

508. Willis, W. Downes. The speech of the Rev. W. Downes Willis,
A.M., at the great annual meeting of the Bath Conservative
Association, on Tuesday, Dec. 20, 1836. Bath: H. E. Carrington, n.d. ST30.13. "Re-published from the Bath Chronicle
under the direction of the Association." A speech attacking
Parliamentary proposals to reform the Church of Ireland, by
one of its clergymen.

509. Wilson, Thomas. The private meditations and prayers of the
Right Rev. Thomas Wilson, D.D., Lord Bishop of Sodor and Man.
New York: Protestant Episcopal Tract Society, 1837. ST15.3.
Tract No. 141.

510. Wiseman, Nicholas. Dissertazione sullo stato attuale del
protestantesimo in Inghilterra e massime sulle opinioni che
esprime intorno alla regola di fede recitata il dì 16 guigno
1837 nell'Accademia di Religione Cattolica da Niccola Wiseman,
Censore della medesima. Rome: Salviucci, 1837. P6.6.
"Estratto dagli Annali delle Scienze Religiose, Fasc. XIV."

511. Woodgate, Henry Arthur. The study of morals vindicated and
recommended in a sermon preached before the University of
Oxford, February 5, 1837. Oxford: J. H. Parker, 1837. T38.1.
Cf. 470. Duplicate copy: T14.16.

512. Woodhouse, George Windus. A sermon, preached in the Collegiate Church of Wolverhampton, on Sunday, April 9, 1837, in aid
of the congregational expences. Wolverhampton: Thomas Simpson,
1837. T32.8.

513. Wordsworth, Christopher. The Ecclesiastical Commission and
the universities; a letter to a friend. London: J. G. & F.
Rivington, 1837. T24.10. I.

WORKS BY UNIDENTIFIED AUTHORS

514. Anon. Introductory discourse on revelation. N.l., n.p.,
n.d. T46.8. Lacks title-page. Consists of 4 lectures on
Romans 1:1-7, delivered in Nov. and Dec. 1837.

515. Anon. Statistics of Popery in Great Britain and the colonies;
illustrated with a map, shewing the situation of each Roman
Catholic chapel, college, and seminary, throughout England,
Scotland, and Wales. 3rd ed. London: James Fraser, 1839.
T35.14. "Reprinted from 'Fraser's Magazine' for March and
April, 1839." The author is possibly John Cumming, according
to Wellesley.

516. Anon. Supplement to the Church Catechism. ST10.3. No title-
page. D?

517. Anon. Thoughts and hints for Conservative electors. [London:
Ibotson and Palmer,] 1837. T10.17. Probably by the same
author as 521.

518. Anon. What is Christian unity? London: J. Hatchard and Son,
      1837. ST28.13. A mildly ecumenical Anglican tract.

519. A., M. A letter to the Hon. & Rev. Baptist W. Noel, M.A.,
      containing a scriptural examination of his tract, entitled
      "The Unity of the Church," &c.· London: James Nisbet, 1837.
      ST31.9. An Evangelical Anglican tract.

520. A Conservative Elector, pseud. Fruits of Whig legislation as
      already ripened in the new Poor Law and Marriage Acts;
      addressed to electors; July, 1837. London: [Ibotson and Pal-
      mer,] 1837. T10.16. Signed at end "A Conservative Elector."
      Cf. 517. Duplicate copy: T22.8.

521. A Layman, pseud. [M.] Questions and answers for young people
      of the Church of England, to guard them against its enemies;
      with hints on the misuse of the word catholic. 6th ed., with
      additions. London: Roake & Varty, 1837. ST10.4. First pub-
      lished 1828. The author wants to "counteract the fatal apathy
      . . . (falsely called liberality) which prevails in our days,
      and which may be partly attributed to the perusal of Sir Wal-
      ter Scott's fascinating novels . . . ." One addition in ink.

522. One of His Constituents, pseud. Thoughts on some of the rec-
      ommendations of the Ecclesiastical Commissioners, and on popu-
      lar views of the Church; in a letter to Sir Robert Harry Inglis
      Bart. M.P. for the University of Oxford, by one of his consti-
      tuents. London: J. G. & F. Rivington, 1837. T24.9.

1838

523. Ainslie, Robert. The neglect of souls; a sermon preached in
      behalf of the Norwich City Mission, August 15, 1837; and in
      behalf of the Pimlico Association, Buckingham Chapel, in aid
      of the London City Mission, November 19, 1837; with an appen-
      dix of the ecclesiastical statistics of the city and liberty
      of Westminster. London: Ward, 1838. ST7.11.

524. Ainslie, Robert. Our home population; a discourse delivered
      at Buckingham, on the twentieth anniversary of the North Bucks
      Association of Independent churches and ministers, June 5,
      1837 [sic; date corrected in ink to 1838]. London: Ward, 1838.
      ST7.12.

525. Ainslie, Robert. The snares of the metropolis. London: Ward,
      1838. ST7.13.

526. Atkinson, William. The state of the science of political
      economy investigated; wherein is shewn the defective character
      of the arguments which have hitherto been advanced for eluci-
      dating the laws of the formation of wealth. London: Whit-
      taker, 1838. T37.5.

527. Bagot, Richard. A charge delivered to the clergy of the Dio-
      cese of Oxford by Richard Bagot, D.D., Bishop of Oxford, and
      Chancellor of the most noble Order of the Garter; at his third
      visitation, July and August, 1838. Oxford: J. H. Parker, 1838.

T28.4.

528. Baines, Peter Augustine. The course of studies and method of instruction, together with the rules and regulations followed in the Colleges of SS. Peter and Paul, Prior Park. Prior Park: n.p., 1838. T68.4.

529. [Baines, Peter Augustine.] The course of studies, and method of instruction, used in St. Peter's College, Prior Park. N.l., n.p., n.d. T68.5.

530. [Baines, Peter Augustine.] Provisional rules for the secular academicians at St. Paul's College. N.l., n.p., n.d. T68.7.

531. [Baines, Peter Augustine.] Rules and regulations for St. Peter's College, Prior Park. N.l., n.p., n.d. T68.6.

532. Banerjee, Krishna Mohana. A funeral sermon preached at the Old Church, Calcutta, on Thursday, October 12, 1837, on the decease of Baboo Mohesh Chunder Ghose. Chelmsford: Chalk, Meggy, and Chalk, 1838. ST10.6. Rpt. of 1st ed. (Calcutta: Bishop's College Press, 1837).

533. Baxter, John Alexander. Scriptural knowledge the source of national stability; a sermon, preached in St. George's Chapel, Kidderminster, in behalf of the National Society for Promoting the Education of the Poor in the Principles of the Established Church; to which is added, an examination of the principles mentioned in the publications of the Central Society, and embodied in Lord Brougham's Bill. London: Hamilton, Adams, 1838. T23.1.

534. Beaven, James. Warnings from history, political and ecclesiastical; a discourse delivered before the University of Oxford on the thirtieth of January, 1838, being the day of King Charles's martyrdom. Oxford: J. H. Parker, 1838. T27.3.

535. Bird, Charles Sumner. The Oxford tract system considered with reference to the principle of reserve in preaching, in a letter to a friend abroad. London: J. Hatchard, 1838. T27.4.

536. Bird, Edward. The Christian ministry: a sermon preached on Oct. 1, 1838, in the cathedral at Chester, at the triennial visitation of the Right Rev. John Bird, Lord Bishop of Chester. Chester: J. Seacome, 1838. T33.4. Sent to N as editor of British Critic.

537. Blomfield, Charles James. A charge delivered to the clergy of the Diocese of London at the visitation in October, 1838. London: B. Fellowes, 1838. T34.4.

538. Blomfield, Charles James. National education; a sermon preached in the Church of St. Martin in the Fields, on Sunday, February 18, 1838, in compliance with the Queen's letter on behalf of the National Society for Educating the Children of the Poor in the Principles of the Established Church. London: B. Fellowes, 1838. T23.10. Blomfield was Bishop of London.

539. Boone, James Shergold. The educational economy of England; Part I: on the external economy of education; or the means of providing instruction for the people. London: John W. Parker,

1838. T23.5.

540. Bramston, John. The Church and ministry a provision for man's
twofold nature; a sermon preached in Chelmsford church, at the
visitation of Charles James, Lord Bishop of London, Oct. 15,
1838. London: Hatchard and Son, n.d. ST6.3.

541. Browne, Robert William. The daily service: a sermon, preached
in Lincoln's Inn Chapel, on Quinquagesima Sunday, 1838. London: J. G. & F. Rivington, 1838. T27.7.

542. Burton, Frances Barbara. Astronomy simplified; or, distant
glimpses of the celestial bodies, described in familiar language, setting forth the power and goodness of the Creator,
through astronomical facts. London: Simpkin, Marshall, 1838.
ST5.4. I.

543. Catholic Institute of Great Britain. Declaration of the
Catholic Bishops, the Vicars Apostolic and their Coadjutors in
Great Britain. New ed. London: Catholic Institute of Great
Britain, 1838. T35.6. A defense of Roman Catholic beliefs
against common English misrepresentations of them.

544. Christie, John Frederick. The ministry a call to endure hard-
ness; a sermon, preached at Cheltenham, at the triennial visitation of the Right Reverend the Lord Bishop of Gloucester and
Bristol, August 15, 1838. Cheltenham: William Wight, 1838.
T33.1.

545. [Churton, Edward.] A Reformed Catholic, pseud. Letters of a
reformed Catholic; No. I: on the leading principle of the Reformation. London: J. G. & F. Rivington, 1838. NL:D4.5.1.

546. [Churton, Edward.] A Reformed Catholic, pseud. Letters of a
reformed Catholic; No. II: on private judgment and authority
in matters of faith. London: J. G. & F. Rivington, 1838.
NL:D4.5.2.

547. Collyer, John Bedingfeld. A sermon preached in the Cathedral
Church, at Norwich, on Saturday, June 30th, 1838, at the primary visitation of the Right Reverend Edward, Lord Bishop of
the Diocese, and dedicated by permission to His Lordship.
Norwich: Josiah Fletcher, 1838. T32.18.

548. Cooper, James. The claims of the unendowed churches; two sermons on the duty of maintaining public worship, delivered at
St. Paul's Chapel, Stonehouse, on Sunday, September 23rd,
1838. Stonehouse: E. W. Cole, n.d. ST7.14.

549. Coxe, R. C. The lowly station dignified: a sermon, preached
at St. James's Church, Piccadilly, on behalf of the Burlington Schools. London: J. G. & F. Rivington, 1838. T32.17.

550. Dealtry, William. Obligations of the national Church: a charge
delivered at the visitation in Hampshire, September, 1838, by
W. Dealtry, D.D., Chancellor of the Diocese of Winchester;
with an appendix, consisting chiefly of extracts from an article in the fourth number of The New York Review, "On the State
of the Church of England." London: J. Hatchard and Son, 1838.
T34.6.

551. Dean, James. Religion an essential element of education; an
address to his congregation, on behalf of "The National Society
for the Education of the Poor in the Principles of the Established Church, throughout England and Wales," Jan. 21st, 1838.
Derby: The National School in Derby, 1838. T10.9. I.

552. Denison, Stephen Charles. Is the ballot a mistake? 2nd ed.
James Ridgway and Sons, 1838. T38.4. Cf. 636.

553. Doane, George Washington, et al. An address to the people of
New Jersey, on the subject of common schools. [Burlington,
N.J.: J. L. Powell, 1838.] T20.8.

554. Doane, George Washington. Bishop Doane's letter to the young
ladies of St. Mary's Hall: read to them at the close of the
second winter term; Wednesday evening, Oct. 3, 1838. Burlington, N.J.: J. L. Powell, 1838. T20.5.

555. Doane, George Washington. Episcopal address to the annual convention of the Diocese of New Jersey, May 30, 1838. Burlington, N.J.: Missionary Press, 1838. T20.17.

556. Doane, George Washington. Speaking the truth in love; the
spirit of the Church and the duty of her ministers: the sermon
before the clergy of the Northern Convocation of the Diocese
of New Jersey, in St. Matthew's Church, Jersey City, Saturday,
November 17, 1838. Burlington, N.J.: J. L. Powell, 1838.
T20.11.

557. Dublin University. Dublin University examinations, M.DCCC.
XXXVII. Dublin: William Curry, 1838. ST5.3.

558. Eden, Robert. Religious declension: a sermon, preached before
the University of Oxford, January 14th, 1838. London: James
Burns, 1838. ST28.8. I.

559. Episcopal Church of Scotland. The Code of Canons of the Episcopal Church in Scotland, as revised, amended, and enacted, by
an ecclesiastical synod, holden for that purpose, at Edinburgh,
on the 29th day of August, and continued by adjournment till
the 6th of September, inclusive, in the year of Our Lord M.
DCCC.XXXVIII. Edinburgh: Robert Grant and Son, 1838. NL:D4.6.
6.

560. Faussett, Godfrey. The revival of Popery; a sermon preached
before the University of Oxford at St. Mary's, on Sunday, May
20, 1838. Oxford: J. G. & F. Rivington, 1838. NL:D4.5.6.
T28.1 is a copy of the 3rd ed. (1838) of this sermon.

561. Fox, Samuel. The apostolical commission a motive to fidelity:
a sermon preached on the 5th of July, 1838, in the parish
church of All Saints', Derby, at the visitation of the Venerable the Archdeacon of Derby. Derby: William Bemrose, 1838.
T32.20.

562. Fulford, Francis. The interpretation of law, and the rule of
faith: an Assize sermon, preached in Winchester Cathedral,
July 13, 1838, before the Right Hon. Sir James Parke, Knt.
(one of the barons of Her Majesty's Court of Exchequer,) and
the Hon. Sir Thomas Coltman, Knt. (one of the justices of Her
Majesty's Court of Common Pleas). London: J. G. & F.

Rivington, 1838. T32.21. I.

563. Giles, John Eustace. Socialism, as a religious theory, irrational and absurd; the first of three lectures on socialism, (as propounded by Robert Owen and others,) delivered in the Baptist Chapel, South-Parade, Leeds, September 23, 1838. London: Simpkin, Marshall, 1838. T19.9.

564. Girdlestone, Charles. God's word and ministers: a sermon, preached in St. Michael's Church, Macclesfield, at the fourth triennial visitation of the Right Reverend the Bishop of Chester. London: J. G. & F. Rivington, 1838. T32.16. I.

565. Goode, William. Reply to the article on Church rates in the Edinburgh Review, No. CXXXIV; reprinted from the British magazine. London: J. Hatchard and Son, 1838. T13.17.

566. Gray, James. Church union; a sermon preached in Holy Rhood Church, Southampton, on Friday, the 14th September, 1838, at the visitation of the Worshipful the Chancellor of Winchester, of the clergy of the Deanery of Southampton, and published at their request. Southampton: Coupland and Nightingale, 1838. T33.2.

567. Guizot, François. Democracy in modern communities. London: C. & H. Senior, 1838. C1.8. S. Second-hand copy, probably acquired in 1860s. Pencil scorings beside passages dealing with law and the will of the individual in democracies. Anonymous translation.

568. Hall, Joseph. Episcopacy by divine right, asserted. London: Hatchard and Son, 1838. ST14.2. Edited by W. B. of Bath.

569. Hampden, Renn Dickson, and William Howley. Correspondence between the Rev. Dr. Hampden, Regius Professor of Divinity in the University of Oxford, and the most Rev. Dr. Howley, Lord Archbishop of Canterbury. 3rd ed. London: B. Fellowes, 1838. T18.24.

570. Hart, Richard. Purgatory: or, a quire of argument in answer to a ream of calumny & misrepresentation, affectionately addressed to all Roman Catholics who, believing that truth will not suffer by investigation, dare to hear both sides! Norwich: Josiah Fletcher, 1838. T35.5.

571. Hawkins, Edward. The duty and the means of promoting Christian knowledge without impairing Christian unity; a sermon preached at Newbury, July 25th, 1838, for the district committee of the Societies for Promoting Christian Knowledge, and the Propagation of the Gospel. London: B. Fellowes, 1838. ST29.1. I.

572. Hawkins, Edward. The duty of private judgment; a sermon preached before the University of Oxford, Nov. 11, 1838. Oxford: J. H. Parker, 1838. T28.9.

573. Hebert, Charles. An appeal of a minister of Christ in behalf of the divine institution of Holy Matrimony; occasioned, partly, by the new Marriage Act; being a sermon preached in Cheltenham Parish Church, on Sunday afternoon, November 4, 1838. Cheltenham: William Wight, 1838. T22.9.

574. Hook, Walter Farquhar. A call to union on the principles of the English Reformation; a sermon, preached at the primary visitation of Charles Thomas, Lord Bishop of Ripon; with notes and an appendix, containing copious extracts from the Reformers. London: J. G. & F. Rivington, 1838. T28.5. Cf. 797.

575. Hook, Walter Farquhar. Hear the Church: a sermon preached in the Chapel Royal, St. James' Palace, on the first Sunday after Trinity, June 17, 1838. Burlington, N.J.: J. L. Powell, 1838. T20.27.

576. Hook, Walter Farquhar. A letter to his parishioners on the use of the Athanasian Creed. Oxford: D. A. Talboys, n.d. T39.3. I. Cf. 666.

577. Irwin, Alexander. A digest of the evidence taken before the select committees of the two Houses of Parliament, appointed to inquire into the progress and operation of the new plan of education in Ireland, 1837; with notes: Part I--principles of the system. Dublin: William Curry, 1838. T23.2.

578. Jacob, George Andrew. National education on a Christian basis; a letter to the Right Honourable Sir Robert Peel, Bart. M.P. &c. &c. London: J. G. & F. Rivington, n.d. T23.3.

579. Jarvis, Samuel Farmar. The first annual address of a rector to his parishioners, delivered in Christ Church, Middletown, Connecticut, on Easter Monday, April 16, 1838. Middletown: n.p., 1838. T21.2.

580. Johns, John. The annual sermon, before the bishops, clergy and laity, constituting the Board of Missions of the Protestant Episcopal Church in the United States of America; preached in St. Paul's Church, Boston, Wednesday evening, June 28, 1838. New York: William Osborn, 1838. T21.10.

581. Lancaster, Thomas William. Strictures on a late publication of Dr. Hampden; the second edition, revised and enlarged; to which is prefixed, a letter to P. B. Duncan, Esq. M.A. Fellow of New College. London: J. G. & F. Rivington, 1838. T18.25.

582. Laurence, Richard. An attempt to illustrate those articles of the Church of England, which the Calvinists improperly consider as Calvinistical, in eight sermons preached before the University of Oxford, in the Year MDCCCIV, at the lecture founded by John Bampton, M.A. 3rd ed. Oxford: John Henry Parker, 1838. Tre6.1.

583. Laurence, Richard. The doctrine of the Church of England upon the efficacy of baptism vindicated from misrepresentation. Oxford: John Henry Parker, 1838. Tre6.2. T28.10 is the 3rd ed. (1838) of this tract.

584. Leeke, William. A few suggestions for increasing the income of many of the smaller livings, for the almost total abolition

of pluralities, and for promoting the residence of ministers in
the several parishes; more particularly addressed to the members of both Houses of Parliament. Derby: William Bemrose,
1838. T22.13. I.

585. Loughborough and Ashby Protestant Tract Society. The penal
laws of Queen Elizabeth and her successors were enacted, not
for the sake of violating the rights of conscience, but for
the safety of the throne and government; with proofs that a
general confederacy of Roman Catholic states with the Papacy to
extirpate Protestants, and the seditions and treasons of English Romanists, rendered those laws necessary. Ashby-de-la-
Zouch: W. and J. Hextall, 1838. ST10.10.

586. M'Ghee, Robert James. Letter to the Duke of Wellington. London: Protestant Association, 1838. T35.2. Sent to N as editor of the British Critic. No. 14 of Publications of the
Protestant Association about the Irish Church Bill.

587. McIlvaine, Charles Pettit. The apostolical commission; the
sermon at the consecration of the Right Reverend Leonidas
Polk, D.D., Missionary Bishop for Arkansas; in Christ Church,
Cincinnati; December 9, 1838. Gambier, Ohio: G. W. Myers,
1838. T21.18.

588. MacLaurin, William Cowper Augustine. The blessedness of the
pious dead; a sermon, occasioned by the decease of the Right
Reverend Father in God, Alexander [Jolly], Bishop of Moray; and
delivered in the Chapel of the Holy Trinity, Elgin. Aberdeen:
A. Brown, 1838. T32.23.

589. Manning, Henry Edward. The principle of the Ecclesiastical
Commission examined, in a letter to the Right Rev. Lord Bishop of Chichester. London: J. G. & F. Rivington, 1838. T24.
12.

590. Manning, Henry Edward. The rule of faith; appendix to a sermon preached in the Cathedral Church of Chichester, June 13,
1838, at the primary visitation of the Right Rev. William,
Lord Bishop of Chichester, containing an examination of certain popular objections, and further proofs of the statements
advanced in the sermon. London: J. G. & F. Rivington, 1838.
T27.6.

591. Martin, Montgomery. The history, antiquities, topography, and
statistics of eastern India; comprising the districts of Behar,
Shahabad, Bhagulpoor, Goruckpoor, Dinajepoor, Puraniya, Rongo-
poor, and Assam, in relation to their geology, mineralogy,
botany, agriculture, commerce, manufactures, fine arts, population, religion, education, statistics, etc., surveyed under
the orders of the supreme government, and collated from the
original documents at the E. I. house with the permission of
the Honourable Court of Directors. London: Wm. H. Allen, 1838.
T53.16. "Circulated by the Aborigines Protection Society."
This is the introduction to vol. III bound separately.

592. Maurice, Frederick Denison. The responsibilities of medical
students; a sermon preached in the Chapel of Guy's Hospital,
on Sunday, March 4th. London: Darton and Clark,

1838. T23.6.

593. Meade, William. Sermon preached at the opening of the general
      convention of the Protestant Episcopal Church, in Philadelphia,
      September 5, 1838. Philadelphia: Episcopal Recorder Press,
      1838. T21.15.

594. [Miller, Charles.] Tithe Commutation Act; some observations
      on the dangerous principles and tendency of the Tithe Act: in
      a letter to George Palmer, Esq., M.P. of Nazing Park; by one
      of his clerical constituents. London: J. G. & F. Rivington,
      1838. T22.14.

595. Miller, John. Church opportunities of praise and thanksgiving
      illustrated in the instance of harvest; a sermon preached in
      the parish church of Benefield in the county of Northampton,
      on Sunday, September 30th, 1838. Oundle: R. Todd, 1838. T33.
      3.

596. Mines, Flavel Scott. The Church the pillar and ground of the
      truth. New York: John S. Taylor, 1838. T20.25.

597. Monk, James Henry. A charge delivered to the clergy of the
      Diocese of Gloucester and Bristol, in August and September,
      1838, at the triennial visitation. London: J. G. & F. Riving-
      ton, 1838. T34.5. I.

598. Mortimer, Thomas. An attempt to promote the peace and edifi-
      cation of the Church by uniting the admirers of Leighton and
      Laud: a sermon preached before the University of Cambridge,
      on Sunday, May 13, 1838. Cambridge: J. and J. J. Deighton,
      1838. T32.15.

599. [Mozley, Thomas.] A dissection of the queries on the amount
      of religious instruction and education, circulated by Lord
      John Russell, through the Poor Law Commissioners; addressed
      to Sir R. H. Inglis, Bart., M.P. by a clergyman of South Wilts.
      Salisbury: Heam & Whitmarsh, 1838. T23.4. I.

600. Murray, John. Considerations on the vital principle; with a
      description of Mr. Crosse's experiments. 2nd ed. London:
      Effingham Wilson, 1838. T37.3. Andrew Crosse was an amateur
      scientist who lived at Broomfield near Taunton.

601. Newman, John Henry. A letter to the Rev. Godfrey Faussett,
      D.D., Margaret Professor of Divinity, on certain points of
      faith and practice. Oxford: J. H. Parker, 1838. T28.2.
      Signed: "John H. Newman. June 25. 1838." Now V.M., II,
      187-249. A reply to 560.

602. Newman, John Henry. A letter to the Rev. Godfrey Faussett,
      D.D., Margaret Professor of Divinity, on certain points of
      faith and practice. 2nd ed. Oxford: J. H. Parker, 1838.
      T28.3. Signed: "J.H.N. July 30. 1838." Duplicate copy: NL:
      D4.5.7.

603. Oakeley, Frederick. Christians, the salt of the earth, and
      the light of the world; a sermon preached in conformity with
      the Queen's letter, on behalf of the Society for the Propa-
      gation of the Gospel in Foreign Parts, in the parish churches

of Adderbury and Deddington, in the county of Oxford, in the
morning and afternoon of Sunday, November the fourth, 1838.
Oxford: J. H. Parker, 1838. ST11.2.

604.   Onderdonk, Henry Ustick. Thoughts on some of the objections to
       Christianity, and some of the causes of unbelief: an address,
       delivered at the commencement in the General Theological Semi-
       nary of the Protestant Episcopal Church in the United States,
       held in St. Peter's Church, New York, on Friday, June 29, 1838.
       Philadelphia: J. Van Court, 1838. T21.6.

605.   Otey, James Hervey. The triennial sermon, before the bishops,
       clergy and laity constituting the Board of Missions of the
       Protestant Episcopal Church in the United States of America,
       preached in St. Stephen's Church, Philadelphia, Thursday eve-
       ning, September 6, 1838. Philadelphia: C. Sherman, 1838.
       T21.13.

606.   Otter, William. A charge delivered to the clergy of the Dio-
       cese of Chichester, in June, 1838, by William Otter, D.D.,
       Lord Bishop of Chichester, at his primary visitation. London:
       B. Fellowes, 1838. T34.2.

607.   Palmer, William (of Worcester College, Oxford). Supplement to
       the Treatise on the Church, by the Rev. W. Palmer, M.A., con-
       taining replies to various objections against that work. N.l.,
       n.p., n.d. NL:D.4.6.3.

608.   Paterson, James. Pietas Londinensis: an abridgment of Pater-
       son's Ecclesiastical State of London in 1714; shewing the set
       times of public prayers and sacraments in all the churches and
       chapels of ease in and about the cities of London and West-
       minster at that time; with the Postscript, recommending the
       duty of public prayer. London: James Burns, 1838. ST11.1. A
       gift to N from the editor, W[illiam] U[pton] R[ichards].

609.   Perceval, Arthur Philip. The Christian priesthood, and the
       Church of England, vindicated from the attack of a pamphlet
       entitled, "Via Media," &c. in a letter to the author. London:
       J. G. & F. Rivington, 1838. T27.9. A reply to 672.

610.   Perceval, Arthur Philip. Observations on a pamphlet entitled,
       "Consensus Omnium." London: J. G. & F. Rivington, 1838. T27.
       11. I. A reply to 671.

611.   Perceval, Arthur Philip. The plain English Churchman guarded
       against the priests of Rome: in a letter to my neighbours in
       Surrey. London: J. G. & F. Rivington, 1838. ST10.7. I.

612.   Perry, Samuel. The powers under the new Poor Law, of the ves-
       try meetings, the boards of guardians, justices of the peace,
       and the Poor Law Commissioners; considered in a letter to Lord
       John Russell, Secretary of State for the Home Department.
       London: J. Souter, 1838. T22.10.

613.   Phillpotts, Henry. The Church Discipline Bill; speech of the
       Lord Bishop of Exeter, in the House of Lords, on the 26th
       July, 1838, on moving that the Church Discipline Bill be read
       that day six months. London: Painter, 1838. T24.8.

614.   Phillpotts, Henry. The Roman Catholic oath: speech of the

Bishop of Exeter, on Thursday, March 1, 1838, in the House of Lords, on presenting a petition from certain inhabitants of the city of Cork. London: Protestant Association, 1838. T35. 4. Sent to N as editor of British Critic. No. 13 of Publications of the Protestant Association.

615. Poole, George Ayliffe. An exposure of an attack upon the Tracts for the Times by the Rev. Miles Jackson, of Leeds. London: J. G. & F. Rivington, 1838. ST31.10. A reply to Jackson's Oxford Tracts Unmasked (London: Hatchard and Son, 1838), and to his letter signed "Clericus," to the editor of the Leeds Intelligencer, dated 27 Feb. 1838.

616. The Prayer Book and Homily Society. The form and order of the service performed, and ceremonies observed, in the coronation of Her Majesty Queen Victoria, in the Abbey Church of St. Peter, Westminster, on Thursday, the 28th of June 1838. London: Prayer Book and Homily Society, 1838. ST10.9.

617. Pressley, Charles. An inheritor of the promises, through faith and patience: a sermon, preached in the Episcopal Chapel, Fraserburgh, on the fourth Sunday after Trinity, 1838; on occasion of the death of the Right Rev. Alexander Jolly, D.D., Bishop of Moray. Aberdeen: A. Brown, 1838. T32.22.

618. Protestant Episcopal Church in the United States. Canons for the government of the Protestant Episcopal Church in the United States of America: being the substance of various canons adopted in general conventions of the said Church, (from A.D. 1789 to A.D. 1832,) and set forth, with alterations and additions, in general convention, A.D. 1832; also, the canons passed in general conventions, A.D. 1835 and 1838; to which are annexed the constitution of the Church, and the course of ecclesiastical studies, established by the House of Bishops, in the general convention of 1804. New York: Swords, Stanford, 1838. T21.17.

619. Protestant Episcopal Church in the United States. Journal of the proceedings of the bishops, clergy and laity of the Protestant Episcopal Church in the United States of America, in a general convention, held in the city of Philadelphia, from September 5, to September 17, inclusive, A.D. 1838; together with the constitution and canons for the government of the Protestant Episcopal Church. New York: Swords, Stanford, 1838. T21.16.

620. Protestant Episcopal Church in the United States. A pastoral letter to the clergy and other members of the Protestant Episcopal Church in the United States of America, from the bishops of the said Church, assembled in general convention in the city of Philadelphia, Sept. 5, 1838. New York: Swords, Stanford, 1838. T21.12.

621. Protestant Episcopal Church in the United States, Board of Missions. Proceedings of the Board of Missions of the Protestant Episcopal Church in the United States of America, at their first triennial meeting; held in the city of Philadelphia, on the 6th day of September, A.D. 1838, and continued by adjournments to the 17th of the same month; together with the

reports of the domestic and foreign committees, the report of
the Board to the general convention, and the report of a special committee, made by the Rev. Jarvis. New York: William
Osborn, 1838. T21.14.

622. Protestant Episcopal Church in the United States, Board of
Missions. Proceedings of the Board of Missions of the Protestant Episcopal Church in the United States of America, at
their third annual meeting; held in the city of Boston, on the
20th day of June, A.D. 1838, and continued by adjournments to
the 22nd of the same month; together with the reports of the
domestic and foreign committees, and the accounts of their
respective treasurers. New York: William Osborn, 1838. T21.9.

623. Protestant Episcopal Church in the United States, Board of
Missions. The Spirit of Missions; edited for the Board of
Missions of the Protestant Episcopal Church of the United
States of America, 3, No. 9 (Aug. 1838), 225-96. T21.11.

624. Protestant Episcopal Church in the United States, Diocese of
New Jersey. Journal of the fifty-fifth annual convention of
the Protestant Episcopal Church in the state of New Jersey;
held in Trinity Church, Newark, on Wednesday the 30th and
Thursday the 31st days of May, 1838. Burlington, N.J.: n.p.,
1838. T20.16.

625. Protestant Episcopal Church in the United States, General Theological Seminary. The General Theological Seminary of the
Protestant Episcopal Church of the United States: proceedings
of the Board of Trustees, at their stated annual meeting held
from the 25th to the 29th June, 1838. New York: Swords, Stanford, 1838. T21.5.

626. Pusey, Edward Bouverie. Appendices to the sermon preached by
the Rev. E. B. Pusey, D.D., on the fifth of November, 1837;
containing, I: an explanation of the points mistaken by the
author of "Passive Obedience Contrary to Holy Scripture"; II:
remarks on the Revolution of 1688, and the principles involved
or not involved in its condemnation, in answer to an article
of the Edinburgh Review; III: the Oxford Decree of 1683.
Oxford: J. H. Parker, 1838. T27.2. A sequel to 497.

627. Pusey, Edward Bouverie. The Church the converter of the
heathen; two sermons preached in conformity with the Queen's
letter in behalf of the Society for the Propagation of the
Gospel, at St. Mary's Church, Melcombe Regis, September 9,
1838. Oxford: J. H. Parker, 1838. Tre13.2.

628. Pusey, Edward Bouverie. The Royal and Parliamentary Ecclesiastical Commissions. London: C. Roworth and Sons, n.d. T36.
1. Rpt. of B.C., 23 (1838), 455-562. "Reprinted for Private
Distribution."

629. Ratramnus. Ratramni presbyteri et monachi Corbeiensis, qui
vulgo Bertramus nuncupatur, Liber de Corpore et Sanguine
Domini. Oxford: J. H. Parker, 1838. ST12.4. Latin original
of first part of 12.3, by the same editors.

630. [Ratramnus, and Ælfric.] The book of Ratramn the priest and
monk of Corbey, commonly called Bertram, On the Body and Blood

of the Lord; to which is added an appendix, containing the Saxon homily of Ælfric. Oxford: John Henry Parker, 1838. ST 12.3. Edited by H. W. and W. C. C.

631. Roberson, Hammond. National education; an address on national and village schools, delivered on Easter Monday, 1838, on the occasion of laying the foundation stone of the National School at Birkenshaw (a hamlet in the Parish of Birstal, near Leeds). London: R. Groombridge, n.d. ST30.12.

632. Roden, Thomas Clarke. The valvular structure of the veins, anatomically and physiologically considered, with a view to exemplify or set forth, by instance or example, the wisdom, power and goodness of God, as revealed and declared in Holy Writ; The Warneford Prize Essay, for the year 1838. Oxford: W. Baxter, 1839. T23.8. The last leaf of the pamphlet was accidentally rebound between T23.6 and T23.7.

633. St. Mary's Hall, Burlington, N.J. Notices of St. Mary's Hall. [Burlington, N.J.:] n.p., n.d. T20.4. D?

634. St. Mary's Hall, Burlington, N.J. St. Mary's Hall, Green Bank, Burlington, New Jersey, for female education, on Christian principles: under the patronage and immediate superintendence of the bishop of the diocese; second semi-annual catalogue. Burlington, N.J.: J. L. Powell, 1838. T20.6.

635. Sankey, William S. Villiers. Epitome of Christian institutions, and appendix. Edinburgh: W. S. Villiers Sankey, 1838. T19.8.

636. Scott, Robert. The Athenian ballot and secret suffrage. Oxford: J. H. Parker, 1838. T38.5. A sequel to 556.

637. Search, John, ed. What? and who says it? An exposition of the statement that the established Church "destroys more souls than it saves," by the Rev. Thomas Chalmers, D.D., Professor of Theology in the University of Edinburgh; the Right Rev. the Bishop of Calcutta; Rev. Samuel Charles Wilks; Rev. Henry Budd; Rev. Charles Bridges; Rev. Henry Melvill; editor of the Record; editor of the Christian Observer; and others; in a letter to "one of the clergy who signed the late requisition to the Archdeacon of Worcester"; edited by John Search. 2nd ed. Worcester: J. H. d'Egville, n.d. T19.7. D?

638. Selwyn, William. The substance of an argument maintained before the Archdeacon of Leicester, against those clauses of the Benefices Plurality Bill, which confer additional powers on the Ecclesiastical Commissioners for England, to the great prejudice of the Right Reverend the Bishops of England and Wales. Cambridge: J. & J. J. Deighton, 1838. T36.2.

639. Sinclair, William. A discourse, preached in the parish church of Huddersfield, December 26th, 1838, at the opening of the Church of England Collegiate School, in that town. 2nd ed. Leeds: T. Harrison, n.d. T33.7.

640. Stephens, Abednego. Address to the Alumni Society of Nashville University, on the influence of institutions for high letters on the mental and moral character of the nation, and

the obligation of government to endow and sustain them. Nashville, TN: B. R. McKennie, 1838. T20.26.

641. Sumner, John Bird. A charge delivered to the clergy of the Diocese of Chester at the triennial visitation in 1838. London: J. Hatchard and Son, 1838. T34.3.

642. Thomas, Vaughan. An address delivered at the Birmingham Royal School of Medicine and Surgery, at the third anniversary meeting, August 29, 1838. Oxford: W. Baxter, 1838. T23.9.

643. Todd, Henry John. An authentic account of our Authorized Translation of the Holy Bible, and of the translators; with testimonies to the excellence of the translation. 3rd ed. Oxford: John Henry Parker, 1838. ST6.5.

644. Trower, Francis Charles. Hannibal, patriæ defensionem suscepturus, ab Italia accitus; carmen latinum, Cancellarii Præmio donatum, et in Theatro Sheldoniano recitatum, MDCCCXXX-VIII; auctore Francisco Carolo Trower, e Collegio Balliolensi. Oxford: J. Vincent, 1838. NL28.11.

645. Tyrwhitt, Richard Edmund. Baptism instituted by our Lord himself; a sermon; to which is added a critical discussion of John III.5. Oxford: John Henry Parker, 1838. T37.4.

646. Vogan, Thomas S. L. The doctrine of the Apostolical Succession developed and proved, in a sermon, preached at the primary visitation of the Right Reverend Edward, Lord Bishop of Norwich, in the parish church of North Walsham, on Wednesday, July 4, 1838. London: J. G. & F. Rivington, 1838. T32.19.

647. Walters, William Clayton. Notes on the sign or sacrament of Holy Baptism. London: John W. Parker, 1838. ST6.6. A defense of infant baptism.

648. Ward, Richard. The testimony of Bishop Jeremy Taylor, to the seven propositions selected by the Rev. M. Jackson as contrary to the doctrine of the Church of England. London: James Burns, 1838. T27.12.

649. Whittingham, William Rollinson. A letter from the Rev. Professor Whittingham, of the General Theological Seminary, to a clergyman of Western New York, in relation to the division of the Diocese of New York; June, 1838. N.l., n.p., 1838. T21.4.

650. Wilberforce, Samuel. The power of God's word needful for national education; a sermon, preached at St. John's Chapel, Portsea, October 28, 1838. Portsea: W. Woodward, 1838. T33.6. I.

651. Wilson, William. A brief examination of Professor Keble's visitation sermon, entitled "Primitive Tradition Recognised in Holy Scripture," and preached in the Cathedral Church of Winchester, September 27, 1836. Oxford: J. H. Parker, 1837. T26.16. M*. A reply to 462.

652. Wodehouse, Charles N. A sermon, preached in the Cathedral Church of Norwich, at the ordination of the Right Reverend Edward, Lord Bishop of the Diocese, on Sunday, March 11th,

1838, and printed at his request. Norwich: John Stacy, 1838.
T32.14. I.

WORKS BY UNIDENTIFIED AUTHORS

653. Anon. Are cathedral institutions useless? A practical answer
to this question. Eton: n.p., 1838. T24.4. Inscription: "Oriel."

654. Anon. A catechism on the holy catholick and apostolick Church;
I: on the unity of the Church; II: on the ministry and discipline of the Church: III.: on the Communion of Saints in the
Church; with an appendix, containing a list of the Archbishops
of Canterbury, from the time of Augustin to the present day;
for the instruction of such as have learned the Church Catechism. 2nd ed. Oxford: J. H. Parker, 1838. ST11.11.

655. Anon. The Christian week. London: Rivingtons, 1838. ST19.9.
Seven hymns.

656. Anon. Extracts illustrating the extent of instruction which
might be afforded by the university. Oxford: Baxter, n.d.
T38.6. D? I. S.

657. Anon. A few verses, printed for sale at the bazaar in aid of
new rooms for the Derby National School, March 8th and 9th,
1838. N.1., Henry Mozley and Sons, n.d. ST7.18. The author
is female, possibly Anne Mozley.

658. Anon. India, Great Britain, and Russia. London: A. H. Baily,
1838. T53.1.

659. Anon. Is baptismal regeneration a doctrine of the Church of
England? London: James Burns, 1838. ST10.8. Sent to N as
editor of the British Critic.

660. Anon. A letter to His Grace the Archbishop of Canterbury
occasioned by the late meeting in support of the Society for
the Propagation of the Gospel in Foreign Parts. London:
Stewart, 1838. NL28.18. By a supporter of the SPCK.

661. Anon. On the admission of lay members to the Ecclesiastical
Synods of the Protestant Episcopal Church in Scotland. Edinburgh: R. Grant & Son, 1838. T22.7. I.

662. Anon. Popular errors. ST5.5. Lacks title-page. D?

663. Anon. The prebendary; or cathedral establishments, ancient
and modern; Part. II: modern cathedral establishments. London: J. Hatchard & Son, 1838. T24.6.

664. Anon. Remarks on the breaking and eating of bread and drink-
ing of wine in remembrance of the Passion of Christ. London:
Houlston, 1838. ST30.14. A Low Church tract.

665. Anon. The voice of the Church, or a weak defender gently re-
buked. Newcastle: Currie and Bowman, 1838. ST28.7. Inscribed "To the Editor of the Brit. Critic." Anti-Tractarian,
by a clergyman in the Diocese of Durham.

666. Christologus Neoptolemus, pseud. A letter to the Rev. Walter
F. Hook, D.D., on his defence and exposition of the damnatory
clauses of the Athanasian Creed. London: Ridgway, 1838. T39.4.

667. A Country Clergyman, pseud. A letter to the Rev. Sydney Smith,
      Canon Residentiary of St. Paul's. London: James Burns, 1838.
      ST28.6. Sent to N by the author. A reply to Smith's letter
      to Lord John Russell on the Clergy Residence and Plurality
      Bill.

668. A Lady, pseud. Remarks on a pamphlet, entitled, "On Proposals
      for Reviving the Convocation Addressed to All Classes":
      printed for the benefit of the National School, and sold at
      the bazaar, held in the New Lecture Hall, Derby, March 8th and
      9th, 1838; by a lady. Derby: William Bemrose, 1838. T22.4.

669. A Layman, pseud. The independence of the Universities and
      colleges of Oxford and Cambridge. Oxford: J. H. Parker, 1838.
      T67.3. Sent to N. Duplicate copy: T16.21.

670. A Layman, pseud. Observations on the illegal and unconstitu-
      tional character of the Ecclesiastical Commission. Oxford:
      J. H. Parker, 1838. T36.3. An anti-Erastian tract.

671. A Member of Oxford Convocation, pseud. Consensus omnium; or,
      the test of orthodoxy; by a member of Oxford Convocation.
      London: J. Ridgway, 1838. T27.10. Cf. 610.

672. A Member of Oxford Convocation, pseud. The via media; or,
      Anglican orthodoxy; by a member of Oxford Convocation. Lon-
      don: James Ridgway, 1838. T27.8. Cf. 609.

673. Parrhesiastes, pseud., and Henry Phillpotts. The Bishop of
      Exeter's speech in the House of Lords, upon the violation of
      the Roman Catholic oath, with an original article by Parrhesi-
      astes. London: C. Mitchell, 1838. ST6.4. An anti-Catholic
      tract. The Bishop of Exeter was Henry Phillpotts.

1839

674. Aborigines Protection Society. Extracts from the papers and
      proceedings of the Aborigines Protection Society; No. 1: May,
      1839. London: William Ball Arnold, and Co., 1839. T53.15.

675. Aborigines Protection Society. Report on the Indians of upper
      Canada. London: William Ball Arnold, 1839. T53.14. Lacks
      title-page.

676. Aborigines Protection Society. The second annual report of
      the Aborigines Protection Society, presented at the meeting
      in Exeter Hall, May 21st, 1839; with list of officers, sub-
      scribers, benefactors, and honorary members. London: P. White
      & Son, 1839. T53.17.

677. Armstrong, John. Church endowment; a sermon preached at Clif-
      ton Church, in aid of the endowment of the new chapel of ease,
      at Durdham Down. London: J. G. F. & J. Rivington, 1839. T33.21.

678. Baines, Peter Augustine. Faith, hope, and charity; the sub-
      stance of a sermon preached at the dedication of the Catholic
      Chapel at Bradford, in the County of York, on Wednesday, July
      27, 1825. London: P. & M. Andrews, 1839. T35.8. "A publica-
      tion of the Catholic Institute of Great Britain." Duplicate

copy: T35.9.

679. Bickersteth, Edward. The real dangers of London: with the duty
      of Christian exertion, and the hope of a divine blessing; a
      sermon, preached before the London City Mission, on Thursday,
      May 2, 1839, at St. John's Chapel, Bedford Row. London: L.
      & G. Seeley, 1839. ST28.10.

680. Bickersteth, Edward. Remarks on the dangers of the Church of
      Christ; its final triumph and our present duties; designed as
      a call to watchfulness and prayer. London: R. B. Seeley, and
      W. Burnside, 1839. NL18.12. I.

681. Binney, Thomas. Conscientious clerical nonconformity; a dis-
      course, delivered at Chadwell Street Chapel, Pentonville, on
      Monday, April 15, 1839, on occasion of its reopening, for the
      use of Ridley H. Herschell, a converted Jew. 2nd ed. London:
      Jackson and Walford, 1839. T19.14.

682. Brougham, Henry Peter. A letter on national education, to the
      Duke of Bedford, K.G., from Lord Brougham. Edinburgh: Adam and
      Charles Black, 1839. T52.6. Sent to N as editor of British
      Critic.

683. Burgh, William. Antichrist; a discourse on the thirteenth
      chapter of the Apocalypse; preached in the chapel of the Dublin
      Female Penitentiary, April 7, 1839; with some additional mat-
      ter, and an appendix, containing an answer to the sermon of
      the Rev. Hugh M'Neile, of Liverpool, bearing same title. Dub-
      lin: W. Curry, 1839. ST29.3.

684. Campbell, Augustus. A speech on the subject of national educa-
      tion, delivered at a public meeting in Liverpool, on the 3rd
      April, 1839, with an appendix, as to the influence of educa-
      tion on morals and crime. London: John Hatchard, n.d. T51.28.

685. Catholic Institute of Great Britain. The widow Woolfrey versus
      the Vicar of Carisbrooke: or, prayer for the dead; a tract for
      the times. London: C. Richards, 1839. T35.10.

686. Chandler, George. An address delivered at the opening of the
      Church of England Metropolitan Commercial School, Rose Street,
      Soho Square, January 28, 1839. 2nd ed. London: John W. Par-
      ker, 1839. T23.12.

687. Chandler, George. A charge delivered to the clergy of the
      peculiar jurisdiction of the Dean of Chichester, at the visita-
      tion holden in the cathedral, May 21, 1839. London: John W.
      Parker, 1839. T34.7. I.

688. [Churton, Edward.] A Reformed Catholic, pseud. Letters of a
      reformed Catholic; Nos. I. & II.: on the leading principle of
      the Reformation: and on private judgment and authority in
      matters of faith. 2nd ed. London: J. G. & F. Rivington,
      1839. T29.7.

689. [Churton, Edward.] A Reformed Catholic, pseud. Letters of a
      reformed Catholic; No. III: on Apostolical Succession; with a
      preface, containing a notice of the Presbyterian attack on Dr.
      Hook, published in Fraser's Magazine. London: J. G. & F. Riv-
      ington, 1839. T29.8. S. Cf. 798. See 545, 546.

690. Cole, Henry. The principles of modern dissentient Evangelism disclosed, and the Church of England proved to be the only conservatrix of the national faith! The only safe instructrix of the poor! Indestructible but by her own hands! being series of letters (originally published in the "Times," and just concluded,) to Dr. Pye Smith on "Geology and Revelation," and on dissentient "Popular Education"; with a summary refutation of Dr. Wardlaw's late lectures on "Church Establishments." London: Nisbet & Co., 1839. T19.17.

691. Committee of Council. Recent measures for the promotion of education in England. London: Ridgway, 1839. T52.2.

692. Cornish, Charles Lewis. An attempt to illustrate the connection between the Catechism and articles of the Church, in a letter to a friend. Oxford: John Henry Parker, 1839. NL:D.4. 6.2.

693. Courtney, John. The poor widow; a sermon preached in the parish church of Sanderstead, Surrey, on Sunday, the 27th of October, 1839. London: J. G. & F. Rivington, 1839. T33.18.

694. Curie, Paul Etienne François Gustave. Dr. Curie's clinical lecture on homœopathy. [London: Palmer & Clayton,] n.d. T47.13. A publication advertising the London Homœopathic Dispensary.

695. Denison, Edward. A charge delivered to the clergy of the Diocese of Salisbury, at the primary visitation of Edward, Lord Bishop of Salisbury, in August and September, 1839. Salisbury: W. B. Brodie and Co., n.d. T34.9.

696. Denison, Edward. The Church, the teacher of her children; a sermon preached at St. Margaret's, Westminster, on Sunday, May 12, 1839. London: John Cochran, 1839. T34.8. I. Denison was Bishop of Salisbury.

697. Doane, George Washington. The beauty and blessedness of early piety: an address to the persons confirmed in St. Mary's Church, Burlington, on the fourteenth Sunday after Trinity, MDCCCXXXIX, thirteen of whom were pupils of St. Mary's Hall. Burlington, N.J.: Powell and George, 1839. T20.7.

698. Doane, George Washington. Episcopal address to the annual convention of the Diocese of New Jersey, May 29, 1839. Burlington, N.J.: Missionary Press, 1839. T20.19.

699. Doane, George Washington. Looking unto Jesus: a sermon preached in St. Mary's Church, Burlington, on the Sunday before Advent, MDCCCXXXIX, being the next after the decease of the Rev. Benjamin Davis Winslow, assistant to the rector. Burlington, N.J.: J. L. Powell, 1839. T20.13.

700. Doane, George Washington. The pastoral office: the third charge to the clergy of the Diocese of New Jersey; at the opening of the annual convention, in St. Mary's Church, Burlington, May 29, 1839, with appendix. Burlington, N.J.: Powell and George, 1839. T20.14.

701. Dodsworth, William. Romanism successfully opposed only on Catholic principles; a sermon. London: J. Burns, 1839.

T29.12. Duplicate copy: NL:D4.5.5.

702. Douglas, James. The revival of religion. Edinburgh: Adam and Charles Black, 1839. T39.6. Sent to N as editor of the British Critic.

703. Eller, Irvin. A few plain words to plain people, on the duty of Christian unity; and on the proper exercise of the right of private judgment. 2nd ed. Grantham: S. Ridge, 1839. ST7.7.

704. Episcopal Church of Scotland. A pastoral letter addressed to the clergy and laity of the Episcopal Communion in Scotland, by the Bishops of that Church. Edinburgh: Robert Grant and Son, 1839. T34.13. Sent to N by the publishers.

705. The Episcopal Magazine and Church of England Warder, 1, No. 9 (Sept. 1839), 525-88. T19.2.

706. Fitzgerald, William. Episcopacy, Tradition, and the Sacraments, considered in reference to the Oxford Tracts, with a postscript upon fundamentals. Dublin: William Curry, 1839. T29.10.

707. Gibbons, George B. A sermon, preached in the parish church of St. Mary Magdalene, Launceston, before the Right Reverend, Henry Bishop of Exeter, at his triennial visitation, September 23, 1839. Launceston: T. & W. R. Bray, 1839. T33.15. A pro-Tractarian sermon.

708. Goode, William. Church rates, colonial Church, and national education; a reply to the answer of the Edinburgh Review to the two following publications; I: A Brief History of Church Rates, Proving the Liability of a Parish to Them to Be a Common Law Liability; II: A Reply to the Article on Church Rates in the Edinburgh Review, no. 134; in two letters to the editor; letter two. London: J. Hatchard, 1839. T22.18.

709. Graves, Robert Perceval. The system of the Church, and the consequent obligations of her ministers; a sermon preached in Kendal Parish Church, April 29th, 1839, before the commissary and clergy, at the visitation of the Venerable and Worshipful James Thomas Law, A.M., Commissary of the Archdeaconry of Richmond. London: Whittaker, n.d. T33.11.

710. Gresley, William. Some thoughts on the means of working out the scheme of diocesan education, in a letter, addressed to the Archdeacons of Stafford, Salop, and Derby. London: J. G. & F. Rivington, 1839. ST21.10. On title-page: "please let me have this again. Might it no[t] lead the article? JHN." Duplicate copy: ST19.7.

711. [Haffreingue, A., ed.] Bénédiction et pose de la première pierre; la nouvelle église Notre-Dame de Boulogne, édifiée sur les ruines de l'ancienne cathédrale par les soins et sur les plans de M. l'Abbé A. Haffreingue, à l'aide d'une souscription volontaire, et destinée a devenir l'église paroissiale de la haute-ville de Boulogne-sur-Mer. (Article extrait du journal l'Annotateur du 11 Avril 1839.); suivi d'un appel en faveur de la souscription, par M. le Baron d'Ordre; et d'un appendice renfermant le procès-verbal de cette pose,

le discours prononcé à cette occasion par M. l'Abbé Sergeant,
aûmonier de l'hospice, et des notes archéologiques et
historiques sur la crypte ou chapelle souterraine de l'ancienne
cathédrale récemment découverte. Boulogne-sur-Mer: F. Birlé,
1839. T45.11.

712. Hawkins, Edward. Church extension in England and Wales; a sermon preached at the Cathedral Church of Rochester, September
22, 1839, in aid of the Incorporated Society for Promoting the
Enlargement, Building, and Repairing of Churches and Chapels.
London: B. Fellowes, 1839. ST29.2.

713. Head, Henry E. Apostolic Succession considered in relation to
national education; in a letter, to the Rt. Hon. Lord John
Russell. London: Nisbet, 1839. T30.2.

714. Hobson, Leonard Jasper. Ecclesiastical colloquies; or dialogues on the nature and discipline of the Church of England;
with a particular reference to certain popular objections; designed to establish the young members of the Church in the
principles of conformity. London: Roake & Varty, 1839. Tre
10.2.

715. Hook, Walter, Farquhar. The novelties of Romanism; or, Popery
refuted by Tradition; a sermon, preached in St. Andrew's
Church, Manchester. London: F. C. & J. Rivington, 1839. T30.
9.

716. [Hook, Walter Farquhar.] A Presbyter of the Church of England,
pseud. Presbyterian rights asserted; by a presbyter of the
Church of England. London: James Burns, 1839. T29.3.

717. Hook, Walter Farquhar. "Who are the Catholics?" answered in
an account of the Protestant Episcopal Church in England, extracted from a sermon preached before the Queen. New York:
Protestant Episcopal Tract Society, 1839. ST15.5. Tract No.
139.

718. Horsley, Heneage. "The pillar and ground of the truth"; a
sermon, preached in the Chapel of St. Paul, Dundee, on Sunday,
17th March 1839; and addressed to the serious consideration
of the members of the Episcopal communion in Scotland at the
present crisis. Dundee: J. Chalmers, 1839. T33.10. Corrections in ink. A defense of Apostolic Succession and Tracts
for the Times.

719. The Inquirer, 2 (January 1839), 1-48. N.l., n.p., n.d. T46.
10.

720. The Inquirer, 2 (Sept. 1839), 421-68. T19.3.

721. The Inquirer, 2 (October 1839), 469-524. T19.5.

722. Jarvis, Samuel Farmar. The long home of man: a sermon,
preached in St. Stephen's Church, East Hadham, on Tuesday,
the 16th day of January, 1838, at the funeral of the Rev.
Stephen Beach, late rector of that parish. New York: Louis
Sherman, 1839. T21.1.

723. Jebb, John. A tract for all times, but for the present,
peculiar character of the Church of England, both from other
branches of the Reformation, and from the modern Church of

Rome. London: Rivingtons, 1839. NL:D4.5.4.

724. Jones, Joseph. An essay on episcopacy. London: John Hatchard and Son, 1839. T30.3.

725. Kay, James Phillips. The training of pauper children; a report published by the Poor Law Commissioners in their fourth annual report. London: William Clowes and Sons, 1839. T51.26.

726. Kay, James Phillips, and Edward Carleton Tufnell. Reports on the training of pauper children together with instructional letter from the Poor Law Commissioners to the chaplain at Mr. Aubin's establishment, Norwood. London: W. Clowes and Sons, 1839. T51.27.

727. Keble, John. Primitive tradition recognised in Holy Scripture: a sermon, preached in the Cathedral Church of Winchester, at the visitation of the Worshipful and Reverend William Dealtry, Chancellor of the Diocese, September 27, 1836; fourth edition, with a postscript, illustrative of some points in the argument of the sermon: to which is subjoined Catena Patrum No. III. (being No. LXXVIII of the "Tracts for the Times"). London: J. G. & F. Rivington, 1839. T26.15. Cf. 651, 467.

728. Lancaster, Thomas William. An earnest and resolute protestation against a certain inductive method of theologizing, which has been recently propounded by the King's Professor of Divinity in Oxford; with other matter. London: J. G. and F. Rivington, 1839. T39.2. A reply to R. D. Hampden's 1832 Bampton Lectures.

729. [Lathburg, Thomas.] One of the Clergy of the Archdeaconry, pseud. Observations on certain statements advanced by the Venerable the Archdeacon of Bath, in his primary charge, respecting one of the sacramental rubrics, and the question of congregational psalmody. London: Simpkin and Marshall, 1839. T48.1. Marginalia, some obliterated in binding, not in N's hand.

730. Lee, Samuel. The duty of Christian ministers taking heed to the ministry which they have received in the Lord, urged in a sermon, preached at the visitation holden by the Lord Bishop of London, at Bishop's Stortford, in October, 1838; in which some notice is taken of the Oxford Tracts, and of the true use of Tradition as subservient to the interpretation of Holy Scripture, and to a just discharge of the duties of priesthood: but, more particularly, of the seventh lecture of Dr. Wiseman, and the groundless assumptions and erroneous statements there made. Cambridge: John W. Parker, 1839. T29.1.

731. LeMesurier, Henry. A recent tract upon reserve in communicating religious knowledge compared with Scripture. Oxford: J. Munday, 1839. T27.5. A reply to Isaac Williams, Tracts for the Times, No. 80 (1837).

732. Lockhart, John Gibson. The Ballantyne-humbug handled, in a letter to Sir Adam Fergusson. Edinburgh: Robert Cadell, 1839. ST14.3. A reply to Fergusson's pamphlet, Refutation of the Misstatements and Calumnies Contained in Mr. Lockhart's Life of Sir Walter Scott, Bart., Respecting the Messrs. Ballantyne

(London, 1838).

733.   Lowe, Thomas Hill. The divine commission and authority of the
       Christian priesthood, asserted and explained; a sermon preach-
       ed in the church of St. Mary Major, Exeter, on the 30th of
       April, 1839, at the visitation of the Venerable John Moore
       Stevens, Archbishop of Exeter. Exeter: W. Spreat, 1839.
       ST28.9.

734.   Lucas, Frederick. Reasons for becoming a Roman Catholic; ad-
       dressed to the Society of Friends. London: Booker and Dolman,
       1839. T35.11. Sent to N as editor of British Critic.

735.   M'Ghee, Robert James. No Popery; extract from a speech of the
       Rev. R. J. M'Ghee, at Sheffield, November 13, 1839. N.l., n.
       p., n.d. T45.16. Protestant Association Handbills, No. 7.

736.   Maitland, Samuel Roffey. A letter to the Rev. W. H. Mill,
       D.D., late principal of Bishop's College, Calcutta; containing
       some strictures on Mr. Faber's recent work, entitled, "The
       Ancient Vallenses and Albigenses." London: J. G. & F. Riving-
       ton, 1839. T37.6. A reply to George Stanley Faber's An En-
       quiry into the History and Theology of the Vallenses and
       Albigenses (1838).

737.   Maude, Thomas. The two states; consequences of the Fall and of
       the Redemption; a sermon preached in the parish church of
       Saint Paul, Covent Garden, on Friday, March 1st, 1839. Lon-
       don: J. Hatchard and Son, 1839. T33.9. An "Easter Ode" is
       appended, pp. 25-27.

738.   Medley, John. The union of the members in Christ's body; a
       sermon, preached in the Cathedral Church of St. Peter, Exeter,
       on Thursday, October 10, M.DCCC.XXXIX., at the triennial
       visitation of the Right Rev. Henry, Lord Bishop of Exeter.
       Exeter: P. A. Hannaford, 1839. T33.16. I.

739.   Merewether, Francis. The ministerial succession; a sermon,
       preached at Broadstairs, in the Parish of St. Peter's, Kent,
       (in the Diocese and Province of Canterbury) on Sunday,
       October 7th, 1838. Ashby-de-la-Zouch: W. & J. Hextall, 1839.
       T33.5. I.

740.   Merewether, Francis. Strictures on the four sermons on tradi-
       tion and episcopacy, preached in the Temple Church, by the
       Rev. Christopher Benson, Master. Oxford: John Henry Parker,
       1839. T30.13.

741.   Merivale, Charles. The Church of England, faithful witness
       of Christ; not destroying the law, but fulfilling it; four
       sermons preached before the University of Cambridge, in Novem-
       ber, 1838. Cambridge: John W. Parker, 1839. T38.7. S*. M.

742.   Miller, Charles. The principles of Mr. Shaw Lefevre's Paro-
       chial Assessments Bill, and the Tithe Commutation Act, com-
       pared in a letter to the Rev. Richard Jones, M.A. one of the
       Tithe Commissioners for England and Wales. London: J. G. &
       F. Rivington, 1839. T22.16.

743.   Moore, Henry. The Church and the Holy Scriptures; a sermon
       preached in the Parish Church of Walsall at the visitation of

the Venerable George Hudson, M.A., Archdeacon of Stafford, May 27, 1839; with notes. London: J. C. & F. Rivington, n.d. T33.12. I. Corrections in ink.

744. National Society for Promoting the Education of the Children of the Poor in the Principles of the Established Church, throughout England and Wales. Prospectus with a list of subscribers and copy of address by the Archbishop of Canterbury. London: Robson, Levey and Franklyn, 1839. T19.1.

745. Norris, Henry Handley. The good shepherd; a sermon, preached in the parish church of Hackney, on Sunday, June 23, 1839, being the Sunday next following the funeral of the Ven. John James Watson, D.D., Archdeacon of St. Alban's and Rector of Hackney. London: J. G. F. & J. Rivington, 1839. T33.13.

746. Oakeley, Frederick. Christ manifested to the faithful through His Church; a sermon preached at Margaret Chapel, St. Marylebone, on the twenty-fifth Sunday after Trinity, MDCCCXXXIX. Oxford: John Henry Parker, 1839. ST11.3.

747. Oakeley, Frederick. Preface to Whitehall Sermons; a few copies of this preface have been printed separately from the sermons to which it belongs, for private distribution only. N.l., n.p., 1839. T29.2.

748. Otter, William. Substance of the Bishop of Chichester's speech in the House of Lords, the 15th. of July, on the plan of national education proposed by Lord Brougham and Vaux. Chichester: William Hayley Mason, 1839. T23.11.

749. Oxford Society for Promoting the Study of Gothic Architecture. The rules and proceedings of the Oxford Society for Promoting the Study of Gothic Architecture. Oxford: n.p., 1839. T37.8. N is listed as a member and as the donor of two books.

750. Parr, John Owen. A few remarks on the state and improvement of popular education, in connexion with the Church of England. Salisbury: W. B. Brodie & Co., 1839. T23.13. Signed: "J.H.N. Jan. 1839."

751. Petty-Fitzmaurice, Henry. Substance of the Marquess of Lansdowne's speech in the House of Lords, July 5, 1839, on the government plan for promoting national education; reprinted from Hansard's Parliamentary Debates. 6th ed. London: Ridgway, 1839. T52.5.

752. Phillpotts, Henry. Charge delivered to the clergy of the Diocese of Exeter by the Right Reverend Henry, Lord Bishop of Exeter, at his triennial visitation in the months of August, September, and October, 1839. London: John Murray, 1839. T34.11.

753. Phillpotts, Henry. National education; speech of the Bishop of Exeter in the House of Lords, July 5, 1839. London: Roake & Varty, 1839. ST22.15.

754. Poole, George Ayliffe. The Church the teacher of her children, and the preaching of the gospel to the poor a sign of Christ's presence with his Church; two sermons, preached in behalf of the Sunday school of St. James' Church, Leeds, on Sunday,

March 2, 1839. London: Burns, 1839. ST13.5. Date of sermon
is corrected in ink to March 3.

755. Poole, George Ayliffe. Strictures, on "An Address Delivered
on Occasion of Laying the First Stone of East Parade Chapel,
Leeds, on Monday, Sept. 2, 1839, by the Rev. John Ely."
Leeds: T. Harrison, 1839. T30.10.

756. Powell, Baden. Tradition unveiled: or, an exposition of the
pretensions and tendency of authoritative teaching in the
Church. Oxford: J. W. Parker, 1839. T29.9.

757. Prevost, George. Corruption and schism hindering the free
course of the Gospel: a sermon in behalf of the Society for
the Propagation of the Gospel, preached at the parish church
of St. Augustine, Bristol, on Sunday, the 13th of October,
1839. London: J. G. F. & J. Rivington, 1839. T33.17.

758. [Protestant Association.] The Jesuits exposed. N.l., n.p.,
n.d. T35.13. Sent to N as editor of British Critic.

759. Protestant Episcopal Church in the United States, Diocese of
New Jersey. Journal of the fifty-sixth annual convention of
the Protestant Episcopal Church in the state of New Jersey;
held in St. Mary's Church, Burlington, on Wednesday the 29th
and Thursday the 30th days of May, 1839. Burlington, N.J.:
n.p., 1839. T20.18.

760. Protestant Episcopal Church in the United States, Diocese of
Vermont. Journal of the proceedings of the forty-ninth annual
convention of the Protestant Episcopal Church in the Diocese
of Vermont; being the seventh annual convention since the full
organization of the diocese: held in St. Stephen's Church,
Middlebury, on the eighteenth and nineteenth days of September,
1839. Burlington, VT: Chauncey Goodrich, 1839. T20.22.

761. Protestant Episcopal Tract Society. Degrees of bliss in heaven. New York: Protestant Episcopal Tract Society, 1839.
ST15.6. Tract No. 141.

762. Pugin, Augustus Welby. A letter on the proposed Protestant
memorial to Cranmer, Ridley, & Latymer, addressed to the subscribers to and promoters of that undertaking. London:
Booker & Dolman, 1839. NL:D.4.5.10. Scoring and marginalia,
not by N. Duplicate copy: T19.10.

763. Pusey, Edward Bouverie. The day of judgement; a sermon,
preached on the twentieth Sunday after Trinity, in S. Peter's
Church, Brighton. Oxford: John Henry Parker, 1839. Tre13.3.

764. [Pusey, Edward Bouverie, ed.] Extracts from the Tracts for
the Times, the Lyra Apostolica, and other publications; showing that to oppose ultra-Protestantism is not to favour Popery.
London: J. G. & F. Rivington, 1839. NL:D4.5.8.

765. Pusey, Edward Bouverie. A letter to the Right Rev. Father in
God, Richard, Lord Bishop of Oxford, on the tendency to
Romanism imputed to doctrines held of old, as now, in the
English Church. Oxford: J. H. Parker, 1839. Tre14.2.

766. Raikes, Henry. "The man of God": a sermon preached at the

ordination held by the Right Reverend the Lord Bishop of
Chester, in the Cathedral of Chester, on Sunday, February 24,
1839. Chester: J. Seacome, 1839. T33.8. Sent to N as editor
of the British Critic.

767. Roberts, Samuel. The Rev. Dr. Pye Smith and the new Poor Law.
London: Whittaker & Co., 1839. T22.11.

768. Russell, John. Substance of Lord John Russell's speech in the
House of Commons, June 20th, 1839; on the government plan for
promoting national education. 6th ed. London: Ridgway, 1839.
T52.4.

769. Russell, Michael. The historical evidence for the apostolical
institution of episcopacy; a sermon, preached at Stirling, on
Sunday the 7th March, 1830, at the consecration of the Right
Rev. James Walker, D.D. 3rd ed. Edinburgh: Oliver & Boyd,
1839. T30.7.

770. Sadler, Michael Thomas. Roman Catholic question: speech of
Michael Thomas Sadler, Esq., M.P. for Neward, in the House of
Commons, on Tuesday, March 17, 1829, at the second reading of
the Roman Catholic Relief Bill. London: Protestant Association, 1839. T35.12. Sent by Rivingtons (publishers) to N as
editor of British Critic. No. 20 of Publications of the Protestant Association.

771. Scott, Robert. A sermon preached on Sunday, Jan. 20, 1839,
in the parish church of Holywell, Oxford, in behalf of the
Society for the Propagation of the Gospel in Foreign Parts.
Oxford: John Henry Parker, 1839. ST11.5. I.

772. Sewell, Richard Clarke. Vindiciae Ecclesiasticae; or a legal
and historical argument against the abolition of the Bishops'
Courts in causes or corrections of clerks, as proposed by the
Church Discipline Bill. Oxford: Henry Slatter, 1839. T24.2.
Dedicated to Rev. Martin Joseph Routh, D.D.

773. [Sewell, William.] "Oxford theology," Quarterly Review, 63
(1839), 525-72. T39.9. Separatum of a review of Tracts for
the Times and 11 other Tractarian works.

774. Silver, Thomas. A letter to Sir R. H. Inglis, Bart., M.P. for
the University of Oxford, on the spoliation and captivity of
the cathedrals of England. Oxford: J. H. Parker, 1839. T24.7.
Inscribed: "John H. Newman from the Author. April 12. 1839."
Cf. 1091.

775. Sinclair, John. Copy of a letter addressed by the Rev. John
Sinclair to the Rev._____, an applicant for aid from the
Parliamentary Grant for the year 1839. N.l., n.p., n.d.
Pl.1. Lacks title-page.

776. Sinclair, John. Correspondence of the National Society with
the Lords of the Treasury and with the Committee of Council
on Education. London: John Murray, 1839. T52.1. I.

777. Sinclair, John. Vindication of the episcopal or apostolical
succession. London: J. G. & F. Rivington, 1839. ST13.7.

778. Symons, Jelinger Cookson. The tendency of the Tithe Act

considered with reference to the Corn-Law question; accompanied by a plain statement of the point at issue with respect to tithe rate assessments. London: C. J. G. & F. Rivington, 1839. T22.15. I.

779. Talbot, H. Fox. The antiquity of the Book of Genesis illustrated by some new arguments. London: Longman, Orme, Green, Brown, and Longman, 1839. T46.3. I.

780. Taylor, Emily. Help to the schoolmistress, or village teaching. London: Harvey and Darton, 1839. ST23.1.

781. Thelwall, Algernon Sidney. To all those who are interested in the circulation of the Word of God. London: Macintosh, 1839. T45.15. A criticism from Exeter Hall of P. A. Pereira de Figueiredo's Portugese version of the Bible. Thelwall was secretary of the Trinitarian Bible Society.

782. Thom, John Hamilton. The practical importance of the Unitarian controversy; a lecture, delivered in Paradise Street Chapel, Liverpool, on Tuesday, February 12, 1839; being the first of a series, to be delivered weekly, in answer to a course of lectures against Unitarianism, in Christ Church, Liverpool, by thirteen clergymen of the Church of England. Liverpool: Willmer and Smith, 1839. T19.11.

783. Turton, Thomas. Observations on the Rev. Dr. Wiseman's reply to Dr. Turton's Roman Catholic Doctrine of the Eucharist considered. Cambridge: John W. Parker, 1839. Tre12.3.

784. Vevers, William. A summary of the doctrines of the Papal and Protestant Churches, compiled from the decrees of general councils, and the articles and homilies of the Church of England. Leeds: R. Inchbold, n.d. ST13.2. Anti-Catholic.

785. Wackerbath, Francis Diedrich. The alleged connexion between the Church of England and Lutheranism examined, in a short review of some statements contained in the visitation sermon, (fourth edition,) of the Rev. George Croly, LL.D., preached at St. Paul's Cathedral, on Monday, October 9, 1838; edited, with an appendix. London: John W. Parker, 1839. T30.5.

786. Wackerbath, Francis Diedrich. The revival of monastic institutions, and their bearing upon society, considered with reference to the present condition of the Anglican Church. Colchester: W. Totham, 1839. T30.6.

787. Ward, George Robert Michael. An appeal to the Bishop of Winchester, Visitor of Trinity College, Oxford, on the misappropriation of the endowments of that society, with hints towards a history of "The Poor Man's Church" in the University of Oxford. Oxford: Henry Alden, 1839. T38.8. See K.C., 56-57.

788. Watson, John James. The Divine Commission and perpetuity of the Christian priesthood: as considered in a charge to the clergy of the Archdeaconry of St. Alban's, at his primary visitation, A. D. 1816. London: J. G. F. & J. Rivington, 1839. T34.12.

789. Wesleyan Missionary Notices, &c., N.S. 1, no. 9 (Sept. 1839),

133-48. T19.4.

790. Wesleyan Missionary Notices, &c., N.S. 1, no. 10 (Oct. 1839), 149-64. T19.6.

791. Whately, Richard. A charge delivered to the clergy of the Dioceses of Dublin and Glendalagh, at the visitation in October, 1839. N.l., n.p., 1839. T34.10. "Not published."

792. Wilberforce, Henry William. The building of the house of God; a sermon, preached in the Church of All Saints, Southampton, on Tuesday, August 13, 1839, at the rebuilding of the ancient Church of St. Lawrence. Southampton: William Smart, [1839]. T33.14. I.

793. Wilberforce, Robert Isaac. A letter to the Most Noble the Marquis of Lansdowne, on the establishment of a board of education. London: John Murry, 1839. ST29.5. Cf. 957.

794. Wiseman, Nicholas. The High-Church claims: or, a series of papers on the Oxford controversy, the High-Church theory of dogmatical authority, Anglican claim to apostolical succession, &c.; No. 1: occasioned by the controversy respecting Dr. Hampden's appointment to the theological chair at Oxford in 1836. London: C. Richards, [1839]. T35.7. Tract 15 of the Catholic Institute of Great Britain. See also 678.

WORKS BY UNIDENTIFIED AUTHORS

795. Anon. An attempt to illustrate the connection between the Catechism and Articles of the Church; in a letter to a friend. Oxford: John Henry Parker, 1839. T39.5. Sent to N. The letter was written from Oxford, 18 Sept. 1837.

796. Anon. A dialogue between John Thoroughgood and Thomas Simple; August, 1839. [Birmingham: H. C. Langbridge,] 1839. ST13.4. A Churchman's tract against Chartism and socialism.

797. Anon. Dr. Hook's "Call to Union" answered; reprinted from "Fraser's Magazine" for January, 1839. London: James Fraser, .1839. T28.6. A reply to 574. Cf. 798, 689.

798. Anon. Dr. Hook's "Call to Union" defended: a reply to Fraser's answer. London: James Burns, 1839. T28.7. A reply to 796.

799. Anon. Introductory lecture on the study and use of history. [London: Samuel Bentley,] n.d. ST14.1.

800. Anon. John Wesley vindicated by himself: an allegory for the Wesleyan centenary. 2nd ed. Leeds: T. Harrison, 1839. ST 13.1. I. Urges Methodists to return to the Church of England. Also contains mixed criticism of Tracts for the Times.

801. Anon. A letter to the Hon. and Rev. A. P. Perceval, B.C.L., Chaplain in Ordinary to the Queen: occasioned by his recent publication on what is commonly denominated Apostolical Succession. London: S. Cornish, 1839. T30.1.

802. Anon. On Apostolic Succession; with some introductory remarks on the special and distinctive character of the present dispensation. London: Whittaker, Arnot, 1839. ST13.6. "This tract is intended to give the substance of two papers in the

Christian Witness, entitled 'The Secret of God,' and 'The
Character of Office in the present dispensation . . . .'"

803. Anon. On baptism. [Trowbridge: J. S. Sweet], n.d. ST13.3.
D? An Anglican view of baptism as a "covenant."

804. Anon. The popery of Methodism; or, the enthusiasm of papists
and Wesleyans compared; with an appendix, containing John Wesley's reasons against separating from the Church. Leeds: T.
Harrison, 1839. ST10.13 Sent to N from Leeds.

805. Anon. Preface to the tenth edition of a pamphlet entitled
Recent Measures for the Promotion of Education in England.
London: Ridgway, 1839. T52.3.

806. Anon. Restitution to the Church; a sacred duty; or, how can
the Church be made to meet the wants of the nation? London:
James Burns, 1839. ST29.4. I. Sent to N as editor of the
British Critic.

807. Anon. The rubric: its strict observance recommended. London:
James Burns, 1839. T30.4.

808. Anon. Vox Ecclesiae; the judgment of the bishops of the Church
of England, against the Ecclesiastical Commission. London: J.
W. Parker, 1839. T36.5. Contains an anonymous preface and
the visitation charges or other statements by various Anglican
bishops regarding the Ecclesiastical Commissions of England
and Ireland.

809. A Churchman, pseud. A few remarks on the idolatrous tendency
of some parts of the Oxford Tracts; including the substance of
a suppressed letter to the editor of the "Morning Post"; with
some observations on baptismal regeneration, private judgement,
Tradition, &c.; by a Churchman. London: J. Hatchard, 1839.
T29.11. Inscription: "The Revd. J. H. Newman. See pages 16 &
27!!" Heavy pencil annotations throughout in the same hand
as the inscription.

810. A Churchman, and a Friend to Unity, pseud. Letters to the Rev.
Walter Farquhar Hook, D.D., Vicar of Leeds, and Chaplain in
Ordinary to Her Majesty; and to the Rev. Philip N. Shuttle-
worth, D.D., Warden of New College, Oxford. Oxford: J. H.
Parker, 1839. T30.8.

811. A Clergyman, pseud. Plan for a more extensive application to
divine service, of the hitherto unoccupied portions of the
cathedrals of England, but more especially of St. Paul's Cathedral: in a letter to the Right Reverend the Dean, and the Rev.
the Prebendaries of St. Paul's. London: J. G. & F. Rivington,
1839. T37.7. Contains a diagram for remodeling St. Paul's
to make it more suitable for religious services.

812. A Dignitary of the Church, pseud. Ecclesiastical Commission;
a letter to the Bishop of Exeter, with considerations on the
letter of the Bishop of Lincoln, and the charges of the Bishops of London, Lincoln, and Gloucester & Bristol. London:
J. G. & F. Rivington, 1839. T36.4. I.

813. A Member of the Established Church, pseud. Evangelicalism
generally: and more especially as it exists in the parish of

St. Mary, Islington; by a member of the Established Church.
London: G. Mann, 1839. ST10.12.

814. A Norfolk Clergyman, pseud. The justice and equity of assess-
ing the net profits of the land for the relief of the poor,
maintained, in a letter to the Poor Law Commissioners: with
some remarks on the celebrated case of Rex v. Jodrell; by a
Norfolk clergyman. London: Roake & Varty, n.d. T22.12.

815. An Observer, pseud. [Loughborough and Ashby Protestant Tract
Society]. Answer to a pamphlet signed "A Catholic," and en-
titled "A Reply to Remarks," &c.; by an observer. Ashby-de-la-
Zouch: W. and J. Hextall, 1839. ST10.11.

816. A Parson, pseud. The Church of England defended against the
Church of England Quarterly Reviewer: a letter to the laity;
by a parson. London: James Burns, 1839. T28.8.

817. A Presbyter of New York, pseud. Thoughts on the division of
dioceses, in a letter to a clergyman, by a presbyter of New
York. New York: A. Hanford, 1838. T20.24.

818. A Presbyter of the Episcopal Church in Scotland, pseud. The
Oxford Tracts vindicated from the misrepresentations of the
Edinburgh Review, Christian Instructor, &c., and proved, from
internal evidence, not Popish; by a Presbyter of the Episcopal
Church in Scotland. Edinburgh: Bell & Bradfute, 1839. NL:D4.
5.9. I. Duplicate copy: T29.4.

819. Scottish Churchmen, anon. ed. Episcopacy tested by the voice
of the primitive Church, &c.; tracts for all places and all
times; edited by Scottish Churchmen; No. 2. Edinburgh:
R. D. Davidson, 1839. T29.6. I. Sent to N as editor of
British Critic.

820. Scottish Churchmen, anon. ed. Tracts for all places and all
times; edited by Scottish Churchmen; No. I. Edinburgh: R. D.
Davidson, 1839. T29.5. I. Sent to N as editor of the British Critic.

1840

821. Acland, Arthur Henry Dyke. A letter to the Right Reverend
Fathers in God, the Lord Bishops of Exeter and Salisbury, and
through them to the Reverend their clergy, on the present
state of religious societies and the mode of obtaining contributions in aid of Christian objects. 2nd ed. Exeter:
P. A. Hannaford, 1840. T22.19. I. Henry Phillpotts was
Bishop of Exeter; Edward Denison, of Salisbury.

822. Acland, Thomas Dyke. Ecclesiastical duties and revenues;
speech of T. D. Acland, Esq., M.P., in the House of Commons,
Monday, June 29, 1840. London: n.p., 1840. T52.8. I.
Against the Ecclesiastical Duties and Revenues Bill.

823. Adams, Richard Newton. The duty and the spirit of the Chris-
tion ministry: a sermon, preached at the Church of St. Mary,
Nottingham, on Friday, July 31, 1840, at the primary

visitation of the Right Reverend John, Lord Bishop of Lincoln,
and published at the request of the bishop and clergy. London:
J. W. Parker, 1840. T33.29.

824. Addison, Berkeley. Christ all and in all; or, the teaching of
the Church vindicated from the charge of not preaching Christ;
a sermon, preached on the fourteenth Sunday after Trinity, in
S. Peter's Church, Brighton. Brighton: Henry S. King, 1840.
ST28.5. Anglo-Catholic.

825. Alford, Henry. The clergy, watchmen unto the people; a sermon
preached in the parish church of Melton Mowbray, on Thursday,
July 30, 1840, at the primary visitation of the Lord Bishop of
Peterborough and published in compliance with a requisition
from the clergy. London: Rivingtons, 1840. T51.8.

826. Anderson, Robert. The Christian planted together with Christ;
a sermon preached at the Parish Church of St. Nicholas,
Brighton, on Sunday, July 26th, 1840, being the day after the
funeral of Mary Sikes Wagner, the wife of the Rev. Henry
Mitchell Wagner, M.A., (Vicar of Brighton) and the only child
of Joshua Watson, Esq., D.C.L. Brighton: Henry S. King, 1840.
ST28.2.

827. Baines, Peter Augustine. A history of the Pastoral addressed
to the faithful of the Western District, on occasion of the
fast of Lent 1840. N.l., n.p., n.d. T66.2. "Not published."
N has written on the title-page: "not given to me by a Catholic." Privately printed. Baines is explaining a controversy
that arose when his Lenten Pastoral was denounced to Propaganda and he was invited to Rome.

828. Barrett, Elizabeth B. A night-watch by the sea. N.l., n.p.
n.d. T31.3. D? A poem; p. 297 of an unidentified periodical.

829. Beaven, James. A calm exposure of the unfairness of the "Gen-
eral Reply to All Objections" of the author of "Ancient
Christianity." London: J. G. F. & J. Rivington, 1840. T31.9.
I. A reply to Isaac Taylor's Ancient Christianity, Part 5.
Cf. 830. Duplicate copy: T58.8.

830. Beaven, James. The doctrine of Holy Scripture, and of the
Primitive Church, on the subject of religious celibacy; with a
vindication of the early Church from the mistakes of the
author of "Ancient Christianity." London: J. G. F. & J. Rivington, 1840. T31.7. The first of two parts.

831. Beaven, James. The doctrine of Holy Scripture, and of the
Primitive Church, on the subject of religious celibacy; with a
vindication of the early Church from the mistakes of the
author of "Ancient Christianity"; Part II. London: J. G. F.
& J. Rivington, 1840. T31.8.

832. Beaven, James. On intercourse between the Church of England
and the Churches in the East; and on the ecclesiastical condition of the English abroad. London: J. G. F. & J. Rivington, 1840. T58.9. I. "Reprinted, with alterations from The
British Magazine. . . ." Duplicate copy: T37.12.

833. Beeston, William. Observations on the genealogies contained

in the Gospels of Saint Matthew and Saint Luke. London: John Hearne, 1840. T46.5.

834. Bennett, William J. E. "If any provide not for his own"; a sermon preached in All Souls' Church, St. Marylebone, on the third Sunday in Lent, 22nd March, 1840; in aid of the funds of the North-West London Provident Dispensary. London: W. J. Cleaver, 1840. ST7.19.

835. Bickersteth, Edward. Come out of Rome; the voice from heaven to the people of God; a sermon preached before the Protestant Association, on Wednesday evening, April 22, 1840, at St. Clement Danes Church. London: Protestant Association, 1840. T35.15. I. No. 31 of Publications of the Protestant Association. Duplicate copy: T45.18.

836. Bickersteth, Edward. Feed my lambs; the claim of infants, on all those who love the Saviour: the annual sermon, preached before the Home and Colonial Infant School Society, in Saint John's Chapel, Bedford Row, on Wednesday evening, May 27, 1840. London: n.p., n.d. ST22.14.

837. Bickersteth, Edward. France: the present duty and blessedness of Britons, to relieve its spiritual necessities; the substance of two sermons preached at Clapham, on Sunday, Feb. 23, 1840, in St. James's, and in the parish churches; in behalf of the Sociétés Évangéliques of France and Geneva; with an appendix containing recent intelligence. London: L. and G. Seeley, 1840. ST28.1.

838. Blunt, John James. An introduction to a course of lectures on the early Fathers, now in delivery in the University of Cambridge. Cambridge: J. & J. J. Deighton, 1840. T31.2.

839. Blunt, Walter. Dissenters' baptisms and church burials; strictures upon the decision of the late Sir John Nicholl; with an attempt at an investigation of the judgment of the Church of England upon the subject. Exeter: P. A. Hannaford, 1840. T36.9. Opposes the Arches Court decision in Kemp v. Wickes, 11 Dec. 1809.

840. Butler, William Archer. Church education in Ireland, its claims and its adversaries; two sermons, preached in behalf of the Church Education Society for Ireland, in St. Stephen's Church, Dublin, January 19 and 26, 1840. Dublin: Grant and Bolton, 1840. T30.16.

841. Butt, Isaac. A speech delivered at the official dinner of High Sheriff Tomlinson, in the city of Dublin, on Tuesday, the 14th of July, 1840. London: James Fraser, 1840. T35.17. Butt, Professor of Political Economy in the University of Dublin, rebutted accusations by Lord Lansdowne in the House of Lords that the Corporation of Dublin was mismanaging funds.

842. Cargill, William. Address of William Cargill, Esq. to the South Shields Chamber of Commerce, May 4, 1840, on the foreign policy of England. London: T. Brettell, 1840. T53.4.

843. Cargill, William. Mehemet Ali, Lord Palmerston, Russia, and France; position of England, Turkey, and Russia--Egypt and

Turkey--negotiations at Alexandria--objects of Russia--Treaty
of July 15, 1840, rupture of the Anglo-French alliance--insur-
rection and convulsion in the Ottoman Empire--way prepared for
the occupation of Constantinople by Russia--stipulation to
that effect by Four Powers in Europe--prospects of India.
London: John Reid, 1840. T53.2.

844. Carr, T. W. Another gospel; a sermon, preached at South-
borough Church, Kent, November 10, 1839. London: W. H. Dalton,
1840. ST22.4. Low Church and anti-Tractarian.

845. Cator, Charles. A citizen of no mean city; a sermon preached
in the Parish Church of St. Lawrence Jewry, before the Right
Hon. the Lord Mayor, the worshipful the aldermen, the recorder,
the sheriffs, the Common Council of the City of London, the
liveries of the several companies, and the city officers, on
Saturday, September 28, 1839, prior to the election of a Lord
Mayor; to this sermon is prefixed an advertisement, containing
a reply to The Wesleyan Methodist Magazine, for December, 1839;
and to the appendix is added, the correspondence between the
late Lord Mayor's chaplain and Sir Peter Laurie, Kt., upon the
minutes of the Court of Common Council. London: J. G. F. & J.
Rivington, n.d. T45.6. Sent to N as editor of British Critic.
Cator was chaplain to the Lord Mayor.

846. Chandler, George. Christian goodness; a sermon preached in
the Cathedral Church of Chichester, on the 30th. of August,
1840, being the Sunday immediately following the funeral of
the Right Reverend William Otter, late Bishop of Chichester.
Chichester: William Hayley Mason, 1840. T34.16.

847. Collison, Frederick William. The Church, the guide to truth
and unity; a sermon, preached before the university on Sunday, September 27, 1840. Cambridge: John William Parker,
1840. T33.24.

848. Courtney, John. A sermon, preached in the parish church of
Sanderstead, Surrey, in aid of the incorporated Society for
Promoting the Enlargement and Building of Churches, on Sun-
day, December 22, 1839. London: J. G. & F. Rivington, 1840.
T33.19. Corrections in ink. Contains extracts of two of
Courtney's 1832 sermons on the First Reform Bill and on aboli-
tion of slavery.

849. Coxe, Arthur Cleveland. Athanasion: an ode pronounced before
the Associate Alumni of Washington College, in Christ Church,
Hartford, on the day before commencement, 1840. Hartford,
Ct.: The Association, 1840. T54.5. Coxe was the Bishop of
Western New York.

850. Cranmer, Thomas, John Jewel, Alexander Nowel, Launcelot Andrews, Richard Bancroft, William Laud, and Charles I. Tracts
of the Anglican fathers; part I: Cranmer. London: W. E.
Painter, 1840. T35.1. A collected edition of all four parts
of Tracts of the Anglican Fathers: Parts I and II originally
published 1838; Part III, 1839; Part IV, 1840. Contains "No.
I: Holy Baptism; a Sermon," by Cranmer, edited in Cambridge
by R.; "No. II: The Apostolical Succession and the Power of
the Keys; a Sermon," by Cranmer, edited in Oxford by I.; "No.

III: The Blessed Sacrament of the Altar; a Sermon," by Cranmer, edited in Oxford by S.; "No. IV: The Gifts of the Holy Ghost, in the Holy Catholic Church; a Sermon," by Cranmer, edited in Cambridge by R.; "No. V: Of Sacraments; and Chiefly Concerning Baptism; a Tract," by Jewel, edited in Cambridge by M.; "No. VI: Of Sacraments, and Chiefly Concerning the Holy Eucharist; a Tract," by Nowel, edited in Oxford by I.; an anonymous preface following a title page "Tracts of the Anglican Fathers; Part III: Andrews and Bancroft"; "No. VII: Of Remission of Sins in the Church; and Chiefly Concerning Absolutions; a Sermon," by Andrews, edited in Cambridge by B.; "No. VIII: Of the Church, Her Doctrines, and the Opposing Heresies; a Sermon," by Bancroft, edited in Cambridge by R.; a preface by I. following a title page "Tracts of the Anglican Fathers; Part IV: Laud and Charles I"; No. IX: The Great Peril of Popery, Especially in the Matter of the Blessed Eucharist; a Tract," by Laud, edited in Oxford by I.; "No. X: The Succession, and Spiritual Supremacy of the Episcopate; a Tract," by Charles I, edited in Cambridge by R. Nos. V and VI comprised Part II, but there is no title-page for that Part.

851. Craps, John. A concise view of Christian baptism. 7th ed. London: G. Wightman, 1840. ST22.12. D?

852. Daniel, C. An exposure of "The Vindication of the Church of England," by the Rev. H. Townsend Powell, Vicar of Stretton-on-Dunsmore; addressed to the Protestants of the said parish, by C. Daniel, shoe-maker; part II. London: P. & M. Andrews, 1840. ST9.9. A reply to 928.

853. Dansay, William. A letter to the Archdeacon of Sarum, on ruri-decanal chapters, occasioned by a pamphlet lately published, entitled "Thoughts on the Projected Revival of Decanal or Rural Chapters, by a Wiltshire Incumbent." London: James Bohn, 1840. T48.3. Sent to N as editor of British Critic. The Archdeacon of Sarum was Francis Lear. The pamphlet is against the Church Discipline Act.

854. Doane, George Washington. Episcopal address to the annual convention of the Diocese of New Jersey, May 27, 1840, and episcopal address to the Convention of the Diocese of Maryland, May 27, 1840. Burlington, N.J.: Missionary Press, 1840. T20.21.

855. Doane, George Washington. Isaiah's prospect of the Church: the sermon at the consecration of the Right Rev. Christopher Edwards Gadsden, D.D., Bishop of the Diocese of South Carolina; in Trinity Church, Boston, on the first Sunday after Trinity, MDCCCXL. Burlington, N.J.: J. L. Powell, 1840. T20.12.

856. [Doane, George Washington.] Pastoral letter to the clergy and laity of the Diocese of New Jersey, on the rights and duties of churchwardens and vestrymen. Burlington, N.J.: n.p., 1840. T20.15.

857. [Dodsworth, William.] A few words on keeping the Church festivals. London: James Burns, 1840. ST31.11.

858. Drummond, Henry. Letter to Thomas Phillips, Esq., R.A., on

the connection between the fine arts and religion, and the
means of their revival. London: James Fraser, 1840. T38.10.

859. Eden, Charles Page. Early prayer; a sermon preached at St.
Mary's, Oxford, before the University, on the third Sunday
after Easter, 1840. Oxford: W. Baxter, 1840. T38.9. I.

860. Elrington, Charles R. Apostolical succession; a sermon
preached in the chapel of Trinity College, Dublin, on the
Feast of St. Matthias; second edition with an appendix of the
transmission of orders through the Church of Rome. Dublin:
Milliken and Son, 1840. T30.17.

861. Faber, Frederick William. The office of this generation in
the Church of Christ; a sermon on education. London: J. G. F.
& J. Rivington, 1840. T31.12.

862. Faber, Frederick William. The Reformation and the duty of
keeping to its principles, altered from a tract. New York:
Protestant Episcopal Tract Society, 1840. ST15.8. Tract No.
151.

863. Farley, Thomas. The case of St. Paul, and the necessity of
appointment to the ministerial office: considered in a sermon,
preached in the parish church of Witney, at the visitation of
the Venerable and Reverend C. C. Clerke, B.D., Archdeacon of
Oxford, on Monday, June 22nd, 1840. London: James Burns,
1840. T33.28. A defense of Apostolic Succession.

864. Fitzgerald, William. An essay on the impediments to knowledge
created by logomachy, or the abuse of words. Dublin: William
Curry, Jun., 1840. T47.8.

865. Frere, John. Fasting: an inquiry into its antiquity, uses,
and obligations: to which is added, a sermon for the Ember
Weeks. London: J. G. F. & J. Rivington, 1840. ST14.4.

866. [Gordon, Alexander.] Should we petition Parliament to adopt
measure of Church extension? This question answered in the
affirmative. London: Hatchards, 1840. ST7.15. "Printed for
the Christian Influence Society." Includes formularies for
petitions asking Parliament to provide for the construction of
new churches in large cities. Gordon was the secretary of
the Church Influence Society.

867. Grant, Alexander. The edification of the Church; a sermon
preached in the Archiepiscopal Chapel of Lambeth, on Sunday,
September XX, MDCCCXL, on occasion of the consecration of the
Right Rev. Philip Nicholas, Lord Bishop of Chichester. London: James Burns, 1840. T33.31. The Bishop of Chichester
was Philip Nicholas Shuttleworth.

868. Groser, William. What can be done to suppress the opium trade.
London: The Anti-Opium Society, 1840. T53.9.

869. Haight, Benjamin I. An address delivered before the Philo-
lexian Society, of Columbia College, May 17th 1840; being the
anniversary of the society. New York: William C. Martin,
1840. T54.3. Duplicate copy: T57.1.

870. Haldane, Robert. The duty of paying tribute enforced, in

letters to the Rev. Dr. John Brown, occasioned by his resisting the payment of the annuity tax. London: Simpkin and Marshall, 1840. T19.15.

871. Hawkins, Edward. The ministry of men in the economy of grace, and the danger of overvaluing it; a sermon preached before the University of Oxford, Oct. 25, 1840. Oxford: J. H. Parker, 1840. T31.13. I.

872. Henderson, Thomas. The catechist; or, the Church Catechism explained: in three parts; I: a table containing a general view of all its parts; II: a series of questions and answers on its doctrines and on the office of Confirmation; III: a list of words, with directions for its use. London: J. G. F. & J. Rivington, 1840. ST9.12. Duplicate copy: ST21.6.

873. Hinds, Samuel. The argument for episcopacy considered; a sermon preached in Whitehall Chapel, on Sunday, March 1, 1840, at the consecration of the Right Rev. Henry Papys, D.D., Lord Bishop of Sodor and Man. London: B. Fellowes, 1840. T56.13.

874. Hope, James Robert. Ecclesiastical Duties and Revenues Bills; substance of a speech delivered in the House of Lords, on behalf of the deans and chapters petitioning against the Bill, 24 July 1840. London: James, Luke G. & Luke J. Hansard, 1840. T36.7. Title-page headed "John H. Newman from the author," in N's hand.

875. Hopwood, Henry, ed. The Order of Confirmation or laying on of hands upon those that are baptised and are come to years of discretion: illustrated by select passages from Holy Scripture, the Baptismal and Eucharistic offices of the English Church, and the writings of Catholic Fathers and doctrines. London: James Burns, 1840. ST28.4.

876. Hopwood, Henry. Principles of national education. London: James Burns, 1840. T52.11.

877. Howley, William. A charge delivered at his ordinary visitation in September 1840; by William, Lord Archbishop of Canterbury. London: J. G. F. & J. Rivington, 1840. T56.2.

878. Inglis, John. The claim of the Society for the Propagation of the Gospel, upon all members of the Church; a sermon. London: Henry Wix, 1840. T51.6. Inglis was Bishop of Nova Scotia.

879. The Inquirer, 3 (April 1840), 145-92. T46.11.

880. Irons, William Josiah. Church Discipline Bill; a letter to the Right Reverend Father in God, the Lord Bishop of Exeter. London: William Edward Painter, 1840. T24.5.

881. Ives, Levi Silliman. Humility, a ministerial qualification: an address to the students of the General Theological Seminary of the Protestant Episcopal Church of the United States; delivered at the seventeenth annual commencement, in St. Peter's Church, New York, June 28, 1840. New York: Swords, Stanford, & Co, 1840. T21.7.

882. [Kennedy, Tristram.] First report on the progress of legal education in Ireland, from the principal of the Dublin Law

Institute, to the council of the society; with suggestions
for extending the beneficial influence of the institution.
Dublin: Hodges & Smith, 1840. T52.20.

883. Kilvert, Francis. The whole counsel of God declared by the
Society for Promoting Christian Knowledge: a sermon preached
in the parish church of Wrington, October 14, 1840, at the
anniversary meeting of the district committee of the Society;
with an appendix. Bath: Riviere, 1840. T33.25. I.

884. King, Robert. The Psalter of the Blessed Virgin Mary illustrated: or a critical disquisition and enquiry concerning the
genuineness of the parody on the Psalms of David, commonly
ascribed to St. Bonaventure; comprehending the first fifty
psalms of the Psalter of the B. V. M., with selections from
the remainder. Dublin: Grant and Bolton, 1840. T35.18.

885. Knill, Richard. A dialogue between a Romish priest and
Richard Knill, missionary. London: J. Snow, 1840. ST7.17.

886. Knollis, Francis Minden. The Church her own revivalist; a
sermon, preached in the parish church of St. Martin's, Leicester, before the Right Reverend Father in God, George,
Lord Bishop of Peterborough, and the Clergy of the Deaneries
of Gartree and Sparkenhoe, on Wednesday, July 29, 1840, being
the day of His Lordship's primary visitation. London: J. G.
& F. Rivington, 1840. ST31.3.

887. Littlehales, Thomas. A letter on the education of the middle
classes; addressed (by permission of the Bishop) to the
landed proprietors and other residents in the Deaneries of
Kineton and Warwick. Stratford: J. Ward, 1840. T23.14.

888. M'Neile, Hugh. Jezebel: speech of the Rev. Hugh M'Neile, at
Market Drayton, Salop, December 19, 1839. N.l., n.p., n.d.
T45.17. Publications of the Protestant Association, No. 27.

889. Magdalen College, Oxford University. Poems by members of
Magdalen College School, Oxford. Oxford: W. Baxter, 1840.
ST23.2.

890. Mann, Joseph. Notes on the Epistle of St. Paul to the Romans.
Cambridge: J. and J. Deighton, 1840. T46.7.

891. Manning, Henry Edward. The preservation of unendowed canon-
ries; a letter to William, Lord Bishop of Chichester. London:
n.p., 1840. T24.3.

892. Markland, James Heywood. Remarks on the sepulchral memorials
of past and present times with some suggestions for improving
the condition of our churches, in a letter addressed to the
Reverend the President, and the members of the Oxford Society
for Promoting the Study of Gothic Architecture. Oxford: John
Henry Parker, 1840. T37.10.

893. Marriott, Charles. A lecture delivered at the Diocesan College, Chichester, at the opening of Lent term, 1840, by the
Reverend Charles Marriott, M.A. fellow of Oriel College Oxford,
Principal; together with the rules of the college, and an appendix containing a list of books used and referred to in the
course of study. Chichester: William Hayley Mason, 1840. T47.3.

I. M.

894. [Marriott, Charles.] Rules of the Diocesan College, Chichester. Chichester: William Hayley Mason, 1840. T47.2.

895. Medley, John. How are the mighty fallen! A sermon preached at the visitation of the Archdeacon Moore Stevens, holden at Exeter, May 8, 1840. N.l.: P. Hannaford, n.d. T31.4. I.

896. Melvill, Henry. Angels rejoicing in the Gospel: a sermon, preached on Tuesday, January 28, 1840, in the Church of St. John the Evangelist, Brighton, on the occasion of its consecration by the Right Rev. the Lord Bishop of Worcester. London: J. G. F. & J. Rivington, 1840. T33.22. Copy split in binding; pp. 17-32 are found following T33.27.

897. Melvill, Henry. Christianity the guardian of human life; a sermon, preached in the Church of St. Nicholas, Deptford, on Trinity Monday, June 15, 1840, before the corporation of Trinity House. London: J. G. F. & J. Rivington, 1840. T51.7. I.

898. Metcalf, Charles T. P. A synopsis of some of the leading arguments in favor of the doctrine of universal restoration. London: Wm. S. Orr, 1840. T46.9.

899. Mill, William Hodge. Observations on the attempted application of pantheistic principles to the theory and historic criticism of the Gospel; part I on the theoretic application being the Christian Advocate's publication for 1840. Cambridge: J. and J. J. Deighton, 1840. Trell.3.

900. Miller, Charles. The petition of the Rev. Charles Miller, Vicar of Harlow, Essex, respecting the Tithe Commutation Act, presented to the House of Lords, by the Bishop of London, during the session of MDCCCXL. London: J. G. F. & J. Rivington, 1840. T22.17.

901. Miller, George. A letter to the Rev. E. B. Pusey, D.D., in reference to his Letter to the Lord Bishop of Oxford. London: Duncan and Malcolm, 1840. T31.11.

902. Mirehouse, John. Crime and its causes: with observations of Sir Eardley Wilmot's bill, authorizing the summary conviction of juvenile offenders in certain cases of larceny and misdemeanour. 2nd ed. London: W. J. Cleaver, 1840. T47.6. Sent to N as editor of the British Critic.

903. Molesworth, John Edward Nassau. Letter to the Lord Bishop of Chester, upon certain sectarian designs in the Pastoral Aid Society; and upon the catholic, comprehensive, and Church regulations of the Society for Promoting the Employment of Additional Curates in Populous Places. London: J. G. F. & J. Rivington, 1840. ST11.6. John Bird Sumner was Bishop of Chester.

904. Monteith, Robert, and William Brown. Reasons for demanding investigation into the charges against Lord Palmerston. Glasgow: William Collins, 1840. T53.3. I. Duplicate copy: T53.7.

905. New York Protestant Episcopal City Mission Society. The ninth

annual report of the board of managers of the New York Protestant Episcopal City Mission Society. New York: Depository, 1840. T54.2.

906. New York Protestant Episcopal Tract Society. The claims of the Holy Week: a plain address to Churchmen. N.l., n.p., n.d. ST22.13. New York Protestant Episcopal Tract Society, No. 155.

907. The Newcastle Journal. Relations with France and Russia. London: T. Brettell, 1840. T53.8. Includes a speech by William Cargill.

908. Newman, John Henry. The Church visible and invisible. London: James Burns, 1840. ST11.8. "The following pages are extracted, by permission, from the third volume of 'Parochial Sermons,' by the Rev. J. H. Newman, B.D., Vicar of St. Mary the Virgin's, Oxford, and Fellow of Oriel College." Now P.S., III, 220-35. An appendix was added, consisting of a long extract from the next sermon, in Vol. III, "The Visible Church an Encouragement to Faith."

909. Nixon, Francis Russell. The duty of the members of the Church of England to adhere to her doctrine and discipline; a sermon, preached in the Cathedral of Christ, Canterbury, before His Grace the Archbishop, at the triennial visitation of the deaneries of Bridge and Elham; on Saturday, September XXVI, MDCCCXL. London: Henry Wix, 1840. T33.23. A defense of the Athanasian Creed.

910. Oakeley, Frederick. The dignity and claims of the Christian poor: two sermons; the latter preached in aid of the Middlesex Hospital. London: James Burns, 1840. ST11.4. Duplicate copy: ST21.11.

911. [Palmer, William (of Magdalen College, Oxford).] In XXXIX Articulos. N.l., n.p., n.d. T42.5.

912. Perceval, Arthur Philip. An apology for the doctrine of apostolical succession: with an appendix, on the English orders. New York: Protestant Episcopal Tract Society, 1840. ST15.9. Author's name spelled "Percival" on title-page.

913. Perceval, Arthur Philip. Mr. Perceval's speech at the meeting of the Society for Promoting Christian Knowledge, held in June, MDCCCXL, with observations connected therewith. London: Gilbert & Rivington, 1840. ST8.8. I. "Private Impression." Perceval's speech upon withdrawing from the S.P.C.K.

914. [Perceval, Arthur Philip.] On the claims of dissenters to the privileges of Churchmen; on the case Mastin v. Escott; from the Episcopal Magazine, No. XXIV. N.l., n.p., n.d. T36. 8.

915. Phillpotts, Henry. Correspondence between the Lord Bishop of Exeter and members of the Commission of Ecclesiastical Enquiry. London: John Murray, 1840. T36.6. Discussions of various Church-state issues.

916. [Pole, Edward Sacheverell Chandos.] A Layman, pseud. An inquiry respecting the destiny of the Ten Tribes. London: J. G. F. & J. Rivington, 1840. T37.13. I. S. Faded, illegible

marginalia in N's hand. Duplicate copy: T46.4 (also with scoring).

917. Poole, George Ayliffe. The Anglo-Catholic use of two lights upon the altar, for the signification that Christ is the very true Light of the World, stated and defended. London: Burns, 1840. T30.12. I.

918. [Poole, George Ayliffe.] An appendix, to "Strictures on an 'Address delivered on Occasion of Laying the First Stone of East Parade Chapel, Leeds, by the Rev. John Ely,' by Geo. Ayliffe Poole, M.A. Incumbent of St. James' Church, Leeds"; with a letter to Mr. John Ely, by the author of the Strictures. Leeds: T. Harrison, 1840. T30.11. I. A sequel to 755.

919. Powell, Baden. State education considered with reference to relevant misconceptions on religious grounds. London: John W. Parker, 1840. T23.15.

920. [Powell, Henry Townsend.] Adoration of the Host, concluded. [London: W. E. Painter,] n.d. ST9.8. The last of the Stretton Tracts and the sequel of 925. See 922, 926.

921. Powell, Henry Townsend. A letter to the inhabitants of Stretton-on-Dunsmore and Princethorpe, shewing that the episcopal succession of the Catholic Church has been continued in the bishops of the Church of England to the present time; with an account of a conference on the same subject, (second edition); to which is added remarks by a Roman Catholic, on the above letter, and a postscript in reply, (more particularly addressed to Roman Catholics,) in which the succession of the Church of England is proved to be Catholic and canonical, by reference to the canons of the Catholic Church. 2nd ed. London: Hamilton, Adams, 1840. ST9.10.

922. [Powell, Henry Townsend.] Roman fallacies and Catholic truths; No. I: angel worship. 3rd ed. London: William Edward Painter, n.d. ST9.1. This is one number of the retitled 3rd ed. of the Stretton Tracts. See 926.

923. [Powell, Henry Townsend.] Roman fallacies and Catholic truths; No. VII: worship of the Virgin Mary. London: William Edward Painter, n.d. ST9.5. I. See 922, 926.

924. Powell, Henry Townsend. Roman fallacies and Catholic truths; No. VIII: canonization of saints. London: William Edward Painter, n.d. ST9.6. I. See 922, 926.

925. [Powell, Henry Townsend.] Roman fallacies and Catholic truths; No. IX: adoration of the Host. London: William Edward Painter, n.d. ST9.7. I. See 922, 926.

926. [Powell, Henry Townsend.] Stretton tracts; No. IV: relic worship. Coventry: Rollason, n.d. ST9.2. One number of the second edition of a series of tracts that were originally untitled. See 922, 927, 928, 923, 924, 925, 920.

927. [Powell, Henry Townsend.] Stretton tracts; No. V: relic worship, continued. Coventry: Rollason, n.d. ST9.3. See 926.

928. [Powell, Henry Townsend.] Stretton tracts; No. VI: saint

worship. Coventry: C. A. N. Rollason, n.d. ST9.4. See 926.

929. [Pring, J.] A Supernumerary, pseud. On the principles of common, or inceptive discipline; the eighth of a series of letters to a brother curate on professional topics of various interest and importance. London: Thomas Cadell, 1840. T47.7.

930. Protestant Association. The settlement of the Constitution in 1688. London: Protestant Association, 1840. T35.16. No. 28 of Publications of the Protestant Association.

931. Protestant Episcopal Church in the United States, Diocese of New Jersey. Journal of the fifty-seventh annual convention of the Protestant Episcopal Church in the State of New Jersey; held in Grace Church, and Trinity Church, Newark; on Wednesday the 27th and Thursday the 28th days of May, 1840. Burlington, N.J.: n.p., 1840. T20.20.

932. Protestant Episcopal Tract Society. The Church almanac for the year of our Lord 1842: containing besides the usual calendar and celestial phenomena, statistics respecting the Church, and alphabetical lists of the clergy, of the United States and the British Provinces. New York: Protestant Episcopal Tract Society, 1840. ST16.3.

933. Protestant Episcopal Tract Society. The Church, the "nursing mother" of her people. New York: Protestant Episcopal Tract Society, 1840. ST15.7. Tract No. 145.

934. Pusey, Edward Bouverie. Preface to the fourth edition of the "Letter to the Right Rev. Father in God, Richard, Lord Bishop of Oxford, on the Tendency to Romanism Imputed to Doctrines Held of Old, as Now, in the English Church"; on the doctrine of Justification. Oxford: J. H. Parker, 1840. T31.10.

935. Radcliffe Infirmary, Oxford. Case and opinion on the will of the Reverend George Powell, deceased, ex-parte the president and governors of the Radcliffe Infirmary, Oxford. Oxford: F. Trash, 1840. T37.11. I. Contains the legal opinion of Richard Clarke Sewell.

936. Ross, John Lockhart. The Christian Church and priesthood; two sermons preached in the Cathedral City of Chester. Chester: J. Seacome, n.d. T33.20. D?

937. Russell, John Fuller. The city of God: a sermon preached in St. Peter's Church, Walworth. London: James Burns, 1840. T 33.26.

938. St. Paul's School, London. Prolusiones literariæ, præmiis quotannis propositis dignatæ, et in D. Pauli Schola; recitatæ comitiis maximis, A. S. H. MDCCCXL. London: Gilbert and Rivington, 1840. T47.11.

939. Sandford, G. B. A divine commission necessary to the minister of religion; a sermon. London: J. G. F. & J. Rivington, 1840. ST11.7. I.

940. Selwyn, William. An attempt to investigate the true principles of cathedral reform; part II. Cambridge: J. & J. J. Deighton, 1840. Tre9.2.

941. Sherard, George. A sermon, in which the duty and blessing of
     Church-membership are considered. Huntingdon: Robert Edis,
     1840. T33.30.

942. Sinnott, John. A letter to the Right Rev. Dr. Phillpotts,
     Lord Bishop of Exeter, by the Rev. John Sinnott, president of
     St. Peter's College, Wexford, on ordination in the Church of
     England: the Lambeth Register examined; the account of the
     Nag's-Head consecration; Bishop Barlow's consecration not
     proved; the formula of King Edward's Ordinal examined; Arch-
     bishop Parker not validly consecrated; no valid ordination of
     bishops and priests in the established Church of England; the
     ministry of the established clergy to the living, inconsistent
     with Protestant principles; the ministry of the established
     clergy useless to the dying, as acknowledged by the Most Rev.
     Doctor Whately, Protestant Archbishop of Dublin, in the time
     of cholera. Wexford: printed at "The Independent" office,
     1840. ST9.11.

943. Skinner, James. The observance of Lent; a letter to the Right
     Hon. the Earl of Uxbridge, &c. &c., Lord Chamberlain of Her
     Majesty's household, &c. &c. &c. London: James Burns, 1840.
     T31.1.

944. Smith, Culling Eardley. Nonconformity within the Church; a
     letter of expostulation addressed to the Rev. Thomas Spencer,
     M.A., perpetual curate of Hinton Charterhouse. London: Thomas
     Ward, n.d. ST7.16. Reprinted with corrections from the
     Christian Reformer. An answer to the latitudinarian Spencer's
     Clerical Conformity and Church Property (1840). Duplicate
     copy: ST21.12.

945. Smith, Herbert. A letter to the Poor Law Commissioners in
     behalf of the deserving poor, with an appendix. London: F.
     and J. Rivington, n.d. T51.23. D? Sent to N as editor of
     British Critic.

946. Steel, John. The truly great man: one who uses his riches for
     God's glory; a sermon preached in the parish church of Tewin,
     on the Sunday after the funeral of Henry Cowper, Esquire, of
     Tewin Water. Hertford: E. W. Cobb, 1840. T51.4.

947. Stone, Thomas. The affairs of this world all ordered with a
     reference to the welfare of the Church: a sermon preached in
     the Parish Church of St. John the Evangelist, Westminster, on
     Sunday, June 21st, 1840, being the day appointed as a Day of
     National Thanksgiving for Her Majesty's escape from assassina-
     tion. London: James Burns, 1840. ST31.1.

948. Storrs, William. Facts and evidence relating to the opium
     trade with China. London: Pelham Richardson, 1840. T53.10.

949. Sumner, John Bird. Eternal life in Jesus Christ: a sermon
     preached at the consecration of St. Luke's Church, Cheetham
     Hill. 2nd ed. London: J. Hatchard and Son, 1840. T34.14.

950. Temple, Henry John, and Adolphe Thiers. Letter from Lord
     Palmerston to M. Thiers, dated Foreign Office, August 31,
     1840; reply of M. Thiers to Lord Palmerston, dated Paris,
     October 3, 1840: with the additional memorandum. London: T.

Brettell, 1840. T53.6.

951. Thorp, Thomas. The student's walk; a sermon preached in the
      chapel of Trinity College, Cambridge, on Sunday, Oct. 18, 1840.
      Cambridge: Pitt Press, 1840. T51.9. I.

952. Trevelyan, E. Otto. A letter to the editor of the British
      Magazine, on the proceedings of the Bible Society and some
      clergy, members of it, in the parish of Hungerford: (reprinted
      from the British Magazine). London: J. G. F. & J. Rivington,
      1840. T19.13.

953. Urquhart, David. Exposition of the boundary differences be-
      tween Great Britain and the United States, subsequently to
      their adjustment by arbitration. Glasgow: John Smith & Son,
      1840. T53.13.

954. Urquhart, David. La crise; la France devant les Quatre Puis-
      sances; Paris, le 20 Septembre 1840. Paris: P. Dufart, 1840.
      T53.5.

955. Walker, G. A. The way which they call heresy; a sermon,
      preached at the evening lecture in St. Andrew's Church, New-
      castle-upon-Tyne, on Sunday, January 12th, 1840. Newcastle: M.
      A. Richardson, 1840. T30.14.

956. Whiteley, Henry. Verbatim reprint of a pamphlet, entitled
      Three Months in Jamaica, in 1832: comprising a residence of
      seven weeks on a sugar plantation. London: Anti-slavery
      Society, n.d. ST14.5.

957. Wilberforce, Robert Isaac. A second letter to the Most Noble
      the Marquis of Lansdowne, on the system of inspection best
      adapted for national education. London: J. Hatchard and Son,
      1840. ST29.6. Cf. 793. Duplicate copy: ST22.1.

958. Wilberforce, Samuel. A charge delivered to the clergy of the
      Archdeaconry of Surrey, by Samuel Wilberforce, M.A., at his
      primary visitation in September and October, 1840; and pub-
      lished at their request. London: James Burns, 1840. T34.15.

959. Wilberforce, Samuel. A letter to the Right Hon. Henry, Lord
      Brougham, on the government plan of education. London: James
      Burns, 1840. T52.7.

960. Wood, Thomas. The mission of Jesus Christ; a lecture preached
      in Brixton Unitarian Chapel, October 18, 1840. London: John
      Green, n.d. T46.12.

961. Wordsworth, William. England in 1840! N.l., n.p., n.d. ST28.
      11. No title-page. A collection of eight political poems.

WORKS BY UNIDENTIFIED AUTHORS

962. Anon. The Bath Rectory Hymn Book examined and exposed. [Bath:
      Carrington,] n.d. ST21.7. A High Church criticism of John
      East's Bath Rectory Hymn Book (Bath, 1840).

963. Anon. ed. Calendar of days for united prayer, being the fes-
      tivals appointed by the Church of England. [London: T. C.
      Johns], n.d. ST28.3. D? A gift of Pusey.

964. Anon. Lessons for the days of the week. London: James Burns, 1840. ST23.8.

965. Anon. A letter to the Right Hon. Lord Brougham, and to the educated and intellectual classes, on the excellencies and consolations of "divine philosophy." London: James Nisbet, 1840. ST19.11.

966. Anon. Mother of St. Augustine: a true story. London: James Burns, 1840. ST23.4.

967. Anon. On a proposal to withhold out-door relief from widows with families, contained in the last annual report of the Poor Law Commissioners for England and Wales; [read at a meeting of the Manchester Statistical Society, December 8th, 1840]. [Manchester: John Harrison,] n.d. T51.24.

968. Anon. On the moral state and political union of Sweden and Norway, in answer to Mr. S. Laing's statement. London: John Murray, 1840. T53.12. A reply to Samuel Laing's Journal of a Residence in Norway (1836) and Tour of Sweden (1838).

969. Anon. Oxford theology; (from the New York Review for January, 1840). New York: Alexander V. Blake, 1840. T30.15. Review of 1st volume of the 2nd ed. of Tracts for the Times, Pusey's Letter to the Bishop of Oxford, and Hook's Call to Union.

970. Anon. Quelques mots sur l'Université Catholique de Louvain. Brussels: Ve. J.-J. Vanderborght, 1840. P4.1.

971. Anon. A sermon: Acts c. xi.v. 24.; For he was a good man. N.l., n.p., n.d. T51.5. D? Lacks title-page.

972. Anon. Some account of Durham College, Oxford, suppressed by Henry the Eighth; together with the Priory, in Durham, with which it was connected. Durham: F. Humble, 1840. C7.5.

973. The Churchman, pseud. The Churchman's protest against the National Society. London: James Nisbet, 1840. T52.10.

974. A Clergyman, pseud. A second letter to the Earl of Chichester, on the subject of the Church Missionary Society. London: Smith, Elder, 1840. T48.9. Defends the Church Missionary Society against charges of excessive land holdings in New Zealand.

975. A Clergyman, pseud. Thoughts, few and brief, touching the government plan of education, and the parliamentary debates thereon. London: Ball, Arnold, and Co., n.d. T52.9. D? Sent to N as editor of British Critic.

976. A Clergyman of the Archdeaconry of Dorset, pseud. A hospital is a religious institution; remarks upon the true character of works of mercy as set forth in the Holy Scripture, and respectfully submitted to the consideration of those who are, or who may become, the supporters of the Dorset County Hospital. Dorchester: G. Clark, 1840. T51.22.

977. A Clergyman of the Diocese and a Resident Member of the University, pseud. A letter to the Right Reverend Father in God, Richard, Lord Bishop of Oxford, containing strictures upon certain parts of Dr. Pusey's letter to His Lordship. Oxford:

John Henry Parker, 1840. T31.6.

978. A Dissenter, pseud. A dissenter's apology for an established
      Church, in a letter to his minister. London: Hatchard and Son,
      1840. T19.16.

979. An English Layman, pseud. The duty of abiding in the ancient
      faith addressed to his countrymen. Malta: Izzo, 1840. ST21.9.

980. A Layman, pseud. Remarks on evangelical preaching, (exclusive-
      ly so called), as exhibited in a published sermon of the Rev.
      Henry Melvill, by a layman. London: William Edward Painter,
      1840. T19.12.

981. A Member of the Church, pseud. An appeal in behalf of Church
      government: addressed to the prelates and clergy of the United
      Church of England and Ireland being remarks on the debate in
      the House of Lords respecting that subject, on 26th May, 1840.
      London: Houlston and Stoneman, 1840. T39.7. Sent to N as
      editor of British Critic.

982. A Minister of the Established Church, pseud. A voice for
      China to my countrymen, the government, and my Church. London:
      Nisbet and Co., 1840. T53.11.

983. One Born and Bred a Churchman, pseud. A short account of the
      Baptists. [London: John Haddon, 1840.] ST22.11.

984. [One of Their Own Number, Provincial Medical and Surgical
      Association, pseud.] [Nuces philosophicæ.] N.l., n.p., n.d.
      T47.9. Lacks title-page; incomplete copy. A dialogue on
      moral philosophy and philology.

985. [P., P.] A bait for "the bull" that bullied Lord Lyttleton.
      N.l., n.p., n.d. T48.2. A letter dated 14 Nov. 1840, to the
      editor of John Bull taking him to task for supporting Lord
      Lyndhurst over Lord Lyttleton in a recent election in Cam-
      bridge. P. P. takes Lyttleton to be a defender of the pre-
      rogatives of the established Church.

986. A Priest of the Church of England, pseud. A letter to the
      clergy upon the speech of the Right Rev. the Lord Bishop of
      Norwich, in the House of Lords, May 26, 1840. London: J. G.
      F. & J. Rivington, 1840. T39.8. Inscribed: "From the author."

987. [Y., O., ed.] One of the People Called Christians, pseud. A
      chapter on duelling, by one of the people called Christians.
      London: James Fraser, 1840. ST31.2. "Reprinted from Fraser's
      Magazine for May 1840, with alterations and additions." Sent
      to N as editor of British Critic.

                              1841

988. [Acland, Arthur Henry Dyke.] Baptismal regeneration; a doc-
      trine of the Church of England, shewn by a comparison of the
      baptismal services, and the practical effects of a belief in
      that doctrine considered. London: James Burns, 1841.
      ST31.12. I.

989. Baggs, C. M. Funeral oration delivered at the solemn obsequies of the Lady Gwendaline Talbot, Princess Borghese, in the Church of S. Charles in the Corso on the 23rd of December, MDCCCXL. Rome: Joseph Salviucci and Son, 1841. Pl.12.

990. Barter, William Brudenell. Lord Morpeth's remarks on "The Tracts for the Times" considered. 2nd ed. London: J. G. F. & J. Rivington, 1841. T40.19. I.

991. Beaufort, Daniel Augustus. Scripture sufficient without Tradition: of the doctrine of the Sixth Article of the British Churches maintained; an essay which obtained the Norrisian Gold Medal for the year 1840, in the University of Cambridge. Cambridge: J. & J. J. Deighton, 1841. T45.1. I.

992. Bickersteth, Edward. The scriptural guide for ministers in these days; a visitation sermon preached at Hatfield, May 25, 1841. 2nd ed. London: Messrs. Seeley and Co., 1841. T51.18. I. Contains measured criticisms of <u>Tract</u> <u>90</u>.

993. Bossuet, Jacques Benignus. An exposition of the Catholic faith on matters of controversy. 2nd ed. London: n.p., 1841. T45. 10. A publication of the Catholic Institute of Great Britain.

994. Bowdler, Thomas. Quid Romæ faciam? No need to join the Romish communion on account of the want of discipline in the Church of England: a letter to a friend, Fellow of_____College, Oxford. London: J. G. F. & J. Rivington, 1841. T43.8.

995. Calder, Robert. The true difference betwixt the principles and practices of the Kirk and the Church of Scotland, exemplified in several instances. 1712; rpt. London: Andrew Moffat, 1841. ST21.2. I. Edited by Thomas Short.

996. Chandler, George. A sermon on the decoration of churches preached at the re-opening of St. Andrew's Church, Chichester, on Friday, the 1st. of January, 1841. Chichester: William Hayley Mason, 1841. ST11.12.

997. <u>Christian</u> <u>Magazine</u>, No. 2, pp. 17-40. ST20.9. Lacks title-page. Contains two chapters of a novel, <u>Esther</u> <u>Simmonds</u>, and other items.

998. Collison, Frederick William. A vindication of the Anglican reformers; in an examination of Prof. Scholefield's discourses. Cambridge: J. & J. J. Deighton, 1841. T48.15. A defense of Anglo-Catholic doctrine by a writer who takes pains to point out that he is not a Tractarian. Cf. 1032, 1102. James Scholefield was curate of St. Michael's, Cambridge.

999. Copleston, William James. The household of God; a sermon, preached at Chipping-Sodbury, on Tuesday, Sept. 7, 1841, at the visitation of the Lord Bishop of Gloucester and Bristol. Oxford: John Henry Parker, 1841. T51.13.

1000. Curtis, John Harrison. The present state of ophthalmology: with new modes of treating the diseases of the eye. 2nd ed. London: John Churchill, 1841. T47.14. Sent to N as editor of the <u>British</u> <u>Critic</u>.

1001. Doane, George Washington. A brief examination of the proofs, by which the Rev. Mr. Boardman attempts to sustain his charge, that "A large and learned body of the clergy of the Church" (of England) "have returned to some of the worst errors of Popery;" with a word or two as to his attempt, without proof, to cast the suspicion of Popery on the Protestant Episcopal Church in the United States of America. Burlington, New Jersey: J. L. Powell, 1841. T43.15.

1002. Doane, George Washington. The Church, the fullness of Christ; the sermon, preached by request of the vicar, with the consent of the Lord Bishop of the diocese, at the consecration of the parish church, Leeds, on Thursday, September 2nd, 1841. Leeds: T. W. Green, 1841. T51.12. Doane was bishop of New Jersey.

1003. Dodsworth, William. Allegiance to the Church; a sermon. London: James Burns, 1841. T51.15.

1004. Dodsworth, William. The Church of England a protester against Romanism and dissent; No. II: On the mortification of the flesh. London: James Burns, 1841. ST31.4. Cf. 479.

1005. Dodsworth, William. On the Holy Communion: three discourses. London: James Burns, 1841. ST31.5.

1006. Dyer, Thomas Henry. Tentamina Æschylea; or, an attempt to restore some passages in Æschylus. London: George Bell, 1841. T47.10.

1007. Fanshawe, Francis. Viæ per Angliam ferro stratæ; carmen Latinum in Theatro Sheldoniano recitatum die Junii XV MDCCCXLI. Oxford: Francis Macpherson, 1841. NL28.1.

1008. Faussett, Godfrey. The Thirty-Nine Articles considered as the standard and test of the doctrines of the Church of England, chiefly with reference to the views of No. 90 of the Tracts for the Times; a lecture delivered before the University of Oxford, in the Divinity School, on Thursday, June 3, 1841. Oxford: John Henry Parker, 1841. T42.7.

1009. Feild, Edward. Report on the state of parochial education in the Diocese of Salisbury, addressed to the Right Reverend the Lord Bishop of the diocese. 2nd ed. London: James Burns, 1841. ST20.6.

1010. Freeman, Philip. Church principles as bearing upon certain statutes of the University of Cambridge: addressed to all persons in statu pupillari. Cambridge: J. & J. J. Deighton and T. Stevenson, 1841. T52.18. Cf. 1238.

1011. French, Daniel. Speech delivered at the annual meeting of the Catholic Institute, held at the Freemason's Tavern, on Thursday, May 13th, 1841. [London: T. Jones,] n.d. ST27.5. A Roman Catholic response to Tract 90.

1012. Golightly, Charles Portales. Brief remarks upon No. 90, second edition, and some subsequent publications in defence of it. Oxford: William Graham, 1841. T40.18. I. Cf. 1049.

1013. Gostick, Joseph. Christ indwelling; a sermon (on Eph. iii 17) preached in Oxford-Place Chapel, Leeds, and Wesley Chapel, Coventry. Coventry: R. C. Tomkinson, 1841. ST20.5.

1014. Hansell, Peter. A letter to the Right Reverend the Lord Bishop of Bath and Wells, on the occasion of his recent circular to the clergy of his diocese. Bath: H. E. Carrington, 1841. ST19.6. Anti-Tractarian, in response to a letter from the bishop recommending he not interfere in the condemnation of Tract 90.

1015. Harle, Charles Ebenezer, ed. Three discourses of the Rev. Joseph Mede, B.D., late fellow of Christ's College, Cambridge; the Church: the offertory. London: James Burns, 1841. T46.2. Taken from the 1672 ed. of Mede's works.

1016. [Hawkins, Edward.] Appendix to the Bampton Lecture for 1840, (being the additional notes, except mere references, footnotes, &c., introduced into the second edition, 1841). N.l., n.p., n.d. T59.2. I. An appendix to Hawkins' An Inquiry into the Connected Uses of the Principal Means of Attaining Christian Truth (Oxford, 1840).

1017. Heathcote, William Beadon. Documentary illustrations of the principles to be kept in view in the interpretation of the Thirty-Nine Articles. Oxford: John Henry Parker, 1841. T42.6. Heathcote was "Fellow and Tutor of New College, Oxford; a Priest of the Church-Catholic in England," according to the title-page.

1018. Highton, Henry. Essays towards a right interpretation of the last prophecy of our Lord concerning the destruction of Jerusalem and the end of the present world. Oxford: Joseph Vincent, 1841. T46.6.

1019. Hook, Walter Farquhar. Letter to the Right Reverend the Lord Bishop of Ripon, on the state of parties in the Church of England. London: J. G. F. & J. Rivington, 1841. T43.10. Cf. 1142, 1040.

1020. Hope, James Robert. The bishopric of the United Church of England and Ireland at Jerusalem considered in a letter to a friend. London: C. J. Stewart, 1841. T49.3. I. Cf. 1186, 1178.

1021. Hussey, Robert. The great contest; a sermon, preached in the Cathedral of Christ Church, on Easter Day, April 11, 1841. Oxford: John Henry Parker, 1841. T51.11. I.

1022. [Jackson, Miles.] Clericus, pseud. A letter to the Hon. & Rev. Baptist W. Noel, containing some remarks on his pamphlet, entitled "A Plea for the Poor." London: Hatchard and Sons, 1841. ST21.4. A response to Noel's "A Plea for the Poor" (London, 1841). Cf. 615.

1023. Jordan, J. The crisis come, being remarks on Mr. Newman's letter to Dr. Jelf, and on Tract for the Times, No. 90. Oxford: J. L. Wheeler, 1841. T40.12.

1024. Journal of Christian Education, and Family and Sunday-School Visiter. Parochial schools: Male Parochial School of All Saints Church, New York. N.l., n.p., n.d. T54.4. Separatum from Journal of Christian Education and Family and Sunday-School Visiter, 3 (Jan. 1841), 1-21.

1025. Jowett, Benjamin. De Etruscorum cultu moribus et legibus
      eorumque apud Romanos vestigiis; oratio in Theatro Sheldoniano
      habita die Junii XV MDCCCXLI. Oxford: Francis Macpherson,
      1841. NL28.13.

1026. Keble, John. The case of Catholic subscription to the Thirty-
      Nine Articles considered: with especial reference to the duties
      and difficulties of English Catholics in the present crisis:
      in a letter to the Hon. Mr. Justice Coleridge. London: pri-
      vately printed, 1841. T40.21.

1027. Ken, Thomas. The Lenten fast; a pastoral letter from the Bis-
      hop of Bath and Wells to his clergy, concerning their behavior
      during Lent, 1687; also, a sermon on the beloved Daniel,
      preached in the King's Chapel, Whitehall, 1685, by the Right
      Reverend Father in God, Thomas Ken, D.D., sometime Bishop of
      Bath and Wells. London: B. Wertheim, 1841. T46.1. Anonymous
      editor.

1028. Lacordaire, Jean-Baptiste Henri. Sermon du R. P. F. Lacordaire
      à Notre-Dame. N.l., n.p., n.d. T45.13. An offprint from
      L'Univers, 16 and 17 Feb. 1841. See L.D., XI, 304-05.

1029. Le Bas, Charles Webb. A sermon, preached in Harlow Church,
      May XXVIII, MDCCCXXXIX, in which some uses of the offertory
      are considered. London: J. G. F. & J. Rivington, 1839. ST11.
      9. A gift from the author.

1030. Longley, Charles Thomas. A charge delivered to the clergy of
      the Diocese of Ripon, at his triennial visitation, in July &
      August, 1841; by the Right Rev. Charles Thomas, Lord Bishop of
      Ripon. London: J. G. F. & J. Rivington, 1841. T56.6. Anti-
      Tractarian, with remarks against Tract 90 and N's "Letter to
      Dr. Jelf."

1031. [Lowe, Robert.] The Articles construed by themselves. Ox-
      ford: W. Baxter, 1841. T43.6.

1032. Lowe, Robert. Observations suggested by a few more words in
      support of No. 90. Oxford: W. Baxter, 1841. T40.16. See
      1103.

1033. Macara, James. A treatise on the scriptural doctrines of re-
      demption and salvation; and shewing that the doctrine of
      Justification by faith alone is the abomination of desolation
      standing in the Holy Place. Edinburgh: Guthrie & Tait, 1841.
      ST21.3. I.

1034. Maltby, Edward. A charge delivered to the clergy of the Dio-
      cese of Durham, at the visitation in July and August, MDCCCXLI,
      by Edward, Lord Bishop of Durham. London: T. Cadell, 1841.
      NL79.25. Part of the Tract 90 controversy.

1035. Maltby, Edward. A charge to his clergy, delivered at St.
      Nicholas' Church, Newcastle-upon-Tyne, on Monday, August 9,
      1841, by the Right Rev. the Lord Bishop of Durham. Newcastle:
      J. Blackwell, 1841. ST24.3.

1036. Manning, Henry Edward. The moral design of the apostolic
      ministry; a sermon preached on Trinity Sunday, 1841, at an
      ordination held by the Right Reverend Philip Nicholas, Lord

Bishop of Chichester, in the Cathedral Church. London: John Murray, 1841. T51.10.

1037. [Marriott, Charles, ed.] Canones SS. Apostolorum græce; cum versione anglica et notis Johnsoni. Oxford: John Henry Parker, 1841. T47.1. I. The second part, a translation into English, is entitled "The Canons, Commonly Called Apostolical or Eccele-siastical," and is reprinted from John Johnson's Clergyman's Vade Mecum (2nd ed., 1714).

1038. Marriott, Charles. The Church's instruments for the work of the Holy Spirit; a sermon preached before the University of Oxford, on the feast of St. Barnabas, MDCCCXLI. Oxford: John Henry Parker, 1841. T51.16. I.

1039. Marriott, Charles. The Church's method of communicating divine truth: a lecture delivered at the Diocesan College, Chichester, at the opening of Lent term, 1841. Chichester: William Hayley Mason, 1841. T47.4. I.

1040. Maurice, Frederick Denison. A letter to the Ven. Samuel Wil-berforce, Archdeacon of Surrey: suggested by the Rev. Dr. Hook's letter to the Bishop of Ripon, on the state of parties in the Church of England. London: J. G. F. & J. Rivington, 1841. T43.11. A response to 1019.

1041. Merewether, Francis. The Roman plea of candour considered: in a letter to the Rev. L. Gentili, LL.D. Ashby-de-la-Zouch: W. & J. Hextall, 1841. ST19.4. I.

1042. Miller, George. A second letter to the Rev. E. B. Pusey, D.D., in reference to his letter to the Rev. R. W. Jelf, D.D., Canon of Christ Church. London: Duncan and Malcolm, 1841. T42.2. A response to 1077.

1043. Newman, Francis William. Manchester New College; introductory lecture, by F. W. Newman, Esq., B.A., formerly fellow of Balliol College, Oxford, Classical Professor; being the first of the series of inaugural lectures delivered by the several professors at the opening of the College, in October, 1840. London: Simpkin, Marshall, 1841. T38.12.

1044. [Newman, John Henry.] A letter addressed to the Rev. R. W. Jelf, D.D., Canon of Christ Church, in explanation of No. 90, in the series called the Tracts for the Times. Oxford: John Henry Parker, 1841. T40.6. Later V.M., II, 351-77. See Apo., p. 123.

1045. [Newman, John Henry.] A letter addressed to the Rev. R. W. Jelf, D.D., Canon of Christ Church, in explanation of No. 90, in the series called the Tracts for the Times. 2nd ed. Ox-ford: John Henry Parker, 1841. T40.7.

1046. [Newman, John Henry.] A letter addressed to the Rev. R. W. Jelf, D.D., Canon of Christ Church, in explanation of Tract No. 90, in the series called the Tracts for the Times. 3rd ed. Oxford: John Henry Parker, 1841. T40.8.

1047. Newman, John Henry. A letter to the Right Reverend Father in God, Richard, Lord Bishop of Oxford, on occasion of No. 90,

in the series called the Tracts for the Times. Oxford: John
Henry Parker, 1841. T40.20. Later <u>V.M.</u>, II, 381-410.

1048. [Newman, John Henry.] Remarks on certain passages in the
       Thirty-Nine Articles; Tracts for the Times, No. 90. [London:
       J. G. F. & J. Rivington, 1841.] T39.12. M. S. 1st ed.

1049. [Newman, John Henry.] Remarks on certain passages in the
       Thirty-Nine Articles; Tracts for the Times, No. 90. 2nd ed.
       [London: J. G. F. & J. Rivington, 1841.] T40.1. Cf. 1012.

1050. [Newman, John Henry.] Catholicus, pseud. The Tamworth
       Reading Room; letters on an address delivered by Sir Robert
       Peel, Bart., M.P., on the establishment of a reading room at
       Tamworth. London: John Mortimer, 1841. T39.11. One marginal
       query by N, regarding a choice of words. A reply to 1066.

1051. Nicholson, Patrick Charles. Unity, the effect of true reli-
       gion; or, Jerusalem, under David, the model of a well ordered
       state; a sermon, preached in the Cathedral Church of Carlisle,
       on Wednesday, August 4, 1841, before the High Sheriff of the
       County of Cumberland, and the Judges of Assize. London: J.
       G. F. & J. Rivington, 1841. T51.14.

1052. Ogle, James Adey. A letter to the Reverend the Warden of Wad-
       ham College, on the system of education pursued at Oxford;
       with suggestions for remodeling the examination statutes.
       Oxford: J. Vincent, 1841. T52.17. I.

1053. Oxenham, Henry Nutcombe. Two sermons preached in the Parish
       Church of Modbury, in November, 1841. Plymouth: Edward
       Nettleton, 1841. ST20.4. I. On the Eucharist.

1054. Oxford, Diocese of; Board of Education. Second annual report
       of the Oxford Diocesan Board of Education, adopted at the pub-
       lic meeting of subscribers, held in the Town Hall, Reading, on
       Thursday, March 4, 1841; the Lord Bishop of the Diocese in the
       chair. Oxford: Thomas Combe, 1841. NL28.2.

1055. Palmer, William (of Magdalen College, Oxford). Aids to re-
       flection on the seemingly double character of the Established
       Church, with reference to the foundation of a "Protestant
       Bishopric" at Jerusalem, recently announced in the Prussian
       State Gazette. Oxford: John Henry Parker, 1841. T49.6. Cf.
       1186.

1056. Palmer, William (of Magdalen College, Oxford). A letter to
       the Rev. C. P. Golightly, occasioned by his communication to
       the Standard newspaper, charging making use of their posi-
       tions within the pale of the Established Church in order to
       propagate Popery. Oxford: John Henry Parker, 1841. T49.4. I.
       A response to Golightly's letter published 26 Nov. 1841.
       Cf. 1186.

1057. Palmer, William (of Worcester College, Oxford). An enquiry
       into the possibility of obtaining means for Church extension
       without parliamentary grants. London: J. G. F. & J. Riving-
       ton, 1841. T48.10. I.

1058. Palmer, William (of Worcester College, Oxford). A letter to

N. Wiseman, D.D. (calling himself Bishop of Melipotamus), containing remarks on his letter to Mr. Newman. Oxford: John Henry Parker, 1841. T41.4. A response to 1114.

1059. Palmer, William (of Worcester College, Oxford). A second letter to N. Wiseman, D.D., on the foundation of the Romish doctrines of satisfactions, indulgences, Purgatory, and suffrages for the dead. Oxford: John Henry Parker, 1841. T41.5. A sequel to 1058.

1060. Palmer, William (of Worcester College, Oxford). A third letter to N. Wiseman, D.D., on the Romish doctrine of satisfactions. Oxford: John Henry Parker, 1841. T41.6. A sequel to 1059.

1061. Palmer, William (of Worcester College, Oxford). A fourth letter to N. Wiseman, D.D., on the Romish doctrine of satisfactions (concluded). Oxford: John Henry Parker, 1841. T41.7. A sequel to 1060.

1062. Palmer, William (of Worcester College, Oxford). A fifth letter to N. Wiseman, D.D., containing a reply to his remarks on letter 1; with additional proofs of the idolatry and superstition of Romanism. Oxford: John Henry Parker, 1841. T41.9.

1063. Palmer, William (of Worcester College, Oxford). A sixth letter to N. Wiseman, D.D., on the doctrine of Purgatory. Oxford: John Henry Parker, 1841. T41.10. A sequel to 1062.

1064. [Parker, John Henry.] Some observations on the domestic architecture of the Middle Ages. N.l., n.p., n.d. T37.9. D? "From the Third Edition of the 'Glossary of Architecture'" (Oxford: John Henry Parker, 1840-41).

1065. Parkinson, Richard. On the present condition of the labouring poor in Manchester; with hints for improving it. London: Simpkin, Marshall & Co., 1841. T51.25. I.

1066. Peel, Robert. An inaugural address, delivered by the Right Hon. Sir Robert Peel, Bart., M.P., president of the Tamworth Library and Reading Room, on Tuesday, 19th January, 1841. London: James Bain, 1841. T39.10. Cf. 1050. Duplicate copy: T67.2.

1067. Perceval, Arthur Philip. A letter to the Rev. Thomas Arnold, D.D., head master of Rugby School; with a reprint of one which appeared in the "Irish Ecclesiastical Journal." London: J. G. F. & J. Rivington, 1841. T43.9. I. Scoring by a comment on R. H. Froude's Remains.

1068. Perceval, Arthur Philip. A letter to the Right Rev. John-Bird, Lord Bishop of Chester: with remarks on his late charge, more especially as relates to the doctrine of Justification; with a reference to the state of things in the University of Oxford. London: J. G. F. & J. Rivington, 1841. T48.19. A response to John Bird Sumner's charge against Tract 90.

1069. Perry, Charles. Clerical education, considered with an especial reference to the universities; in a letter to the Right Reverend the Lord Bishop of Lichfield. London: John W.

Parker, 1841. T52.16. Bishop of Lichfield was James Bowstead. Sent to N as editor of <u>British</u> <u>Critic</u>.

1070. Phillipps, Ambrose Lisle. Some remarks on a letter addressed to the Reverend R. W. Jelf, D.D., Canon of Christ Church, in explanation of No. 90 in the series called the Tracts for the Times. London: Charles Dolman, 1841. T41.1. A response to 1044.

1071. Poole, George Ayliffe. On the present state of parties in the Church of England: with especial reference to the alleged tendency of the Oxford School to the doctrines and communion of Rome. London: James Burns, 1841. T43.14. S.

1072. [Powell, Henry Townsend.] Roman fallacies and Catholic truths. London: William Edward Painter, 1841. ST18.2. Contains twelve tracts; including 920, 922, 923, 924, 925, 926, 927, and 928.

1073. Pretyman, Richard. A review of No. 90 of the Tracts for the Times, with observations upon the Articles to which it relates. Oxford: Joseph Vincent, 1841. T43.7.

1074. Protestant Episcopal Church, U.S.A. Canons for the government of the Protestant Episcopal Church in the United States of America: being the substance of various canons adopted in general conventions of said Church, (from A.D. 1789, to A.D. 1832,) and set forth, with alterations & additions, in general convention, A.D. 1832; also, the canons passed in general conventions, A.D. 1835, 1838, and 1841, to which are annexed, the constitution of the Church, and the course of ecclesiastical studies, established by the House of Bishops, in the general convention of 1804. New York: Swords, Stanford, 1841. T54.12.

1075. Protestant Episcopal Church, U.S.A. Journal of the proceedings of the bishops, clergy, and laity of the Protestant Episcopal Church in the United States of America, in a general convention held in the city of New York, from October 6th to October 19th, inclusive, A.D. 1841; together with the constitution and canons for the government of the Protestant Episcopal Church. New York: Swords, Stanford, 1841. T54.11.

1076. Protestant Episcopal Tract Society. The Church almanac for the year of our Lord 1842. New York: Protestant Episcopal Tract Society, 1841. ST16.4.

1077. Pusey, Edward Bouverie. The articles treated on in Tract 90, reconsidered and their interpretation vindicated in a letter to the Rev. R. W. Jelf, D.D., Canon of Christ Church; with an appendix from Abp. Ussher on the difference between ancient and modern addresses to saints. Oxford: John Henry Parker; J. G. F. & J. Rivington, 1841. T42.1. Duplicate copy: NL11.1.

1078. Pusey, Edward Bouverie. Christ, the source and rule of Christian love; a sermon, preached on the Feast of S. John the Evangelist, MDCCCXL, at St. Paul's Church, Bristol, in aid of a new church to be erected in an outlying district in that parish; with a preface on the relation of our exertions to our needs. Oxford: John Henry Parker, 1841. Tre13.5.

1079. Pusey, Edward Bouverie. The preaching of the Gospel, a preparation for our Lord's coming; a sermon preached at the parochial Church of St. Andrew's, Clifton, in conformity with the Queen's letter, in behalf of the Society for the Propagation of the Gospel. Oxford: John Henry Parker, 1841. Tre13.4.

1080. Ram, Pierre François Xavier de. Oratio de doctoris catholici dignitate et officio, quam die secunda mensis Augusti MDCCCXLI habuit Petrus Franc. Xav. de Ram, Rector Universitatis in Oppido Lovaniensi, quum virum eruditissimum Augustum Kempeneers, ex Montenaken, dioecesis Leodiensis presbyterum, sacrorum canonum doctorem, more majorum renuntiaret. Louvain: Vanlinthout et Vandenzande, n.d. P5.1.

1081. Rathborne, Joseph. Are the Puseyites sincere? A letter most respectfully addressed to a Right Reverend Catholic Lord Bishop, on the Oxford Movement. London: T. Jones, 1841. T44.4.

1082. [Robertson, James Burton.] Verax, a Catholic Layman, pseud. A letter to the Rev. William Palmer, M.A., of Worcester College, Oxford. London: T. Jones, 1841. T41.12.

1083. [Robertson, James Burton.] Verax, a Catholic Layman, pseud. Second letter to the Rev. William Palmer, M.A., of Worcester College, Oxford; demonstratively proving the Church of England to be an heretical and schismatical church, the mere creature of human invention. London: T. Jones, 1841. T41.13.

1084. [Robertson, James Burton.] Verax, a Catholic Layman, pseud. Third letter to the Rev. William Palmer, M.A., of Worcester College, Oxford; on auricular confession, and the absolute necessity thereof; also the nullity of the Church of England's ordinations, notes, etc. London: T. Jones, 1841. T41.14.

1085. [Robertson, James Burton.] Verax, a Catholic Layman, pseud. The triumph of truth, being a reply to "A Short Inquiry into the Doctrines of the Churches of England and Rome." London: T. Jones, 1841. ST18.1. An answer to various anti-Catholic works of Walter Farquhar Hook.

1086. St. Paul's School, London. Prolusiones literariæ, præmiis quotannis propositis dignatæ, et in D. Pauli Schola; recitatæ comitiis maximis A. S. H. MDCCCXLI. London: Gilbert and Rivington, 1841. T47.12.

1087. Scott, Robert. Christian quietness: a sermon. London: J. G. F. & J. Rivington, 1841. ST27.4. I.

1088. Sewell, William. A letter to the Rev. E. B. Pusey, D.D., Regius Professor of Hebrew, and Canon of Christ Church, on the publication of No. 90 of the Tracts for the Times. Oxford: John Henry Parker, 1841. NL11.2.

1089. Sewell, William. A letter to the Rev. E. B. Pusey, D.D., Regius Professor of Hebrew, and Canon of Christ Church, on the publication of No. 90 of the Tracts for the Times. 2nd ed., with a postscript. Oxford: John Henry Parker, 1841. T40.9. Cf. 1100.

1090. Sibthorp, Richard Waldo. The claims of the Catholic Church; a sermon preached in the Chapel of St. Mary Magdalen College

before the University of Oxford on the feast of St. Mark the
Evangelist A.D. MDCCCXLI. Oxford: John Henry Parker, 1841.
T44.8.

1091. Silver, Thomas. A second letter to Sir Robert Harry Inglis,
Bart., M.P. for the University of Oxford, on the origin and
importance of the Church rate. Oxford: John Henry Parker,
1841. T48.4. Cf. 774.

1092. Stafford, J. C. The offertory, or the duty of making gifts
of charity an offering to God, according to the directions of
the rubric in the Communion Service; a sermon preached in Harlow Church October XI, MDCCCXL. Oxford: John Henry Parker,
1841. ST11.10.

1093. Strachan, John. A charge delivered to the clergy of the Diocese of Toronto, at the primary visitation, held in the Cathedral Church of St. James, Toronto, on the 9th September, 1841.
Toronto: H. & W. Rowsell, 1841. T56.4. I.

1094. Sumner, Charles Richard. A charge delivered to the clergy of
the Diocese of Winchester, at his fourth visitation in September, 1841. London: J. Hatchard and Son, 1841. T56.3. Anti-
Tractarian, with an attack on *Tract* 90.

1095. Sumner, John Bird. A charge delivered to the clergy of the
Diocese of Chester, at the visitation in June and September,
MDCCCXLI; by the Right Reverend John Bird, Lord Bishop of
Chester. London: J. Hatchard and Son, 1841. T56.7. S. Anti-
Tractarian.

1096. Talbot, John, 16th Earl of Shrewsbury. Letter from the Earl
of Shrewsbury to Ambrose Lisle Phillipps, Esq., descriptive
of the Estatica of Caldaro and the Addolorata of Capriana.
London: Charles Dolman, 1841. T44.1. See also 1097.

1097. Talbot, John, 16th Earl of Shrewsbury. Second letter to Ambrose Lisle Phillipps, Esq., from the Earl of Shrewsbury; on
the present posture of affairs. London: Charles Dolman, 1841.
T44.2. A sequel to 1096.

1098. Tarbutt, Arthur. The observance of Lent explained and enforced; a sermon. London: Simpkin, Marshall, and Co., 1841.
ST20.12.

1099. Thorp, Thomas. Two charges delivered at the general visita-
tions of the Archdeaconry of Bristol held in June 1839 and
July 1840. Cambridge: J. G. F. & J. Rivington, 1840. T55.6.
I.

1100. Thorpe, William. A review of a letter from the Rev. W. Sewell,
A.M., Professor of Moral Philosophy in the University of Oxford, to the Rev. Dr. Pusey: to which are added remarks on Mr.
Sewell's treatise on Christian morals, and also an article
attributed to him, entitled "Romanism in Ireland," which
appeared in a late number of the Quarterly Review. London: J.
Hatchard and Sons, 1841. T40.10. See 1088. The article is
in *Quarterly Review*, 67 (1840), 117-71.

1101. [United Church of England and Ireland, The.] Statement of
proceedings relating to the establishment of a bishopric of

the United Church of England and Ireland in Jerusalem. London: Rivingtons, 1841. T49.1. N quotes from this document in Apo., pp. 132-33.

1102. Ward, William George. Appendix to a few more words in support of No. 90 of the Tracts for the Times, in answer to Mr. Lowe's pamphlet. Oxford: John Henry Parker, 1841. T40.17. See 1103, 1032.

1103. Ward, William George. A few more words in support of No. 90 of the Tracts for the Times. Oxford: John Henry Parker, 1841. T40.15. Cf. 1104, 1032, 1102.

1104. [Ward, William George.] A few words in support of No. 90 of the Tracts for the Times, partly with reference to Mr. Wilson's letter. Oxford: John Henry Parker, 1841. T40.14. A review of 1112.

1105. Watson, Alexander. The ministerial blessing; a farewell sermon, preached at St. Andrew's, Ancoats, Manchester, December 6th, 1840. London: Burns, 1841. T33.27. A defense of Apostolic Succession.

1106. Whitaker, S. The Church--the ark of salvation; a sermon, preached in the Parish Church of Tipton, Staffordshire, on Sunday, March 21, 1841. London: J. G. F. & J. Rivington, 1841. ST22.2. I. A High Church sermon on Apostolic Succession.

1107. Wilberforce, Robert Isaac. A primary charge to the clergy of the Archdeaconry of the East Riding. London: James Burns, 1841. T55.7.

1108. Wilkins, George. A charge to the clergy of the Archdeaconry of Nottingham, delivered at Nottingham, Retford, and Newark, in May, 1841, by George Wilkins. London: J. G. F. & J. Rivington. T55.5. I.

1109. [Williams, Isaac.] A few remarks on the Charge of the Lord Bishop of Glocester [sic] and Bristol on the subject of reserve in communicating religious knowledge as taught in the Tracts for the Times, No. 80, and No. 87; by the writer of those Tracts. Oxford: John Henry Parker, 1841. T48.17. The Bishop of Gloucester was James Henry Monk. Duplicate copy: T48.20.

1110. Williams, Isaac. A sermon preached at the consecration of the church of Llangorwen, in the Diocese of St. David's, December 16, MDCCCXLI. Aberystwith: J. Cox, 1841. T51.19.

1111. Wilson, Daniel. The sufficiency of Holy Scripture as the rule of faith; a sermon preached at the Cathedral Church of St. John, Calcutta, at an ordination, holden on Sunday, May 2, 1841, by Daniel, Bishop of Calcutta and Metropolitan of India. London: J. Hatchard and Son, 1841. T56.5. Anti-Tractarian with remarks against Tract 90.

1112. [Wilson, Henry Bristow.] A letter to the Rev. T. T. Churton, M.A., fellow and tutor of Brasenose College. Oxford: W. Graham, 1841. T40.13. Cf. 1104. Against Tract 90 and the Letter to Dr. Jelf. Wilson and Churton were two of the

Four Tutors who signed the original protest against Tract 90.

1113. Wiseman, Nicholas. A letter on Catholic unity, addressed to the Right Honorable, the Earl of Shrewsbury. London: Charles Dolman, 1841. T44.3. I. A response to 1096 and 1097.

1114. Wiseman, Nicholas. A letter respectfully addressed to the Rev. J. H. Newman, upon some passages in his letter to the Rev. Dr. Jelf. London: Dolman, 1841. T41.2. A response to 1044. Duplicate copy: NL14.12.

1115. Wiseman, Nicholas. A letter respectfully addressed to the Rev. J. H. Newman, upon some passages in his letter to the Rev. Dr. Jelf. 2nd ed. London: Charles Dolman, 1841. T41.3.

1116. Wiseman, Nicholas. Remarks on a letter from the Rev. W. Palmer. London: Charles Dolman, 1841. T41.8. A reply to 1058, 1059, 1060, and 1061.

1117. Wordsworth, Charles. Evangelical repentence: a sermon preached in the Cathedral Church of Winchester, in aid of the Society for Promoting Christian Knowledge, and the Society for the Propagation of the Gospel in Foreign Parts; on Thursday, Nov. 11, 1841. Oxford: John Henry Parker, 1841. T45.3.

WORKS BY UNIDENTIFIED AUTHORS

1118. Anon. ed. Certain documents, &c. &c. connected with Tracts for the Times, No. 90. Oxford: W. Baxter, 1841. T40.2. Contains: "The Resolution of the Hebdomadal Board"; "Letter to the Editor of the Standard from 'Academicus'"; "Letter to the Same from 'Academicus Alter'"; "The Letter of the Four Tutors"; "Mr. Newman's Letter to the Vice-Chancellor, with Remarks"; "Letter to the Editor of the Times from 'A Protestant'"; "Opinions of the People, from the Morning Chronicle"; "Opinions of Bishops, from the Standard"; "Letter to the Editor of the Standard from 'A Member of Convocation'"; "Letter to the Same, Likewise from 'A Member of Convocation.'" Cf. 1128, 1129.

1119. Anon. The Church of England and in America compared. New York: Robert Craighead, 1841. T45.5. An offprint of an article in The New York Review (April 1841).

1120. Anon. The controversy between Tract No. XC and the Oxford tutors. London: How & Parsons, 1841. T43.5.

1121. Anon. The doctrine of the Catholic Church in England on the Holy Eucharist, illustrated by extracts from her great divines, with an appendix on various other points of faith and practice. Oxford: John Henry Parker, 1841. T44.7.

1122. Anon. The honor of the sanctuary: a few words to the inhabitants of_____ where a new church is to be built. London: James Burns, 1841. ST20.10.

1123. Anon. A letter to the author of the Tract for the Times, No. 90. [Oxford: J. Vincent], n.d. T40.11.

1124. Anon. Quelques mots sur la proposition de MM. Du Bus Aîné et Brabant, tendante à déclarer l'Université de Louvain

personne civile; deuxième édition, suivie du rapport présenté
par M. De Decker, au nom de la section centrale chargée de
l'examen de la proposition. 2nd ed. Brussels: Ve. J. J.
Vanderborght, 1841. P4.2. Cf. 1225.

1125. Anon. The reformer; Church notions: high and low. N.1., n.p.,
n.d. ST20.13. High Church.

1126. Anon. Remarks on the Churches of Rome and England, respect-
fully addressed to the Right Rev. Dr. Wiseman and the Rev.
William Palmer. London: J. Hatchard and Son, 1841. T41.17.
An ecumenical treatise. Cf. 1058, 1116.

1127. Anon. The rights of laymen, their privilege and duty to receive blessings equally in every Orthodox Church. London: J.
Hatchard and Son, 1841. Tre10.3.

1128. Anon. ed. Some documents, &c. &c. connected with Tract for
the Times, No. XC. 3rd ed. Oxford: W. Graham, 1841. T40.3.
Contains: "The Resolution of the Hebdomadal Board," "The Rev.
Mr. Newman's Letter to the Vice-Chancellor," "Letter of
Oxoniensis Catholicus to the Editor of The Times," "Letter to
the Editor of the Morning Post from Discipulus Ecclesiae Angli-
canae," "The Object of the Tracts for the Times, from the
Morning Post," "Remarks on the late Revival of Catholic Principles, from The Times Newspaper." Cf. 1118, 1129.

1129. Anon. ed. Some papers illustrative of Tract for the Times,
No. 90, &c.; with an appendix and notes. Oxford: W. Graham,
1841. T40.4. Contains: "Testimony to Mr. Newman's View of
the Yearnings of the Age, from a Work Published in 1830,"
"Remarks on Mr. Newman's Letter, from the Morning Post,"
"Rev. W. B. Barter's Letter on the Tracts for the Times, their
effects, and the Spirit of Their Opponents, from the Conserva-
tive Journal," "The Sixth Article of Religion, with the
Church's Comment," "Quotations from Chillingworth, Bishop
March, &c." T40.4. Cf. 1118, 1128.

1130. Anon. What is Puseyism? N.1., n.p., n.d. T60.2. D? An
anti-Tractarian broadside.

1131. A British Subject, pseud. The penalty of death retained for
cruel atrocities; part the first, the divine sanction. London:
Edmund Lloyd, 1841. T47.5.

1132. A Catholic of the Anglican Church, pseud. A short letter
respectfully addressed to the Right Reverend Father in God,
Richard, Lord Bishop of Oxford, respecting a remarkable passage in a letter of the Rev. J. H. Newman to the Rev. Dr.
Jelf, having an important bearing on the interests of the
Church. London: J. Hatchard and Son, 1841. T43.4. N has
noted that the scoring in this pamphlet is not his.

1133. A Churchman, pseud. The case stated with reference to the
late meeting of the Society for the Employment of Additional
Curates in Populous Places; and to the attacks which have been
made thereon. Leeds: T. W. Green, 1841. ST20.8. S. A High-
Church tract against the Pastoral Aid Society and in defense
of W. F. Hook.

1134. A Clergyman of the Church of England, pseud. Help to self examination. Durham: F. Andrews, 1841. ST23.6. Gift of the publisher.

1135. An English Catholic, pseud. Oxford or Rome? A letter to the Rev. J. H. Newman, on No. 90 of the "Tracts for the Times." London: James Ridgway, 1841. T44.6. M. S.

1136. Laicus, and Clerus, pseuds. Revival of old Church principles: or, a defence of the doctrine of Catholic tradition and authority in matters of faith, as held of old by our reformers, and as taught in our formularies: in a letter to the Morning Post, by "Laicus"; with an answer to the same, and in defence of ultra-Protestantism, by "Clerus"; and a rejoinder from "Laicus"; the whole reprinted from the columns of "The Morning Post"; with an appendix. London: James, Burns, 1841. T40.5.

1137. A Layman, pseud. Remarks on the best means of increasing the number of bishoprics in England and Wales, in connexion with the remodeling of cathedral institutions. Newbury: W. Lewis, 1841. ST21.13. Duplicate copy: ST22.5.

1138. A Member of the Church, pseud. A few humble remarks on the great question: how is England to become Catholic? London: C. Dolman, 1841. T44.5.

1139. A Member of the Church of Scotland, pseud. Present state of the Church of England exposed. London: Whittaker and Co., 1841. ST20.7. Anti-Tractarian.

1140. A Member of the University of Oxford, pseud. Strictures on No. 90 of the Tracts for the Times. Oxford: J. Vincent, 1841. T43.2. See 1141.

1141. A Member of the University of Oxford, pseud. Strictures on No. 90 of the Tracts for the Times, Part II. Oxford: J. Vincent, 1841. T43.3. Part II of 1140.

1142. One of the Original Subscribers to the Tracts for the Times, pseud. New and strange doctrines extracted from the writings of Mr. Newman and his friends, in a letter to the Rev. W. F. Hook, D.D. Oxford: W. Baxter, 1841. T43.1. I. A response to 1019.

1143. A Presbyter of the Church, pseud. The Rhode Island cottage; or a gift for the children of sorrow; a narrative of facts. New York: W. B. & T. Smith, 1841. ST19.10. An account of Cynthia Taggart.

1842

1144. Abeken, Heinrich. A letter to the Rev. E. B. Pusey, D.D., in reference to certain charges against the German Church, contained in his letter to His Grace the Archbishop of Canterbury. London: John W. Parker, 1842. T49.2. Abeken was chaplain to the legation at Rome of the King of Prussia. Cf. 1204.

1145. Bagot, Richard. A charge delivered to the clergy of the Diocese of Oxford by Richard Bagot, D.D., Bishop of Oxford, and Chancellor of the Most Noble Order of the Garter; at his fourth visitation, May, 1842. 3rd ed. Oxford: John Henry Parker, 1842. T56.9. A long discussion of the controversy surrounding Tracts for the Times, with a specific condemnation of Tract 90.

1146. Biber, George Edward. Catholicity v. Sibthorp; or, some help to answer the question, whether the Rev. R. W. Sibthorp, B.D., is now or ever was a Catholic? In a series of letters addressed to him by the Rev. G. E. Biber, LL.D., Presbyter of the Anglo-Catholic Church: letter the second. London: F. G. F. and J. Rivington, 1842. T44.15. I. See 1210, 1147, 1148, 1149.

1147. Biber, George. Catholicity v. Sibthorp; or, some help to answer the question, whether the Rev. R. W. Sibthorp, B.D., is now or ever was a Catholic? In a series of letters addressed to him by the Rev. G. E. Biber, LL.D., Presbyter of the Anglo-Catholic Church: letter the third. London: J. G. F. and J. Rivington, 1842. T44.16. I. See 1210, 1146.

1148. Biber, George Edward. Catholicity v. Sibthorp; or, some help to answer the question, whether the Rev. R. W. Sibthorp, B.D., is now or ever was a Catholic? In a series of letters addressed to him by the Rev. G. E. Biber, Presbyter of the Anglo-Catholic Church: letter the fourth. London: J. G. F. and J. Rivington, 1842. T44.17. I. See 1210, 1146.

1149. Biber, George Edward. Catholicity v. Sibthorp; or, some help to answer the question, whether the Rev. R. W. Sibthorp, B.D., is now or ever was a Catholic? In a series of letters addressed to him by the Rev. G. E. Biber, Presbyter of the Anglo-Catholic Church: letter the fifth. London: J. G. F. and J. Rivington, 1842. T44.18. I. See 1210, 1146.

1150. Biber, George Edward. Our day of sifting; a plain sermon for these perplexing times, preached on New Year's Day, 1842, at St. Andrew's, Ham. London: J. G. F. and J. Rivington, 1842. T44.14. I. On Justification.

1151. Bickersteth, Edward. The divine warning to the Church, at this time, of our present enemies, dangers, and duties, and as to our future prospects; a sermon preached before the Protestant Association, at St. Dunstan's, Fleet-Street, on Saturday, November 5, 1842, with notes and an appendix, containing information respecting the present diffusion of infidelity, lawlessness, and Popery. London: Protestant Association, 1842. T59.22. I. Publications of the Protestant Association, No. 37.

1152. Bickersteth, Edward. The permanence and progress of divine truth; or, the truths of the Reformation brought fourth by the Church of England, according to the direction of our Lord; a sermon preached before the Prayer Book and Homily Society, on Thursday evening, May 5, 1842, (being Ascension-Day): at St. Dunstan's Church, Fleet Street. London: Prayer-Book and Homily Society, 1842. T45.20. I.

1153. British Society for Promoting the Religious Principles of the
Reformation. The contradictions of the Fathers, respectfully
addressed to Roman Catholics and Tractarians. London: British
Society for Promoting the Religious Principles of the Reformation, 1842. ST19.2.

1154. British Society for Promoting the Religious Principles of the
Reformation. The fanaticism of the fourth and fifth centuries,
or Tractarian inconsistency. London: British Society for Promoting the Religious Principles of the Reformation, 1842.
ST19.3.

1155. British Society for Promoting the Religious Principles of the
Reformation. Where was the universal voice of the visible
Church in the Nicene age? Or, a brief sketch of the principal
heresies and division of the fourth and fifth centuries, designed as an antidote to Tractarianism. London: British
Society for Promoting the Religious Principles of the Reformation, 1842. ST24.4.

1156. Butler, William Archer. Primitive Church principles not inconsistent with universal Christian sympathy; a sermon
preached at the visitation of the United Dioceses of Derry
and Raphoe, on Thursday, September 22, 1842. London: J. G. F.
& J. Rivington, 1842. T48.26.

1157. Caswall, Henry. The city of the Mormons; or, three days at
Nauvoo, in 1842. London: J. G. F. & J. Rivington, 1842.
ST22.3. I.

1158. [Episcopal Church of Scotland.] The office for the Holy Communion according to the use of the Scottish Church. Edinburgh: Grant and Son, 1842. ST23.5.

1159. Clarke, H. Poems: chiefly relating to the present state and
prospects of the Church. London: Rivingtons, 1842. ST19.8.

1160. Coleridge, Derwent. A letter on the National Society's
Training-College for Schoolmasters, Stanley Grove, Chelsea;
addressed to the Rev. John Sinclair, M.A., secretary of the
society. London: John W. Parker, 1842. T52.13. Coleridge
was principal of the college.

1161. Collison, Frederick William. Remarks on a sermon by Professor
Scholefield, entitled The Christian Altar: being a vindication
of the Catholic doctrines therein impugned. Cambridge: T.
Stevenson: 1842. T48.16. Cf. 1103, 1102.

1162. Copleston, Edward. A charge delivered to the clergy of the
Diocese of Llandaff, at the triennial visitation, in October,
1842, by Edward, Lord Bishop of Llandaff. 2nd ed. London:
J. G. F. & J. Rivington, 1842. T55.3. A mildly anti-Tractarian charge.

1163. [De Bary, Richard B.] Veles, a Non-Commissioned Member of the
Holy Catholic Church, pseud. Col. Mitchell's argument for the
abolishment of promotion by purchase in the army: considered
in a letter respectfully addressed to the editors of "The
British Critic," "The British Magazine," and "The Christian
Remembrancer." London: James Burns, 1842. T48.8. A response
to a letter to The Times of Nov. 1841 from Col. John Mitchell,

who advocated abolishing the purchase of military promotions.

1164. Denison, Edward. A charge delivered to the clergy of the Diocese of Salisbury, by Edward Denison, D.D., Bishop of Salisbury, at his second visitation, September, 1842. 3rd ed. London: J. G. F. & J. Rivington, 1842. T56.8. M. Specifically attacks Tract 90. Duplicate copy: T56.10.

1165. De Vere, Aubrey. Inaugural address delivered on the evening of the eighth of February, 1842, at the house of the Limerick Philosophical and Literary Society. Dublin: Grant and Bolton, 1842. T52.21.

1166. Doane, George Washington. Ancient charity, the rule and the reproof of modern: a sermon, in St. Mary's Church, Burlington, on the first Sunday after the epiphany, M DCCC XLII; the Sunday after the reading of the pastoral letter, on systematic charity. Burlington: J. L. Powell, 1842. T54.9. Duplicate copy: T57.5 (lacks title-page).

1167. Doane, George Washington. The glorious things of the city of God: the first sermon (sixteenth Sunday after Trinity, 26th September, 1841.) in St. Mary's Church, Burlington, after a brief pilgrimage to the Church of England. Burlington, New Jersey: J. L. Powell, 1842. T54.8.

1168. Dodsworth, William. Remarks on the second letter of the Rev. Richard Waldo Sibthorp, B.D., entitled "A Further Answer to the Inquiry, Why Have You Become a Catholic?" London: James Burns, 1842. T44.13. See 1210, 1169.

1169. Dodsworth, William. Why have you become a Romanist? A letter to Rev. Richard Waldo Sibthorp, B.D., occasioned by his letter entitled "Some Answer to the Inquiry, Why Are You Become a Roman Catholic?" London: James Burns, 1842. T44.12. See 1210.

1170. Elrington, Charles R. Subscription to the XXXIX. Articles; a sermon, preached in the chapel of Trinity College, Dublin, on Sunday the 20th of February, 1842. Dublin: Andrew Milliken, 1842. T42.3. See 1197.

1171. Froude, James Anthony. The influence of the science of political economy on the moral and social welfare of a nation; a prize essay read in the Sheldonian Theatre, Oxford, June 8, 1842. Oxford: J. Vincent, 1842. T68.8.

1172. [Fund for the Endowment of Additional Bishoprics in the Colonies.] Additional colonial bishoprics; declaration of the archbishops and bishops of the United Church of England and Ireland, with a list of subscribers to the fund. London: n.p., 1842. T48.11.

1173. Hawkins, Edward. The Apostolical Succession; a sermon preached in the Chapel of Lambeth Palace, on Sunday, February 27, 1842, at the consecration of the Right Rev. Ashurst Turner, Lord Bishop of Chichester. London: B. Fellowes, 1842. T43.13. I.

1174. Hawkins, Ernest. Christian forbearance; a sermon, preached before the University of Oxford, at St. Mary's, on Sexagesima

Sunday, MDCCCXLII. Oxford: J. H. Parker, 1842. T48.21

1175. Herschell, Ridley H. Reasons why I, a Jew, have become a
      Catholic and not a Roman Catholic; a letter to reply to the
      Rev. R. W. Sibthorp, B.A., late of Ryde. London: J. Unwin,
      1842. T44.19. See 1210.

1176. Hook, Walter Farquhar. Peril of idolatry; a sermon. London:
      J. G. F. & J. Rivington, 1842. T48.24.

1177. Hook, Walter Farquhar. Reasons for contributing towards the
      support of an English bishop at Jerusalem, stated in a letter
      to a friend. London: J. G. F. & J. Rivington, 1842. T49.9.

1178. Hope, James Robert. Postscript; the Bishopric of the United
      Church of England and Ireland at Jerusalem, considered in a
      letter to a friend. London: C. J. Stewart, 1842. T49.8. I.
      A sequel to 1020.

1179. James, William. A second appendix to "Four Sermons on the
      Benefit and Necessity of the Sacraments, and the Obligation of
      the Moral Law and the Sabbath, with Remarks on Helyn's History
      of the Sabbath"; being a reply to seeming objections from more
      recent publications. London: J. G. F. & J. Rivington, 1842.
      T51.2. Partly against Tracts for the Times, Nos. 67, 68, and
      69, on Baptismal Regeneration, by Pusey.

1180. Jelf, Richard William. Via media: or the Church of England
      our providential path between Romanism and Dissent; a sermon,
      preached before the University of Oxford in Christ Church
      Cathedral, on Sunday, Jan. 23, 1842. Oxford: John Henry Par-
      ker, 1842. T43.12. I.

1181. Johnson, Samuel Roosevelt. The testimony of Jesus; a sermon
      preached in St. Paul's Church, New Albany, Indiana; at the
      ordination of the Rev. Andrew Wylie, D.D., President of
      Indiana University, on the second Sunday in advent, A.D. 1841.
      Lafayette: John B. Seman's, 1842. T54.10.

1182. Lambert, John. A lecture on the music of the Middle Ages,
      especially in relation to its rhythm and mode of execution,
      with illustrations; delivered before the members of the
      Wiltshire Archeological Society, at their third annual meeting
      and published at their request. Devizes: H. Bull, 1842.
      T68.14.

1183. [Luscombe, Matthew, and William Palmer (of Magdalen College,
      Oxford).] Litteræ commendatoriæ reverendissimi patris in
      Christo Matthæi, Scotorum, Anglorum, aliorumque in Gallia
      habitantium episcopi, a Scotiæ episcopis consecrati. Oxford:
      William Baxter, 1842. T49.12. An Anglo-Catholic reaction
      against the Jerusalem Bishopric.

1184. Maguire, John. Protestantism and churches in the East; a
      tract for the times. London: Catholic Institute of Great
      Britain, n.d. NL23.5. I. Tract No. 42 of the Catholic
      Institute of Great Britain.

1185. Marriott, Charles. Numbering our days; a sermon preached in
      Bradfield Church, on the twenty-second Sunday after Trinity,
      MDCCCXLII, being the day after the funeral of the Rev. H.

Stevens, forty-two years rector of that parish. Oxford: I. Shrimpton, 1842. T51.17.

1186. Maurice, Frederick Denison. Three letters to the Rev. W. Palmer, fellow and tutor of Magdalen College, Oxford, on the name 'Protestant;' on the seemingly ambiguous character of the English Church; and on the bishopric at Jerusalem; with an appendix, containing some remarks on a pamphlet of J. R. Hope, Esq., entitled "The Bishopric of the United Church of England and Ireland, at Jerusalem, considered in a letter to a Friend." London: J. & G. Rivington, 1842. T49.7. Cf. 1020, 1056, 1055.

1187. Miller, Charles. Prospectus of a publication entitled A Catalogue of Authorities, Ecclesiastical and Civil, Taken from the Writings of the Ancient Fathers, from the Laws of England, and from Other Sources, Bearing Uniform Witness to the System of Tithes, as a Divine Institution of Perpetual Obligation: with Introductory Observations. London: J. G. F. & J. Rivington, 1842. T58.10. I.

1188. Muhlenburg, William A. An account of the grammar school, or junior department of St. Paul's College. New York: F. C. Gutierrez, 1842. ST16.5.

1189. Muhlenburg, William A., ed. Devotions for the Holy Week. N.l., n.p., n.d. ST22.6.

1190. Musgrave, Thomas. A charge delivered to the clergy of the Diocese of Hereford, June, 1842, at the second visitation of Thomas, Lord Bishop of Hereford. Hereford: Webb & Phillips, 1842. T55.2.

1191. [Palmer, William (of Magdalen College, Oxford).] Analysis of letters commendatory, from the Right Rev. Matthew, (consecrated in 1825 to be Bishop of the Scots, English, and others resident in France, by the Bishops of Scotland,) addressed to all Orthodox and Catholic bishops. Oxford: Baxter, 1842. T49.13. A sequel to 1183. Endorsed "Private."

1192. [Palmer, William (of Magdalen College, Oxford).] A Member of the Church of England, pseud. Examination of an announcement made in the Prussian State Gazette, concerning "the relations of the Bishop of the United Church of England and Ireland in Jerusalem," with "the German Congregation of the Evangelical Religion in Palestine." Oxford: John Henry Parker, 1842. T49.10.

1193. Palmer, William (of Magdalen College, Oxford). A letter to a Protestant-Catholic. Oxford: John Henry Parker, 1842. T49.5. A response to an anonymous letter published 11 Dec. 1841 in The Oxford Herald.

1194. Palmer, William (of Worcester College, Oxford). An examination of the Rev. R. W. Sibthorp's reasons for his secession from the Church. Oxford: John Henry Parker, 1842. T44.10. See 1210.

1195. Palmer, William (of Worcester College, Oxford). A seventh letter to N. Wiseman, D.D., on the doctrine of indulgences. Oxford: John Henry Parker, 1842. T41.11. A sequel to 1063.

1196. Palmer, William (of Worcester College, Oxford). A supplement
to An Examination of Mr. Sibthorp's Pamphlet, comprising observations on his "Further Answer," &c. Oxford: John Henry
Parker, 1842. T44.11. See 1210, 1194.

1197. Perceval, Arthur Philip. On subscription to the XXXIX. Articles; letter to the Rev. Charles Elrington, D.D., Regius Professor of Divinity in the University of Dublin; occasioned by
his sermon in Trinity College Chapel. London: J. G. F. & J.
Rivington, 1842. T42.4. See 1170.

1198. Phillips, Ambrose Lisle. An appeal to the Catholics of England
in behalf of the Abbey Church of Saint Bernard, Charnwood
Forest, Leicestershire. London: Charles Dolman, 1842. T45.12.

1199. Phillips, John Bartholomew. Prayers for the dead; a sermon
preached at the parish church of Saint Woollos, Newport,
Monmouthshire, on Sunday, March 13, 1842. London: J. G. F. &
J. Rivington, 1842. T51.20. Partly a reply to Pusey's letter
to the Bishop of Oxford. Phillips was a distant relative of
Newman.

1200. [Powell, Henry Townsend, ed.] "Faith, hope, and charity";
extract from a sermon preached at the dedication of the Catholic chapel at Bradford, in the county of York, on Wednesday,
July 27, 1825, (and republished by the Catholic Institute in
1840,) by Peter Augustine Baines, D.D., Bishop of Siga, &c.:
or, the Bishop's appeal to the Catholic Church against the
Pope and the Church of Rome, founded upon Holy Scripture, contrasted with quotations from the Missal and the Breviary and
other approved authorities and books of devotion in the Church
of Rome. London: W. E. Painter, 1842. ST17.3. Cf. 827 and
922.

1201. Protestant Episcopal Church of the United States, General
Theological Seminary. Catalogue of the officers and students
of the General Theological Seminary of the Protestant Episco-
pal Church of the United States located in the city of New
York, 1841-42, to which is added a catalogue of the alumni.
New York: R. Craighead, 1842. ST16.2.

1202. [Pusey, Edward Bouverie, ed.] Appendix; extracts from the
Tracts for the Times, the Lyra Apostolica, and other publications; showing that to oppose ultra-Protestantism is not to
favour Popery. London: J. G. & F. Rivington, n.d. Tre14.3.
D?

1203. Pusey, Edward Bouverie. A letter to His Grace the Archbishop
of Canterbury, on some circumstances connected with the present crisis in the English Church. Oxford: John Henry Parker,
1842. T50.1. A response to the controversies over Tract 90
and the Jerusalem Bishopric. The Archbishop of Canterbury was
William Howley.

1204. Pusey, Edward Bouverie. Notes added to the third edition of a
letter to His Grace the Archbishop of Canterbury, by the Rev.
Dr. Pusey. [Oxford: Baxter,] n.d. T50.2. Sent to N. See
1203. Includes a reply to 1144.

1205. [Pusey, Edward Bouverie.] Scriptural views of Holy Baptism, as established by the consent of the ancient Church, and contrasted with the systems of modern schools. 2nd ed., enlarged. N.l., n.p., n.d. Tre3.2. D? Tracts for the Times, No. 67. Offprint from Tracts for the Times, vol. II, Part II for 1834-35. Regarding the date of this edition, see Blehl, pp. 115-16.

1206. Ram, Pierre François Xavier de. Discours prononcé au cimetière de l'Abbaye de Parc-lez-Louvain, le 10 octobre 1842, par P. F. X. de Ram, Recteur de l'Université Catholique de Louvain, sur la tombe de M. Jean-Gérard-Joseph Ernst, professeur ordinaire à la Faculté de Droit. Louvain: Vanlinthout et Vandenzande, n.d. P5.2.

1207. Ratisbonne, Marie Alphonse. Lettre de M. Marie-Alphonse Ratisbonne, a M. Desgenettes, curé de N.-D.-des-Victoires, à Paris. [Lyon: L. Lesne,] n.d. ST23.3. About Marian devotion.

1208. [Robertson, James Burton.] Verax, a Catholic Layman, pseud. Fourth letter to the Rev. William Palmer, M.A., of Worcester College, Oxford; on the way to find out the true Church of Christ on earth, on satisfaction, on indulgences, on the supremacy of the See of Rome, infallibility, Eucharist, etc., etc. London: T. Jones, 1842. T41.15.

1209. Scott, Robert. A letter to Lewis Lyne, Esq., on apostolical episcopacy. London: James Burns, 1842. ST21.5. I. A reply to Lyne's Apostolical Succession and the Church of Christ (1842).

1210. [Seager, Charles.] Academicus, pseud. Auricular confession: six letters in answer to the attacks of one of the City Lecturers on the Catholic principle and practice of private confession to a priest; in which are embodied some of the principal testimonies as well of the primitive Fathers as of the highest Anglican authorities in favour of that practice; with a preface, notes, and a general postscript. Oxford: John Henry Parker, 1842. T45.8. I. The controversy was chiefly between William Simcox Bricknell and Seager.

1211. Sibthorp, Richard Waldo. Some answer to the inquiry: why are you become a Catholic? In a letter to a friend. London: Charles Dolman, 1842. T44.9. Cf. 1194.

1212. Sinclair, John. Letter to a member of Parliament on national education. London: J. G. F. and J. Rivington, 1842. T52.12. I.

1213. Street, Alfred Wallis. Details explanatory of the minutes of the managing committee of Calcutta High School, at their meeting of June 15, 1842. Calcutta: William Rushton, 1842. T45.7. Another outbreak of the Tractarian controversy in India; cf. 1111.

1214. Thirlwall, Connop. A charge to the clergy of the Diocese of St. David's, by Connop, Lord Bishop of St. David's, delivered at his primary visitation, October, 1842. 2nd ed. London: Rivingtons, 1842. T56.11. Generally a defense of N's Jfc. and Tract 90, although N's interpretation of Article 22 is condemned. Pusey's and Isaac Williams' tracts are also defended, with some reservations.

1215. T[homas], V[aughan], ed. Letters addressed by large bodies of the clergy to those members of Convocation who met in the Common Room of Corpus Christi College, during the controversy of 1836, together with the answers returned to the same. Oxford: W. Baxter, 1842. T50.4.

1216. Townsend, George. Remarks on the errors of Mr. Maitland, in his notes on the contributions of the Rev. Geo. Townsend to the new edition of Foxe's Martyrology; part I: on the memoir of Foxe ascribed to his son. Durham: Andrews, 1842. T48.13. I.

1217. Whittingham, William Rollinson. The priesthood in the Church, set forth in two discourses, delivered, the first, in St. Paul's Church, Baltimore, at the ordination of the Rev. Thomas James Wyatt, and the Rev. John N. McJilton, deacons, to the Holy Order of priesthood, on the twenty-third Sunday after Trinity; the second, in Christ Church, Baltimore, at the institution of the Rev. Henry Van Dyke Johns, to the rectorship, on the twenty-fourth Sunday after Trinity. Baltimore: Knight & Colburn, 1842. T54.16.

1218. Wilberforce, Henry William. Christian unity. London: James Burns, 1842. ST20.11. I.

1219. Williams, John. The priesthood: a sermon preached in St. John's Church, Hartford, on the autumnal ordination Sunday, MDCCCXLII; when the Bishop of Connecticut admitted to the Holy Order of priests the minister of the parish. Hartford: Belknap & Hamersley, 1842. T54.14.

1220. Willis, William Downes. Simony; a sermon preached July 5th, 1842, in the Cathedral Church of Chichester, at the visitation of the Ven. H. E. Manning, M.A., Archdeacon of Chichester; with an appendix, containing some account of the Simeon Trustees for the purchase of Advowsons, A.D. 1836, and also of the Puritan feoffees for the buying in of impropriations, A.D. 1626. London: J. G. F. & J. Rivington, n.d. T51.21. An extended criticism of the sale of benefices.

1221. Wilson, Daniel. Report of the new Cathedral of St. Paul, Calcutta, from June 1839 to October 1841, with a list of the English subscribers. London: Compton and Ritchie, 1842. ST20.14. Wilson was Bishop of Calcutta.

WORKS BY UNIDENTIFIED AUTHORS

1222. Anon. Bishop Butler an avowed Puseyite, & suspected Catholic. N.l., n.p., n.d. T58.12. S. An ironic pamphlet by an Anglo-Catholic, or possibly a Roman Catholic, satirizing puritanical Protestantism.

1223. Anon. The censure of 1836 still necessary; the following considerations are suggested to members of Convocation on the subject of the proposed repeal of the statute affecting Dr. Hampden. [Oxford: Baxter,] n.d. T50.5. D?

1224. Anon. The confession of a true Churchman, at the present juncture. N.l., n.p., n.d. T58.13. A broadside by an irenical Anglican. T58.13. D?

1225. Anon. Du retrait de la proposition des MM. Dubus [sic] et Brabant. N.l., n.p., n.d. P4.3. Lacks title-page. Cf. 1124.

1226. Anon. Edward Trueman, or false impressions. London: James Burns, 1842. ST23.7. A novella.

1227. Anon. The Hampden question revived by the Hebdomadal Board. [Oxford: Baxter, 1842.] A Tractarian appeal not to rescind the 1836 censure of R. D. Hampden. Includes a reprint of documents relating to the original issue.

1228. Anon. ed. The Lent-fast, with appropriate prayers. Bath: H. E. Carrington, 1842. ST23.9.

1229. Anon. A letter to certain members of Convocation. [Oxford: Vincent,] n.d. T50.6. A pamphlet favoring rescindment of the 1836 censure against R. D. Hampden.

1230. Anon. Plain words to plain people on the present dissensions in the Church. London: James Burns, 1842. ST20.3. Pro-Tractarian.

1231. Anon. Pro Ecclesia Dei: an appeal to English Churchmen against the union of the two bishoprics of North Wales. Oxford: John Henry Parker, 1842. T48.5. Against the Ecclesiastical Commission's projected union of the sees of Bangor and St. Asaph.

1232. Anon. Thoughts on Matt. XVI. 18; or Rome tested by her own weapon, "Thou art Peter and upon this rock I will build my Church"; with some additional considerations on Protestant systems. London: D. Walther, 1842. T45.19. Sent to N.

1233. Anon. La vraie Église. Paris: Marc-Aurel Frères, 1842. ST17.4. A tract by a bishop of the Reformed Catholic Church.

1234. Americo-Catholicus, pseud. A letter to the Hon. and Rev. George Spencer on the Oxford Movement in the United States. New York: Casserly and Sons, 1842. T45.9. I. Pencil corrections in margin. "Americo-Catholicus" was a Catholic convert, formerly an American Episcopalian.

1235. An Anglo-Catholic, pseud. A letter to the Rev. Philip Gell, M.A., minister of St. John's Church, Derby, and Rural Dean; containing remarks on his sermon preached at the visitation of the Venerable the Archdeacon of Derby, in All Saints' Church, June 21, 1842. Derby: Henry Mozley and Sons, 1842. T58.11. I.

1236. A Clergyman of the Church of England, pseud. A union between the Roman Catholic & Protestant Churches rendered practicable; in a series of discourses, by a clergyman of the Church of England; first number: the Eucharist or celebration of the Lord's Supper proved to be a feast upon a sacrifice. London: Burns, 1842. T45.4.

1237. A Clergyman of the Established Church, pseud. Humbling recollections of my ministry. London: L. and G. Seeley, 1842. ST22.16. Low Church.

1238. A Fellow of a College, pseud. Some consideration of Church
principles, and obedience to them the safest rule of conduct
during an university career. Cambridge: J. & J. J. Deighton,
1842. T52.19. A reply to 1010.

1239. An Incumbent in His Lordship's Diocese, pseud. A letter to
the Lord Bishop of Lincoln, occasioned by some recent lay-
addresses to His Grace the Archbishop of Canterbury. London:
J. G. F. & J. Rivington, 1842. T48.22. A defense of Anglo-
Catholic doctrines. The Bishop of Lincoln was John Kaye.

1240. No Tract-Writer, pseud. A letter to certain lay-members of
the Church of England, who have memorialized His Grace the
Primate, on the subject of the "Tracts for the Times," and
the controversy arising out of them. London: J. G. F. & J.
Rivington, 1842. T48.23. I. Argues against the request for
a synodical act against certain Tracts for the Times, especially Nos. 80 and 87 (by I. Williams) and 90 (by N).

1241. One Who Never Contributed to the Former Series, pseud. Number
ninety-one; a tract for the present times. London: James Nisbet, 1842. ST19.5. Against the re-publication of Tracts for
the Times.

1242. A Squire, pseud. Tract for squires. London: James Burns,
1842. ST20.15. High Church.

1243. W., S., ed. Contributions of S. T. Coleridge to the revival
of Catholic truths. N.l., n.p., n.d. T45.2. A brief compendium of excerpts from Coleridge's works, with an epigraph
from N's Letter to Dr. Jelf.

1843

1244. Anthon, Henry, ed. The true Churchman warned against the
errors of time; edited with notes, by the Rev. Henry Anthon,
D.D., Rector of St. Mark's Church, New York. New York: Harper
& Brothers, 1843. T57.16. Cf. 1250. A reprint, with preface
by Anthon, of Henry Hughes, ed., The Voice of the Anglican
Church, Being the Declared Opinion of Her Bishops on the
Doctrines of the Oxford Tract Writers, Collected, with an
Introductory Essay (Oxford, 1843). Contains comments of 18
Anglican bishops on Tracts for the Times.

1245. Ball, John. The Church's thanksgiving for her twofold de-
liverance; a sermon, preached in the Church of St. Lawrence,
Reading, on Sunday, November 5th, 1843. Reading: Richard
Welch, 1843. ST26.5. Sent to N by Ball. Scoring, probably
by the anti-Tractarian Ball.

1246. Beaufort, Daniel Augustus. The customs of the Church; a sermon preached in Portman Chapel, St. Marylebone, on Sunday,
the 1st of January, 1843, being the Feast of the Circumcision,
upon making certain changes consequent upon the Bishop's
charge. London: W. J. Cleaver, 1843. ST20.1.

1247. Blomfield, Charles James. A charge delivered to the clergy of

the Diocese of London at the visitation in October, 1842.
London: B. Fellowes, 1843. ST24.2. Anti-Tractarian and specifically against <u>Tract 90</u>.

1248. Bowden, John William. A few remarks on pews. London: J. G. F.
& J. Rivington, 1843. T48.7. I. Against pew-renting.

1249. Carden, James. Two essays: the style and composition of the
books of the New Testament are in no way inconsistent with the
belief that the writers of them were divinely inspired,
MDCCCXLIII; the influence of the science of political economy
upon the moral and social welfare of a nation, MDCCCXLII. Oxford: John Henry Parker, 1843. T67.7.

1250. Carey, Arthur. A letter to a parishioner, relative to the recent ordination of Mr. Arthur Carey. New York: James A.
Sparks, 1843. T57.12. A defense of Arthur Carey against
accusations of Roman Catholic tendencies. Cf. 1251.

1251. Carey, Arthur, and Onderdonk, Benjamin T. A full and true
statement of the examination and ordination of Mr. Arthur
Carey; taken from The Churchman of July 8, 15, 22, 29, and
August 5, 12, 19, and 26, with an appendix. New York: James
A. Sparks, 1843. T57.13. Carey was ordained by B. T. Onderdonk. Both men were High Churchmen, and references are made
in these documents to <u>Tracts for the Times</u>.

1252. [Chase, Drummond Percy.] A Bachelor of Arts, pseud. Should
public examiners be private tutors? A question respectfully
addressed to members of Convocation by a bachelor of arts.
Oxford: William Graham, 1843. P7.3. S. Inscribed "W. H.
Scott Esqr From the Author." Corrections of errata in ink.

1253. Cheyne, Patrick. The authority and use of the Scottish Communion Office vindicated. Aberdeen: A. Brown, 1843. T59.3.

1254. Clerke, Charles Carr. Uniformity in teaching: a charge delivered at the ordinary visitation of the Archdeaconry of Oxford, by the Venerable Charles Carr Clerke, B.D., Archdeacon
of Oxford, in June and July, 1843. Oxford: John Henry Parker,
1843. T55.9. I.

1255. Close, Francis. The written tradition; or the only divine
rule of faith and practice, vindicated against the Tractarians;
a sermon preached in the parish church, Cheltenham, November
5th, 1842. 2nd ed. London: Hatchard and Son, n.d. T59.20.
D?

1256. Collison, Frederick William. Some further remarks on the
Christian altar and eucharistic sacrifice: with strictures on
Vedelius and Williams. Cambridge: T. Stevenson, 1843. T48.18.
Cf. 1103, 1032.

1257. Collisson, Marcus, trans. Psellus' Dialogue on the Operation
of Daemons; now, for the first time, translated into English,
from the original Greek, and illustrated with notes. Sydney:
James Tegg, 1843. ST25.1.

1258. De Bary, Richard B. Thoughts upon certain leading points of
difference between the Catholic and Anglican Churches.
Leamington: W. Reeve, 1843. T50.13. Scoring by references to

Newman and Pusey.

1259. De Lancey, William H. A charge to the clergy of the Diocese of Western New York, delivered August 17, 1842, at the opening of the convention in St. Paul's Church, Syracuse, on the extent of redemption. Geneva, Western New York: Sooten, Merrell & Stow, 1843. T54.17.

1260. Doane, George Washington. The Church upon her knees: the sermon before the offertory, in St. Mary's Church, Burlington, on Quinquagesima Sunday, MDCCCXLIII; when, at the request of the Board of Missions, the offerings of the Church, in the United States, were devoted to the missionary work. Burlington: J. L. Powell, 1843. T57.2.

1261. Doane, George Washington. Diocese of New Jersey: episcopal address to the sixtieth annual convention, in St. Mary's Church, Burlington, June 1, 1843. Burlington, New Jersey: Missionary Press, 1843. T54.18.

1262. Doane, George Washington. To the parishioners of St. Mary's Church, from their affectionate rector; a pastoral for Lent: being a plea for the daily service. N.1., n.p., n.d. T57.3.

1263. Duer, John. Speech of Mr. John Duer, delivered in the convention of the Protestant Episcopal Church of the Diocese of New York, on Friday, the 29th of September, 1843, in support of the resolutions offered by Judge Oakley. New York: Harper and Brothers, 1843. T57.18. Cf. 1250. A protest against the ordination of Arthur Carey.

1264. Eastburn, Manton. The faithful steward: a sermon, preached in the Church of the Ascension, New York, on Sunday, March 19, 1843, by the request of the bishop of the diocese, on occasion of the Rev. Gregory Thurston Bedell, M.A., being instituted rector of that parish. New York: Carvill and Co., 1843. T54.13.

1265. Fletcher, John. A short historical view of the rise, progress, and establishment of the Anglican Church. London: Dolman, 1843. ST27.14. A view of the Anglican Church as schismatic.

1266. Gray, John Hamilton. Letter to the Right Hon. and Rev. the Lord Bishop of London, on the state of the Anglican congregations in Germany. London: J. G. F. & J. Rivington, 1843. T48.6.

1267. Griswold, Alexander Viets. The Reformation: a brief exposition of some of the errors and corruptions of the Church of Rome. Boston: James B. Dow, 1843. ST16.6.

1268. Hamilton, James. The dew of Hermon; or, the true source of Christian unity. London: James Nisbet, 1845. ST26.31.

1269. Hawkins, Edward. The presence of God in the Church by the Holy Spirit; a sermon preached before the University of Oxford, on Whitsunday, June 4, 1843. London: B. Fellowes, 1843. T59.1. I. Cf. 1288.

1270. Henn, William. The coming of Christ; a sermon, preached in the Cathedral Church of St. Columbkille, Derry, on Advent

Sunday, 1842; with an appendix, relating chiefly to the Holy Eucharist. Dublin: Grant and Bolton, 1843. T48.27. A defense of Anglo-Catholic doctrines.

1271. Hicks, James. The poor and their guardians; or, the law of Christ a witness against selfishness, oppression, and cruelty, a sermon preached at Piddletrenthide, on Sunday, January 15th, 1843. London: J. G. F. & J. Rivington, 1843. T58.17. I.

1272. Kempis, Thomas à. On the Holy Communion: from the fourth book of the Imitation of Christ. London: James Toovey, 1843. ST22.7.

1273. Knollis, Francis Minden. The blessedness of the dead which die in the Lord; a sermon, preached in the Parish Church of Teversal, on the Sunday after Ascension Day, May 28, 1843, occasioned by the lamented death of the Reverend Edward Blencowe, M.A., curate of Teversal, Nottinghamshire, and formerly Fellow of Oriel College, Oxford. London: Rivingtons, 1843. ST22.8.

1274. Knollis, Francis Minden. A few words to the flock. N.l., n.p., n.d. ST22.9. High Church rules and regulations for his congregation.

1275. Knollis, Francis Minden. Man's responsibility for Gospel privileges; a sermon, preached in the Parish Churches of Llangollen, Denbighshire, and Congerstone, Leicestershire, in the years 1842 and 1843. London: Rivingtons, n.d. ST26.6. With an appendix defending the Tractarian interpretation of baptismal regeneration.

1276. The Leeds Wesleyan Deputation. On the amended educational clauses of Sir James Graham's Factory Bill; a second letter to the Hon. John Stuart Wortley, member of Parliament for the West-Riding of the County of York. N.l., n.p., 1843. T48.28. The letter is signed by William Lord and Francis A. West. This copy was mailed to N.

1277. Lingen, Ralph Robert Wheeler. Quænam fuerit certaminum publicorum apud antiquos vis et utilitas? Oratio in Theatro Sheldoniano habita die Junii XXVIII MDCCCXLIII. Oxford: Francis Macpherson, 1843. NL28.12.

1278. Loch, John D. An account of the introduction and effects of the system of general religious education established in Van Diemen's Land in 1839. Hobart Town (Australia): J. C. Macdougall, 1843. Pl.3. Corrections, not by N.

1279. McIlvaine, Charles Pettit. The chief danger of the Church in these times: a charge delivered to the clergy of the Diocese of Ohio, at the twenty-sixth annual convention of the same, in Rosse Chapel, Gambier, September 8th, 1843. New York: Harper and Brothers, 1843. T57.17. Anti-Tractarian.

1280. Manning, Henry Edward. A charge delivered at the ordinary visitation of the Archdeaconry of Chichester in July, 1843. 2nd ed. London: John Murray, 1843. T55.8.

1281. Morris, Thomas Edward. A sermon preached on the day of our
      blessed Lord's Ascension, MDCCCXLIII., before the University
      of Oxford, in the Cathedral Church. Oxford: John Henry Parker,
      1843. T50.7. I. See K.C., pp. 229-30, and Apo., pp. 163-64.

1282. O'Brien, James Thomas. A charge delivered to the clergy of
      the United Dioceses of Ossory, Ferns, and Leighlin, at his
      primary visitation in September 1842. London: Seeley, Burn-
      side, and Seeley, 1843. T55.1. An anti-Tractarian tome
      (294 pp.).

1283. O'Connell, Timothy John. A letter to the Reverend Doctor
      Pusey, on the true mode of the real presence, or transubstan-
      tiation. London: Charles Dolman, 1843. T50.14. A Catholic
      response to 1293.

1284. Onderdonk, Benjamin T. Address of the Rt. Rev. B. T. Onder-
      donk, D.D., Bishop, to the fifty-ninth annual convention of
      the Protestant Episcopal Church in the Diocese of New York,
      September 28, A.D. 1843. New York: Church Depository, 1843.
      T57.4.

1285. Overbeck, Johann Friedrich. An account of the picture of
      Frederick Overbeck, representing religion glorified by the
      fine arts; now in Stadel's Art-Institute at Frankfort-on-the-
      Maine; written in German by the painter himself, and trans-
      lated by John Macray. Oxford: John Henry Parker, 1843. T67.6.

1286. Oxford Society for Promoting the Study of Gothic Architecture.
      Proceedings of the Oxford Society for Promoting the Study of
      Gothic Architecture: Michaelmas Term, MDCCCXLIII. N.l., n.p.
      n.d. NL28.14. Sent to N.

1287. Palin, William. The weekly offertory: its obligation, uses,
      results; a sermon, preached in the Parish-Church of St. Mary,
      Stifford, Essex, Septuagesima Sunday, 1843; with notes. Lon-
      don: J. Burns, 1843. T58.14.

1288. [Palmer, William (of Worcester College, Oxford).] Church
      development; or, how to repress romanizing tendencies. Lon-
      don: James Burns, 1843. T59.4. I. A rpt. of an article in
      the Christian Remembrancer (Nov. 1843). Cf. 1289.

1289. Palmer, William (of Worcester College, Oxford). A narrative
      of events connected with the publication of the Tracts for the
      Times, with reflections on existing tendencies to Romanism,
      and on the present duties and prospects of members of the
      Church. Oxford: John Henry Parker, 1843. T60.4.

1290. Perceval, Arthur Philip. A collection of papers connected
      with the theological movement of 1833. 2nd ed. London: J.
      G. F. & J. Rivington, 1843. T60.3.

1291. Perceval, Arthur Philip. Two sermons: I: on Christian duty
      in time of danger or anxiety; II: on the means of providing
      the religious education of the people. London: J. G. F. & J.
      Rivington, 1843. T50.10. I. These sermons are dedicated to
      Pusey, after his suspension: see 1293, 1319.

1292. Perceval, Arthur Philip. A vindication of the proceedings
      relative to the mission of Bishop Alexander to Jerusalem.

London: J. G. F. & J. Rivington, 1843. T49.11. I.

1293. Pusey, Edward Bouverie. The Holy Eucharist a comfort to the penitent; a sermon preached before the university, in the Cathedral Church of Christ, in Oxford, on the fourth Sunday after Easter. Oxford: John Henry Parker, 1843. T50.8. I. See K.C., pp. 233-38, and Apo., pp. 163-64.

1294. [Robertson, James Burton.] Verax, a Catholic Layman, pseud. Fifth letter to the Rev. William Palmer, M.A., of Worcester College, Oxford. London: T. Jones, 1843. T41.16.

1295. [Robertson, James Burton.] Verax, a Catholic Layman, pseud. The supremacy and jurisdiction of the Roman pontiffs, demonstratively proved from Scripture, from Tradition, and from the writings of some of the most eminent Catholic and Protestant authors who have treated on this subject; in six letters, addressed to the Lord Archbishop of Canterbury, and dedicated with the most profound humility to the Most Holy Father Gregory XVI., the reigning pontiff. London: T. Jones, 1843. T50.12.

1296. Rutherfurd, J. The city of refuge; 5th ed.; no. 19 [Kelso: J. Rutherfurd,] n.d. ST26.22 D?

1297. Rutherfurd, J. Electing love; 5th ed.; no. 8. [Kelso: J. Rutherfurd,] n.d. ST26.15. D?

1298. Rutherfurd, J. Jehovah our righteousness; 7th ed.; no. 4. [Kelso: J. Rutherfurd,] n.d. ST26.21. D?

1299. Rutherfurd, J. The Lord's Supper; 5th ed.; no. 16. [Kelso: J. Rutherfurd,] n.d. ST26.28 D?

1300. Rutherfurd, J. The love of the spirit; 3rd edition; no. 24. [Kelso: J. Rutherfurd,] n.d. ST26.17.

1301. Rutherfurd, J. Now; 10th ed.; no. 10. [Kelso: J. Rutherfurd, n.d.] ST26.32 D?

1302. Rutherfurd, J. Righteous reconciliation; 3rd ed.; no. 26. [Kelso: J. Rutherfurd,] n.d. ST26.25.

1303. Rutherfurd, J. The well of living water; 9th ed.; no. 3. [Kelso: J. Rutherfurd,] n.d. ST26.23. D?

1304. Rutherfurd, J. Words of warning; 9th ed.; no. 7. [Kelso: J. Rutherfurd,] n.d. ST26.33. D?

1305. Rutherfurd, J. The works of the Holy Spirit, as recorded in the Scriptures; no. 9. [Kelso: J. Rutherfurd,] n.d. ST26.20. D?

1306. Rutherfurd, J. The works of the Holy Spirit; 4th ed.; no. 13. [Kelso: J. Rutherfurd,] n.d. ST26.24. D?

1307. St. Paul's School, London. Prolusiones literariæ, præmiis quotannis propositis dignatæ, et in D. Pauli Schola habitæ A.S.H. MDCCCXLIII, subjiciuntur et nonnullæ comitiis Hibernis nuper recitatæ. London: B. Fellowes, 1843. T67.8.

1308. Sandys, George William. A letter to the Right Honourable Sir James R. G. Graham, Bart., M.P., Secretary of State for the

Home Department, occasioned by a recent debate in the House
of Commons on the subject of national education. London:
James Ridgway, 1843. T52.14. I.

1309. Smith, Hugh, and Henry Anthon. A statement of facts in relation to the recent ordination in St. Stephen's Church, New
York. New York: Harper and Brothers, 1843. T57.14. Cf.
1250: Smith and Anthon had opposed Arthur Carey's ordination
because of his supposed Roman Catholic sympathies.

1310. Ullathorne, William Bernard. The blessing of the Calvary on
the Grace Dieu Rocks; a sermon preached on the occasion.
London: Charles Dolman, 1843. T45.14.

1311. Westmacott, Richard. Letter on the appropriate disposal of
monumental sculpture, addressed to the Rev. Henry Hart Milman,
M.A., Prebendary of Westminster and rector of St. Margaret's.
London: W. Clowes & Sons, 1843. T67.5.

1312. Whately, Richard. A charge to the clergy of Dublin and Glandelagh, delivered in St. Patrick's Cathedral, June 1843; by
Richard Whately, D.D. Archbishop of Dublin; to which is
appended a petition to the House of Lords, praying for a
Church government; together with the report of the debate on
its presentation and some additional remarks. London: B.
Fellowes, 1843. T55.4. An anti-Tractarian charge.

1313. Whittingham, William Rollinson. The body of Christ; a charge
delivered to the clergy of the Diocese of Maryland, by William
Rollinson Whittingham, Bishop of the Diocese, at the annual
convention in Baltimore, Thursday, June 1st, 1843. Baltimore:
Joseph Robinson, 1843. T54.15.

1314. Wilberforce, Robert Isaac. Church courts and Church discipline. London: John Murray, 1843. Tre12.2.

1315. Williams, John. Primitive Tradition: a letter to the editor
of the Edinburgh Review by Mr. Archdeacon Williams, rector of
the Edinburgh Academy, &c. Edinburgh: R. Grant and Son, 1843.
T48.14. I. A reply to a review by William Mure of Williams'
Homerus, Part I (1843) in the Edinburgh Review, 77 (Feb. 1843),
44-71.

1316. Woodgate, Henry Arthur. Considerations on the position and
duty of the University of Oxford, with reference to the late
proceeding against the Regius Professor of Hebrew. Oxford:
John Henry Parker, 1843. T50.11. A protest against Pusey's
suspension: see 1293, 1319.

1317. Wodehouse, Charles Nourse. Subscription the disgrace of the
English Church. London: Longman, Brown, Green, and Longmans,
1843. T48.25.

1318. Wray, Cecil. The suppression of any portion of the truth,
in the work of education, unjustifiable; a sermon, preached
in the Church of St. Martin's-in-the-Fields, Liverpool; upon
the feast of St. Mark the Evangelist, 1843. London: J. Burns,
1843. T52.15. I.

WORKS BY UNIDENTIFIED AUTHORS

1319. Anon. The plea of the six doctors examined. Oxford: W. Baxter, 1843. T50.9. A protest against Pusey's suspension from preaching by action of the Oxford Board of Heresy, as a result of his sermon, 1293.

1320. Anon. Tracts for the last days, no. I: the one Holy Catholic and Apostolic Church. [London: W. E. Painter,] n.d. T58.15. D?

1321. Anon. A voice from Rome. London: James Burns, 1843. ST24.6. A High Church report on the corrupted Roman Catholic Church.

1322. A., C., pseud. The daily service; the Order for Morning Prayer daily (not weekly) throughout the year; the Order for Evening Prayer daily (not weekly) throughout the year. London: James Burns, 1843. ST22.10.

1323. A Clergyman of the Diocess of Raphoe, pseud. Enquiry and consideration, being a reply to Vigilance and Steadfastness, in a letter addressed to the Rev. George Scott, A. M. rector of Balteagh, Diocess of Derry, in which the "Romanizing tendency" attributed by him to certain specified religious views asserted to be held within the united Diocess of Derry and Raphoe is examined. Dublin: Grant and Bolton, 1843. ST21.8.

1324. A London Clergyman, pseud. A remonstrance addressed to the Quarterly reviewer, respecting his recent article on the rubrics. London: J. G. F. & J. Rivington, 1843. T48.29. I. An Anglo-Catholic response to J. W. Croker, "Rubrics and Ritual of the Church of England," Quarterly Review, 72 (May 1843), 232-90.

1325. A Member of the Protestant Episcopal Church in the Diocess of New York, ed., pseud. The true issue sustained; or, an exhibit of the views and spirit of the Episcopal press in relation to the recent ordination in St. Stephen's Church, New York. New York: Harper & Brothers, 1843. T57.15. Cf. 1250. Opposes Arthur Carey's ordination. Contains an appendix entitled "The Progress of Puseyism--Puseyism and Its Champions."

1326. A Parish Priest, pseud. A letter to His Grace the Archbishop of Canterbury, on the collection of funds for the endowment of the Bishopric of Manchester. London: n.p., 1843. T48.12. I. Opposes the union of the Sees of Bangor and St. Asaph proposed by the Ecclesiastical Commission for the Established Church Bill, 1836.

1327. [W., B. W.] A Presbyter of the Church of England, pseud. "The beacon of hope" at the present crisis; with some signals of an approaching display of providential and retributive power on behalf of the Church, and the literal Israel; by a presbyter of the Church of England. 3rd ed. London: James Nisbet, 1843. ST26.10.

1844

1328. Auriol, Edward, et al. The list of clergymen in priests'
orders resident in England and Wales, who have affixed their
names to the following declaration and protest; revised and
corrected to June, 1844. N.l., n.p., n.d. T60.5. Inscribed
"From a D[ear] Friend," by the donor. An anti-Tractarian protest and petition from Exeter Hall.

1329. [Bower, George.] An exposition of the Church Catechism, for
the use of teachers in Sunday schools. London: James Burns,
1844. ST26.9. I.

1330. Episcopal Church of Scotland. The Church of Scotland's claim
of right, to which are prefixed the speeches of Dr. Chalmers,
Dr. Gordon, and Mr. Dunlop in the General Assembly, in support
of the same, May 24, 1842. Edinburgh: John Johnstone, 1844.
T70.1. Contains speeches by Thomas Chalmers and Alexander
Murray Dunlop.

1331. Coleridge, Derwent. A second letter on the National Society's
Training Institution for Schoolmasters, St. Mark's College,
Chelsea, addressed to the Ven. Archdeacon Sinclair, treasurer
of the Society. T67.4. The cover is endorsed: "To John
Newman/ From: the Author: Private and confidential. The Para-
graphs marked with an asterisk are withdraw[n] on pages 48-53-
63-55." Those paragraphs deal with ecclesiastical ritual.
Coleridge was Principal of St. Mark's College.

1332. [Doane, George Washington.] A pastoral for the season of Confirmation: baptism; Confirmation; the Supper of the Lord.
Burlington, N.J.: n.p., 1844. ST27.7.

1333. Doane, George Washington. The shepherd of the sheep: a sermon, in St. John's Church, Salem, commemorative of the late
rector elect,the Reverend Edward Gordon Prescott, Wednesday,
10 July, 1844. Burlington, N.J.: Missionary Press, 1844.
T57.6.

1334. Gladstone, William Ewart. Speech of the Right Hon. W. E.
Gladstone, on the second reading of the Dissenters' Chapels
Bill, on the 6th of June 1844. London: Richard Kinder, n.d.
T70.2. I.

1335. Haley, W. T. Lies of the League refuted and denounced, in a
series of Corn-Law essays. London: published by the author,
1844. T67.13. Title-page epigraph: "Pooh, pooh, gentleman!
pish, pooh, pooh, pshaw! [Colman the younger.]" Against the
Anti-Corn Law League.

1336. Hawker, Robert Stephen. The offertory; to J. Walter, Esq.,
Bearwood. [London: Eneas Mackenzie,] n.d. ST26.8.

1337. Irons, William Josiah. Our blessed Lord, regarded in his
earthly relationships; four sermons (preached in 1842 and
1844). London: J. G. & F. Rivingtons, 1844. T59.11.

1338. Lambruschini, Aloysius. A polemical dissertation on the Immaculate Conception of the Most Blessed Virgin Mary;

translated from the original Italian. Rome: S[acred] C[ongregation] of Propaganda Fide, 1844. C6.1. Incomplete copy: contains only the anonymous translator's dedication to James Philip Cardinal Fransoni.

1339. MacMullen, Richard Gell. Two exercises for the degree of B.D. read in the Divinity School, Oxford, April 18, and 19, 1844. Oxford: John Henry Parker, 1844. T60.6. I. MacMullen was a Fellow of Corpus Christi College and an ardent Tractarian. He had applied to enter for a B.D., which normally would have meant that he would have to debate on two given subjects in front of the Regius Professor of Divinity, R. D. Hampden. Hampden saw an opportunity to deal a further blow to the Tractarians, and, instead of oral debate, asked MacMullen to submit two essays on highly controversial subjects to him. MacMullen refused and insisted on his right to a public debate. When Hampden continued to resist, MacMullen published these two disputations and demanded that Hampden preside over their public presentation. There was prolonged litigation, and, eventually, in 1844, MacMullen received his B.D.

1340. [Mathison, Gilbert Farquhar Graeme.] A Member of the National Society, pseud. How can the Church educate the people? The question considered with reference to the incorporation and endowment of colleges for the middle and lower classes of society; in a latter addressed to the Lord Archbishop of Canterbury, by a member of the National Society. London: Francis and John Rivington, 1844. Pl.2. Author identified by N on title-page.

1341. Montalembert, Charles, Count. A letter addressed to a Rev. member of the Camden Society, on the subject of Catholic literary societies on the architectural, artistical, and archaeological movements of the Puseyites. Liverpool: Booker and Co., 1844. ST27.6.

1342. Onderdonk, Benjamin T. A pastoral letter, to the clergy and people of his spiritual charge. New York: Onderdonk & Forrest, 1844. T57.10.

1343. Onderdonk, Benjamin T. Pastoral letter: to the laity of my pastoral charge. N.l., n.p., n.d. T57.11.

1344. Perceval, Arthur Philip. Two plain sermons on fasting. London: J. Leslie, 1844. T59.5.

1345. Pusey, Edward Bouverie. God is love; whoso receiveth one such little child in my name, receiveth me; two sermons preached (with the sanction of the Lord Bishop) in the Church of the Holy Trinity, Ilfracombe, in behalf of a new Church, and of the parochial schools, on the tenth and twelfth Sundays after Trinity, 1844. Oxford: John Henry Parker, 1844. Tre14.1.

1346. Rutherfurd, J. The chosen one; No. 32. [Kelso: J. Rutherfurd,] n.d. ST26.19.

1347. Rutherfurd, J. The throne of grace; No. 27. [Kelso: J. Rutherfurd,] 1844. ST26.16.

1348. Rutherfurd, J. The true heart; No. 28. [Kelso: J. Rutherfurd,] n.d. ST26.18.

1349. Rutherfurd, J. Without God; No. 29 [Kelso: J. Rutherfurd,] n.d. ST26.27.

1350. St. Paul's School, London. Oratiuncula latina; reginæ serenissimæ Victoriæ ad forum mercatorium proficiscenti a Divi Pauli Scholæ alumnis dedicata; die Octobris XXVIII, MDCCCXLIV; subjiciuntur et versiculi nonnulli. N.l., n.p., n.d. T67.9.

1351. Todd, James Henthorn. University of Dublin; remarks on some statements attributed to Thomas Wyse, Esq., M.P., in his speech in Parliament on academical education in Ireland, July 19th, 1844. Dublin: Hodges and Smith, 1844. T70.4. I.

1352. Triebner, T. F. A letter to the Very Revd. J. W. Kirwan, D.D., Vicar-General in Galway, on some variations from the more ancient liturgies of the Church, in the form prescribed in the canon of the Mass, for the consecration of the most Holy Eucharist. London: William Spooner, 1844. T59.12. I.

1353. [Wake, William.] A sketch of the origin and character of Convocation, and of the canonical synods and councils; (extracted from "Archbishop Wake's State of the Church and Clergy of England") p. 1, Chap. i. [Chichester: Mason,] n.d. T59.8. Anon. ed. Wake's work was first published in 1703.

1354. Walter, Henry. A letter in defence of those members of the Church of England who hold that not all the baptized, but 'as many as are led by the spirit of God, are the sons of God,' intended as some reply to the attack made upon their faith and character, in a tract entitled "Baptismal Regeneration, a Doctrine of the Church of England," with a brief appendix of notes upon Newman on Justification, and Pusey on baptism. London: Seeley, Burnside and Seeley, 1844. ST26.7. I. Anti-Tractarian, with appendices on N's Lectures on Justification and E. B. Pusey's Tract 67.

1355. White, John William. Ecclesiastical law; the constitutions of Otho, with notes. London: J. G. F. & J. Rivington, 1844. T59.6. I. Some pages uncut. "A summary of the Legatine Constitutions . . . 1236 . . . ."

1356. White, John William. Ecclesiastical law; the Constitutions of Othobon. London: William Benning & Co., 1844. T59.7. I. "A summary of the Legatine Constitutions . . . 1268 . . . ."

WORKS BY UNIDENTIFIED AUTHORS

1357. Anon. The amelioration of Ireland contemplated, in a series of papers; I: on the use of the Irish language in religious worship and instruction. London: W. J. Cleaver, 1844. T70.3.

1358. Anon. Appeal to the members of the Society for Promoting Christian Knowledge, on doctrinal changes lately introduced into the series of tracts circulated under their authority. London: Burns, 1844. T59.10. An objection to SPCK Tract No. 619, by John Bird Sumner, The Doctrine of Justification

Briefly Stated by John Bird, Lord Bishop of Chester (1844).

1359. Anon. An exposition of the Church Catechism, for the use of
teachers in Sunday schools. London: James Burns, 1844. ST26.9.
I.

1360. Anon. God is love; comfort and teaching for the sick and the
sorrowful. [London: James Nisbet,] n.d. ST26.29.

1361. Anon. Oxford parish burial grounds; statement. N.l., n.p.,
n.d. T67.14. Attacks proposals for a commercially-run central
cemetery on ecclesiastical grounds.

1362. Anon. Plain words to the sick, to enable them to enter into
the spirit of the Visitation Service in the Book of Common
Prayer; No. 1. [Bristol: J. Chilcott,] n.d. ST26.2.

1363. Anon. Plain words to the sick; No. II. [Bristol: J. Chilcott,] n.d. ST26.3.

1364. Anon. Plain words to the sick, No. III. [Bristol: J. Chilcott,] n.d. ST26.4.

1365. A Clergyman of the Church of England, pseud. A letter to the
Rev. the Dean and Chapter of Westminster, on the intended al-
terations in the interior of Westminster Abbey. London: J. G.
F. & J. Rivington, 1844. T59.9.

1366. M.A., pseud. Mr. Ward and the new test; or, plain reasons why
those who censure Mr. Ward should not vote for the New Statute,
which limits the Thirty-Nine Articles. N.l., n.p., n.d. T60.7.

1845

1367. Angelin, T. Réponse aux attaques de la presse protestante
genevoise contre les catholiques par M. l'Abbé T. Angelin,
directeur du Pensionnat Saint-François à Onex. Geneva:
Libraires Catholiques, 1845. T59.23.

1368. Barter, William Brudenell. A letter to the Hebdomadal Board
on Mr. Ward's case, and the new test. London: James Burns.
1845. T60.13. I. A protest against the proposed degradation
of W. G. Ward.

1369. Barter, William Brudenell. Some remarks on the Exeter Hall
agitation and the Maynooth Grant. London: James Burns, 1845.
T70.8. I. A defense of the Maynooth Grant by an Anglican
priest.

1370. Bricknell, William Simcox. Oxford: Tract No. 90; and Ward's
Ideal of a Christian Church: a practical suggestion respect-
fully submitted to members of Convocation, with an appendix
containing the testimonies of twenty-five prelates of the
English Church; extracts from Ward's Ideal; conduct of Mr.
Ward compared with that of Luther; and the resolutions of the
Hebdomadal Board. 4th ed. Oxford: J. Vincent, 1845. T61.11.
An attack on Newman's and Ward's works.

1371. Burgon, John William. Petra; a prize poem, recited in the

Theatre, Oxford, June IV, MDCCCXLV. Oxford: W. Baxter, 1845.
NL18.31. I.

1372. [Congregational Union of England and Wales.] Leeds Tracts,
New Series. ST20.2. A Church dictionary. Contains Tracts
6-15, with articles from "Church of Ireland" through "Evens."

1373. Doane, George Washington. Diocese of New Jersey: episcopal
address to the sixty-second annual convention, in St. Mary's
Church, Burlington, May 28, 1845. Burlington, New Jersey:
Missionary Press, 1845. T57.9.

1374. Doane, George Washington. Incorporation with Christ, the
source and channel of the spiritual life: the fifth charge
to the clergy of the Diocese of New Jersey; in St. Mary's
Church, Burlington May 28, 1845. Burlington, New Jersey:
Missionary Press, 1845. T57.8.

1375. Doane, George Washington. Jesus of Nazareth, who went about
doing good, the model for the Church and for the ministry: the
sermon at the annual commencement of the General Theological
Seminary of the Protestant Episcopal Church in the U.S. of
America. Burlington: Edmund Morris, 1845. T57.7.

1376. Dodson, John, and Richard Bethell. Case as to the proposed
degradation and declaration in the statute of Feb. 13, submitted to Sir Dodson, Knt. Queen's Advocate; and R. Bethell,
Esq. Q. C., with their opinion of its decided illegality:
accompanied with notes on the history and nature of academical
degrees, and on the history of subscription in the University
of Oxford. Oxford: W. Baxter, 1845. T61.4.

1377. Donkin, William Fishburn. A defense of voting against the
propositions to be submitted to Convocation on Feb 13, 1845.
Oxford: John Henry Parker, 1845. T60.15. A protest against
the proposed degradation of W. G. Ward.

1378. Dupanloup, Félix Antoine Philibert. De la pacification
religieuse: Quelle est l'origine des querelles actuelles?
Quelle en peut être l'issue? Paris: Jacques Lecoffre, 1845.
P3.1.

1379. Foster, William H. A supplication upon Church affairs
addressed to the Rev. Fathers in God, the Lords Archbishops
and Bishops of the United Church of England and Ireland. Dublin: George Folds, 1845. T59.15. Foster is an anti-Erastian
advocate of Prayer Book reform.

1380. Garbett, James. The University, the Church, and the New Test,
with remarks on Mr. Oakeley's and Mr. Gresley's pamphlets;
a letter to the Lord Bishop of Chichester. London: J. Hatchard
and Son, 1845. T61.7. A reply to 1401.

1381. Gladstone, William Ewart. Substance of a speech for the
second reading of the Maynooth College Bill, in the House of
Commons, on Friday, April 11, 1845. London: John Murray,
1845. T70.9. Pencil correction.

1382. Goulburn, Edward Meyrick. A reply to some parts of Mr. Ward's
defence, justifying certain parties in recording their votes

against him. Oxford: W. Baxter, 1845. T61.5. A reply to
1415.

1383. Gresley, William. Suggestions of the new statute to be proposed in the University of Oxford. London: James Burns, 1845.
T61.1. Against the proposed university statute concerning
subscription.

1384. Hale, William Hale. The approaching contest with Romanism
considered, in a charge addressed to the clergy of the Archdeaconry of London, at the visitation, April 29, 1845; by
the Venerable William Hale Hale, M.A., Archdeacon of London.
London: Francis & John Rivington, 1845. T56.12. M. S.
Hale's Erastian charge concerns the Maynooth Grant.

1385. Hawker, Robert Stephen. The field of Rephidim; a visitation
sermon in the Diocese of Exeter, written by the Vicar of
Morwenstow, in Cornwall; delivered, in the Church of Saint
Mary Magdalene, Launceston, June 27, 1845, by T. N. Harper,
B.A., Curate of Stratton. London: Edwards and Hughs, 1845.
T62.2. I. The sermon was only delivered, not written, by
T. N. Harper.

1386. Hull, William Winstanley. MDCCCXLV; the month of January;
Oxford. London: Seeley, Burnside, and Seeley, n.d. T61.6.
Opposes the measures proposed to Convocation against W. G.
Ward.

1387. Hussey, Robert. Reasons for voting upon the third question to
be proposed in convocation on the 13th inst. Oxford: John
Henry Parker, 1845. T61.10. Sent to N. Opposes censure of
Tract 90.

1388. Keble, John. Heads of consideration on the case of Mr. Ward.
Oxford: John Henry Parker, 1845. T60.14. A defense of W. G.
Ward.

1389. Marshall, Thomas William. Twenty-two reasons for entering the
Catholic Church. London: Thomas Richardson and Son, n.d.
ST25.3. D?

1390. Maurice, Frederick Denison. The new statute and Mr. Ward; a
letter to a non-resident member of Convocation. Oxford: John
Henry Parker, 1845. T60.16. A protest against the proposed
degradation of W. G. Ward.

1391. Maurice, Frederick Denison. Thoughts on the rule of conscientious subscription, on the purpose of the Thirty-Nine
Articles, and on our present perils from the Romish System:
in a second letter to a non-resident member of Convocation.
Oxford: John Henry Parker, 1845. T60.11. A sequel to 1390,
and a reply to 1413.

1392. Moberly, George. The proposed degradation and declaration,
considered in a letter addressed to the Rev. the Master of
Balliol College. Oxford: John Henry Parker, 1845. T60.12.
Corrections in ink. A defense of W. G. Ward.

1393. [Mozley, James Bowling.] An Oxford M.A., pseud. The proposed
decree on the subject of No. XC. Oxford: W. Baxter, 1845.
T61.9. Opposes University censure of Tract 90. Mailed to N

at Littlemore by Mozley.

1394. Neale, Edward Vansittart. The Real Property Acts of 1845;
being the acts to render the assignment of satisfied terms
unnecessary; to amend the law of real property; to facilitate
the conveyance of real property; and to facilitate the granting of certain leases; with introductory observations and
notes. London: V. & R. Stevens and G. S. Norton, 1845. NL24.4.

1395. [Newman, Francis William.] A grammar of the Berber language.
N.l., n.p., n.d. T67.11. A page of the author's handwritten
corrections and notes is bound with the pamphlet, and there
are many pencil corrections in the text.

1396. Norman, John Paxton. Some observations on the jurisdiction of
the House of Convocation. Oxford: J. Vincent, 1845. T61.2.
A professional legal opinion on the charges against W. G. Ward.

1397. Oakeley, Frederick. The claim to "hold as distinct from teaching," explained in a letter to a friend. London: James Toovey,
1845. T61.15. A sequel to 1399.

1398. Oakeley, Frederick. A letter on submitting to the Catholic
Church. London: James Toovey, 1845. ST25.4.

1399. Oakeley, Frederick. A letter to the Lord Bishop of London, on
a subject connected with the recent proceedings at Oxford.
London: James Toovey, 1845. T61.13. A reply to charges that
Oakeley did not wholeheartedly subscribe to the Thirty-Nine
Articles and to criticisms of his "innovations" at Margaret
Street Chapel. Cf. 1400, 1397. The Bishop of London was C.
J. Blomfield.

1400. Oakeley, Frederick. A second letter to the Lord Bishop of
London, containing an earnest and respectful appeal on the
subject of Margaret Chapel. London: James Toovey, 1845.
T61.14. Title-page endorsed in Oakeley's hand: "Suppressed
for the present. [Not published]." The place, publisher, and
date are crossed through in ink. This is a sequel to 1399.

1401. Oakeley, Frederick. The subject of Tract XC; historically
examined, with the view of ascertaining the object with which
the Articles of the Church of England were put out, and the
sense in which they are allowed to be subscribed; together with
testimonies of English divines to Catholic doctrines; to which
is added, the case of Bishop Mountague, in the reign of King
James I. 2nd ed., revised, with a preface on the measure about
to be submitted to the Oxford convocation. London: James
Toovey, 1845. T61.12. A republication of this tract, occasioned by the proposed censure of Tract 90. Duplicate copy:
NL81.12.

1402. The Oxford Magazine, 1, No. 1 (May 1845). Oxford: J. Vincent,
1845. NL25.6. Deals with the question of the Maynooth Grant.

1403. Parks Smith, W. G. A letter addressed to William Kitson, Esq.,
churchwarden of the parish of Tormoham, by the Rev. W. G.
Parks Smith, A. M. incumbent of St. John's, Torquay, in answer
to a remonstrance sent to him by the churchwardens and certain
members of his congregation; also the requisition presented to

him by the chapelwardens of St. John's Chapel of East Torquay. Torquay: E. Cockrem, n.d. T59.14. Parks Smith's congregation was concerned that some of his ritual reminded them of "the Superstitions and Corruptions of Rome."

1404. Protestant Episcopal Church in the United States, Diocese of New York. The constitution and canons of the Protestant Episcopal Church in the Diocese of New York; published by order of the Convention. New York: Henry M. Onderdonk, 1845. C4.11.

1405. Pusey, Edward Bouverie. A letter on the Catholic position of the English Church and the duty of remaining in her communion. N.l., n.p., n.d. NL11.4. The addressee is not identified.

1406. Rogers, Frederic. A short appeal to members of Convocation, upon the proposed censure of No. 90. London: James Burns, 1845. T61.8. Duplicate copy: C6.15.

1407. Roussel, Napoléon. La religion d'argent; or, the religion of money; second part; translated from the French of the Rev. N. Roussell [sic], a French pastor. N.l., n.p., 1845. T59.21. Anon. trans. Incomplete copy.

1408. Rutherfurd, J. God's purpose of grace; No. 31. [Kelso: J. Rutherfurd,] n.d. ST26.26.

1409. Ryder, George Dudley. Subscription to the Articles. London: James Toovey, 1845. T61.16.

1410. St. Paul's School, London. Apposition; St. Paul's School, 1845. London: B. Fellowes, 1845. NL26.11. I.

1411. St. Paul's School, London. Prolusiones literariæ, præmiis quotannis propositis dignatæ, et in D. Pauli Schola comitiis majoribus habitæ die Aprilis XXX A.S.H. MDCCCXLV, subjicitur et carmen alcaicum latinum comitiis hibernis recitatum. London: B. Fellowes, 1845. T67.10.

1412. Sewell, Richard Clarke. A letter to the members of the venerable House of Convocation, in the University of Oxford. London: Owen Richards, 1845. T61.3. Opposes the charges against W. G. Ward.

1413. Tait, Archibald Campbell. A letter to the Rev. the Vice-Chancellor of the University of Oxford, on the measures intended to be proposed to Convocation on the 13th of February, in connexion with the case of the Rev. W. G. Ward, M.A., fellow of Balliol College. Edinburgh: William Blackwood and Sons, 1845. T60.17. An argument in favor of degradation of W. G. Ward and censure of The Ideal of a Christian Church. Cf. 1391.

1414. Wakeham, I. The Church advancing; a popular address to Roman Catholics, on the present encouraging aspect of affairs, designed to stimulate the faithful to retrieve the error, and efface the crime, of the Reformation. London: Aylott and Jones, n.d. T59.13. Inscribed "From a Protestant Church of England Layman." The Protestant "editor" is supposedly printing an "address" by a militant English Roman Catholic. D?

1415. Ward, William George. An address to members of Convocation in

protest against the proposed statute. London: James Toovey,
1845. T60.8. Ward's self-defense against the proposed condemnation of his The Ideal of a Christian Church and his degradation. Duplicate copy: NL8.1.

1416. Watson, Alexander. The folly of "looking earnestly" on man,
and the wisdom of serving God by abiding where we are called;
a sermon, preached in St. John's Church, Cheltenham. N.l.,
n.p., n.d. T62.1. "This sermon was preached . . . in reference to certain rumoured secessions from the Anglican to
the Roman Communion."

1417. Woodgate, Henry Arthur. An earnest appeal to members of the
Oxford Convocation, on the proposed assumption of ecclesiastical powers by the University. 2nd ed. London: James Burns,
1845. T60.9. A defense of W. G. Ward.

1418. [Woodgate, Henry Arthur.] Reasons for voting against the
measures to be proposed in Convocation at Oxford on February
13, 1845, respectfully suggested for the considerations of
members of Convocation. London: James Burns, 1845. T60.10.
A defense of W. G. Ward.

WORKS BY UNIDENTIFIED AUTHORS

1419. Anon. Church principles and Church measures; a letter to Lord
John Manners, M.P., with remarks on a work entitled, "Past and
Present Policy of England towards Ireland." London: Francis
& John Rivington, 1845. T70.6. By the author of 1421, 1422.

1420. Anon. Effect of the misuse of familiar words on the character
of men, and the fate of nations; freedom--constitution. London: John Ollivier, 1845. T67.12. "From the Portfolio, No.
XVII. Dec. 1844, revised."

1421. Anon. Maynooth, the Crown, and the country; or, a protest,
on behalf of the monarchy and the nation, against the new,
augmented, permanent, and uncontrolled endowment of the Roman
Catholic College of Maynooth; the constitution and influence
of which is shown, by evidence derived from itself, to be in-
compatible with allegiance to the Crown; and fraught with danger to the country, both from within and from without. 2nd
ed. London: Francis & John Rivington, 1845. T70.5. By the
author of 1419, 1422.

1422. Anon. A review of the Maynooth Endowment Bill, shewing its
fatal tendencies, and of the debates in the Commons, on the
first and second reading, with a proposal for the conciliation
of contending parties in Ireland. London: Francis & John
Rivington, 1845. T70.7. By the author of 1421, 1419.

1846

1423. Allies, Thomas William. The Church of England cleared from
the charge of schism, upon testimonies of councils and Fathers
of the first six centuries. London: James Burns, 1846.

Tre15.1.

1424. Barter, William Brudenell. A postscript to The English Church Not in Schism: containing a few words on Mr. Newman's Essay on Development. London: Francis & John Rivington, 1846. P8.1. I. A hostile review of Dev.

1425. Faber, Frederick William. Grounds for remaining in the Anglican Communion; a letter to a friend. London: James Toovey, 1846. T62.3. Duplicate copy: NL9.3.

1426. [Grottanelli de' Santi, Eugenio Stanislao.] Compendio della vita della beata Chiara Gambacorti Pisana, fondatrice del Monastero di S. Domenico della città di Pisa. Pisa: Pieraccini, 1846. P6.4. Inscribed: "Al M. R. John Bapt [sic] Newman Rettore dell'Università Cattolica di Dublino in segno di stima ed affetto l'autore 23.Giugno 1856."

1427. Hewitt, N. A. A few thoughts concerning the theories of High-Churchmen and Tractarians; with reasons for submitting to the authority of the Holy See. Charleston, South Carolina: Burges and James, 1846. T57.19. Two corrections in ink (not N's). Hewitt was a convert to Roman Catholicism influenced by Dev.

1428. Marshall, Thomas William. A letter to the Rev. Cecil Wray. M.A., upon his recent "Address" to the congregation of St. Martin's, Liverpool entitled "The Scandal of Permitted Heresy and A Violated Discipline." London: Charles Dolman, n.d. T62.6.

1429. Murray, Patrick Aloysius. The divine institution and obligation of confession; a letter addressed to the Rev. Dr. Pusey, on occasion of his recently published sermon, entitled "Entire Absolution of the Penitent." T59.16. I. Murray was Professor of Dogmatic and Moral Theology at Maynooth. Duplicate copy: NL11.5.

1430. Northcote, James Spencer. The fourfold difficulty of Anglicanism, or the Church of England tested by the Nicene Creed; in a series of letters. London: Thomas Richardson and Son, 1846. T62.4. I.

1431. [Perrone, Giovanni.] "Articolo II." P6.2. D? Title-page and first thirty pages missing. Author identified on first page by N. Apparently this is the second part (pp. 31-74) of a review of Mgr. Malou's La Lecture de la Sainte Bible (Louvain, 1846).

1432. St. John's College, Bishop's Auckland, New Zealand. Industrial System. Eton: E. P. Williams, 1846. ST24.5. I. "For Private Circulation." A gift of Edward Coleridge.

1433. Thompson, Edward Healy. Remarks on certain Anglican theories of unity. London: Charles Dolman, 1846. T62.5.

WORK BY UNIDENTIFIED AUTHOR

1434. Anon. The Church in the house. London: James Nisbet. 1846. ST26.30.

1847

1435. Annali delle Scienze Religiose. Serie di pubblicazioni contro
L'Indicatore Maltese, giornale protestante anglicano; estratto
dagli Annali delle Scienze Religiose. Rome: Tipografia Salviucci, 1847. P6.1.

1436. Archiconfrérie du Très-Saint et Immaculé Cœur de Marie pour la
Conversion des Pécheurs. Annales de l'Archiconfrérie du Tres-
Saint et Immaculé Cœur de Marie pour la Conversion des
Pécheurs, 1, no. 6 (2 Feb. 1847), 409-94. N.l., n.p., n.d.
T61.17. Contains significant commentary, by French Catholics,
on the Oxford Movement.

1437. Archiconfrérie du Très-Saint et Immaculé Cœur de Marie pour
la Conversion des Pécheurs. Statue de l'Archiconfrérie.
Paris: n.p., n.d. T61.18. D?

1438. Belgium, Ministère des Affaires Étrangères. Organisation du
Corps Diplomatique; réglement: examens pour le grade de
secrétaire de légation. Brussels: J.-A. Lelong, 1847. C13.2.
The following works are underlined or otherwise marked from
among the recommended readings for the examination: "l'Histoire politique de Heeren, le tableau de l'histoire politique
de l'Europe, par Ancillon"; "L'Almanach de Gotha"; and
"l'ouvrage de M. Villeneuve de Bargemont."

1439. Fitzalan Howard, Henry Granville, 14th Duke of Norfolk, Earl
of Arundel and Surrey. A few remarks on the social and political condition of British Catholics. London: C. Dolman,
1847. T66.3. One correction in ink. Distinguishes between
allegiance to the Queen and "spiritual allegiance" to the
Pope. Duplicate copy: C7.10.

1440. Gondon, Jules. Conversion de cent cinquante ministres angli-
cans, membres des universités anglaises, et personnes de distinction, avec une notice sur MM. Newmann [sic], Ward et
Oakeley. 2nd ed. Paris: Sagnier et Bray, 1847. ST25.2. I.

1441. Gordon, John Joseph. Some account of the reasons of my con-
version to the Catholic Church; by a late clergyman of the
Anglican Communion; in letters to a friend. London: Levey,
Robson, and Franklyn, 1847. T62.9. I. See Henry Tristram,
Newman and His Friends (London: John Lane, The Bodley Head,
1933), p. 113.

1442. Gordon, John Joseph. Some account of the reasons of my conversion to the Catholic Church, in nine letters to a friend.
7th ed. London: Burns, Lambert, and Oates, n.d. NL21.13.

1443. Lewis, David. Notes on the nature and extent of the royal
supremacy in the Anglican Church. London: James Toovey,
1847. T63.1. Duplicate copy: T62.7.

1444. Ram, Pierre François Xavier de. De laudibus quibus veteres
Lovaniensium theologi eferri possunt; oratio quam die vigesima
sexta mensis julii MDCCCXLVII habuit Petrus Franc. Xav. de
Ram, Rector Universitatis Cath. in Oppido Lovaniensi, quum
viros eruditissimos Henricum Joannem Feye, SS. canonum

doctorem, et Carolum de Blieck, S. theologiæ doctorem, more
majorum renunciaret. Louvain: Vanlinthout et Vandenzande,
n.d. P5.3. Contains "Statuta Facultatis Theologiæ Lovanien-
sis."

1445. Renouf, Peter Le Page. The Greek and Anglican communions; a
letter respectfully addressed to the Rev. T. Allies, Rector
of Launton. London: James Toovey, 1847. T62.8.

1446. Waterworth, J. At press, to be ready early in 1848, in one
large volume, octavo, dedicated by permission, to the Right
Rev. Nicholas Wiseman, Bishop of Melipotamus, The Canons and
Decrees of the Sacred and Oecumenical Council of Trent, Celebrated under the Sovereign Pontiffs, Paul III, Julius III,
and Pius IV; translated by the Rev. J. Waterworth: to which
are prefixed essays on the external and internal history of
the Council: Preface. N.l., n.p., n.d. C7.11.

1447. Wiseman, Nicholas. Conversion: a letter to Mr. Alexander
Chirol and his family, on their happy admission to the communion of the Holy Catholic Church; and on some publications
to which it has given rise. 2nd ed. London: James Burns,
1847. NL13.1.

1848

1448. The British Magazine, 34 (1 Dec. 1848), 601-74, 715-16. P2.1.
Cf. 1451. Principally of interest because of an anonymous
review-article on pp. 615-74, "Illustrations of Roman-Catholic
Unity," which uses the controversy surrounding F. W. Faber's
life of St. Rose of Lima in The Lives of the Saints to illustrate the disunity of English Catholics. Edward Price's
critical review is reprinted from Dolman's Magazine, together
with responses from Faber, Ullathorne, and N. (See L.D.,
XXII, passim.) This also contains "A Puzzling Coincidence,"
which concerns the controversy in The Tablet surrounding the
authenticity of a relic of St. Thomas of Canterbury in the
possession of George Talbot. The first article in the issue
is "Cramp Rings," by J. Lathbury.

1449. Cayol, Jean Bruno. Relation de la blessure et de la mort de
Mgr l'Archevêque de Paris, suivie du procès-verbal de l'em-
baumement du corps et de l'examen médico-légal de la plaie.
Paris: Adrien Leclère, 1848. T66.4. Reprinted from La Revue
Médicale Française et Etrangère (June 1848). The Archbishop
of Paris was Denis Affre, who was wounded during the 1848
riots in Paris and later died.

1450. [Daman, Charles.] A Tutor, pseud. Ten letters introductory
to college residence; by a tutor. Oxford: I. Shrimpton, 1848.
P7.4. "Not published."

1451. Dolman's Magazine, Dec. 1848, pp. 1-2. P2.2. Contains a
"Notice to Subscribers and Correspondents" from Edward Price,
the editor, regretting "whatever scandals may have arisen from
the review of Mr. Faber's Lives of the Saints." Cf. 1448.

1452. Laing, Francis Harry. Catholic the same in meaning as sover-
      eign, in which the genuine nature of Catholicity is relieved
      from the false notions with which the Protestant usurpation of
      the word has embarrassed it. London: Thomas Richardson and
      Son, 1848. ST24.13. I.

1453. [Perceval, Arthur Philip.] Working of the Tithe Commutation
      Act. London: J. G. & F. Rivington, 1838. ST27.8.

1454. Pius IX, Pope. Allocution of His Holiness, Pope Pius IX.,
      delivered in secret consistory, April 29, 1848; SS. Domini
      Nostri Pii divina providentia Papae IX: allocutio habita in
      consistorio secreto die XXIX April an.MDCCCXLVIII. London:
      James Burns, 1848. T66.6. On the relations between the
      Papacy and the European powers in 1848.

1455. Sconce, Robert Knox. Reasons for submitting to the Catholic
      Church. Sydney: St. Julian & Hawksley, 1848. T62.10. A
      gift to N from the Archbishop of Sydney.

1456. Ullathorne, William Bernard.   Funeral oration on the Rev.
      William Richmond, delivered at his Solemn Requiem, in Saint
      Mary's Church, Brewood, November 16, 1848. London: James
      Burns, 1848. Pl.13. I.

1457. Wiseman, Nicholas. Words of peace and justice, addressed to
      the Catholic clergy and laity of the London District, on the
      subject of diplomatic relations with the Holy See. London:
      Charles Dolman, 1848. T66.5.

WORKS BY UNIDENTIFIED AUTHORS

1458. Anon. Protestant defamation, its causes and effects; an essay
      dedicated to the Association of St. Thomas of Canterbury, for
      the vindication of Catholic rights. London: Jones, 1848.
      ST24.7. Inscribed "To the Religious Community of Oratorians
      at St. Mary's Vale."

1459. Anon. Remarks on Noble's appeal in behalf of the doctrines
      of Swedenborg. London: Thomas Richardson and Son, 1848.
      T59.19. Inscribed: "Very Revd. J. H. Newman from J. Walker"--
      who may be the author.

1460. A Lay Member of the English Church, pseud. Publications of
      the Birmingham Protestant Association, No. 3; an answer to a
      layman's challenge to the Church of England, printed by M.
      Maher, Congreve Street; by a lay member of the English Church;
      to which is appended a challenge to the members of the Church
      of Rome. Birmingham: T. Ragg, 1848. ST27.11.

1461. A Parish Priest, pseud. The Blessed Sacrament; preparation,
      attendance, giving of thanks, spiritual communion; drawn from
      the writings of the saints. London: James Toovey, 1848.
      NL79.8.

1849

1462. Cottrell, Charles Herbert. Religious movements of Germany in the nineteenth century. London: John Petheram, 1849. NL19.19.

1463. Dayman, Alfred Jeken. The houses of God; as they were,--as they are,--and as they ought to be; a sermon, preached, by desire of the ordinary, at the Free Chapel of St. Giles's, Packwood, Warwickshire, on the commemoration of the dedication, September 5th, 1849. London: F. and J. Rivington, 1849. T62.12. I.

1464. The Knight of the Faith, (at Home), no. 3 (10 Feb. 1849), pp. 21-52. ST27.16.

1465. The Knight of the Faith, (at Home), no. 4 (24 Feb. 1840), pp. 53-64. ST27.17. A continuation of 1464.

1466. MacDonnell, Eneas. County of Mayo: its awful condition and prospects, and present insufficiency of local relief. London: John Ollivier, 1849. NL80.22. I.

1467. Mooney, Mrs. The girl's first catechism of manufactures and trades, compiled and arranged for the children of the Irish peasantry. Dublin: John J. O'Shaughnessy, 1849. ST26.13.

1468. Oakeley, Frederick. The teaching and practice of the Catholic Church on the subject of frequent communion, briefly set forth in a letter to the editor of the Christian Remembrancer, occasioned by a passage in the April number of that periodical. London: James Burns, 1849. T66.8. A reply to "On the Theology of the Eighteenth Century," Christian Remembrancer (April 1849); and also to E. B. Pusey's Letter to the Archbishop of Canterbury (1842).

1469. Oeuvre de Notre-Dame-des-Anges. Oeuvre de Notre-Dame-des-Anges. Paris: Bailly, Divry, n.d. ST26.12. An appeal for contributions for a charitable religious foundation begun by Pauline Marie Jaricot.

1470. Ram, Pierre François Xavier de. Pétition adressée à MM. les membres du Sénat par P. F. X. de Ram, Recteur de l'Université Catholique de Louvain, concernant le nouveau projet de loi sur l'enseignement supérieur; (juillet 1849). Brussels: M. Vanderborght, n.d. P5.4.

1471. Scally, Matthew. A sermon on the most ancient and venerable order of the ever blessed Virgin Mary of Mount Carmel: in which is clearly expalined, the devotion peculiar to that same; the duties to be performed by the members of the confraternity correctly expounded; the errors of many uninformed on these duties corrected; and by which all who desire in sincerity the conversion of England are invited to become the Advocates of Devotion to Mary. London: Henry Lucas, 1849. ST24.12.

1472. Scally, Matthew. The surest road to Ireland's prosperity; dedicated to the ministry of England, the landlords of Ireland, and the Catholics of the United Kingdom. London: C. Dolman, 1849. ST27.13. I.

1473. Simpson, R. Invocation of saints proved from the Bible alone; substance of an address delivered by R. Simpson, Esq. B.A., at a discussion between him and Dr. Cumming, at Clapham, Tuesday, July 3d, 1849, with notes and appendix. London: James Burns,

n.d. NL26.29. On title-page, in an unidentified hand: "It
w[oul]d be a shame to allow this tract to go out of print and
circulation. N.B." S.

1474. Weedall, Henry. Funeral oration, delivered at the Solemn
Requiem of the Right Rev. Dr. Walsh, Vicar Apostolic of the
London District, at St. Mary's Church, Moorfields, London,
on Wednesday, the 28th of February, and at the solemn obsequies, at St. Chad's, Birmingham, on Friday, March the 2nd,
1849. London: Charles Dolman, 1849. T66.7. I.

WORKS BY UNIDENTIFIED AUTHORS

1475. Anon. A Christmas gift for thoughtful people, or reflections
suggested by the present state of religious parties in England. London: James Burns, 1849. T62.11.

1476. A Late Member of the University of Oxford, pseud. Four years'
experience of the Catholic religion, with observations on its
effects, intellectual, moral, and spiritual; and on the thral-
dom of Protestantism. London: James Burns, 1849. ST24.14.
Dedicated to N.

1477. A Lay Member of the Birmingham Protestant Association, pseud.
Publications of the Birmingham Protestant Association, No. II;
the secret oath, and a translation of the secret instructions
of the Order of the Jesuits, with a slight sketch of the Society, and the principles and actions of its members; second edition, with an appendix, containing a brief history of the Order
and its founder. Birmingham: Thomas Ragg, 1849. ST27.10.

1850

1478. Allies. Thomas William. The royal supremacy viewed in reference to the two spiritual powers of order and jurisdiction.
London: William Pickering, 1850. T64.5.

1479. Allies. Thomas William. The See of St. Peter, the rock of the
Church, the source of jurisdiction, and the centre of unity.
London: Burns & Lambert, 1850. Cl1.1. I.

1480. Badeley, Edward. Substance of a speech delivered before the
Judicial Committee of the Privy Council, on Monday the 17th
and Tuesday the 18th of December, A.D. 1849, upon an appeal in
a cause of duplex querela, between the Rev. George Cornelius
Gorham, clerk, appellant, and the Right Rev. Henry, Lord
Bishop of Exeter, respondent; with an introduction. London:
John Murray, 1850. T63.3.

1481. Baker, Arthur. A plea for "Romanizers" (so called) in the
Anglican Communion; a letter to the Right Honourable and
Right Reverend the Lord Bishop of London. London: Joseph
Masters, 1850. T64.12.

1482. [Belgium, Chambre des Représentants et Sénat.] Recueil des
discours prononcés à la Chambre des Représentants et au Sénat,
dans la discussion de la loi sur l'enseignement supérieur;

(1849). Brussels: M. Vanderborght, 1850. P4.4.

1483. Bennett, William James Early. The Church, the crown, and the state, their junction or their separation; considered by two sermons, bearing reference to the Judicial Committee of the Privy Council. London: W. J. Cleaver, 1850. T64.6.

1484. Bennett, William James Early. A first letter to the Right Honourable Lord John Russell, M.P., on the present persecution of a certain portion of the English Church; with a sermon preached at St. Paul's, Knightsbridge, on Sunday morning and evening, November 17, 1850. London: W. J. Cleaver, 1850. T64.7.

1485. Bowyer, George. The Cardinal Archbishop of Westminister and the new hierarchy. 4th ed. London: James Ridgway, 1850. T65.5.

1486. Boyle, Richard. Correspondence between the Right Rev. Dr. Wiseman, V.A.L.D., and the Rev. Richard Boyle, in reference to the sudden removal of the latter from the Catholic church of St. John's, Islington; with explanatory observations addressed to the congregation. London: Kent and Richards, 1850. P2.3. Concerns the controversy that arose when Wiseman removed Boyle in favor of Frederick Oakeley, whom Boyle calls "a recently ordained ex-Protestant clergyman."

1487. The British Protestant, 6, No. 42 (Feb. 1850), 17-32. ST26.14. Contains a report of a meeting of the British Reformation Society.

1488. Cavendish, Charles William. Plain directions for private devotion, drawn from the writings of the saints; two sermons. London: Joseph Masters, 1850. T69.2. M. S.

1489. Dodsworth, William. The Gorham case briefly considered in reference to the judgment which has been given, and to the jurisdiction of the court. London: William Pickering, 1850. T64.8.

1490. Dodsworth, William. The things of Cesar [sic], and the things of God; a discourse, preached in Christ Church, S. Pancras, on Sunday, January 27th, 1850; with especial reference to the claim of the state to exercise power over the Church in decisions of doctrine. London: Joseph Masters, 1850. T64.9.

1491. [Drane, Augusta Theodosia.] A. B., pseud. The morality of Tractarianism: a letter from one of the people to one of the clergy. London: William Pickering, 1850. T64.11. An Anglo-Catholic response to 1501.

1492. Garside, Charles Brierley. The impiety of bartering faith for opinion. London: William Pickering, 1850. T69.1. I.

1493. Goode, William. A letter to the Bishop of Exeter; containing an examination of his letter to the Archbishop of Canterbury. London: J. Hatchard and Son, 1850. T63.5. A response to 1507.

1494. Grottanelli de' Santi, Eugenio Stanislao. Elogio di Giuseppe Pianigiani, Senese, detto nei solenni funerali fatti per il medesimo dai professori della Università di Siena nella

chiesa di S. Vigilio il 25. Novembre 1850. N.l., Tipografia
del R. Istituto Toscano dei Sordo-muti, n.d. P6.5.

1495. Irons, William Josiah. The present crisis in the Church of
England; illustrated by a brief inquiry as to the royal supremacy; I: what it was before the Reformation; II: how the Reformation dealt with it; III: how it may now be interpreted.
London: Joseph Masters, 1850. T64.4. On the Gorham case.

1496. [Kent, W. C. M.] An English Journalist, pseud. What shall be
done with Cardinal Wiseman; an inquiry. London: Charles Dolman, 1850. T65.10.

1497. M'Quoin, James and John Connelly. Confraternity of St. Joseph,
Bunhill Row. London: n.p., n.d. ST27.15. See L.D., XIII,
passim.

1498. Manning, Henry Edward. The appellate jurisdiction of the crown
in matters spiritual; a letter to the Right Reverend Ashurst-
Turner, Lord Bishop of Chichester. London: John Murray, 1850.
NL14.3. On the Gorham case.

1499. Maskell, William. A first letter on the present position of
the High Church party in the Church of England, by the Rev.
William Maskell, Vicar of S. Mary Church; the royal supremacy,
and the authority of the Judicial Committee of the Privy
Council. 2nd ed. London: William Pickering, 1850. T64.1.
On the Gorham case. Maskell was chaplain to Henry Phillpotts,
Bishop of Exeter.

1500. Maskell, William. A letter to the Rev. Dr. Pusey, on his prac-
tice of receiving persons in auricular confession. London:
William Pickering, 1850. T66.13. I. A reply to Pusey's
'The Church of England Leaves Her Children Free to Whom to
Open Their Griefs'; A Letter to the Rev. W. Richards (London,
1850).

1501. Maskell, William. A second letter on the present position of
the High Church party in the Church of England, by the Rev.
William Maskell, Vicar of S. Mary Church: the want of dogmatic
teaching in the Reformed English Church. London: William
Pickering, 1850. T64.2. A sequel to 1499.

1502. Mayow, Mayow Wynell. A letter to the Rev. William Maskell,
A.M. London: William Pickering, 1850. T64.3. A response to
1499 and 1501.

1503. Mill, William Hodge. Human policy and divine truth; a sermon
preached on Passion Sunday, March 17, 1850, at Great Saint
Mary's Church, before the University of Cambridge. Cambridge:
J. Deighton, 1850. T64.13.

1504. Monro, Edward. A few words on the spirit in which men are
meeting the present crisis in the Church; a letter to Roundell
Palmer, Esq., Q.C., M.P. Oxford: John Henry Parker, 1850.
T64.14. Chiefly a High-Church criticism of the way of life of
the Anglican clergy.

1505. Neale, John Mason. A few words of hope on the present crisis
of the English Church. London: Joseph Masters, 1850. ST24.9.
High-Church views on the Gorham case.

1506. Phillipps, Ambrose Lisle. A letter to the Right Hon. the Earl
of Shrewsbury, Waterford and Wexford, on the re-establishment
of the hierarchy of the English Catholic Church, and the present posture of Catholic affairs in Great Britain. London:
Charles Dolman, 1850. T65.14.

1507. Phillpotts, Henry. A letter to the Archbishop of Canterbury
from the Bishop of Exeter. London: John Murray, 1850. T63.4.
A High-Church response to the republication of John Bird Sumner's Apostolical Preaching Considered in an Examination of
St. Paul's Epistles (1st ed. 1815). Cf. 1536.

1508. Pius IX, Pope, et al. The Roman Catholic question: the apostolic letter of Pope Pius IX.; Cardinal Wiseman's pastoral;
the two letters to the "Times" by Bishop Ullathorne; Lord John
Russell's letter; the "New Batch of Bishops," from the "Weekly
Dispatch"; two letters by the Rev. G. A. Denison; a letter
from Benjamin D'Israeli, Esq., M.P.; review and extracts from
Ambrose Phillips's "Letter to the Earl of Shrewsbury"; concluded by a biography of Cardinal Wiseman. London: James
Gilbert, n.d. T65.1. An anthology by an anonymous editor.

1509. Privy Council, Judicial Committee. Gorham v. Bishop of
Exeter; the judgment of the Judicial Committee of Privy
Council, delivered March 8, 1850, reversing the decision of
Sir H. J. Fust; third edition; with the appellant's prayer
and reasons, etc. London: Seeleys, 1850. T63.2.

1510. Pugin, Augustus Welby. An earnest appeal for the revival of
the ancient plain song. London: Charles Dolman, 1850.
T66.10.

1511. Pusey, Edward Bouverie. The royal supremacy not an arbitrary
authority but limited by the laws of the Church of which kings
are members. Oxford: John Henry Parker, 1850. Tre15.2.

1512. Ram, Pierre François Xavier de. Discours prononcé à la Salle
des Promotions le 1 février 1850 par P.-F.-X. de Ram, Recteur
de l'Université Catholique de Louvain, après le service funèbre célébré en l'église primaire de Saint-Pierre pour le repos
de l'âme de M. Marien Verhoeven, professeur ord. de Droit
Canon à la Faculté de Théologie. Louvain: Vanlinthout et
Vandenzande, n.d. P5.5.

1513. Russell, John. Letter from Lord John Russell to the Bishop of
Durham; original version. London: Charles Dolman, 1850.
T65.12. I. "Printed from the 'Portefeuille Diplomatique.'"

1514. Scally, Matthew. England with reference to the monastic
institute: an essay upon the restoration of Catholicity to
that country in its full glory. London: Burns and Lambert,
1850. ST26.11.

1515. Sewell, William. Suggestions to minds perplexed by the Gorham
case; a sermon preached at the Royal Chapel, Whitehall, on
Sexagesima Sunday, 1850. Oxford: John Henry Parker, 1850.
ST24.8.

1516. Ullathorne, William Bernard. The office of a bishop: a discourse delivered at the solemn thanksgiving for the

re-establishment of the hierarchy. London: Thomas Richardson
and Son, 1850. NL12.25. I. Duplicate copy: T65.2.

1517. Ullathorne, William Bernard. Remarks on the proposed education
bill. London: Burns and Lambert, 1850. NL12.1. Duplicate
copy: Pl.6.

1518. Ward, William George. The Anglican Establishment contrasted,
in every principle of its constitution, with the Church Catholic of every age; being a second letter to the Editor of the
"Guardian:" with strictures on the articles in that journal
entitled "Anglo-Romanism." London: Burns and Lambert, 1850.
NL8.2. S. Cf. 1546.

1519. Weedall, Henry, ed. Report of a meeting of Catholics, held in
Birmingham, November 18, 1850, in the hall of the bishop's
house, Bath Street, with the addresses agreed to. Birmingham:
M. Maher, 1850. T65.3.

1520. Wiseman, Nicholas. An appeal to the reason and good feeling
of the English people on the subject of the Catholic hierarchy.
London: Thomas Richardson and Son, 1850. T65.4.

1521. Wiseman, Nicholas. Three lectures on the Catholic hierarchy;
lecture I, delivered in St. George's, Southwark, on Sunday,
December 8th, 1850. London: Richardson and Son, 1850. T65.16.
Duplicate copy: T27.12.

1522. Wiseman, Nicholas. Three lectures on the Catholic hierarchy;
lecture II, delivered in St. George's, Southwark, on Sunday,
December 15th, 1850. London: Richardson and Son, 1850. T65.
17.

1523. Wiseman, Nicholas. Three lectures on the Catholic hierarchy;
lecture III, delivered in St. George's, Southwark, on Sunday,
December 22nd, 1850. London: Richardson and Son, 1850. T65.
18.

WORKS BY UNIDENTIFIED AUTHORS

1524. Anon? Church matters in 1850. N.l., n.p., 1850. ST24.10.
Lacks title-page. Protesting the Gorham case.

1525. A Barrister, pseud. Papal aggression considered. London:
Charles Dolman, 1850. T65.9. A Protestant refutation of
charges of "Papal agression." Possibly by George Bowyer.

1526. A Kentish Clergyman, pseud. Popery in the Church! The Archdeacon of Maidstone's Popery Exposed and Refuted; to which
are added some remarks on the deplorable state of our universities, and the approaching downfall of the Church of England.
London: William Edward Painter, 1850. T66.9.

1851

1527. [Bellasis, Edward.] The Anglican bishops versus the Catholic
hierarchy; a demurrer to farther proceedings. London: James
Toovey, 1851. T65.7. A refutation of charges of "Papal

aggression."

1528. Bowyer, George. Observations on the arguments of Dr. Twiss respecting the new Roman Catholic hierarchy. London: James Ridgway, 1851. T65.6. I. A reply to Travers Twiss, The Apostolic Letters of Pius IX, Considered with Reference to the Law of England and the Law of Europe (1851).

1529. The Catholic School, 2, no. 8 (Dec. 1851), 201-32. NL19.2.

1530. DeVere, Stephen Edward. Is the hierarchy an aggression? London: James Ridgway, 1851. T65.8. I.

1531. Dodsworth, William. Anglicanism considered in its results. 2nd ed. London: William Pickering, 1851. T64.10. Written after Dodsworth's conversion to Roman Catholicism. Cf. 1538.

1532. Drummond, Henry. A plea for the rights and liberties of women imprisoned for life under the power of priests; in answer to Bishop Ullathorne. London: T. Bosworth, 1851. T66.17. A response to 1544.

1533. Gaume, Jean Joseph. Le ver rongeur des sociétés modernes; ou, le paganisme dans l'éducation. Paris: Gaume Frères, 1851. P3.2. M*. S*. See L.D., XIV, 358; and also Ian T. Ker's note in Idea, pp. 620-21.

1534. Gladstone, William Ewart. Two letters to the Earl of Aberdeen, on the state prosecutions of the Neapolitan government. 7th ed. London: John Murray, 1851. T66.15. The Earl of Aberdeen was George Gordon. Cf. 1535.

1535. Gondon, Jules. A letter to the Rt. Hon. W. E. Gladstone, M.P., in answer to his Two Letters to the Earl of Aberdeen, on the State Prosecutions of the Neapolitan Government, with a preface written for the English edition. London: Charles Dolman, 1851. T69.3. A reply to 1534 and a defense of Ferdinand II of Naples.

1536. Phillpotts, Henry. A pastoral letter to the clergy of the Diocese of Exeter, on the present stage of the Church. 2nd ed. London: John Murray, 1851. T63.6.

1537. Pugin, Augustus Welby. An earnest address, on the establishment of the hierarchy. London: Charles Dolman, 1851. T66.11. Duplicate copy: NL25.23.

1538. Pusey, Edward Bouverie. A letter to the Right Hon. and Right Rev. the Lord Bishop of London, in explanation of some statements contained in a letter by the Rev. W. Dodsworth. 3rd ed. Oxford: John Henry Parker, 1851. NL11.6. A reply to 1531.

1539. Pusey, Edward Bouverie. The rule of faith, as maintained by the Fathers, and the Church of England: a sermon, preached before the University in the Cathedral Church of Christ, in Oxford, on the fifth Sunday after Epiphany. Oxford: John Henry Parker, 1851. NL11.15.

1540. Ram, Pierre François Xavier de. Discours prononcé à la Salle des Promotions le 14 juillet 1851 par P.-F.-X. de Ram, Recteur de l'Université Catholique de Louvain, après le service funèbre célébré en l'église primaire de Saint-Pierre pour

le repos de l'âme de M. Arnould-Pierre Tits, professeur ord.
de Théologie Dogmatique Générale à la Faculté de Théologie.
Louvain: Vanlinthout, n.d. P5.6.

1541. [Rigby, Nicholas.] Two addresses: one, to the gentlemen of
Whitby, who signed the requisition, calling a meeting to address the Queen, on the late (so called) agression of the
Pope: and the other, to the Protestant clergy, by the Catholic
priest of Ugthorp. Whitby: Horne and Richardson, 1851. T66.
12. One sentence is marked.

1542. Strachey, Richard. On the physical geography of the provinces
of Kumáon and Garhwál in the Himálaya Mountains, and of the
adjoining parts of Tibet. N.l., n.p., n.d. T68.9. "Read
before the Royal Geographical Society of London on the 12th
of May, 1851."

1543. Talbot, John, 16th Earl of Shrewsbury. Letter to the Right
Honorable the Lord John Russell. London: Charles Dolman, 1851.
T65.13. A refutation of charges of "Papal aggression."

1544. Ullathorne, William Bernard. A plea for the rights and liberties of religious women, with reference to the bill proposed
by Mr. Lacy. London: Thomas Richardson and Son, 1851. T66.16.
A protest against the Religious Houses Bill. Cf. 1532.

1545. Van Bommel, Corneille. Lettre de l'Évêque de Liége à monsieur
Piercot, Bourgmestre de la ville de Liége, à l'occasion du
discours prononcé par ce magistrat le 14 octobre 1851, lors
de l'installation de l'Athénée Royal. Liége: H. Dessain, 1851.
P4.6.

1546. Ward, William George. Heresy and immorality considered in
their respective bearing on the notes of the Church; being a
final letter to the Editor of the "Guardian." London: Burns
and Lambert, 1851. NL8.3.

1547. Wharton, John Jane Smith, ed. The statute law now in force
relating to Roman Catholics in England. London: Spettigue and
Farrance, 1851. T65.15.

WORKS BY UNIDENTIFIED AUTHORS

1548. Anon. A continuous confutation of Dr. Newman's view of the
present position of Romanism in England contained in nine
lectures delivered at the Corn Exchange, Birmingham. [Birming-
ham: Wm. Hodgetts,] n.d. T66.14. A polemical response to
Prepos.

1549. Anon. Coroner's inquest and post-mortem examination on the
Inquisition. Glasgow: Hugh Margey, 1851. NL99.14.

1550. Anon. Le Ministère et le clergé dans la question de l'enseignement moyen; observations et documents. Brussels: J.-B.
de Mortier, 1851. P4.5. Primarily a collection of correspondence between the Belgian Minister of the Interior and the
Archbishop of Malines, Victoire Auguste Isidore Dechamps.

1551. Anglo-Catholicus, pseud. A Protestant plea in support of
Cardinal Wiseman's "Appeal." London: Charles Dolman, 1851.

T65.11.

1852

1552. Bondini, Giuseppe, and Wilfrid Faber. Della fondazione dell'
Oratorio in Inghilterra; memorie storiche di Giuseppe Bondini,
con documenti inediti tratti dagli originali; e Dello spirito
e del genio di S. Filippo Neri, apostolo di Roma, per Wil-
frido Faber, della Congregazione dell'Oratorio di Londra.
Rome: Co' Tipi di Bernardo Morini, 1852. P6.7.

1553. Caswall, Henry. Synodal action necessary to the Church; a
letter to the Right Hon. W. E. Gladstone, M. P. London:
John and Charles Mozley, 1852. NL10.14.

1554. Catholic University of Ireland. Report of the Committee, and
list of subscriptions. Dublin: J. M. O'Toole, 1852. P7.7.

1555. Finlason, William Francis. Report of the trial and prelimi-
nary proceedings in the case of the Queen on the prosecution
of G. Achilli v. Dr. Newman; with an introduction containing
comments on the law and on the course and conduct of the trial;
also with the pleadings and affidavits; and copious notes,
particularly on the constitution and practice of the Court of
Inquisition. London: C. Dolman, 1852. P2.5. This copy is
endorsed "H. A. Mills."

1556. Formby, Henry. The march of intellect; or, the alleged hos-
tility of the Catholic Church to the diffusion of knowledge
examined; a lecture delivered to the members of the Catholic
Literary and Scientific Institute in Birmingham. London:
C. Dolman, 1852. P1.7. A reply to utilitarian educators,
including Robert Peel and Lord Brougham, with a reference to
Peel's speech at the opening of the Tamworth reading room.
Duplicate copy: NL80.4.

1557. Grant, Alexander. Sullo stato dell'Anglicanismo negli ultimi
anni; considerazioni. Rome: Tipografia Marini e Morini, 1852.
P6.8. "Estratto dagli Annali delle Scienze Religiose." Grant
was Rector of the Scots College, Rome. See L.D., XII, 36,
432.

1558. Husenbeth, Frederick Charles. The Roman question: a refutation of a treatise professing to be "the truth about Rome."
London: Burns and Lambert, 1852. T69.7. A reply to The Truth
about Rome: A Short Treatise on Supremacy, by the Author of
"Faith and Infidelity."

1559. Laforet, Nicholas Joseph. Principes philosophiques de la
morale. Louvain: C.-J. Fonteyn, 1852. C21.5.

1560. [Louvain, Université de.] Cours universitaires; année
scolaire 1852-1853; extrait du Catalogue général de la
Librairie de Van Esch, 5, Kraeken-straet, à Louvain. C21.4.
A summary of the courses offered.

1561. MacCabe, William Bernard. Religious liberty--proselytism;
the Madiai Case, from the Weekly Telegraph of November 6th,

and November 13th, 1852. Dublin: James Duffy, 1852. T69.4.
A Catholic response to Protestant reports of anti-Protestant
persecution in Florence.

1562. Malen, Jean-Baptiste. Instruction sur l'enseignement de la
religion dans les collèges, adressée par Mgr. l'Évêque de
Bruges, aux professeurs ecclésiastiques et laïques de son
diocèse. 2nd ed. Bruges: Vanhee-Wante, 1852. P4.7.

1563. Manning, Henry Edward. Help nearest when need greatest; a
sermon preached in the Synod of Oscott, on Sunday, July 11th,
1852. N.l., n.p., n.d. NL14.4.

1564. Manning, Henry Edward. The love of Jesus our law; a sermon
preached in the Church of "Our Ladye Star of the Sea," on
Sunday, July 18th, 1852, in behalf of the Greenwich Catholic
Poor Schools. London: Burns & Lambert, 1852. P1.15. Appended
is "A Brief Account of the New Catholic Church, at Croom's
Hill, Greenwich," by J. G. Duplicate copy: P8.7.

1565. Manning, Henry Edward. The name and patience of Jesus; a ser-
mon preached in the Church of the Immaculate Conception on the
Feast of St. Ignatius. London: Burns and Lambert, 1852.
P1.14.

1566. Newman, John Henry. Christ upon the waters; a sermon preached
in substance at St. Chad's, Birmingham, on Sunday, October
27, 1850, on occasion of the establishment of the Catholic
hierarchy in this country; published by desire of the Bishop.
4th ed. Birmingham: M. Maher, n.d. ST24.11.

1567. Northcote, James Spencer. A Pilgrimage to La Salette; or, a
critical examination of all the facts connected with the
alleged apparition of the Blessed Virgin to two children on
the mountain of La Salette, on September 19, 1846. London:
Burns and Lambert, 1852. C6.9. Several pencil scorings
beside the utterances of the apparition. This copy originally
belonged to Henry Austin Mills of the Birmingham Oratory.

1568. Spurrell, James. Miss Sellon and the "Sisters of Mercy"; an
exposure of the constitution, rules, religious views, and
practical working of their society; obtained through a "sis-
ter" who has recently seceded. London: Thomas Hatchard,
1852. P2.6. An "exposure" of an Anglican sisterhood in
Devonport by the vicar of Great Shelford, Cambridgeshire, who
was a Low Churchman.

1569. Ubaghs, Gérard Casimir. Du dynamisme considéré en lui-même
et dans ses rapports avec la Sainte Eucharistie. Louvain:
Vanlinghout, 1852. C9.1.

1570. Wiseman, Nicholas. University education: a sermon delivered
by His Eminence the Cardinal Archbishop of Westminster, in St.
George's Cathedral, Southwark, on Sunday June 27th, 1852,
in behalf of the Catholic University of Ireland. London:
Thomas Richardson and Son, 1852. P7.6. Inscribed "Very Rev.
Dr. Newman President of Catholic University."

1853

1571. Allday, Joseph, ed. True account of the proceedings leading
to, and a full & authentic report of, the searching inquiry,
by Her Majesty's Commissioners, into the horrible system of
discipline practised at the Borough Gaol of Birmingham. Birmingham: John Tonks, n.d. P2.7. This copy is endorsed "H. A.
Mills The Oratory, Birmingham."

1572. Connelly, Pierce. Report of an address delivered by the Rev.
P. Connelly, A.M., with a preface, and dedicated to His Grace
the Duke of Manchester, chairman of the Rev. P. Connelly's
committee. London: James Ridgway, 1853. P2.4. See L.D., XV,
487-88, 515-16. This pamphlet was published by Bertram Arthur
Talbot, seventeenth Earl of Shrewsbury, in order to discredit
Connelly, who had recently converted back to Anglicanism and
who was slandering the Roman Catholic Church. There is a long
anonymous introduction, as well as the text of an address
Connelly had delivered as a Catholic in Baltimore Cathedral
on 27 May 1842.

1573. Cullen, Paul. Pastoral letter to the Catholic clergy and laity
of the Diocess of Dublin, on the Festival of St. Patrick. Dublin: James Duffy, 1853. T70.11.

1574. Faber, Frederick William. An essay on the interest and charac-
teristics of the lives of the saints, with illustrations from
mystical theology. London: Richardson and Son, 1853. NL9.5.

1575. Gainsford, Robert John. Reformatory schools; why and how they
should be established and maintained. London: Cash, n.d.
NL21.8. D?

1576. Hart, A. J. X. The mind and its creations; an essay on mental
philosophy. New York: Appleton, 1853. T68.10. Duplicate
copy: C1.5.

1577. Newman, Francis William. On the intrusive elements of Latin.
N.l., n.p., n.d. T68.11. D? "Extracted from the Classical
Museum."

WORK BY UNIDENTIFIED AUTHOR

1578. P., J. H. The difficulties of "Mariolatry"; an English lay-
man's first letter to the Rev. H. M. S., a minister of the
Anglican establishment. London: Burns and Lambert, 1853.
P8.2.

1854

1579. Formby, Henry. State rationalism in education: or, serious
compromise to the doctrines of revealed religion the inseparable adjunct of state measures of education; an examination of the actual working and results of the system of the
Board of Commissioners of National Education in Ireland.

Dublin: J. Duffy, 1854. Pl.8.

1580. Gillis, James. A letter to the Right Honourable Duncan Mac-
laren, Lord Provost of Edinburgh, on the proposed "voluntary"
amendment of the Lord Advocate's Educational Bill for Scotland.
Edinburgh: Marsh and Beattie, 1854. Pl.4. A Catholic bishop's
protest against mixed education.

1581. Hennessy, Henry. Report to the Cork Harbour Commissioners,
on the great flood at Cork, on Wednesday, 2nd November, 1853.
Cork: George Nash's Printing Establishment, 1854. C13.15.
Hennessy was Librarian of Queen's College, Cork.

1582. Marshall, Henry. The Most Holy Name of Jesus; a sermon,
preached in the Church of St. Francis Xavier, Gardiner Street,
Dublin, on the Festival of the Most Holy Name, 1854. Dublin:
James Duffy, 1854. Pl.16. I.

1583. Neale, John Mason. Confession and absolution: a lecture,
written for delivery in the Town Hall, Birmingham. London:
Joseph Masters, 1854. P2.8. The reply of a noted High
Churchman to a lecture delivered by the Rev. J. C. Miller of
Birmingham on 11 March 1853, which was entitled "The Confes-
sional in the Church of England a Tractarian Development."

1584. Nicol, James. A short account of James Nicol, a private
soldier; stating how he became a Catholic: in a letter to a
friend. London: Charles Dolman, 1854. C6.12. A posthumous
publication, with an anonymous postscript.

1585. Ram, Pierre François Xavier de. Considérations sur l'histoire de l'Université de Louvain; (1425-1797); discours
prononcé à la séance publique de la Classe des Lettres de
l'Académie Royale de Belgique, le 10 mai 1854, par M. le
Chanoine de Ram, Directeur de la Classe des Lettres, Recteur
Magnifique de l'Université Catholique de Louvain. Brussels:
H. Goemaere, 1854. P5.10.

1586. Ram, Pierre François Xavier de. Discours prononcé à la Salle
des Promotions le 25 octobre 1854 par P. F. X. de Ram,
Recteur de l'Université Catholique de Louvain, après le service funèbre célébré en l'église primaire de Saint-Pierre pour
le repos de l'âme de M. Henri Barthélémi Waterkeyn, professeur
ord. à la Faculté des Sciences et Vice-Recteur de l'Université.
Louvain: Vanlinthout, n.d. P5.7.

1587. Ram, Pierre François Xavier de. Discours prononcé à la Salle
des Promotions le 26 octobre 1854 par P. F. X. de Ram, Recteur
de l'Université Catholique de Louvain, après le service funèbre célébré en l'église primaire de Saint-Pierre pour le repos
de l'âme de M. Grégoire Demonceau, professeur ordinaire et
Doyen de la Faculté de Droit. Louvain: Vanlinthout, n.d.
P5.8.

1588. Vaughan, Henry Halford. Oxford reform and Oxford professors:
a reply to certain objections urged against the report of the
Queen's commissioners. London: John W. Parker and Son, 1854.
Trel4.4.

1589. Gastaldi, Fr. Funeral oration delivered at the solemn obsequies of the Very Rev. Anthony Rosmini, founder and first General of the Institute of Charity, celebrated at St. Mary's Church, Rugby, on Tuesday, July 3, 1855. London: C. Dolman, 1855. Pl.17. For N's comments after Antonio Rosmini-Serbati's death, see <u>L.D.</u>, XVI, 504-05.

1590. Jenkins, Robert Charles. The Immaculate Conception, rejected in the Council of Florence; a few words addressed to His Eminence Cardinal Wiseman. Folkestone: J. English, n.d. T69.8. I.

1591. Parker, John Henry. New examination statutes; abstracts of their principal provisions; with a catalogue of books, either expressly mentioned, or treating of the subjects required; with the cash prices charged by John Henry Parker, Broad Street, Oxford. Oxford: John Henry Parker, 1855. P7.1.

1592. Ram, Pierre François Xavier de. Discours prononcé à la Salle de Promotions le 25 octobre 1855 par P. F. X. de Ram, Recteur de l'Université Catholique de Louvain, après le service funèbre célébré en l'église primaire de Saint-Pierre pour le repos de l'âme de M. Jacques Guillaume Crahay, professeur ordinaire de Physique et d'Astronomie à la Faculté des Sciences. Louvain: Vanlinthout, n.d. P5.9.

1593. Saint-Albin, Alexandre de. Lettre à M. Athanase Coquerel, l'un des pasteurs de l'Église Réformée de Paris; à propos de son sermon du 12 novembre 1854. Paris: Charles Douniol, 1855. C22.4. A defense of the doctrine of the Immaculate Conception and a response to Coquerel, who had published his sermon.

1594. Ullathorne, William Bernard. The discourse delivered at the opening session of the second Provincial Synod of Oscott. London: Richardson and Son, 1855. Pl.11.

1595. Wilberforce, Robert Isaac. Seven letters to the editor of the Weekly Register, in reply to the Rev. F. Meyrick's article on Church-authority. London: Burns and Lambert, 1855. T69.9. Frederick Meyrick's review of Wilberforce appeared in the <u>Christian Remembrancer</u>.

1856

1596. Acheson, William. An enquiry into the origin, progress and material of ancient personal ornaments. Dublin: Hodges, Smith, 1856. T68.15. "From the Journal of the Royal Dublin Society, 1856."

1597. Bowyer, George. The differences between the Holy See and the Spanish government. London: Thomas Richardson and Son, 1856. C14.2. "Reprinted from the 'Dublin Review,' No. LXXIX, March 1856." Defends the Temporal Power. Bowyer was M.P. for

Dundalk. See 1598.

1598. Bowyer, George. Rome and Sardinia. London: Thomas Richardson
and Son, 1856. C14.1. "Reprinted from the 'Dublin Review,'
No. LXXVII, September, 1855." See 1597. Duplicate copy:
T69.5.

1599. Bowyer, George. Speech delivered by George Bowyer, Esq., M.P.
for Dundalk, during the adjourned debate on the "Treaty of
Peace"; (reported by Mr. Strang, short-hand writer); House of
Commons, Tuesday, May 6, 1856. [London:] James Ridgway, n.d.
T69.6. Cf. 1598, 1535.

1600. Creagh, Pierse. The Catholic Oath, the temporalities of the
Established Church and the Maynooth Grant, considered in a
letter from Pierse Creagh, Esquire, barrister-at-law, to His
Excellency the Earl of Carlisle, Lord Lieutenant of Ireland.
Dublin: James Wyer, n.d. T70.12.

1601. Gillis, James. A lecture on education, delivered in St.
Mungo's Parish Church, Glasgow, on Sunday the 26th October
1856, in behalf of its Catholic Boys' School. Edinburgh:
Marsh & Beattie, 1856. Pl.5. Cf. 1580.

1602. Grottanelli de' Santi, Eugenio Stanislao. Cenni storici
sulle sepolture pubbliche, e privilegiate e voto medico-
legale sopra alcuni particolari sepolcreti nell'intero, o
nelle vicinanze delle città. Pisa: Pieraccini, 1846. P6.3.
I. Presented to N in 1856, when he was Rector of the Catholic
University of Ireland. See L.D., XVII, 78.

1603. Harpur, Alexander. The nature of visible magnitude; the de-
ductions by which the relative magnitudes of the planets, and
the absolute magnitude of the sun, and consequently the magnitudes of the moon and of the planets, are determined in the
received astronomical system, proved to be fallacious, and
therefore those magnitudes as so determined in the received
system, to be entirely erroneous. Dublin: M'Glashan and Gill,
1856. T68.12.

1604. Hennessy, Henry. On the influence of the earth's internal
structure on the length of the day. London: Taylor and
Francis, 1856. C19.6. "From the Philosophical Magazine for
August 1856." Hennessy was Professor of Natural Philosophy
in the Catholic University of Ireland.

1605. Moseley, Henry. Report on the examination for appointments to
the Royal Artillery & practical class of the Royal Military
Academy at Woolich, held at Burlington House, London, on the
21st of January, 1856, with copies of the examination papers.
London: Harrison, 1856. P7.2. Above "practical class" on
title-page N has written "civil engineering & civil service."
The examiners included R. C. Trench, A. H. Clough, John Tyndall, and T. H. Huxley.

1606. Mosquera, Emmanuel Marie. Apologie de Monseigneur Emmanuel-
Joseph de Mosquera, mort Archevêque de Santa-Fé de Bogotá,
et de sa réponse à l'encyclique de notre Saint-Père le Pape
Pie IX, du 2 février 1849; ou lettre à Son Éminence le
Cardinal Gousset, Archevêque de Reims. Paris: Librairie

d'Auguste Vaton, 1856. C22.3. Cardinal Gousset, in his La
Croyance générale et constante de l'Église touchant l'Immaculée Conception de la Bienheureuse Vierge Marie, had by a mistranslation of one of the Archbishop of Bogotá's letters to the
Pope made it appear that the latter did not believe in the
Pope's prerogative and ability to define a dogma infallibly
and acting alone, as head of the Church. The Archbishop's
brother wrote this pamphlet to correct the error and to affirm
his brother the Archbishop's impeccable ultramontane credentials. An exchange of correspondence in Latin between the
Archbishop of Bogotá and Pope Pius IX is appended.

1607. Murray, Patrick Joseph. Reformatory schools for Ireland; a
letter addressed to the Right Hon. Edward Horsman, M.P.,
Chief Secretary for Ireland. Dublin: W. B. Kelly, 1856.
T70.10.

1608. Ullathorne, William Bernard. A pilgrimage to the Proto-
Monastery of Subiaco and the Holy Grotto of St. Benedict.
London: Robson, Levey, and Franklyn, 1856. P7.8.

1609. Walker, John. Letter to the editor of The Rambler concerning
original sin. London: Richardson and Son, 1856. NL4.10.

WORK BY UNIDENTIFIED AUTHOR

1610. Anon. Mozley's Augustianism; Art. II.--A Treatise on the
Augustinian Doctrine of Predestination, by J. B. Mozley, B. D.,
fellow of Magdalen College, Oxford; London: Murray, 1855.
N.l., n.p., 1856. T69.10. A separatum of an anonymous review
from an unidentified periodical of March 1856, pp. 67-134.

1857

1611. Abraham, George Whitley. The Catholic origin of the British
constitution: a lecture delivered before the Catholic Young
Men's Society of Dublin, on Tuesday, January 8th, 1857. Dublin: James Duffy, 1857. C6.10. I.

1612. [Badeley, Edward Lowth.] A Barrister, pseud. Considerations
on divorce a vinculo matrimonii, in connexion with Holy
Scripture. London: C. J. Stewart, 1857. P2.9. I. Author
identified by N on title-page. A religious argument against
divorce on the grounds of adultery and subsequent remarriage.

1613. Dodsworth, William. Popular delusions concerning the faith
and practice of Catholics. London: Burns & Lambert, 1857.
NL20.6.

1614. Forde, Laurence. De synodis commentarium liturgico-canonicum,
sive, manuale juris et ritus, qui in synodorum convocatione
ac celebratione servari debent; ex caeremoniali episcoporum,
pontificali romano, aliisque documentis authenticis vel
probatis edidit, proemio annotationibusque illustrabit, R. D.
Laurentius Forde, PH. ac S.T.D., Metropolitanæ Ecclesiæ
Dublinensis, S. Patritii canonicus, in Universitate Catholica

Hiberniæ Juris Sacri Professor. Dublin: Apud Jacobum Duffy, 1857. NL80.3.

1615. Formby, Henry. Our Lady of Salette: internal credibility of the miracle of La Salette: or, indications of an identity in the beautiful lady of the apparition, with Mary the mother of Jesus: a discourse, addressed to the Birmingham Confraternity of Our Lady of La Salette, on the occasion of the eleventh anniversary of the apparition. London: Burns and Lambert, n.d. C6.6.

1616. Formby, Henry. State rationalism in education, second series; a digest of the reasons on which certain members of the clergy and religious orders are unable to accept the Privy-Council education grants; gathered from their correspondence and drawn up by the Rev. Henry Formby. London: Levey, Robson, and Franklyn, 1857. P1.9. A sequel to 1579.

1617. Lyons, Robert Spencer Dyer. Outlines of fever, or selections from a course of lectures on fever, being part of a course of theory and practice of medicine . . . ; Lecture I. Dublin: Fannin, 1857. C13.9. I. Lyons was Professor of Practice of Medicine and Pathology in the School of Medicine of the Catholic University of Ireland, having been appointed by N in 1855.

1618. M'Cormac, Henry. On the theory of final causes; three letters addressed by Dr. M'Cormac, to the editor of The Leader newspaper. Belfast: Shepherd and Aitchison, 1857. T68.13.

1619. Maret, Henri Louis Charles. Seconde lettre à M. le professeur Ubaghs. Offprint from the Revue Catholique, 5th series, August 1857. C9.13. Part of a controversy in the Revue Catholique over whether at the creation the first man received knowledge through "infusion" or "revelation."

1620. Phillipps, Ambrose Lisle. On the future unity of Christendom. London: Charles Dolman, 1857. T69.11.

1621. Stanley, Arthur Penrhyn. Three introductory lectures on the study of ecclesiastical history. Oxford: John Henry and James Parker, 1857. Tre15.3.

1622. Ullathorne, William Bernard. Notes on the education question. London: Richardson and Son, 1857. P1.10.

WORK BY UNIDENTIFIED AUTHOR

1623. A Scruple, pseud. The Catholic oath; its meaning explained, in a correspondence between an Elector of Tralee, & a Scruple of Killarney, with a preface, by a Scruple; and an appendix containing the Emancipation Act. Tralee: The Office of the "Tralee Chronicle and Killarney Echo," n.d. T70.13.

1858

1624. Dalgairns, John Bernard. The German mystics of the fourteenth century. London: Thomas Richardson and Son, 1858. P7.9.

1625. Fander, John. The proper use of <u>shall</u> and <u>will</u> fully explained by two short rules and two German words, <u>sollen</u> & <u>wollen</u>, and made intelligible to minds of the smallest capacity; in a letter to an Irish student at an English college. London: David Nutt, 1858. P7.5.

1626. Jenkins, Robert Charles. The judgment of Thomas de Vio, Cardinal Cajetan, against the Immaculate Conception of the Blessed Virgin Mary; translated, with a historical introduction. Canterbury: Thomas Ashenden, 1858. C6.19. A translation of Cajetan's <u>Opuscula</u> (1515). Duplicate copy: P8.3.

1627. Ramière, Henri. De la théologie scolastique. Paris: Julien, Lanier, Cosnard, 1858. C21.3. "Extrait des <u>Études de Théologie, de Philosophie et d'Histoire.</u>" Ramière was a Jesuit.

1628. Stanley, Arthur Penrhyn. The repentance of David; a sermon preached in the church of St. Giles, Oxford, on Ash-Wednesday, 1858. Oxford: John Henry and James Parker, 1858. P8.9.

1629. Tierney, Mark Aloysius. A reply to Cardinal Wiseman's letter to his chapter, to which is prefixed the letter to "The Rambler," which is the subject of His Eminence's strictures. [London: Cox and Wyman,] n.d. C5.6. "Not published." Tierney's letter was entitled, "Was Dr. Lingard Actually a Cardinal?" <u>The Rambler</u>, N.S. 9 (June 1858), 425. See 1632. Duplicate copy: NL13.6.

1630. Walker, John. Essay on the connexion of the soul with the body, as a sequel to the Essay on the Origin of Knowledge. London: Thomas Richardson and Son, 1858. NL27.3. A sequel to 1631.

1631. Walker, John. Essay on the origin of knowledge, according to the philosophy of St. Thomas. London: Richardson and Son, n.d. NL27.4. Cf. 1630.

1632. Wiseman, Nicholas. A letter to the canons of the cathedral chapter of Westminster, in reply to one published in The Rambler for June 1858, relative to a passage in the "Recollections of the Last Four Popes." London: Thomas Richardson and Son, 1858. C5.5. Privately circulated. A reply to Mark A. Tierney's "Was Dr. Lingard Actually a Cardinal," <u>Rambler</u>, N.S. 9 (June 1858), 425-32. Tierney maintained that Leo XII made John Lingard, not Lamennais, a cardinal <u>in petto</u>. See 1629; also <u>L.D.</u>, XIX, 163; also Josef L. Altholz, <u>The Liberal Catholic Movement in England</u> (London: Burns & Oates, [1962]), pp. 76-77; also W. G. Roe, <u>Lamennais and England</u> ([Oxford]: Oxford Univ. Press, 1966), pp. 127-34.

WORK BY UNIDENTIFIED AUTHOR

1633. Anon. L'Empereur Napoléon III et l'Angleterre. Paris: Firmin Didot Frères, Fils, 1858. C24.4.

1859

1634. Bellows, Henry W. The suspense of faith; an address to the
      alumni of the Divinity School of Harvard University, Cambridge,
      Mass., given July 19, 1859. New York: C. S. Francis, 1859.
      P8.6.

1635. Camps, F. F. F. Camps' answer to Dr. Forbes; the Church of
      Rome vindicated from every calumny; with epistle dedicatory to
      Father Dayman. New York: F. A. Brady, 1859. P8.5. An answer
      to a letter in the New York Herald, 22 Oct. 1859, by John
      Murray Forbes, an American Episcopalian who had left his
      church for Roman Catholicism but returned because of the con-
      troversy over the Temporal Power.

1636. Dick, Robert. The spiritual Dunciad; Oxford "Tracks" to pop-
      ery; a satire; with notes and appendix. London: Charles
      Westertin, 1859. NL99.10. Sent to N. Contains verses re-
      lating to most of the Tractarians.

1637. [Döllinger, Johann Joseph Ignaz von.] The paternity of
      Jansenism; to the editor of the Rambler; reprinted from the
      Rambler of December 1858. [London: Robson, Levey, and
      Franklyn,] n.d. C5.7. See 1638.

1638. Gillow, John. Remarks on a letter in the Rambler for December
      1858, entitled "The Paternity of Jansenism." London: Thomas
      Richardson and Son, 1859. C5.8. See 1637. Duplicate copy:
      P8.4.

1639. Manning, Henry Edward. The perpetual office of the Council of
      Trent; a sermon preached in the third provincial council of
      Westminster. London: Burns & Lambert, n.d. P8.8.

1640. Maturin, Edmund. A defense of the claims of the Catholic
      Church, in reply to several recent publications. Halifax,
      Nova Scotia: Compton & Bowden, 1859. NL23.15. I. See 1641.

1641. Maturin, Edmund. A defense of the claims of the Catholic
      Church, in reply to several recent publications; by Edmund
      Maturin, A.M.; part II: the supremacy of the Pope, and other
      articles of faith. Halifax, Nova Scotia: Compton & Bowden,
      1859. NL23.16. A continuation of 1640.

1642. Maturin, Edmund. A letter to the Lord Bishop of Fredericton,
      in reply to some statements in his recent charge. Halifax,
      Nova Scotia: Compton & Bowden, 1859. NL23.18.

1643. Maturin, Edmund. The origin of Christianity in Ireland; a
      lecture delivered before the Halifax Catholic Institute, on
      Tuesday evening, November 1, 1859. Halifax, Nova Scotia:
      Compton & Bowden, 1859. NL23.17.

1644. Montgomery, George. The Oath of Abjuration taken by profes-
      sors and students of Royal College of Maynooth; considered in
      a letter to the Roman Catholic Archbishop of Armagh. London:
      Simpkin, Marshall, 1859. NL23.28.

1645. Paget, James. On the chronometry of life. N.l., n.p., n.d.

P12.8. Proceedings of the weekly evening meeting on Friday, 8 April 1859, of the Royal Institution of Great Britain.

1646. Rhodes, Matthew John. His Holiness Pope Pius IX. and the temporal rights of the Holy See, as involving the religious, social, and political interests of the whole world: (with a notice of some important passages in the history of Pope Pius the Seventh;): being an address delivered at a meeting of the Catholics of Richmond, Yorkshire, November 27, 1859, by M. J. Rhodes, Esq., M.A.; revised and enlarged by the author, with appendix. London: Thomas Richardson and Son, 1859. P8.13. An ultramontane pamphlet.

1647. Rigby, Nicholas. Three sermons on the foundations of religion. 2nd ed. London: Catholic Publishing & Bookselling, 1859. NL26.5. Rigby was the priest at Ugthorpe. Contains a letter by N not included in L.D.

1648. Robertson, William. A paper, showing the cause of the early destruction of the teeth, and how the evil is to be prevented; read before the members of the Odontological Society, London. London: John Churchill, 1859. C13.13. Read 1 June 1857.

1649. Robertson, William. A practical treatise on the human teeth; showing the cause of their destruction, and the means of their preservation. 4th ed. [London: John Churchill], n.d. C13.14. D? Publisher's advertisement.

1650. Russell, Charles Arthur. The Catholic in the workhouse; popular statement of the law as it affects him, the religious grievances it occasions, with practical suggestions for redress. London: Catholic Publishing and Bookselling Company, 1859. NL26.8.

1651. Thiel, Andreas. De Nicolao Papa I; commentationes duae historico-canonicae. Brunsbergae: J. R. Huye, 1859. C1.9. Contains: Commentatio I: De Nicolao Papa I legislatore ecclesiastico; Commentatio II: Nicolao Papae I idea de primatu romani pontificis explicata.

WORKS BY UNIDENTIFIED AUTHORS

1652. Anon. L'Empereur Napoléon III et l'Italie. New ed. Paris: E. Dentu, 1859. C24.5.

1653. Anon. Fictions of our forefathers: Fion Mac Cumhail and his warriors. Dublin: M'Glashan and Gill, n.d. P12.1. "Reprinted from the Irish Quarterly Review, No. XXXV, October, 1859." "By the author of Legends of Mount Leinster." A review of Transactions of the Ossianic Society, I-IV (Dublin: O'Daly, 1854-59).

1654. Anon. Le Pape et le Congrès. Paris: E. Dentu, 1859. C23.1.

1860

1655. La Morcière, Léon Christophe de. Rapport du Général de La

Morcière à Monseigneur de Mérode, Ministre des Armes de Sa Sainteté Pie IX, sur les opérations de l'armée pontificale, contre l'invasion piémontaise dans les Marches et l'Ombrie. Paris: Charles Douniol, 1860. C24.3.

1656. Montgomery, George. "Velimus nolimus, rerum caput Roma erit," Rome and the Papacy now and forever inseparable; this fact made apparent and certain matters therewith connected considered in a letter to the editor of "The Tablet." London: Simpkin, Marshall, 1860. NL80.26.

1657. Ortiz Urruela, Manuel. La verdad, la razón y los hechos. [Cádiz: n.p., 1860.] C23.2. Lacks title-page. An argument in favor of the Temporal Power in response to 1654.

1658. Scott, William Hope. The theory of the picturesque. Dublin: John F. Fowler, n.d. NL82.4. "From the _Atlantis_ of January, 1860."

1659. Stanley, Arthur Penrhyn. Freedom and labour; two sermons preached before the University of Oxford. Oxford: J. H. and Jas. Parker, 1860. P8.10.

1660. Ullathorne, William Bernard. The speech on the question of the Pontifical States, delivered by the Right Rev. Bishop Ullathorne, at the Town Hall, Birmingham, on Tuesday the 14th of February, 1860. London: Burns and Lambert, 1860. P8.11.

WORK BY UNIDENTIFIED AUTHOR

1661. An Ultramontane, pseud. The Pope, the press, and Napoleon III., considered in a letter to Count de Montalembert. London: Edward Lumley, 1860. P8.12.

1861

1662. Bowyer, George. Speech of Sir George Bowyer, Bart. M.P., in the debate in the House of Commons, on the 4th March 1861. N.l., n.p., n.d. C14.3. See 1597 and 1598.

1663. Dupanloup, Félix Antoine Philibert. Discours prononcé par Mgr. l'Évêque d'Orléans en faveur des pauvres catholiques d'Irlande, à Paris, dans l'église Saint-Roch, le Lundi Saint, 25 mars 1861. Paris: Charles Douniol, 1861. C24.7. A plea for Irish freedom.

1664. Dupanloup, Félix Antoine Philibert. Lettre à M. le Vte. de La Guéronnière en réponse à sa brochure La France, Rome et l'Italie, par Mgr. l'Évêque d'Orléans. Paris: Charles Douniol, 1861. C23.4. In response to C23.3., Dupanloup argues that France must not abandon her protection of the Temporal Power.

1665. Laemmer, Hugo. Analecta romana; kirchengeschichtliche Forschungen in römischen Bibliotheken und Archiven; eine Denkschrift. Schaffhausen: Verlag der Fr. Hurter'schen Buchhandlung, 1861. C21.2.

1666. La Guéronnière, Alfred de. La France, Rome et l'Italie.

Paris: E. Dentu, 1861. C23.3. The author was Minister of the
Interior. He argues against continuance of the Temporal Power.
Cf. 1664.

1667. Manning, Henry Edward. The last glories of the Holy See,
greater than the first; three lectures, with a preface. London: Burns & Lambert, 1861. NL14.6.

1668. Veuillot, Louis. Waterloo. Paris: Gaume Frères et J. Duprey,
1861. C13.7. Violent ultramontane invective against the
threat to the Temporal Power posed by the unification of Italy.

WORKS BY UNIDENTIFIED AUTHORS

1669. Anon. The word of an Irish exile. London: Keating & Co.,
1861. NL22.17. Dated "Tournehem, December 20, 1860." A conservative Catholic criticism of Irish politics. Partly a
response to Le Pape et le Congrès.

1670. A Clergyman, pseud. Concerning doubt: a letter to "A Layman."
Oxford and London: J. H. and Jas. Parker, 1861. C15.3. A
reply to 1673.

1671. Justitia, pseud. The discount system: what is it? London:
n.p., 1861. Pl2.12. A letter dated 4 May 1861 to the editor
of The Weekly Register about problems experienced by Catholic
booksellers.

1672. A Layman, pseud. Concerning doubt: a reply to "A Clergyman."
Oxford: J. L. Wheeler, 1861. C15.1.

1673. A Layman, pseud. The suppression of doubt is not faith: a
letter to the Lord Bishop of Oxford, on his two sermons, entitled "The Revelation of God the Probation of Man." Oxford:
J. L. Wheeler, 1861. C15.2. A reply to Samuel Wilberforce.

1862

1674. Anderson, William Henry. Self-education: a lecture delivered
to the Catholic Young Men's Society of Dublin, in their new
hall, Denmark Street, November 4, 1861. Dublin: John F.
Fowler, 1862. NL79.3. I. "To the Little Oratory."

1675. [Challis, Henry William.] The determinist theory of volition:
its statement and history. C9.12. Lacks title-page. The
author is identified by H. I. D. Ryder. Scoring and marginalia by Ryder.

1676. Fowler, R. Solutions of the questions in mixed mathematics
proposed at examinations for admission to the Royal Military
Academy, Woolwich, in 1861 and 1862. London: Longman, Green,
Longman, and Roberts, 1862. C1.1.

1677. Gooch, Charles. The record of creation, considered in an
examination of Mr. Goodwin's essay on Mosaic cosmogony. Cambridge: Deighton, Bell, 1862. Pl0.1. Reprinted from the
Journal of Sacred Literature, July 1862.

1678. Gurney, Archer. Restoration; or the completion of the Reformation. 2nd and enlarged ed. London: J. T. Hayes, n.d. C3.2. I.

1679. Lucas, Edward. On the first two centuries of Christianity: proving the incorruptibility of the Catholic Church, by historical considerations. London: Burns & Lambert, 1862. C19.3. "Read before H. E. Cardinal Wiseman and the Catholic Academia of London."

1680. Mathieu, Jacques Marie Adrien Césaire. Observations du Cardinal Mathieu, Archevêque de Besançon, sur l'ouvrage intitulé Du pouvoir temporel de la papauté, par M. Bonjean. Paris: Librairie d'Adrien Le Clere, 1862. C24.2. Louis Bernard Bonjean's Du pouvoir temporel et de la papauté (1862) was a Gallican attack on the Temporal Power.

1681. Newman, Francis William. Hiawatha: rendered into Latin, with abridgment by Francis William Newman, professor of Latin in University College, London. London: Walton and Maberly, 1862. NL24.1. I.

1682. Porter, G. S. The days or periods of creation; an answer to Mr. Goodwin's essay "On the Mosaic Cosmogony" in "Essays and Reviews." Cambridge: Deighton, Bell, 1862. C6.18.

1683. Reddie, James. Vis inertiæ victa, or fallacies affecting science: an essay towards increasing our knowledge of some physical laws, and a review of certain mathematical principles of natural philosophy. London: Bradbury & Evans, 1862. P12.7.

1684. Roberts, John William, and William George Ward. Correspondence between the Rev. Father Roberts and Dr. Ward, on the relation of intellectual power to man's true perfection. London: Burns and Lambert, 1862. C9.11. Cf. 1687 and 1688. Duplicate copy: P9.3.

1685. Simpson, Richard. Bishop Ullathorne and The Rambler; reply to criticisms contained in "A Letter on The Rambler and Home and Foreign Review, Addressed to the Clergy of the Diocese of Birmingham, by the Right Rev. Bishop Ullathorne." 2nd ed., with Postscript. London: William and Norgate, 1862. P9.6. Endorsed "A St John" in N's hand. A reply to 1686. Cf. 1706.

1686. Ullathorne, William Bernard. A letter on The Rambler and The Home and Foreign Review; addressed to the clergy of the Diocese of Birmingham. London: Thomas Richardson and Son, 1862. P9.5. Duplicate copy: NL12.4. A response to "Cardinal Wiseman and the Home and Foreign Review," by John Acton (with Thomas Frederick Wetherell and Richard Simpson) in the Home and Foreign Review, 1 (Oct. 1862), 501-20; and also to letters by Richard Simpson in The Rambler, N.S. 4 (July 1855), 25-37; and N.S. 5 (May 1856), 327-45.

1687. Ward, William George. The relation of intellectual power to man's true perfection, considered in two essays read before the English Academy of the Catholic Religion; published with notes and appendices, by desire of the Cardinal Archbishop of Westminster and the Academy. London: Burns and Lambert, 1862. C9.9. Duplicate copy: P9.1. On pp. 75-76 Ward quotes from

N's Loss and Gain and comments on the likenesses between his and N's thought. On pp. 77-80 Ward comments on Charles Kingsley and "muscular Christianity." Cf. 1688.

1688. Ward, William George. The relation of intellectual power to man's true perfection, further considered, with reference to a criticism in the Rambler for May 1862. London: Burns and Lambert, 1862. C9.10. Duplicate copy: P9.2. A response to the review of 1687 by John William Roberts. Cf. 1684.

WORKS BY UNIDENTIFIED AUTHORS

1689. Anon. A review of the Rev. H. Venn on St. Francis Xavier and Christian missions. London: Burns & Lambert, 1862. Pll.1. "The following pages are reprinted, with a few additions, from the 'Weekly Register' of Nov. 8th and 15th." A review of Henry Venn's Missionary Life and Labours of Francis Xavier (London, 1862).

1690. A Missionary Priest of Westminster, pseud. Mischievous consequences of Dr. Ward's doctrine of the intellect. Tipton: C. & W. Britten, 1862. P9.4. A review of 1688.

1863

1691. [Acton, John.] Human sacrifice. N.l., n.p., n.d. P12.6. Author is identified on title-page by N. A review of Philip Henry Stanhope's Miscellanies (London, 1863). See The Correspondence of Lord Acton and Richard Simpson, ed. Josef L. Altholz, Damian McElrath, and James C. Holland, vol. III (Cambridge: Cambridge Univ. Press, 1975), 72-73.

1692. Bache, Samuel. Miracles, the credentials of the Christ: five lectures, delivered in the Church of the Messiah, Birmingham, on Sunday mornings in January and February, 1863. London: E. T. Whitfield, 1863. NL18.2. I. Given to N in 1868.

1693. Eden, Robert. Dr. Pusey and Dr. Newman; two letters. N.l., n.p., n.d. P9.8. A response to the prosecution in the Vice-Chancellor's Court at Oxford of Benjamin Jowett, on charges of teaching heresy; the prosecution was instigated by E. B. Pusey. This is also a response to the exchange of letters in The Times between F. D. Maurice and N on the subject of Tract 90. See L.D., XX, 413-17.

1694. Freppel, Charles Émile. Oraison funèbre de Son Éminence Monseigneur le Cardinal Morlot, Archevêque de Paris, Grand Aumonier de l'Empereur, prononcée dans l'Eglise Métropolitaine de Paris le 12 février 1863. Paris: Librairie d'Adrien Le Clere, 1863. Pll.2.

1695. Gooch, Charles. The interpretation of Scripture. London: Williams and Norgate, 1863. P10.2. "Reprinted from The Journal of Sacred Literature and Biblical Record for January 1863." A review of Benjamin Jowett's "A History of the Interpretation of Scripture" in Essays and Reviews.

1696. Gregg, Tresham Dames. The steam locomotive as revealed in the Bible; a lecture delivered to young men in Sheffield, at the Music Hall, on Tuesday, February 24th, 1863. London: Wertheim, Macintosh, and Hunt, 1863. P12.17. "The mariner's compass is in the Bible; gas is in the Bible; photography is in the Bible; telegraphy is in the Bible; but, above all, steam locomotion is in the Bible"--especially in Ezekiel 1:4-25. See L.D., XX, 236-37.

1697. Gregg, Tresham Dames. To [the Most Reverend, Right Reverend, and Right Honourable the Upper House of,] [the Reverend, the Venerable, and Very Reverend, the Lower House of,] the Convocation of the Province of Canterbury, of the United Church of England and Ireland. N.l., n.p., n.d. P12.18. Cf. 1758.

1698. Harrison, George. A letter to Alderman Lloyd, on the extent of the great social evil in our large towns. Birmingham: E. Massey, 1863. P12.14. I. An argument for the regulation of prostitution based on the French legal system.

1699. Leahy, Patrick. Mr. Somes' bill; letter from the Archbishop of Cashel, to the Very Rev. John Spratt, D.D., and James Haughton, Esq. Dublin: James Duffy, 1863. P12.13. The archbishop supports Mr. Somes' bill to close public houses on Sundays, saying that "intemperance is the besetting sin of our people in Ireland . . . ."

1700. Mills, Alexius. The battle of the Church; and Pope Pius the Ninth: two lectures delivered in the Whittington Hall. London: W. H. Giles, 1863. P10.11.

1701. Newman, Francis William. On the Umbrian language. P12.4. Extracted from Transactions of the Philological Society (1863), pp. 167-212. Corrections in ink. Cf. 1729.

1702. Northcote, James Spencer, and Charles Meynell. The 'Colenso' controversy considered from the Catholic standpoint; being five letters about Dr. Colenso's work upon the Pentateuch, and the criticisms which it has called forth on either side. London: Thomas Richardson and Son, 1863. C9.8. Duplicate copy: P10.3.

1703. O'Reilly, Myles William Patrick. Two articles on education. London: Thomas Richardson and Son, 1863. P10.4. I. Reprinted from The Dublin Review, 52 (1863), 423-67. The articles have to do with the Catholic University of Ireland.

1704. Renouf, Peter Le Page. A few words on the supposed Latin origin of the Arabic version of the Gospels. London: Williams and Norgate, 1863. P12.3. "From the Atlantis, Vol. IV."

1705. Sigerson, George. Some remarks on a proto-morphic phyllotype. Dublin: John F. Fowler, 1863. P12.9. I. "Reprinted from the Atlantis, vol. IV."

1706. Ullathorne, William Bernard. On certain methods of The Rambler and The Home and Foreign Review; a second letter to the clergy of the Diocese of Birmingham. London: Thomas Richardson and Son, 1863. P9.7. A reply to 1685. A sequel to 1686. Duplicate copy: NL12.7.

1707. The Union and Emancipation Society, Manchester. Earl Russell
      and the slave power. Manchester: The Union and Emancipation
      Society, 1863. P12.15. A protest against the British govern-
      ment's dealings with the Confederate States of America.

WORKS BY UNIDENTIFIED AUTHORS

1708. Anon. The Church establishment in Ireland, past and present;
      illustrated exclusively by Protestant authorities, with appen-
      dices showing the revenues of the established Church, the
      religious census of the population of Ireland and other re-
      turns bearing on this subject. Dublin: G. P. Warren, 1863.
      P9.10.

1709. Anon. Civil intolerance of religious error; M. de Montalem-
      bert at Malines. London: Burns & Lambert, 1863. P9.9.
      Marginalia on p. 33, partially obliterated in binding. A re-
      print of a review of Charles René Comte de Montalembert,
      L'Église libre dans l'état libre; discours prononcés au
      Congrès Catholique de Malines (Paris: Douniol, Didier, 1863).
      The review originally appeared in Journal de Bruxelles, 25
      and 26 August, 1836.

                              1864

1710. Acland, Thomas Dyke. Agricultural education; what it is, and
      how to improve it: considered in a letter to Sir Edward C.
      Kerrison, Bart., M.P., president of the Royal Agricultural
      Society of England. London: W. Clowes and Sons, 1864. P12.10.

1711. Banting, William. Letter on corpulence, addressed to the pub-
      lic. 3rd ed. London: Harrison, 1864. C19.7. The personal
      history and dietary recommendations of a very fat man.

1712. [Caswell, Edward.] Scriblerus Redivivus, pseud. The art of
      pluck; being a treatise after the fashion of Aristotle; writ
      for the use of students in the universities; to which is
      added fragments from the examination papers. 11th ed. Ox-
      ford: J. Vincent, 1864. NL82.1.

1713. Cummings, J. W. The present state of religious controversy
      in America: an address delivered before the New York Theo-
      logical Society, September 22, 1864. New York: P. O'Shea,
      1864. P11.14.

1714. Davis, Charles Henry. A practical defence of the Evangelical
      clergy: or, the Prayer Book's reputedly "popish" portions
      really Protestant, Dissenters themselves being witnesses.
      London: Seeley, Jackson, and Halliday, 1864. P11.12.
      Marginalia, possibly by Davis.

1715. Dupanloup, Félix Antoine Philibert. Discours prononcé au
      Congrès de Malines par Mgr. l'Évêque d'Orléans le 31 août
      1864 sur l'enseignement populaire. Paris: Charles Douniol,
      1864. P10.12.

1716. Ellicott, C. J. Church work and Church prospects; a charge to
      the clergy of the diocese of Gloucester and Bristol, at his
      primary visitation, in October, 1864. Gloucester: Edmund Nest,
      n.d. Pll.9. Includes comments on Essays and Reviews.

1717. Gregg, Tresham Dames. Leviathan: the iron-clads of the sea re-
      vealed in the Bible; an exposition of Job XLI. London: William
      Macintosh, 1864. Pl2.19. Cf. 1758.

1718. Hawkins, Edward. Notes upon subscription, academical and
      clerical. Oxford: John Henry and James Parker, 1864. C4.2.
      I.

1719. Keane, Augustus Henry. The case of the Irish Catholics in
      Scotland stated: being a memorial on the present state of the
      Catholic Church in Scotland; addressed to His Eminence Cardi-
      nal Alex. Barnabo, Prefect of the Sacred Congregation of
      Propaganda Fide. Glasgow: "Free Press" Office, 1864. Pll.4.

1720. Kingsley, Charles. "What, then, does Dr. Newman mean?" A
      reply to a pamphlet lately published by Dr. Newman. London:
      Macmillan, 1864. NL4.5. M*. S*. Sent to N by the publish-
      ers.

1721. Littledale, Richard Frederick. Religious communities of women
      in the early and mediæval Church. 2nd ed. London: Joseph
      Masters, 1864. Pll.8.

1722. Littledale, Richard Frederick. Unity and the rescript; a re-
      ply to Bishop Ullathorne's pastoral against the A.P.U.C. Lon-
      don: G. J. Palmer, 1864. NL12.10. I. A defense of the Asso-
      ciation for the Promotion of the Unity of Christendom. See
      N's reply to Littledale in L.D., XXI, 349-40. Cf. 1735. Dup-
      licate copy: Pl0.8.

1723. M'Corry, John Stewart. The Church and her trials: being a
      discourse delivered in the church of the Irish College, Rome,
      on the feast of St. Agatha, February 5, 1864; and dedicated to
      His Grace the Most Rev. Dr. Cullen, Archbishop of Dublin,
      Apostolic Delegate, etc., etc. Edinburgh: John Miller, 1864.
      Pll.5. I. A defense of the Temporal Power.

1724. Manning, Henry Edward. The workings of the Holy Spirit in the
      Church of England: a letter to the Rev. E. B. Pusey, D.D.
      London: Longman, Green, Longman, Roberts, & Green, 1864.
      C8.5. Scoring beside a passage that distinguishes between
      "the grace of the Church of England," which Manning belittles,
      and "the working of grace in the Church of England." A reply
      in part to Pusey's Legal Force of the Judgment of the Privy
      Council. Duplicate copy: Pll.8.

1725. Marshall, Henry Johnson. Religion, society, and the press;
      one of a course of lectures, delivered in St. Patrick's
      Church, Edinburgh, on religion and society. London: Burns &
      Lambert, 1864. Pll.3.

1726. Meyrick, Frederick. But isn't Kingsley right after all? A
      letter to the Rev. Dr. Newman from the Rev. Frederick Meyrick.
      London: Rivingtons, 1864. NL4.9. Cf. 1727.

1727. Meyrick, Frederick. On Dr. Newman's rejection of Liguori's doctrine of equivocation. London: Rivingtons, 1864. NL4.8. Embossed "From the author." Cf. 1726.

1728. Morell, John Reynell. The case of Mr. J. R. Morell. London: Mitchell and Hughes, 1864. P12.11. Morell had been dismissed from his position as a School Inspector.

1729. Newman, Francis William. The text of the Iguvine inscriptions with interlinear Latin translation, and notes. London: Trübner, 1864. P12.5.

1730. Oakeley, Frederick. The Catholic religion, considered in reference to national morality; a lecture, delivered for a charitable purpose, at Barnsbury Hall, Islington, on Monday, March 14, 1864. London: W. H. Giles, 1864. P11.6.

1731. Oakeley, Frederick. The question of university education for English Catholics, considered principally in its moral and religious bearings; in a letter to the Right Rev. the Bishop of Birmingham. London: Burns and Lambert, 1864. P10.6.

1732. Pompallier, Jean Baptiste. A letter of the Catholic Bishop of Auckland, to the Catholic fathers of Maori tribes, for the pacification and Christian happiness of New Zealand. Auckland, New Zealand: Philip Kunst, 1864. NL25.22.

1733. Pusey, Edward Bouverie. Everlasting punishment; a sermon preached before the university in the Cathedral Church of Christ, in Oxford, on the twenty-first Sunday after Trinity. Oxford: John Henry and James Parker, 1864. P11.7.

1734. Seeley, John Robert. Classical studies as an introduction to the moral sciences; an introductory lecture delivered on October 13, 1863, at University College, London. London: Bell and Daldy, 1864. C7.16. Takes issue with a lecture of Lord Stanley calling for more sciences in university curricula.

1735. Ullathorne, William Bernard. A letter on the "Association for the Promotion of the Unity of Christendom," addressed to the clergy of the diocese of Birmingham. London: Thomas Richardson and Son, 1864. P10.7. Cf. 1722.

WORK BY UNIDENTIFIED AUTHOR

1736. A Catholic Layman, pseud. University education for English Catholics; a letter to the Very Rev. J. H. Newman, D.D., by a Catholic layman. London: Burns & Lambert, 1864. P10.5. A reply to an article, "The Work and Wants of the Catholic Church in England," Dublin Review (July 1863). Duplicate copy: NL4.6.

1865

1737. Abbotts Smith, W. Observations on hay-fever, hay-asthma, or summer-cattarh. 2nd ed. London: Robert Hardwicke, 1865. C19.8.

1738. Amherst, Francis Kerril. Verbum in optimo, fructus in patientia; a sermon preached in the Cathedral of Northampton, on Sunday, the 19th of February, 1865, on the death of His Eminence Cardinal Wiseman, 1st Archbishop of Westminster. London: Burns, Lambert, and Oates, 1865. NL13.7.

1739. Badeley, Edward. The privilege of religious confessions in English courts of justice considered, in a letter to a friend. London: Butterworths, 1865. C19.1. Argues for the inviolability of confession.

1740. Bonnechose, Henri Marie Gaston Boisnormand de. Sénat: discours prononcé par S. Ém. le Cardinal de Bonnechose sur la Convention du 15 septembre (séance du 17 mars 1865). Paris: Ch. Lahure, 1865. C23.6. A speech in favor of French protection of the Temporal Power.

1741. Bonnechose, Henri Marie Gaston Boisnormand de. Sénat: discours prononcé par S. Ém. le Cardinal de Bonnechose sur les rapports entre l'Église et l'État (séance du 14 mars 1865). Paris: Ch. Lahure, 1865. C24.1.

1742. Buck, Victor de. Mgr. de Ram, Recteur Magnifique de l'Université Catholique de Louvain. Paris: Charles Douniol, 1865. C24.9. "Extrait des Études religieuses, historiques et littéraires. Numéros de Juin, Juillet et Août 1865."

1743. [Clifford, William Joseph Hugh.] Remarks on the encyclical of December 8, 1864, by the Bishop of Clifton. London: Burns, Lambert, and Oates, 1865. P10.10. I.

1744. Connolly, James. Sermon in memory of Nicholas, Cardinal Wiseman, Archbishop of Westminster, preached in St. Joseph's, Bunhill Row, London, on Sunday, February 19th, 1865. Dublin: James Duffy, 1865. P11.13.

1745. Crowe, J. O'Beirne, ed. and trans. Scela na Esergi; a treatise on the Resurrection; now printed for the first time, from the original Irish in Lebor na h-Uidre, a ms. in the library of the Royal Irish Academy; with a literal translation. Dublin: John F. Fowler, 1865. P12.2.

1746. Dupanloup, Félix Antoine Philibert. La Convention du 15 septembre et l'encyclique du 8 décembre, par M. l'Évêque d'Orléans, de l'Académie Française. Paris: Charles Douniol, 1865. C22.1. About a conflict between Church and state in France, in which a government official forbade publication by Church authorities of a papal encyclical which was nevertheless published in the secular press. Dupanloup argues that the Church should not be discriminated against, and that the Catholic clergy should have the same rights as other citizens. The Convention referred to was the agreement between Louis Napoleon and Victor Emmanuel to put the Papal States under Italian protection.

1747. Dupanloup, Félix Antoine Philibert. Oraison funèbre du Général de La Morcière, prononcée dans la cathédrale de Nantes le mardi 17 octobre 1865, par Mgr. l'Évêque d'Orléans. Paris: Ch. Douniol, 1865. C24.6.

1748. Dupanloup, Félix Antoine Philibert. Remarks on the encyclical of the 8th of December, A.D. 1864; trans. from the 32nd Paris ed. by William J. M. Hutchinson. London: Geo. Cheek, 1865. P10.9. Inscribed by the translator.

1749. Hampshire Chronicle. Did William of Wykeham carry the crozier in his right hand--if not, is it correct to represent him so? The restoration of Winchester City Cross, by Mr. G. G. Scott, architect; the statue of William of Wykeham, Bishop of Winchester, from A.D. 1367 to 1404, founder of Winchester College, and of New College, Oxford. Winchester: Jacob & Johnson, n.d. NL82.2. "From the Hampshire Chronicle of Dec. 23, 1865."

1750. Harper, Thomas. The claims of the Anglican establishment to be the representative of the primitive Church, tested by the history and acts of the Council of Ephesus; a sermon, preached at St. Werburga's, Birkenhead, on Sunday, 5th February, 1865. Liverpool: Rockliff Brothers, 1865. P11.11.

1751. Husenbeth, Frederick Charles. On sacramental fonts in Norfolk. C7.6. D? I. An offprint (probably one of Husenbeth's 1,305 contributions to Notes and Queries).

1752. Jenkins, Robert Charles. Documents disclosing a passage in the history of the Twysden family; communicated by the late Rev. L. B. Larking, and illustrated by the Rev. R. C. Jenkins, Rector of Lyminge, and Hon. Canon of Canterbury. Reprinted from Archæologia Cantiana, 8 (1865). C7.4.

1753. [Lockhart, William.] A review of Dr. Pusey's Eirenicon, reprinted from the "Weekly Register," with two letters to the editor from Dr. Pusey on his hopes of the reunion of the Church of England with the Catholic Church: also, letters from Dr. Newman and Canon Oakeley. London: George Cheek, n.d. C8.3. Contains N's letter of 19 Nov. 1865, L.D., XXII, 105-06.

1754. Monsell, William. On some of the impediments to Irish manufacturing industry; containing: I. A lecture given at the Limerick Athenæum, on Tuesday, the 31st of January, 1865; and II. A speech made in the House of Commons on Friday, the 7th of April, 1865, in support of a motion that government should inquire into the Irish railway system by Col. the Right Hon. William Monsell. Dublin: J. F. Fowler, 1865. NL23.25.

1755. Nardi, Francesco. Discorso tenuto nella chiesa del Gesù alla conferenza della Società di S. Vincenzo di Paoli, il dì 8 decembre [sic] 1864. Rome: Sinimberghi, 1865. P10.13.

1756. Newman, Francis William. English institutions and their most necessary reforms; a contribution of thought. London: Trübner, 1865. C1.7. Several corrections and revisions in ink, but not N's.

1757. Newman, Francis William. The good cause of President Lincoln: a lecture. London: The Emancipation Society, n.d. NL81.7.

1758. Newman, Francis William. The Permissive Bill more urgent than any extension of the franchise: an address at Ramsgate, February 17th, 1865. Manchester: Abel Heywood, 1865. P12.16. Inscribed "To Very Rev Dr J H Newman from the writer." A speech in favor of temperance legislation.

1759. Newman, John Henry, Edward Bouverie Pusey, and John Keble.
Tract XC: on certain passages in the XXXIX Articles, by the
Rev. J. H. Newman, B.D., 1841; with a historical preface by the
Rev. E. B. Pusey, D.D.; and Catholic subscription to the XXXIX
Articles considered in reference to Tract XC, by the Rev. John
Keble, M.A., 1841. Oxford: John Henry and James Parker, 1865.
C4.4. Inscribed by Pusey. Pusey's republication of Tract 90
and of Keble's The Case of Catholic Subscription to the Thirty-
Nine Articles Considered: With Especial Reference to the Duties
and Difficulties of English Catholics in the Present Crisis:
In a Letter to the Hon. Mr. Justice Coleridge (privately
printed, 1841). See 1777.

1760. Oxenham, Henry Nutcombe. Dishonest criticism; some remarks on
two articles in the Dublin Review for July and October 1865.
London: Longmans, Green, and Co., 1865. C5.3. I. A reply
to W. G. Ward's hostile review of his book, The Catholic Doctrine of the Atonement (1865). Duplicate copy: NL25.5.

1761. Stevens, William Bacon. A man of God approved in Christ! A
sermon commemorative of the life of the Rt. Rev. William Jones
Boone, D.D., missionary bishop to China; preached in Calvary
Church, New York, January 29, 1865. Philadelphia: Serman,
1865. Pll.15. Stevens was Assistant Bishop of the Protestant
Episcopal Diocese of Pennsylvania.

1762. Tommaseo, Niccolò. Il Parlamento e l'Italia; lettera; di N.
Tommaseo. Florence: G. Cassone, 1865. C23.7. A moderate
Catholic appeal for all citizens to cooperate with the new
Italian government and to vote in the new parliamentary
elections. Scoring on pp. 33 and 34, next to passages about
incidents of anticlericalism.

1763. Ullathorne, William Bernard. The Anglican theory of union,
as maintained in the appeal to Rome and Dr. Pusey's "Eirenicon;" a second letter to the clergy of the Diocese of Birmingham. London: Burns, Lambert, and Oates, n.d. NL12.22. Cf.
1735.

WORKS BY UNIDENTIFIED AUTHORS

1764. Anon. ed. The Catholic Eirenicon, in friendly response to Dr.
Pusey, or "Roman Catholic Principles in Reference to God and
the King": by the loyal profession of which our Roman Catholic ancestors achieved emancipation for themselves and us; reprinted from the edition of 1815. London: J. T. Hayes, 1865.
C8.4. Originally published in 1680 as Roman Catholick Principles in Reference to God and the King, Explained in a Letter
to a Friend, and Now Made Publick, to Shew the Connexion
Between the Said Principles and the Late Popish Plot, by the
recusant Benedictine James Maurus Corker. The 1815 edition
was published by John Kirk as Roman Catholic Principles in
Reference to God and the King; to Which Is Prefixed an Inquiry
Respecting the Editions and the Author of That "Valuable
Tract."

1765. Senex, pseud. "Visible unity:" the price to be paid for it; a letter to the Ven. Christopher Wordsworth, D.D., Archdeacon of Westminster, from Senex, on reading Dr. Pusey's "Eirenicon." London: Hatchard, 1865. C6.17.

1766. U., R. Notes on "University Education in Ireland." Dublin: John F. Fowler, 1865. NL82.18. Printed for private circulation only. A response to 1703.

1866

1767. Allies, Thomas William. Dr. Pusey and the ancient Church. London: Longmans, Green, Reader, and Dyer, 1866. C11.5. I. Part of the Eirenicon controversy.

1768. Attwood, E. W. Preface to a work recently published; entitled, Panacéa Britannica: a series of papers mainly devoted to a vindication of Catholicism against objections founded on scripture, history, policy, civilisation, social conditions, and secular progress; more especially with reference to the necessities and prejudices of Englishmen. London: Burns, Lambert, and Oates, 1866. C6.8. I.

1769. Bedford, Henry. Naples, (part I.). Dublin: John F. Fowler, 1866. NL18.9. I. "Reprinted from the 'Irish Ecclesiastical Record.'"

1770. Bedford, Henry. Naples, (part II.). Dublin: John F. Fowler, 1866. NL18.10. I. "Reprinted from the 'Irish Ecclesiastical Record.'"

1771. Bedford, Henry. Venice. Dublin: John F. Fowler, 1866. NL18.8. I. "Reprinted from the 'Irish Ecclesiastical Record.'" Pages uncut.

1772. Brady, W. Maziere. The alleged conversion of the Irish bishops to the reformed religion, at the accession of Queen Elizabeth; and the assumed descent of the present established hierarchy in Ireland from the ancient Irish Church, disproved. 4th ed. enlarged. London: Longmans, Green, 1866. C21.6.

1773. [Challis, Henry William.] A letter to George Augustus Simcox, Esq. M. A., Fellow of Queen's College, Oxford; from a friend who has lately been received into the Catholic Church. London: Robert Washbourne, 1866. NL19.4.

1774. De Vere, Aubrey. The Church Settlement of Ireland, or, Hibernia Pacanda. London: Longmans, Green, Reader, and Dyer, 1866. NL20.12.

1775. Fitzgerald, J. D., James Spencer Northcote, et al. Report of the proceedings in the case of Fitzgerald v. Northcote and another; together with an introductory narrative and other documents. London: Burns, Lambert, and Oates, 1866. C20.1. The case concerned the explusion from Oscott College of a son of J. D. Fitzgerald (of Dublin) by the President of Oscott, J. Spencer Northcote. Contains a letter of W. B. Ullathorne regarding the nature of anti-Catholic prejudice in the courts.

1776. Gallwey, Peter. The Lady Chapel and Dr. Pusey's peacemaker; the substance of a sermon preached in St. John's Church, Islington, on the 24th Sunday after Pentecost, 1865. London: Burns, Lambert, and Oates, n.d. NL21.11. A reply to Pusey's objections to certain Roman Catholic Marian devotions in his Eirenicon (1865).

1777. Hawkins, Edward. Additional notes on subscription, academical and clerical, with reference to the Clerical Subscription Act of 1865; the republication of Tract XC; the Texts Abolition (Oxford) Bills. Oxford: John Henry and James Parker, 1866. C4.3. I.

1778. Husenbeth, Frederick Charles. A.M.D.G.; the substance of a sermon preached at the funeral of the Right Rev. William Wareing, D.D., Bishop of Retimo (in partibus), assistant at the pontifical throne, in the chapel of St. Mary's Abbey, East Bergholt, January 3, 1866. London: Longmans, Green, and Co., 1866. NL22.12. I.

1779. Jenkins, Robert Charles. The Basilica of Lyminge; Roman, Saxon, and mediæval. N.1., n.p., n.d. Reprinted from Archæologia Cantiana, 9 (1866). C7.2.

1780. Jenkins, Robert Charles. Chilham Castle. N.1., n.p., n.d. NL22.24. Inscribed, with annotation by the author. "Reprinted from Archæologia Cantiana, 7 (1866).

1781. Lockhart, William. Possibilities and difficulties of reunion: a review of Dr. Pusey's Eirenicon. 2nd ed. London: Longmans, Green, 1866. C11.4.

1782. Manning, Henry Edward. The reunion of Christendom; a pastoral letter to the clergy, etc. London: Longmans, Green, and Co., 1866. NL14.7. I. On the Association for Promoting the Unity of Christendom and the Rescript of 1865. See 1783.

1783. Manning, Henry Edward. The reunion of Christendom; a pastoral letter to the clergy, etc. 2nd ed. London: Longmans, Green, 1866. C3.5. Scorings and marginalia regarding revelation, dogma, and infallibility. See 1859, 1782.

1784. Manning, Henry Edward. The Temporal Power of the Pope in its political aspect. London: Longmans, Green, 1866. C14.4.

1785. Nardi, Francesco. Della Chiesa Cattolica in Inghilterra; lettera di Francesco Nardi, allora professore nell'Università di Padova, ora uditore di S. Rota. 4th ed. Rome: S. C. di Propaganda Fide, 1866. NL81.1. Contains comments on Pusey and N.

1786. Oakeley, Frederick. The leading topics of Dr. Pusey's recent work reviewed in a letter addressed (by permission) to the Most Rev. H. E. Manning, D.D. London: Longmans, Green, 1866. C11.3. M. S. Part of the Eirenicon controversy. Duplicate copy: NL11.8.

1787. Oxenham, Henry Nutcombe. Dr. Pusey's Eirenicon considered in relation to Catholic unity: a letter to the Rev. Father Lockhard of the Institute of Charity. London: Longmans, Green, 1866. C11.2. M. S.

1788. Sidden, Joseph. Cardinal Wiseman and Bishop Challoner; a
Christian peace offering; the devotion of Catholics to the
Blessed Virgin truly represented, with the solemn attestation
of the Right Reverend Dr. Challoner, Bishop of Debra and Vicar
Apostolic of the London District; republished with the express
written approbation of Cardinal Wiseman, given by himself to
the Rev. Joseph Sidden. London: Thomas Richardson and Son,
1866. NL13.8. I.

1789. [Stanley, Arthur Penrhyn.] Dr. Pusey's Eirenicon; the substance of a paper read by the Dean of Westminster at a meeting
of London clergy. N.l., n.p., n.d. C8.2. "Reprinted from
The Contemporary Review," 1. (April 1866), 534-50. I.
Scoring beside remarks on Tract 90.

1790. The Tablet. Opinions of the press, letters, and other docu-
ments on the late Oscott trial. N.l., n.p., n.d. C20.2.
"The following Letter and Documents appear in the Tablet of
Feb. 17th [1866]." See 1775.

1791. Ullathorne, William Bernard. The Anglican theory of union,
as maintained in the appeal to Rome and Dr. Pusey's "Eirenicon"; a second letter to the clergy of the Diocese of Birmingham. London: Burns, Lambert, and Oates, n.d. C3.6. Another
denunciation of the Association for Promoting the Unity of
Christendom: see 1859 and 1783. Passage dealing with the position of the Vatican is scored.

1792. Ullathorne, William Bernard. On the management of criminals;
a paper read before the Accademia of the Catholic Religion.
London: Thomas Richardson and Son, 1866. NL12.12.

1793. Ullathorne, William Bernard. The rock of the Church: a discourse delivered in substance at the solemn dedication of St.
Peter's Church, Belfast, on the 14th of October, 1866. Belfast: Owen Kerr, 1866. NL12.13.

1794. Vaughan, Henry. The spirit of the French episcopate on the
papal question; with a preface. London: Burns, Lambert and
Oates, 1866. C14.5. A collection of pastoral letters from
French bishops regarding the threat to the Temporal Power.

1795. Williams, George. Yearnings after unity in the East; (from
the writings of the Most Reverend Gregory of Byzantium,
Metropolitan of Chios); with remarks thereon. Occasional
Paper of the Eastern Church Association, No. 3. London:
Rivingtons, 1866. C3.8.

WORKS BY UNIDENTIFIED AUTHORS

1796. Anon. De la propriété foncière dans l'État Potifical; sub-
division du sol, repeuplement des campagnes; institution
d'une Banque Foncière Romaine. Paris: Paul Grou, 1866.
C23.5. A proposal to prospective investors for an agricultural bank that would finance land reform and agricultural
development in the Papal State.

1797. Anon. The Irish College, Paris. Dublin: John F. Fowler,
1866. C7.8. "Reprinted from the 'Irish Ecclesiastical

Record.'"

1798. Anglo-Saxon, pseud. An ironicon: a reply to an Eirenicon, by
      Rev. E. B. Pusey, D.D., Regius Professor of Hebrew, etc.;
      faithfully and fearlessly addressed to him, and to "all sorts
      and conditions of men" in the British Empire, "who profess and
      call themselves Christians." London: Arthur Hall, 1866. C8.8.
      I. A remarkable piece of anti-Puseyite, anti-Catholic polemic.
      In the copy sent to N, there are pencil corrections and dele-
      tions, evidently by the author.

1799. B., H. The Ambrosian Basilica at Milan. Dublin: John F.
      Fowler, 1866. C7.9. "Reprinted from the 'Irish Ecclesiasti-
      cal Record.'"

1800. R., G. Eisotheism: a protest of unwritten against written
      revelation; prepared, but presented too late, for the Anthro-
      pological Society's missionary discussion of July last; by a
      then member; printed for circulation to those whose position
      justifies the conjecture of fitness to appreciate the dis-
      tinction between the conventionally and the absolutely true.
      London: F. Farrah, 1866. C16.7. The author solicits support
      for his "suggested Congress for Revision of the World's Reli-
      gious Philosophy" and for the construction of a "World's Altar
      TO THE UNKNOWN CAUSE Whereon to consecrate a World's Reli-
      gion . . . ."

                              1867

1801. Barton, F. B. An outline of the Positive Religion of Humanity
      of A. Comte. London: E. Truelove, 1867. C9.6. Inscribed
      "From Mr. Jas H Starling Corbett's Coffee Room New Street
      Birmingham."

1802. [Birmingham, Clergy of the Diocese of, and William Bernard
      Ullathorne.] The address presented to the Right Reverend
      William Bernard [Ullathorne], O.S.B., Bishop of Birmingham, at
      St. Mary's College, Oscott, on Thursday, July 18th, 1867, and
      His Lordship's reply. Birmingham: M. Maher and Son, n.d.
      C6.5.

1803. Challis, Henry William. A letter to John Stuart Mill, Esq.,
      M.P., on the necessity of geometry and the association of
      ideas. Oxford and London: James Parker, 1867. C9.4. On
      p. 6 there is a marginal comment, apparently by H. I. D. Ryder,
      partially obscured in binding.

1804. De Vere, Aubrey. The Church establishment in Ireland, illus-
      trated exclusively by Protestant authorities; with a preface.
      London: Longmans, Green, Reader, and Dyer, 1867. NL79.23.
      I. Cf. 1834, 1806, 1851, 1805.

1805. De Vere, Aubrey. Ireland's Church property, and the right use
      of it. London: Longmans, Green, Reader, and Dyer, 1867.
      NL79.24. Cf. 1834, 1806, 1851, 1804.

1806. De Vere, Aubrey. Pleas for secularization. London: Green,

Reader, and Dyer, 1867. NL79.21. I. An essay on the state
of Irish Catholicism. See 1834.

1807. E[dwards], F[rederick] T[homas] A. A plain appeal to High
Churchmen; by a recent convert. London: Burns, Oates, 1867.
C6.13. Dated by Newman "S.S. Simon & Jude 1867." N mildly
reproved Edwards for publishing this: see L.D., XXIII, 361-62.

1808. Ffoulkes, Edmund Salusbury. An historical account of the
addition of the words "Filioque" to the Creed of the West.
Occasional Paper of the Eastern Church Association, No. 7.
London: Rivingtons, 1867. C10.13. I. S.

1809. Harper, Thomas. A letter from the Rev. F. Harper, S.J., to
the editor of the "Dublin Review." London: Wyman & Sons,
1867. C5.4. I. A reply to the October 1867 Dublin Review.

1810. Jenkins, Robert Charles. Bullam "Ineffabilis" ad veterum
romanorum pontificum judicium revocavit. London: Whittingham
[and] Wilkins, 1867. C14.9. A private printing of the Bull
"Ineffabilis," with a preface in Latin against papal infallibility, dedicated to the Archbishop of Canterbury. See 1877 and
1970.

1811. Jenkins, Robert Charles. From the proceedings of the Society
of Antiquaries, May 16, 1867. N.l., n.p., n.d. NL80.14. I.

1812. Knox, Thomas Francis. When does the Church speak infallibly?
Or, the nature and scope of the Church's teaching office.
London: Burns, Oates, 1867. C14.14. An ultramontane view of
infallibility. Knox was of the London Oratory. Marginalia
by Ryder.

1813. Leahy, Patrick. Pastoral letter of the Most Rev. Patrick
Leahy, Archbishop of Cashel and Emly, to the people of Cashel
and Emly. Dublin: James Duffy, 1867. NL22.32. I.

1814. [MacIvor, James.] To the Rev. the Provost and the Senior
Fellows of Trinity College, Dublin. N.l., n.p., n.d. C9.5.
I.

1815. Manning, Henry Edward. The centenary of Saint Peter and the
General Council: a pastoral letter to the clergy &c. London:
Longmans, Green, and Co., 1867. NL14.8.

1816. Moriarty, David. A letter on the disendowment of the Established Church, addressed to the clergy of the Diocese of
Kerry. Dublin: John F. Fowler, 1867. NL80.29. Moriarty
was the Roman Catholic Bishop of Kerry.

1817. Newman, Francis William. On the philosophical classification
of national institutions; a lecture delivered at the Bristol
Institution for the Advancement of Science, Literature and
the Arts, March 4th, 1867, by F. N. W. Newman, Emeritus
Professor of Univ. Coll., London; formerly Fellow of Balliol
College, Oxford. London: Trübner, 1867. NL24.2. About the
British Constitution, the British Empire, the United States,
and various other historical and political matters.

1818. Newman, Francis William. Why the people ought to have a veto
on the sale of drink? [Manchester: United Kingdom Alliance,]

n.d. NL81.2. "Substance of a speech delivered in Bristol, April 1st, by Professor F. W. Newman."

1819. Parker, John Henry. A catalogue of a series of photographs illustrative of the archæology of Rome, prepared under the direction of John Henry Parker, M.A., F.S.A., in the winters of 1864, 1865, and 1866. Oxford: James Parker, 1867. NL25.14.

1820. Pusey, Edward Bouverie. "Essays on re-union"; the introductory essay. London: J. T. Hayes, n.d. NL11.14.

1821. Pusey, Edward Bouverie. Will ye also go away? A sermon, preached before the University of Oxford, on the fourth Sunday after the Epiphany, 1867. Oxford: James Parker & Co., 1867. NL11.9. I.

1822. Ryder, Henry Ignatius Dudley. Idealism in theology; a review of Dr. Ward's scheme of dogmatic authority. London: Longmans, Green, Reader, and Dyer, 1867. C18.5. A review of W. G. Ward's ultramontane views on papal infallibility in his The Authority of Doctrinal Decisions (London, 1866). Answered by Ward in 1828. See also Wilfrid Ward, William George Ward and the Catholic Revival (London: Macmillan, 1893), pp. 231-32.

1823. Shipley, Orby. Tracts for the day: essays on theological subjects; by various authors; no. 1: priestly absolution, scriptural. London: Longmans and Green, 1867. NL26.18. Pages uncut.

1824. Tondini de Quarenghi, Cesare. Études sur la question religieuse de Russie; première étude: la primauté de Saint Pierre prouvée par les titres que lui donne l'Église Russe dans sa liturgie. Paris: Victor Palmé, 1867. NL26.27. I. Pages uncut.

1825. Tondini de Quarenghi, Cesare. Études sur la question religieuse de Russie; première étude: la primauté de Saint Pierre prouvée par les titres que lui donne l'Église Russe dans sa liturgie. Paris: Victor Palmé, 1867. C25.1. A duplicate copy of 1824.

1826. Ullathorne, William Bernard. The confessional; an address delivered in St. Mary's Catholic Church, Walsall, on Sunday, the 17th of March, and in St. Patrick's Church on the following Sunday. London: Thomas Richardson and Son, 1867. NL12.21.

1827. Ward, William George. A letter; the Rev. Father Ryder on his recent pamphlet. London: Burns & Oates, 1867. NL8.8. See duplicate copy: 1828.

1828. Ward, William George. A letter; the Rev. Father Ryder on his recent pamphlet. London: Burns & Oates, 1867. C14.10. M*. S. A reply to 1822. Contains extensive marginalia, often hostile and sometimes sarcastic, by both N and Ryder. When Ward remarks that he hopes the matter of papal infallibility will "be brought again and again before the notice of Catholics in the Dublin Review," Ryder comments: "usque ad nauseam."

WORKS BY UNIDENTIFIED AUTHORS

1829. Anon. Church reform and true Christianity. London: W. J.
      Golbourn, 1867. C16.9. A confused review of Essays and Re-
      views by a Low Churchman with Socinian tendencies.

1830. A Wrangler, pseud. The theories of Copernicus and Ptolemy.
      London: Longmans, Green, 1867. C5.10.

                              1868

1831. Bottalla, Paul. Pope Honorius before the tribunal of reason
      and history. London: Burns, Oates, 1868. C5.2. A rebuttal
      of 1852.

1832. Cardella, Valerian. Giulio Watts-Russell, pontifical Zouave;
      a biography, written in Italian, by Valerian Cardella, S. J.,
      Professor of Dogmatic Theology in the Roman College; trans-
      lated by William Tylee, B.A., Oriel College, Oxford; with a
      preface by His Grace the Archbishop of Westminster. London:
      John Philip, n.d. NL19.1. Given to N.

1833. Church, Richard William. Civilization and religion; a sermon
      preached before the University of Oxford, at St. Mary's Church,
      on the fifth Sunday in Lent, March 29, 1868. Oxford and Lon-
      don: James Parker, 1868. C17.4. I.

1834. De Vere, Aubrey. Ireland's Church question: five essays.
      London: Longmans, Green, Reader, and Dyer, n.d. NL79.20. I.
      This is the Preface only.

1835. Dupanloup, Félix Antoine Philibert. Lettre sur le futur
      concile œcumenique adressée par Mgr. l'Évêque d'Orléans au
      clergé de son diocèse. Paris: Charles Douniol, 1868. CV5.8.

1836. Estcourt, Edgar Edmund. The dogmatic of the Book of Common
      Prayer on the subject of the Holy Eucharist. London: Long-
      mans, Green, Reader, and Dyer, 1868. C8.1. Answers a review
      in the Jan. 1866 Christian Remembrancer, which criticizes
      Estcourt's criticism of Pusey's Eirenicon.

1837. Ffoulkes, Edmund Salusbury. The Church's creed or the Crown's
      creed? A letter to the Most Rev. Archbishop Manning, etc.,
      etc. 7th ed. London: J. T. Hayes, n.d. C10.14. S*. M*.
      Extensive scoring and indignant marginalia.

1838. Fowler, William. Mozley and Tyndall on miracles; an essay.
      London: Longmans, Green, 1868. C17.3. A criticism of an
      article by John Tyndall in the June 1867 Fortnightly Review.
      Tyndall had criticized J. B. Mozley's 1865 Bampton Lectures
      on miracles.

1839. Fry, Henry. An address to the ministers & members of the
      established and nonconformist Churches. The Evangelical
      Church Union, E.P.B. Tracts, No. 3. London: W. J. Johnson,
      n.d. C13.18. An anti-Catholic pamphlet advocating Protestant
      unity.

1840. Hawkins, Edward. Our debts to Cæsar and to God; a sermon
      preached before the University of Oxford, on Advent Sunday,
      Nov. 29, 1868. Oxford: James Parker, 1868. NL21.43. I.

1841. Hyacinthe, Fr. (Charles Loyson.) Discours pour la profession
      de foi catholique et pour la première communion d'une Pro-
      testante convertie prononcé par le R. P. Hyacinthe, Carme
      déchaussé, dans la Chapelle des Dames de l'Assomption, à Paris
      le 14 juillet 1868. Paris: Joseph Albanel, 1868. NL22.8. I.
      See L.D., XXIV, 140-41.

1842. Ingleby, Clement Mansfield. On some traces of the authorship
      of the works attributed to Shakespeare. N.l., n.p., n.d.
      NL22.15. I. S. Reprinted from the Transactions of the Royal
      Society of Literature, N.S. 9 (1868). See G. A., p. 495.

1843. Ingleby, Clement Mansfield. On the unpublished manuscripts of
      Samuel Taylor Coleridge. N.l., n.p., n.d. NL22.16. I.
      Pages uncut. Reprinted from the Transactions of the Royal
      Society of Literature, N.S. 9 (1868).

1844. Labbé, Pierre L. Souvenirs de M. Bobée, curé d'Yvetot. Havre:
      Eugène Costey, n.d. NL18.13. A memoir of François-Augustin
      Bobée.

1845. Layton, Frederick William Hanham. On the decadence and fall
      of Christendom; an address delivered on Monday, September 7th,
      1868, by the Rev. F. W. H. Layton, B.A., (of St. Peter's
      College, Cambridge), in the New Assembly Room, Agricultural
      Hall, Islington. N.l., n.p., n.d. An offprint from The Penny
      Pulpit, N.S., No. 317 (17 Sept. 1868), pp. 126-32. C13.21. A
      late Irvingite tract. Duplicate copy: C16.6.

1846. Leahy, Patrick, and John Derry. Statement on the university
      question, addressed to the Catholic members of Parliament.
      Dublin: John F. Fowler, 1868. NL80.20. See L.D., XXIV, 51-
      52.

1847. McCarthy, Charles. The lives of the principal Benedictine
      writers of the Congregation of St. Maur: with an historical
      introduction. London: Burns, Oates, 1868. NL23.13. I.

1848. M'Corry, John Stewart. The Madonna: being a discourse on the
      Immaculate Conception, and the maternity of the Blessed Virgin
      Mary; with prefatory notes on Rome and the revolution; dedi-
      cated to the Right Rev. James Chadwick, D.D., Lord Bishop of
      Hexham and Newcastle. London: Burns, Oates, 1868. C6.7.

1849. Mereweather, G. D. [i.e., John David]. La Chiesa Anglicana
      e l'universale unione religiosa, pel reverendo G. D. Mere-
      weather, B.A. Oxford, ministro della Chiesa Cattolica Angli-
      cana in Venezia; tradotto dall'originale inglese. Bergamo:
      Fratello Bolis, 1868. C13.19. I. A carrying to Italy of the
      argument for the catholicity of the Anglican Church.

1850. Meynell, Charles. Padre Liberatore and the ontologists: a
      review. London: Burns, Oates, n.d. C9.7. M*. Review of
      Della conoscenza intellettuale (Rome: Uffizio della Civiltà
      Cattolica, 1858), by Matteo Liberatore. Also contains a
      Postscriptum criticizing 1856. See L.D., XXIV, 234, 281.
      Duplicate copy: NL23.22.

1851. O'Reilly, Myles. Reply to certain strictures by Myles

O'Reilly, Esq., being a postscript to pleas for secularization, by Aubrey De Vere. London: Longmans, Green, Reader, and Dyer, 1868. NL79.22. Inscribed "From the Author See Page 20 & 21," which deal with John Russell and the Irish Church settlement. A sequel to 1806.

1852. Renouf, Peter Le Page. The condemnation of Pope Honorius. London: Longmans, Green, 1868. C5.1. See L.D., XXIV, 90-93. Answered in 1831 by Paul Bottalla. Cf. 1888.

1853. Ryder, Henry Ignatius Dudley. A letter to William George Ward, Esq., D.Ph., on his theory of infallible instruction. London: Longmans, Green, Reader, and Dyer, 1868. C18.6. Answered by Ward in 1828.

1854. Ryder, Henry Ignatius Dudley. Postscriptum to letter to W. G. Ward, Esq., D.Ph. London: Longmans, Green, Reader, and Dyer, 1868. C18.7. Answered by Ward in 1858.

1855. Taylor, Henry. Crime considered in a letter to the Rt. Hon. W. E. Gladstone, M. P. London: Hamilton, Adams, 1868. NL10.8. I.

1856. Walker, John. Essay on first principles. London: Longmans, Green, 1868. C1.4. I. See 1850.

1857. Ward, William George. A brief summary of the recent controversy on infallibility; being a reply to Rev. Father Ryder on his Postscript. London: Burns, Oates, 1868. C14.12. A reply to 1854.

1858. Ward, William George. A second letter to the Rev. Father Ryder. London: Burns, Oates, 1868. C14.11. M*. A reply to 1853. Contains extensive marginalia by N and Ryder.

1859. Ward, William Harry Perceval, and Richard Frederick Littledale. Corporate re-union, not individual secession: two sermons preached at the eleventh anniversary of the foundation of the Association for the Promotion of the Unity of Christendom; the first at All Saints', Lambeth, on the eve of the Nativity of Our Lady, 1868, by the Rev. W. H. Perceval Ward; the second at St. Mary Magdalene's, Munster Square, on the feast of the Nativity of Our Lady, 1868, by the Rev. R. F. Littledale; to which is added a report of the progress of the association from the year 1857 to the year 1868, by the Ex-General Secretary of the A.P.U.C. London: J. T. Hayes, 1868. C3.1. Inscription from F. G. Lee.

1860. Woodlock, Bartholomew. Catholic university education in Ireland: a letter to the Rt. Hon. W. H. F. Cogan, M.P., etc., etc. Dublin: John F. Fowler, 1868. NL82.26. I.

1861. Woodlock, Bartholomew. Educational dangers; or, the bearing of education on the future of Ireland. Dublin: John F. Fowler, 1868. NL82.22. "Reprinted from the Irish Ecclesiastical Record of August and September, 1868."

WORKS BY UNIDENTIFIED AUTHORS

1862. Anon. The alleged "Nunnery Scandal" at Birmingham;

correspondence relating thereto, and refutation of the slander.
N.l., n.p., n.d. C20.3. Contains press accounts and letters
from the perpetrator of the scandal, Thomas Gutteridge, and
W. B. Ullathorne, E. E. Estcourt, and John Poncia.

1863. Anon. Recent secessions and corporate re-union: a letter to
an Anglican friend. London: Burns, Oates, 1868. C3.7.

1864. An Undergraduate Churchman, pseud. Mr. Goldwin Smith and "The
Clerical Reaction." Oxford: W. R. Bowden, n.d. NL26.21. A
letter on the state of Oxford and Cambridge Universities.

1869

1865. Bedford, Henry. Vesuvius in 1868, a lecture delivered before
the Literary, Historical, and Asthetical [sic] Society of the
Catholic University of Ireland, on December 9th, 1868. Dublin:
William B. Kelly, 1869. NL18.11. I.

1866. Christie, Albany J. Union with Rome; five afternoon lectures
preached in the Church of the Immaculate Conception, Farm
Street. London: Burns, Oates, 1869. C3.3. Inscribed by
Christie, a Jesuit: "J. H. N. Not for its value but for
'auld lang syne' in affectionate remembrance, A. J. C."
Duplicate copy: NL19.10.

1867. Cobb, Gerard Francis. A few words on reunion and the coming
council at Rome. London: G. J. Palmer, 1869. CV8.4.

1868. Cobb, Gerard Francis. "Separation," not "schism"; a plea for
the position of Anglican reunionists. London: G. J. Palmer,
1869. C3.4. I. A sequel to 1867.

1869. Dillon, William. Inaugural address delivered before the
Literary, Historical, & Æsthetical Society of the Catholic
University of Ireland. Dublin: Browne & Nolan, 1869. NL20.5.

1870. [Döllinger, Johann Joseph Ignaz von, et al.] Janus, pseud.
The Pope and the Council. London: Rivingtons, 1869. CV3.1.
See L.D., XXV, 19, 47-48.

1871. Feilding, Rudolph William Basil, Earl of Denbigh. [No title.]
Newnham Paddox: n.p., 1869. NL20.2. A printed letter, dated
25 Oct. 1869, concerning a controversy between Fr. Robert
Rodolph Suffield and David Urquhart, on the morality of war.
See 1892.

1872. Gerdil, Giacinto Sigismondo. Brief exposition of the origin,
progress, and marks of the true religion, from the creation of
the world. London: Longmans, Green, Reader, and Dyer, 1869.
C19.4. Translated by Edmond William O'Mahony. See Idea, pp.
7-8, and Ian T. Ker's note, pp. 576-77 (which refers to L.D.,
XXIII, 77).

1873. Gill, Henry Galloway. Plain reasons why I submitted to the
Catholic Church. London: R. Washbourne, 1869. C6.14.

1874. Ingleby, C. M. An introduction to metaphysic; in two books.
London: n.p., 1869. C1.3. Contains only Division II of Book

II; earlier parts were published in 1864.

1875. Irons, William Josiah. Analysis of human responsibility; being three papers read before the Victoria Institute, or Philosophical Society of Great Britain, on February 1st, March 1st, and June 7th, 1869. London: Robert Hardwicke, n.d. Cl.2.

1876. Jenkins, Robert Charles. A letter respectfully addressed to His Holiness Pope Pius IX., in reply to his appeal to the members of the Reformed Churches. Folkestone: J. English, 1869. CV8.5. I. Privately printed.

1877. Jenkins, Robert Charles. What do the Popes say on their alleged infallibility? A letter respectfully addressed to the Most Reverend Archbishop Manning, D.D. London: Winter, 1869. Cl0.6. I. See 2036 and 1961. Duplicate copy: CV4.6.

1878. Lee, Frederick George. The "sour grapes" of dis-union; a sermon preached in substance at All Saints Church, Lambeth, after the first evensong of the Feast of the Nativity of Our Blessed Lady, 1869, being the twelfth anniversary of the foundation of the Association for the Promotion of the Unity of Christendom. NL22.34. I.

1879. M'Corry, John Stewart. Cardinal Beaton, George Wishart, and John Knox: a review. London: Burns, Oates, 1869. C16.3. A Catholic account of the Reformation in Scotland.

1880. Manning, Henry Edward. The Œcumenical Council and the infallibility of the Roman pontiff: a pastoral letter to the clergy. London: Longmans, Green, and Co., 1869. CV5.5. S.

1881. Maret, Henri Louis Charles. Du concile général et de la paix religieuse; première partie: la constitution de l'Église, la périodicité des conciles généraux; mémoire soumis au prochain concile œcuménique du Vatican, vol. I. Paris: Henri Plon, 1869. CV11.1. I.

1882. Maret, Henri Louis Charles. Du concile général et de la paix religieuse; première partie: la constitution de l'Église et la périodicité des conciles généraux; mémoire soumis au prochain concile œcumenique du Vatican, vol. II. Paris: Henri Plon, 1869. CV12.1.

1883. Melly, George. The uneducated children in our large towns; a speech by George Melly, M.P., House of Commons, 12th March, 1869. N.l., Nichols and Sons, 1869. NL23.19.

1884. Monsell, William. Address of Right Hon. Wm. Monsell, M.P. vice-president, at the annual meeting of the Statistical and Social Inquiry Society of Ireland, 22nd January, 1869. [Dublin: R. D. Webb and Son,] n.d. NL23.9. Sent to N.

1885. Newman, Francis William. James and Paul; a tract. Mount Pleasant: Thomas Scott, 1869. NL81.8. Sent by the publisher.

1886. Newman, Francis William. Professor F. W. Newman on vegetarianism; Manchester, October 14th, 1868; [reprinted from the Dietetic Reformer of January, 1869.] Cl3.12. A publication of the Vegetarian Society.

1887. O'Brien, Henry. Endowment of the Irish Catholic, the Anglo-
      Catholic, and the Presbyterian churches in Ireland: a letter
      to the members of the houses of Parliament on Mr. Gladstone's
      Irish Church Bill. Dublin: Hodges, Smith and Foster, 1869.
      NL81.13.

1888. Renouf, Peter Le Page. The case of Pope Honorius reconsidered
      with reference to recent apologies. London: Longmans, Green,
      Reader, and Dyer, 1869. CV8.1. M. S. Cf. 1852.

1889. Ryder, Henry Ignatius Dudley. A critique upon Mr. Ffoulkes'
      "Letter." London: Longmans, Green, 1869. C10.15. M. S*.
      See 1837.

1890. St. Ignatius College, Galway. Galway academical papers: pub-
      lished for St. Ignatius College, Galway; part I: the public
      academy of Christmas, 1868, on the spirit of a language. Dub-
      lin: W. B. Kelly, 1869. NL21.9.

1891. St. Ignatius College, Galway. Galway academical papers: pub-
      lished for St. Ignatius College, Galway; part II: the public
      academy of Shrovetide, 1869, on the oratory of Demosthenes.
      Dublin: W. B. Kelly, 1869. NL21.10.

1892. Urquhart, David. Effect on the world of the restoration of the
      canon law; being the vindication of the Catholic Church against
      a priest. London: Diplomatic Review Office, 1869. C16.1.
      See 1871.

1893. [Urquhart, David.] Explication de L'Appel d'un Protestant au
      Pape. Geneva: Vve. Auguste Garin, 1869. CV8.6. A sequel to
      Urquhart's L'Appel d'un Protestant au Pape.

1894. Valroger, H. de. Petits traités sur l'accord des sciences et
      de la religion; l'age du monde et de l'homme d'après la Bible
      et l'Église. Paris: E. De Soye, n.d. NL27.1. I.

1895. Ward, William George. De infallibilitatis extensione; theses
      quasdam et quæstiones theologorum judicio. London: Burns,
      Oates, 1869. C14.13. Inscribed "H I D Ryder in dono
      auctoris." Extensive marginalia by Ryder.

1896. Weninger, Francis Xavier. On the apostolical and infallible
      authority of the Pope, when teaching the faithful, and on his
      relation to a general council. New York: D. & J. Sadlier,
      1869. CV2.1.

1897. Woodlock, Bartholomew. Catholic University of Ireland;
      religion in education; inaugural discourse at the commencement
      of the academical session, 1869-70, by the Very Rev. Monsignor
      Woodlock, D.D., rector, etc., etc., October, 1869. Dublin:
      Browne & Nolan, 1869. NL82.24. I.

1898. Woodlock, Bartholomew. Memorandum on university education in
      Ireland. N.1., n.p., n.d. NL82.23. Memorandum on university
      education.

WORKS BY UNIDENTIFIED AUTHORS

1899. Anon. Der evangelische Ober-Kirchenrath in Berlin und das
      Concil. Freiburg (Breisgau): Herder'sche Verlagshandlung,

1869. C23.12.

1900. Anon. Is it opportune to define the infallibility of the Pope?
Memorandum addressed to the bishops of Germany; respectfully
offered in translation to the bishops of the United Kingdom
and its colonies and to the bishops of the United States.
[London: Spottiswoode,] n.d. CV9.1. Title-page is signed
"J H Newman October 1869."

1901. Anon. Sermon preached in the chapel of Grace Dieu Manor,
October 22, 1869. N.l., n.p., n.d. NL26.17. The funeral
sermon of Osmund Charles de Lisle.

1902. Anon. Thoughts on some questions of the day. London: Longmans, Green, 1869. C6.16. Criticizes Anglican "ritualism,"
disputes the validity of Anglican orders, and advocates the
disestablishment of the Church of Ireland.

1870

1903. Bache, Samuel. To the members of the congregation of the
Church of the Messiah, Broad Street, Birmingham. N.l., n.p.,
n.d. NL18.3. I. With an additional personal note to N. On
miracles.

1904. Bedford, Henry. Douglas Jerrold; a lecture delivered before
the Literary, Historical, and Æsthetical Society of the Catholic University of Ireland, March 31, 1870. Roehampton: n.p.,
1870. NL18.7. I.

1905. Bianchini, Antonio. De vita V. D. S. I. Iuvenalis Ancina
Salutiarum episcopi e sodalibus Philippianis commentarius.
Rome: Typis S. Congreg. de Propaganda Fide, 1870. Cl.10.

1906. Brown, Thomas Joseph. A pastoral letter addressed to the
clergy and laity of the diocese of Newport and Menevia. N.l.,
n.p., 1870. CV5.6. Attached is a copy of Brown's letter to
the editor of the Saturday Review, dated 18 Oct., 1870.

1907. Case, George. The Vatican Council and a duty of Catholics in
regard to it; a sermon preached on Whit-Sunday 1870. London:
Longmans, Green, 1870. Cl4.15. Case castigates those ultramontanes who were attacking opponents of a definition of papal
infallibility by the Vatican Council. This sermon is ob-
viously influenced by N's reference to the "agressive insolent
faction" of ultramontanes in his letter of 28 January 1870
to Ullathorne, which was public knowledge by mid-March. See
L.D., XXV, 19, 54-55.

1908. Dalgairns, John Bernard Dobrée. On the theory of the human
soul. C9.14. S. Lacks title-page. Reprint of article in
Contemporary Review, 16 (December 1870), 16-43.

1909. De Hefele, Karl Joseph. Causa Honorii Papae. Naples: de
Angelis, 1870. CV5.2. M. S.

1910. [Döllinger, Johann Joseph Ignaz von.] Quirinus, pseud.
Letters from Rome on the Council. London: Rivingtons, 1870.

"Reprinted from the [Augsburg] Allgemeine Zeitung."

1911. Dupanloup, Félix Antoine Philibert. Réponse de Mgr. l'Évêque d'Orléans à Monseigneur Dechamps, Archevêque de Malines. Paris: Charles Douniol, 1870. C23.9. A public reply to a letter from Victoire Auguste Isidore Dechamps that had been published in Belgian, French, and Italian newspapers on 10 December 1869, two days before the opening of the Vatican Council. Dupanloup argues that there are a number of reasons for not defining papal infallibility. Duplicate copy: CV9.2.

1912. Field, Horace. Professor Huxley and the grace of God. London: James Burns, 1870. C1.6. I.

1913. Friedrich, Johann, ed. Documenta ad illustrandum Concilium Vaticanum anni 1870; I: Abtheilung. Nordlingen: C. H. Beck'- sche Buchhandlung, 1871. CV10.1.

1914. Gaillard, Léopold de. Mort et funérailles de M. de Montalembert. Paris: Charles Douniol, 1870. C24.8. "Extrait du Correspondant du 25 mars."

1915. Gallwey, Peter. St. Joseph and the Vatican Council; the substance of a sermon preached at the opening of St. Joseph's Chapel, Roehampton, March 19, 1870. London: Burns, Oates, 1870. CV8.3.

1916. Gerlache, Eugenius de. The last days of the Papal army. Birmingham: D. Kelly, 1870. NL21.12. Anon. trans. Gerlache was chaplain to the Papal Zouaves.

1917. Gordon, Alexander. Ancient and modern Muggletonians: a paper read before the Liverpool Literary and Philosophical Society, April 4th, 1870. N.l., n.p., n.d. C16.12. See 1918.

1918. Gordon, Alexander. The origin of the Muggletonians. C16.13. D? Lacks title-page. A lively account of the sect founded by Lodowicke Muggleton in the seventeenth century. See 1917.

1919. Gordon, Alexander. Our spiritual calling: a sermon, preached before the Provincial Assembly of Presbyterian and Unitarian ministers and congregations of Lancashire and Cheshire, at their annual meeting in Hyde Chapel, Gee Cross, on Thursday, June 16, 1870. London: Edward T. Whitfield, 1870. C16.10. Partly a history of Unitarianism in England.

1920. Gratry, Auguste Joseph Alphonse. Mgr. l'Évêque d'Orléans et Mgr. l'Archevêque de Malines; première lettre à Mgr. Deschamps [sic]. 6th ed. Paris: Charles Douniol, 1870. CV4.1. See L.D., XXV, 47.

1921. Gratry, Auguste Joseph Alphonse. Mgr. l'Évêque d'Orléans et Mgr. l'Archevêque de Malines; deuxième lettre à Mgr. Dechamps. 2nd ed. Paris: Charles Douniol, 1870. CV4.2.

1922. Gratry, Auguste Joseph Alphonse. Mgr. l'Évêque d'Orléans et Mgr. l'Archevêque de Malines; troisième lettre à Mgr. Dechamps. 2nd ed. Paris: Charles Douniol, 1970. CV4.3.

1923. Gratry, Auguste Joseph Alphonse. Mgr. the Bishop of Orleans, and Mgr. the Archbishop of Malines; first letter to Monseigneur Dechamps, by A. Gratry, prêtre [sic] de l'Oratoire,

membre de l'Académie Française; translated from the French by
Thomas John Bailey, B. A., priest of the Church of England.
London: J. T. Hayes, n.d. NL21.14. Translation of 1920.

1924. Gratry, Auguste Joseph Alphonse. Quatrième lettre. 2nd ed.
Paris: Charles Douniol, 1870. CV4.4.

1925. Guéranger, Prosper. De la monarchie pontificale à propos du
livre de Mgr. l'Évêque de Sura. Paris: Victor Palmé, 1870.
CV7.1. A response to 1881 and 1882.

1926. Guéranger, Propser. Défense de l'Église romaine contre les
accusations du R. P. Gratry. Paris: Victor Palmé, 1870.
CV7.2. A reply to 1920.

1927. Guéranger, Prosper. Deuxième défense de l'Église romaine
contre les accusations du R. P. Gratry. Paris: Victor Palmé,
1870. CV7.3. A reply to 1921.

1928. Hart, W. H. A register of the lands held by Catholics and
nonjurors in the County of Kent in the reign of King George I.
London: John Russell Smith, 1870. NL22.6.

1929. [Hugon, Jean.] Ce qui se passe au Concile. Paris: Henri Plon,
1870. CV6.1. Title-page is signed "T. A. Pope." One correction in pencil.

1930. Ingleby, Clement Mansfield. Some account of an Italian miracle play of the sixteenth century, on the legend of St.
Cecilia; [from the Transactions of the Royal Society of Literature, Vol. IX, new series.]; (read December 19, 1866). N.l.,
n.p., n.d. C7.7.

1931. Jenkins, Robert Charles. Christian Stramburger, or the art-
ist's grave, a relic of the Old Gottesacker in Leipzig. Canterbury: A. Ginder, 1870. NL22.25. I. A series of poems.

1932. Jenkins, Robert Charles. Hymns. Canterbury: A. Ginder, 1870.
NL22.23. I.

1933. Kenrick, Peter Richard. Concio Petri Ricardi Kenrick, Archi-
episcopi S. Ludovici in Statibus Foederatis Americae septen-
trionalis, in Concilio Vaticano; habenda at non habita.
Naples: de Angelis, 1870. CV5.4. M.

1934. [Kenrick, Peter Richard.] De pontificia infallibilitate qualis
in Concilio Vaticano definienda proponitur; dissertatio
theologica. Naples: de Angelis, 1870. CV5.3. I.

1935. Keogh, Edward Stephen. A few speciments of "scientific history" from "Janus." London: Longmans, Green, 1870. C10.8.
M*. Keogh was of the London Oratory. This is a response to
1870. See L.D., XXV, 47-48.

1936. [Kleutgen, Joseph.] De Romani Pontificis suprema potestate
docendi; disputatio theologica. Naples: Vincentii Manfredi,
1870. CV5.7. M. S. The author is identified by N on title-
page.

1937. Littledale, Richard Frederick. Pharisaic proselytism: a for-
gotten chapter of early Church history. London: J. T. Hayes,
1870. C8.7. Inscribed, but not acknowledged by N, in con-
trast to Littledale's earlier Unity and the Rescript (see 1722),

for the gift of which N responded with guarded thanks (see
L.D., XXI, 349-50). N's eventual response was perhaps the
sending of a copy of D.A.: see L.D., XXVI, 12, 16.

1938. Martet, S. P. L'ordre des temps divisés d'après l'hébreu et
la Vulgate en sept époques principales depuis Adam jusqu'à la
mort de Notre Seigneur, fixée à l'an 29 de l'ère nouvelle;
lettre de M. l'abbé S. P. Martet à M. Henri de Maguelonne,
rédacteur en chef de la correspondence de Rome. Rome:
Imprimerie de la Chambre Apostolique, 1870. NL23.14.

1939. Mossman, Thomas Wimberley. The primacy of S. Peter: a translation of Cornelius à Lapide, upon S. Matthew XVI.17-19, &
S. John XXI.15-17; with a preface. London: Bull, Simmons,
n.d. C6.11.

1940. Parker, John Henry. Historical photographs; a catalogue of
upwards of eighteen hundred photographs of the antiquities of
Rome, with the dates, historical or approximative, and an index. Oxford: n.p., 1870. C7.3.

1941. Pretyman, John Radclyffe. What is the use of infant baptism?
London: Hamilton, 1870. C16.4. A view of infant baptism as a
"Romish error."

1942. [Rauscher, Josef Othmar.] Observationes quaedam de infallibilitatis Ecclesiae subjecto. Naples: Typographi Sirenae, 1870.
CV9.3. M. S. The author, the Archbishop of Vienna, is identified by N on title-page.

1943. Russell, Charles William. The Irish and Anglo-Irish in the
sixteenth century, with a fac simile of an ancient Irish deed:
two papers read before the Royal Irish Academy, May 24th, and
June 14th, 1869. Dublin: University Press, 1870. NL26.7.

1944. [Schwarzenburg, Friedrich, Cardinal Prince von.] De Summi
Pontificis infallibilitate personali. Naples: de Angelis,
1870. CV5.1. M. S. The author is identified by N on title-
page.

1945. Todd, William Gowan. The kingly office of the Church; a sermon. London: Longmans, Green, 1870. C13.20. Defending the
Temporal Power of the papacy.

1946. Vance, Alexander. Hellenica sacra; Scripture as divested of
Jewish incrustation. 2nd ed. corrected and enlarged. London
and Dublin: Moffat, 1870. C16.8. This "edition" is only a
new introduction to the 1st edition of Hellencia Sacra. Vance
criticizes existing translations of the Bible and calls for a
new translation that will "re-distribute" the Old Testament
Scriptures.

1947. Walker, G. P. Scriptural view of baptism and other religious
observances. London: Simpkin, Marshall, 1870. C16.5.

WORKS BY UNIDENTIFIED AUTHORS

1948. Anon. An appeal to the people of England, on the recognition
and superintendence of prostitution by government, by an
English mother. 2nd ed. Nottingham: Frederick Banks, n.d.

C19.9. Written against the Association for Promoting the Extension of the Contagious Diseases Act to the Civil Population, and against the proposed Sanitary Act.

1949. Anon. Are the Anglican orders valid? N.l., n.p., n.d. C16.2. Against the validity of Anglican orders.

1950. Anon. De infallibilitatis R. Pontificis definitione; synopsis. Rome: Petrus H. F. Marietti, 1870. CV4.5. On title-page N has written, "By an Ex-Jesuit."

1951. Anon. La dernière heure du Concile. Paris: Dentu, 1870. CV6.2. Title-page is signed "T. A. Pope."

1952. Anon. Is it opportune to define the infallibility of the Pope? Memorandum addressed to the bishops of Germany; respectfully offered in translation to the bishops of the United Kingdom and its colonies and to the bishops of the United States. N.l., n.p., n.d. C23.8. An argument against defining Papal infallibility.

1953. Anon. The pontifical decrees against the motion of the earth, considered in their bearing on the theory of advanced ultramontanism. 2nd ed. London: Longmans, Green, Reader, and Dyer, 1870. C5.9. Against W. G. Ward's Authority of Doctrinal Decisions (1866).

1954. An English Catholic, pseud. Papal infallibility and persecution; Papal infallibility and usury. London: Macmillan and Co., 1870. CV8.2. M. S.

1871

1955. Calenzio, Generoso. Metropolitanae Ecclesiae Neapolitanae provisiones consistoriales a saeculo XV ad XIX ex authenticis documentis in lucem editae a Generoso Calentio Neapolitano Romani Oratorii presbytero; accedit inedita nota archiepiscopatuum et episcopatuum regni Neapolitani cum maioribus et minoribus beneficiis cuiuscumque dioecesis. Rome: Guerra et Mirri, 1878. NL79.12. Calenzio was a member of the Roman Oratory.

1956. Defourny. L'armée de Mac-Mahon et la bataille de Beaumont (en Argonne); lettres à madame Urquhart sur la guerre et la situation présente. Brussels: Devaux, 1871. C13.8. Defourny was a priest in Beaumont-en-Argonne. A report from the front on a battle in the Franco-Prussian War.

1957. Döllinger, Johann Joseph Ignaz von, and Father Hyacinthe (Charles Loyson). Déclarations de M. le professeur Döllinger et du R. P. Hyacinthe; publiées avec l'autorisation des auteurs. Paris: E. Dentu, 1871. C23.10. The response of Döllinger and others to the "new doctrine" of papal infallibility and to their excommunication for opposing it. In a section entitled "Ma position et ma conscience," Hyacinthe, a Discalced Carmelite, gives his reasons for having left his order and for refusing to accept the Vatican Decrees. Cf.

L.D., XXIV, 346-47; XXV, 235; XXVI, 120.

1958. Dupanloup, Félix Antoine Philibert. Lettre de M. l'Évêque
d'Orléans à M. Gambetta. [Orléans: Ernest Colas,] n.d.
C6.3. Lacks title-page. A reply to Léon Gambetta's anti-
clerical speech at Saint-Quentin on 16 Nov. 1871. See Guy
Chapman, The Third Republic of France: The First Phase 1871-
1894 (London: Macmillan, 1962), p. 36; and F. Lagrange, Life
of Monseigneur Dupanloup, Bishop of Orleans, trans. Lady Herbert (London: Chapman and Hall, 1885), II, 410.

1959. Friedrich, Johann, ed. Documenta ad illustrandum Concilium
Vaticanum anni 1870; II. Abtheilung. Nordlingen: C. H.
Beck'sche Buchhandlung, 1871. CV10.2.

1960. H[arper,] T[homas Norton]. Dr. Newman's Essay in Aid of a
Grammar of Assent. N.l., n.p., n.d. C17.14. A separatum
(pp. 129-55) from Harper's Difficulties Touching Certain Philosophical Theories Propounded in Dr. Newman's Grammar of Assent
(privately printed, 1871?): see Edmund F. Sutcliffe, Bibliography of the English Province of the Society of Jesus, 1773-
1953 (Roehampton and London: Manresa Press, 1957), pp. 79-80.
Cf. 1970.

1961. Jenkins, Robert Charles. Weak links in the chain of papal
infallibility; a letter to the Venerable John Sinclair, M.A.,
Archdeacon of Middlesex and Vicar of Kensington. London:
Winter, 1871. C10.7. See 2036 and 1877.

1962. La Serre, Henri. Le barde à la France de 1871. Versailles:
Beau, 1871. NL80.19. A poem dedicated to N and prefaced by
one of his letters: see L.D., XXV, 337.

1963. Littledale, Richard Frederick. The secular studies of the
clergy. C22.5. "Reprinted from the 'Contemporary Review,'
December, 1871." I. Littledale predicts that the Church of
England will be disestablished and asserts that the public
schools and universities have made "athletics and physical
training the main subject of study, while science and literature are relegated to the background . . . ." He then argues
the importance of a liberal education for the clergy, and he
points out the evils of a system of seminaries that would turn
out ecclesiastical specialists.

1964. Moriarty, David. Pastoral letter of the Bishop of Kerry for
the Lent of 1871. Dublin: John F. Fowler, 1871. NL22.29. S.
On the Vatican Council.

1965. Moriarty, James J. The Bible and the Catholic Church; a lec-
ture delivered by the Rev. James J. Moriarty, A.M., in the
Church of the Immaculate Conception, New Lebanon, N.Y.
Albany, New York: Van Benthuysen, 1871. NL80.28. I.

1966. Nicholson, T. Cooke. The Catholic churches and chapels of
Newcastle-upon-Tyne, being an historical sketch from the sub-
version of the ancient faith in the sixteenth century down to
the present period, with a descriptive account of the Cathedral Church of St. Mary. Newcastle-upon-Tyne: Henry Savage,
1871. NL19.18. I.

1967. Paley, Frederick Apthorp. Religious tests and national universities. London: Williams and Norgate, 1871. NL25.25.

1968. Perraud, Adolphe, and Félix Antoine Philibert Dupanloup. Les prisonniers de guerre: discours prononcé à Bruxelles, en l'église de Sainte-Gudule, le lundi 26 décembre 1870, par le R. P. Adolphe Perraud, prêtre de l'Oratoire et professeur à la Sorbonne, Aumônier des Ambulances internationales, membre de la Société Internationale de Secours pour les Prisonniers de Guerre; suivi d'une lettre adressée à l'auteur par Mgr l'Évêque d'Orléans. Brussels: H. Goemaere, 1871. C13.5.

1969. Shipley, Orby. Secular judgments in spiritual matters: considered in relation to some recent events. London: Joseph Masters, 1871. C15.4. An Anglo-Catholic protest against the authority of the Judicial Committee of the Privy Council over ecclesiastical matters: "The Gorham judgment, the Liddell prosecution, the decisions in the case of the Essays and Reviews, the S. Alban's suit . . . have materially altered the standing point of the great High Church school of thought, whether represented by the originators of the Oxford Movement, or their lineal successors in the Catholic Revival" (p. 6).

1970. Smith, Sydney Fenn. Essay on causation; in reference to the "Grammar of Assent." N.l., n.p., n.d. C17.15. Argues that N's "view on causality involves scepticism as a necessary consequence." A separatum bound with 1960. Smith's essay was originally the final part (pp. 159-76) of T. N. Harper's Difficulties . . . , described under 1960.

1971. Stapleton, Augustus Granville. The French case, truly stated. London: Edward Stanford, 1871. C13.6. Denies French responsibility for the Franco-Prussian war.

1972. Urquhart, David. Désolation de la Chrétienté par la substitution de la familiarité à la politesse; (éducation, religion, guerre). London: Bureau de la Revue Diplomatique, 1871. C10.1. Inscribed "With Mr. Monteiths respectful Compliments."

WORKS BY UNIDENTIFIED AUTHORS

1973. Anon. The apparition of the Blessed Virgin at Pontmain, in the Diocese of Laval, France, on January 17th, 1871; translated from the French. Deal: Deveson, n.d. C6.2. Translated by the Convent of Deal.

1974. Anon. Are the Anglican orders valid? N.l., n.p., n.d. D?

1975. Anon. Wo ist Europa's Zukunft? Freiburg (Breisgau): Herder'sche Verlagshandlung, 1871. C23.13.

1872

1976. Addis, William Edward. Anglican misrepresentations: a reply to "Roman Misquotations." London: Burns and Oates, 1872. C10.10. A reply to 1998. See L.D., XXVI, 150-51.

1977. Addis, William Edward. Anglicanism and the Fathers, with reference to No. 4 of the "English Church Defence Tracts." London: Burns and Oates, 1872. C10.12. Cf. 1990, 1976, 1989.

1978. Brownlow, W. R. Bernard. The Church of England and its defenders; a letter to Anglican friends who frequent St. John's, Torquay. Torquay: Croydon, 1872. NL18.27. I. See 1999.

1979. Bullerwell, William T., and T. Cooke Nicholson. The Catholic Church: a controversial correspondence on doctrinal and historical subjects, between Mr. W. T. Bullerwell and Mr. T. C. Nicholson. Newcastle-upon-Tyne: H. Savage, n.d. C15.14. An exchange between a High Church Anglican (Bullerwell) and a former Anglican.

1980. Buroni, Giuseppe. Di un equivoco circa l'infallibilità pontificia, con due appendici; relazione d'una conferenza teologica sopra i'infallibilità del Pontefice (tenuta il 1° maggio 1854); discorso per la festa della Immacolata Concezione di Maria sopra lo sviluppo de' dogmi nella Chiesa Cattolica (recitato li 8 dicembre 1862). Turin: Stamperia della Società, L'Unione Tipografico-Editrice Torinese, 1872. C22.2. The last discourse deals with the development of the doctrine of the Immaculate Conception. The main part of the pamphlet is a reply to an article on the Vatican Council's decree on Papal infallibility in Civiltà Cattolica, 6 April 1872, p. 87.

1981. Caldicott, John William. Religious education and religious freedom, from a Churchman's point of view; a letter addressed to the Right Hon. W. E. Gladstone, M.P., First Lord of Her Majesty's Treasury. Birmingham: Cornish Brothers, 1872. C15.9. Discusses the Elementary Education Act of 1870.

1982. Clutton, Henry. A narrative and correspondence relating to the restoration of All Souls College chapel, Oxford. Printed for private circulation, May 18, 1872. C7.1. I. Contains letters of J. W. Nutt.

1983. Dalton, John. Sermon delivered at the funeral of the Very Rev. Provost Husenbeth, D.D., V. G., at St. Walstan's Chapel, Cossey, on the 6th of November, 1872. London: Burns and Oates, n.d. NL20.1. I.

1984. Duplanloup, Félix Antoine Philibert. Les apologistes du Christianisme au XVIIe siècle. N.l., n.p., n.d. C19.2. This is a prefatory letter recommending a series of books to be published as antidotes to atheism.

1985. [Jenkins, Robert Charles.] A Country Clergyman, pseud. The new ducal theology; a letter to His Grace the Duke of Somerset, K.G., from a country clergyman. London: Winter, 1872. C17.5. I. A reply to Christian Theology and Modern Scepticism (1872) by Edward Adolphus Seymour, 12th Duke of Somerset.

1986. Jones, James. The Creed of St. Athanasius: Charlemagne and Mr. Ffoulkes. London: Burns and Oates, 1872. C18.4. A Catholic response to E. S. Ffoulkes' The Athanasian Creed.

1987. Laveleye, Émile de. On the causes of war, and the means of reducing their number. London: Peace Society, 1872. C13.1. "Reprinted by Permission from 'The Cobden Club Essays,' Second Series, 1871-72."

1988. Lee, Frederick George. The abolition and rejection of the Athanasian Creed: a letter to His Grace, Archibald Campbell, Lord Archbishop of Canterbury, Primate of all England and Metropolitan. London: John Hodges, 1872. C15.5. Lee defends the Athanasian Creed. He also calls attention to Campbell's role in the Tract 90 controversy in 1841, by referring to "the action which, as one of the celebrated Four Tutors, your grace took at Oxford against Mr. Newman . . .--action that eventually lost the Church of England a very sensitive and high-minded man, the most masterly, profound, and accomplished theological writer whom our communion has known for many a generation . . ." (p. 9).

1989. [Liddon, Henry Parry, and William Bright.] More about Roman misquotations: with reference to a pamphlet entitled 'Anglican Misrepresentations.' London: Rivingtons, 1872. C10.11. M. S. English Church Defence Tracts, No. 4. Cf. 1990, 1976, and 1977.

1990. [Liddon, Henry Parry, and William Bright.] Roman misquotations. London: Rivingtons, 1872. C10.9. English Church Defence Tracts, No. 1. An Anglican tract disputing Papal infallibility; primarily against F. X. Weninger. Cf. 1976. See L.D., XXVI, 150-51.

1991. Maskell, William. Protestant ritualists. London: James Toovey, 1872. C15.6. I. Accuses the "high-church or ritualist party" of "what, after all, is but bastard Romanism" (p. 4). Also criticizes the English Church Defence Tracts of H. P. Liddon and W. Bright. See 1990, 1989.

1992. Minton, Samuel. The harmony of Scripture on future punishment; or, the truths contained in the views of Origen and Augustine reconciled by the earlier doctrine of conditional immortality; an address, prepared at the request of a ruridecanal chapter. London: Elliot Stock, 1872. C15.11. "Reprinted, with additions, from The Rainbow.

1993. North American Review. A historic survey of international arbitration; (from the North American Review). London: Peace Society, n.d. C13.3 D?

1994. Perraud, Adolphe. Le P. Gratry; ses derniers jours, son testament spirituel. Paris: Charles Douniol, 1872. NL25.7. I.

1995. St. John, Ambrose. A sermon preached at the Catholic Church, Deal, Thursday, March 7, 1872, at the Mass of Requiem celebrated by His Lordship the Bishop of the diocese, for the repose of the soul of Miss Catherine Boys, late of The Orphanage, Deal. London: Burns and Oates, n.d. NL7.8. I.

WORK BY UNIDENTIFIED AUTHOR

1996. Anon. Authentic report of the immortal discussion that took
      place in Rome on the evenings of the 9th and 10th of February,
      1872, between Roman Catholic priests and Evangelical ministers
      regarding the coming of St. Peter to Rome; with three admirable
      engravings of the triumphant disputants, Sciarelli, Ribetti,
      and Gavazzi; accurately translated from the Italian. 2nd ed.
      Dublin: Italian Mission Office, n.d. C10.4. An unsigned
      letter of presentation to N attached.

1873

1997. Amherst, William J. Words spoken in the Chapel of the Ursu-
      lines of Jesus, St. Margaret's Convent, Edinburgh, on the 7th
      day of May, 1873, at the funeral of James Robert Hope Scott,
      Q.C. N.1., n.p., n.d. NL26.16. I.

1998. Blair, W. T. A lecture on ritualism. London: William Hunt,
      1873. C15.12. An Evangelical view, replying on Jacob's The
      Ecclesiastical Polity of the New Testament.

1999. Brownlow, W. R. Bernard. The Church of England and its de-
      fenders, a second letter to Anglican friends who frequent St.
      John's, Torquay; in reply to the Rev. J. W. Patterson, and
      Rev. J. Walter Moore. Torquay: Cockrem, 1873. NL18.28. I.
      A sequel to 1978.

2000. Coleridge, John Duke. Wordsworth. N.1., n.p., n.d. NL19.12.
      I. "A lecture delivered before the Literary Society of
      Exeter, in April 1873."

2001. Gladstone, William Ewart. Address delivered at the distribu-
      tion of prizes in the Liverpool Collegiate Institution, Decr.
      21, 1872. London: John Murray, 1873. C17.1. Some reflec-
      tions on education and religion.

2002. Harper, Thomas. Three lectures on Papal infallibility,
      preached in the Church of the Holy Name, Manchester, by the
      Rev. Thomas Harper, S.J., in reply to the Right Rev. James
      Fraser, D.D., Protestant Bishop of Manchester. Manchester:
      Thomas Walker, n.d. C14.7.

2003. Hoole, Charles H. St. Peter's visit to Rome. Oxford: J. Vin-
      cent, 1873. C10.5.

2004. Ingle, John. The Roman meeting house in the Mint; a letter
      to his parishioners. London: G. J. Palmer, n.d. C16.14.
      Inscribed "Revd. R. Wilkins From the Author." Ingle, rector
      of S. Olave, Exeter, had been accused of "imitating Rome"
      and was an Anglo-Catholic and evidently a ritualist. This is
      a fiercely anti-Roman Catholic pamphlet.

2005. Jenkins, Robert Charles, ed. The Bull of Pope Paul IV.
      against heretics, "Cum ex Apostolatûs Officio"; translated
      from the authentic Roman edition, 1559, with an introduction
      and notes. Folkstone: R. Goulden, n.d. NL99.3.

2006. Jenkins, Robert Charles. The extravagant of Pope Julius II,
      "On the Simoniacal Election of a Pope," "Cum tam divino quam

humano jure"; with extracts from the commentary thereupon of
Petrus Andreas Gammarus, auditor of the Rota, and vicar of
the Pope in the city of Rome (A.D. 1527); and a brief consideration of its results upon the modern Church of Rome. Folkstone: R. Goulden, n.d. NL99.1. I. About the Vatican Council and Papal infallibility.

2007. Lambert, George. A few particulars relative to the Hon. and
Rev. John ffrench, S. J., who died in Rome on the 31st day of
May, 1873. Dublin: Dollard, n.d. NL22.31.

2008. Maccoll, Malcolm. Papal infallibility and its limitations.
N.l., n.p., n.d. Cl4.6. "Reprinted from the 'Church Review.'"

2009. Pannilini, Giuseppe. The perils of the (so called) "devotion
of the Sacred Heart of Jesus," from the pastoral of Monsignore
Giuseppe Pannilini, Bishop of Chiusi and Picnza, and Count
Palatine of the Holy Roman Empire; published in the assembly
of bishops in the "Sala de Novissimi" of the Palazzo de' Pitti
in Florence, May 1787; translated by Robert C. Jenkins, M.A.,
Rector of Lyminge, Hon. Canon of Canterbury. Folkstone: J.
English, n.d. NL22.21. I. "Not published." A gift of the
translator.

2010. [Peace Society.] International arbitration and the improvement of international law; the debate in the House of Commons,
on Tuesday, July 8th, 1873, on the motion of Mr. Henry Richard
for an address to the Crown. London: Hodder & Stoughton,
n.d. C13.4.

2011. Roman Catholic Church, Province of Westminster. Pastoral
letter of the archbishops and bishops of the Province of
Westminster in provincial council assembled. N.l., n.p.,
1873. NL14.13.

2012. Sweetman, Walter. Some thoughts on free-will; to which is
added a short personal statement. Dublin: Hidges, Foster,
1873. NL82.13. The first part is a critique of J. S. Mill;
the second part is Sweetman's explanation of his conviction
for assault with a pistol. Marginalia, not by N. Duplicate
copy: C17.10.

2013. White, Thomas. Our great West: a lecture delivered under the
auspices of the Young Men's Christian Association of Christ
Church Cathedral, on the evening of the 27th February, 1873.
Montreal, n.p., 1873. C13.16.

2014. Young, Hugo J. Monastic and conventual institutions: their
legal position, property, and disabilities. London: Burns
and Oates, 1873. NL27.22.

WORK BY UNIDENTIFIED AUTHOR

2015. Anon. Apostolic lordship and the interior life; a narrative
of five years' communion with Catholic Apostolic Angels. N.l.,
n.p., 1873. C16.11. An anti-Irvingite pamphlet by a former
Irvingite converted to Catholicism.

1874

2016. Beresford Hope, Alexander James Beresford. The place and influence in the Church movement of Church congresses; a paper
read at Sion College, London, February 25, 1874. London:
Edward Stanford, 1874. C15.8.

2017. Brown, William Henry. The Babylonian captivity. 2nd ed.
London: Harrison and Sons, 1874. C17.8. Brown was a member
of the Society of Biblical Archæology.

2018. Capel, Thomas John. A reply to the Right Hon. W. E. Gladstone's 'Political Expostulation.' London: Longmans, Green,
1874. C12.3. "Reprinted, with additions, from 'The Weekly
Register and Catholic Standard.'" Capel makes use of Joseph
Fessler's The True and False Infallibility of the Popes, although he cannot have used Ambrose St. John's translation of
1875. On p. 11 Capel quotes from a letter of N to Samuel
Walshaw, priest of Sheffield, which was printed in the Sheffield Daily Telegraph of 11 April 1870. Capel mistakenly
describes the source as the Standard. N had originally included this passage, concerning his unwavering trust in the
Catholic Church and the Holy See, in his letter to the Globe
newspaper of 28 June 1862. See L.D., XX, 215-16.

2019. Clifford, William Joseph Hugh. A pastoral letter of William
Clifford, Bishop of Clifton, November 25th, 1874. Bristol:
Austin & Oates, 1874. C12.8. N has marked a passage on p.
19 in which Clifford states that before the decree on infallibility "the Pope had no right, in any way, to interfere, in
the civil government of England . . . ; so neither has he any
such right now." See L.D., XXVII, 172-73.

2020. Coleridge, Henry James. The abomination of desolation; a sermon, preached in the Church of the Immaculate Conception, Farm
Street, on the last Sunday after Pentecost, Nov. 23, 1874.
London: Burns and Oates, 1874. C23.14. A response to Gladstone's Expostulation, accusing Gladstone of misrepresentation
through mistranslation.

2021. Dupanloup, Félix Antoine Philibert, and Pope Pius IX. Letter
from the Right Reverend the Lord Bishop of Orleans to M.
Minghetti, Minister of Finance to King Victor Emmanuel, on the
spoliation of the Church at Rome and throughout Italy; together with the brief of the Pope to the Bishop of Orleans on
the occasion of this letter. London: Burns and Oates, 1874.
C18.1.

2022. Dupanloup, Félix Antoine Philibert, and Pope Pius IX. Lettre
de M. l'Évêque d'Orléans à M. Minghetti, Ministre des Finances
du Roi Victor-Emmanuel, sur la spoliation de l'Église à Rome
et en Italie. 6th ed. Paris: Ch. Douniol, 1874. C23.11.
The French edition of 2013, except that it also contains a
letter from Dupanloup to the editor of the newspaper France.

2023. Dykes, John Bacchus. Eucharistic truth and ritual; a letter
to the Right Reverend the Lord Bishop of Durham, occasioned
by His Lordship's reply to an address from certain laymen in

the diocese. London: Masters, 1874. C15.13. I. A High-Church view of the ritualist controversy and of the Public Worship Bill. The Bishop of Durham was Charles Baring.

2024. Gasquet, J. R. The madmen of the Greek theatre. Lewes: G. P. Bacon, 1874. C17.9. "Reprinted from the Journal of Mental Science."

2025. Gladstone, William Ewart. The Vatican decrees in their bearing on civil allegiance: a political expostulation. London: John Murray, 1874. C2.1. One minor marginal remark, in pencil.

2026. The Intellectual Repository and New Jerusalem Magazine. "The Lord's miracles illustrative rather than evidential." An article extracted by N from The Intellectual Repository and New Jerusalem Magazine of 1874 (pp. 4-12) and so labeled by N. C9.2.

2027. The Intellectual Repository and New Jerusalem Magazine. "The miracles recorded in the New Testament." A hostile review of Supernatural Religion: An Inquiry into the Reality of Divine Revelation, 3rd ed. (London: Longmans, 1874), reputedly by William Bouverie Pusey, the brother of E. B. Pusey. Like 2026 extracted by N from The Intellectual Repository and New Jerusalem Magazine of 1874 (pp. 555-65). C9.3.

2028. Monsell, William, Lord Emly. Address to the Statistical and Social Inquiry Society of Ireland, at the annual meeting for the inauguration of the twenty-eighth session, on Tuesday, the 24th November, 1874. N.l., n.p., n.d. NL20.10. I.

2029. Moriarty, James J. The Catholic Church in its relations to human progress; a lecture by the Rev. James J. Moriarty, A. M., Chatham Village, N. Y.; published for the benefit of the Church of the "Sacred Heart," to be erected in Philmont, N. Y. Albany, New York: Van Benthuysen, 1874. NL80.27. I.

2030. Newman, Francis William. Ancient sacrifice. London: Thomas Scott, 1874. NL81.5.

2031. Newman, Francis William. "And now abideth faith, hope, and charity"; a lay sermon, preached at St. George's Hall, Langham Place, May 3rd, 1874. N.l., n.p., n.d. NL24.9. Corrections in ink.

2032. Newman, Francis William. Comments on Herbert Spencer as a writer on religion. N.l., n.p., n.d. NL81.6.

2033. Newman, Francis William. The political side of the vaccination system; an essay read at the Birmingham Anti-Vaccination Conference, October 26th, 1874. Cheltenham: G. F. Poole, n.d. C13.11. A publication of the National Anti-Compulsory Vaccination League.

2034. O'Carroll, J. J. Clongweswood College Historical Debating Society; inaugural address: delivered at the opening of the academical session, 1874-5. Dublin: McGlashan & Gill, 1874. NL25.3. On rhetoric.

2035. O'Hagan, John. Queen's Bench: the Rev. Robert O'Keeffe <u>v.</u>

His Eminence Cardinal Cullen: speech of John O'Hagan, Esq.,
Q.C., summing up for defendant. Dublin: J. M. O'Toole & Son,
1874. C17.12. I. See L.D., XXVII, 28-29. See also 1838.

2036. O'Reilly, Edmund J. The relations of the Church to society.
C14.8. Extracted by N from The Irish Monthly, April 1874, pp.
219-26. On papal infallibility. P. 219 also contains a poem,
"Pastor Aeternus," by Aubrey De Vere.

2037. O[rnsby], R[obert.] On the correct treatment of ancient history. N.1., n.p., n.d. C7.14. I. "A Lecture delivered before the Catholic University of Ireland, on April 30, 1874."

2038. O[rnsby], R[obert.] The personal character of Homer, as
traced in his poetry. N.1., n.p., n.d. C7.15. "Delivered
before the Catholic University of Ireland on May 4, 1874."

2039. Oxford Union Society. A verbatim report of the speeches at
the banquet in the Corn Exchange, Oxford, on occasion of the
fiftieth anniversary of the Oxford Union Society, October 22nd,
1873; to which is prefixed a sketch of the history of the society. Oxford: T. Shrimpton and Son, 1874. C19.10. Contains speeches by A. C. Tait and J. D. Coleridge, among
others, and a brief remark by Matthew Arnold.

2040. [Redemptorist Fathers.] Vindiciarum Alphonsianarum; alterius
editionis præfatio apologetica; accedunt dissertatio de
auctoritate doctrinæ moralis S. Alphonsi et altera dissertatio
de morali systemate ejusdem s. doctoris. Paris: H. Casterman,
n.d. C21.1. Defenses of the moral theology of St. Alphonsus
Liguori.

2041. Ryan, Daniel. A reply to Mr. Gladstone's Expostulation. Dublin: McGlashan & Gill, 1874. C12.6. I. Ryan was a priest
and taught at St. Patrick's College, Thurles.

2042. Stewart, James. Socrates: a sketch. N.1., n.p., n.d. C7.13.
D? Stewart was of the Catholic University of Ireland. He
concludes this lecture by insisting on the necessity to
classical studies of "the guidance of the Catholic religion,
and in a Catholic University . . . ."

2043. Tondini de Quarenghi, Cesare. L'avenir de l'Église Russe;
études sur la question religieuse de Russie. Paris: Librairie
de la Société Bibliographique. C25.2. I.

2044. [Tondini de Quarenghi, Cesare, ed.] Duxovnyj reglament Petra
Pervago. Paris: Institut de la Société Bibliographique, 1874.
C25.4. The Russian version of 2045 but without the introduc-
tion and notes.

2045. Tondini de Quarenghi, Cesare, ed. Règlement ecclésiastique de
Pierre le Grand. Paris: Librairie de la Société Bibliographique, 1874. C25.3. I. Edited and translated from the Russian
by Tondini with a long introduction and notes. See 2044.

2046. Ullathorne, William Bernard. A pastoral letter to the faithful of the Diocese of Birmingham. [Birmingham], n.p., 1874.
C12.7. Partly a response to Gladstone. This letter, dated
17 Nov. and read on 22 Nov., almost prevented N from writing
the Letter to the Duke of Norfolk: see L.D., XXVII, 155-56.

See also 2089.

2047. Wagner, A. D. Christ or Caesar? A letter to the Most Reverend the Lord Archbishop of Canterbury. London: Rivingtons,
1874. C15.10. A High-Church protest to Archbishop A. C. Tait
against the authority of the Judicial Committee of the Privy
Council in ecclesiastical matters.

2048. Yeatman, John Pym. The history of the common law of Great
Britain and Gaul from the earliest period to the time of
English legal memory; part I. London: Stevens & Sons, 1874.
C19.5.

WORKS BY UNIDENTIFIED AUTHORS

2049. Anon. Convocation: as it is, and as it might be; a letter to
two friends. N.l., n.p., n.d. C15.7. "Printed for Private
Circulation." Calls for regular elections of Anglican bishops
and a wide toleration of various "liturgies." Signed by "One
who takes a Statesman's point of view."

2050. Anon. A letter to the Right Hon. W. E. Gladstone, M.P., by a
Scotch Catholic layman. London: William Ridgway, 1874.
C20.10. A response to Gladstone's Expostulation by a dis-
appointed admirer.

2051. Anon. The Liberal Party and the Catholics. London: Longmans,
Green, 1874. C20.5.

2052. Anon. The Mosaic cosmogony; a case of conscience. Oscott,
n.p., 1874. C17.6. Catholic views on Genesis and geology,
possibly by Charles Meynell. Cf. 2054. Duplicate copy:
NL23.8.

2053. Anon. Some remarks on modern free thought and scepticism;
and, the testimony of Scripture to the Atonement of Christ.
N.l., n.p., n.d. C17.11. Lacks title-page. The second part
of this pamphlet is a reprint of a tract published 30 years
earlier. The first "remarks" are a criticism of James Mill
and Matthew Arnold.

2054. Ignotus, pseud. Thoughts on spiritual ethnology. London:
Saml. Harris, 1874. C17.7. Argues that Genesis 2:7 is "the
record of how the original man of Genesis i . . . passed into
a higher form of existence." Cf. 2052.

2055. A Layman, pseud. Present position of the High Church party;
a few words. London: Rivingtons, 1874. NL24.6.

1875

2056. Bright, William. The Roman claims tested by antiquity; a
paper read before the Oxford branch of the E. C. U. in 1875.
London: English Church Union Office, n.d. NL18.22.

2057. Burgon, John William. Plea for the study of divinity in
Oxford. Oxford: James Parker, 1875. NL18.32. I.

2058. Clarke, Richard H. Mr. Gladstone and Maryland toleration.
New York: Catholic Publication Society, 1875. NL10.11. A
reply to Gladstone's Rome and the Newest Fashions in Religion
(1875).

2059. Cooke, Robert. Catholic memories of the Tower of London; first
series: I. Bishop Fisher; II. Sir Thomas More; being the substance of two lectures delivered at the temporary Church of
the English Martyrs, Tower Hill. London: Burns and Oates,
1875. NL19.13.

2060. Craven, Augustine. Deux incidents de la question Catholique
en Angleterre. Paris: Didier, 1875. NL19.20.

2061. Cullen, Paul. Letter of the Cardinal Archbishop of Dublin to
the Catholic clergy and laity of the diocese. [Dublin:
M'Glashan & Gill,] n.d. C12.5. Refers to the Letter to the
Duke of Norfolk and to "the venerable Dr. Newman, for many
years the great and pious and learned rector of the Catholic
University, whom Ireland will ever revere."

2062. Curry, John. Catholicity, liberty, allegiance: a disquisition
on Mr. Gladstone's "Expostulation"; written for the Bradford
Catholic Club. 2nd ed. London: Burns & Oates, 1875. C20.9.

2063. De Lisle, Ambrose Phillips. The Council of the Vatican in its
bearings on civil allegiance. N.l., n.p., n.d. C20.7. I.
From the Union Review (1875). A review of Gladstone's Expostulation (2025), William Clifford's Pastoral Letter (2019), and
Herbert's A Pastoral Letter on Submission to a Divine Teacher
Neither Disloyalty nor the Surrender of Mental and Moral Freedom (London: Burns and Oates, 1875). De Lisle concludes with
a brief review of N's Letter to the Duke of Norfolk, which had
just appeared.

2064. Feesler, Joseph. The true and the false infallibility of the
Popes; a controversial reply to Dr. Schulte. 2nd ed. revised
[of the English trans.]. London: Burns and Oates, 1875. C18.3.
Translated by Ambrose St. John.

2065. Foster, Balthazar. How we die in large towns; a lecture on
the comparative mortality of Birmingham and other large towns.
London: Statham & Co., "Public Health" Office, n.d. C13.10.
I.

2066. Gladstone, William Ewart, and Philip Schaff. The Vatican
decrees in their bearing on civil allegiance; a political
expostulation, by the Right Hon. W. E. Gladstone, M.P., to
which are added a history of the Vatican Council; together
with the Latin and English text of the Papal Syllabus and the
Vatican decrees, by the Rev. Philip Schaff, D.D., from his
forthcoming 'History of the Creeds of Christendom.' New York:
Harper & Brothers, 1875. C12.1. S.

2067. Gladstone, William Ewart. Vaticanism: an answer to replies
and reproofs. London: John Murray, 1875. C2.4. M*.

2068. Kavanagh, James. A reply to Mr. Gladstone's Vaticanism. Dublin: James Duffy and Sons, 1875. C22.6. N has noted that he
received this pamphlet from the author on 4 April 1875.

2069. Lee, Frederick George. Recent legislation for the Church of England, and its dangers: a letter to the Right Reverend the Lord Bishop of Winchester, D.D., Prelate of the Order of the Garter, &c. &c. &c. London: A. R. Mowbray, 1875. NL22.35. I. Opposing the Public Worship Regulation Bill.

2070. Manning, Henry Edward. "Dominus illuminatio mea:" a sermon preached at Oxford, Nov. 23, 1875. London: Longmans, Green, 1875. NL14.10. A controversial sermon preached at the opening of the Church of St. Aloysius.

2071. Manning, Henry Edward. The Vatican decrees in their bearing on civil allegiance. London: Longmans, Green, 1875. C2.3. With card "From the Author." Attached to original dust jacket, a short review of N's Letter to the Duke of Norfolk.

2072. Mélot, D. Des lettres pontificales et de la portée qu'elles ont dans la pensée du Saint Père; trois lettres à un jeune homme. Louvain: Veuve Charles Fonteyn, 1875. NL23.20. Letters on Papal infallibility.

2073. Meyrick, Frederick. Does Dr. Newman deserve Mr. Gladstone's praises, or not? London: William Wells Gardner, 1875. C20.11. Meyrick criticizes N bitterly for having abandoned his fellows in the Oxford Movement and inquires "whether [N] does not enjoy an undeserved reputation for candour and fairness as a controversialist." Meyrick levels specific charges at the Apologia and A Letter to the Rev. E. B. Pusey, D.D., on His Recent Eirenicon (1866; now in Diff., II). Meyrick considers Gladstone's Vaticanism to be a full refutation of the critics of his Expostulation.

2074. Moriarty, David, Robert Ffrench Whitehead, Aubrey De Vere, and Joseph Farrell. The laying of the stone: a sermon by the Most Rev. David Moriarty, D.D., Bishop of Kerry, with commemorative verses by the Very Rev. Robert Ffrench Whitehead, D.D., Aubrey De Vere, Esq., and Rev. Joseph Farrell, on occasion of laying the first stone of a new church, in St. Patrick's College, Maynooth, on Sunday, October 10th, 1875, the feast of the dedication of all the churches of Ireland. Dublin: McGlashan & Gill, 1875. C6.4. Contains a Latin hymn by Whitehead, "Sonnets on the Laying of the Foundation Stone of the New Church in St. Patrick's College, Maynooth" by De Vere, and "The Laying of the Stone" by Farrell.

2075. Nettleship, Henry. Suggestions introductory to a study of the Aeneid. Oxford: Claredon Press, 1875. NL24.7.

2076. Neville, Henry. A few comments on Mr. Gladstone's Expostulation. London: B. M. Pickering, 1875. NL10.9. I.

2077. Neville, Henry. A few comments on Mr. Gladstone's Expostulation; with some remarks on "Vaticanism." 2nd ed. London: B. M. Pickering, 1875. C12.2. I. Cf. 2067.

2078. Newman, Francis William. Re-organization of English institutions: a lecture by emeritus professor F. W. Newman; delivered in the Manchester Athenæum, on Friday, October 15, 1875. Manchester: John Heywood, n.d. NL81.4. Corrections in ink.

2079. Newman, John Henry. A letter addressed to His Grace the Duke of Norfolk on occasion of Mr. Gladstone's recent Expostulation. London: B. M. Pickering, 1875. C2.2.

2080. Overbeck, J. J. The Bonn conferences; impressions produced by their transactions. London: Trübner, 1875. C10.3. A criticism of Döllinger and a reply to a review in the Saturday Review.

2081. Pearson, Samuel. Conscience & the Church in their relations to Christ and Caesar; thoughts suggested by Dr. J. H. Newman's pamphlet on the Vatican Decrees. London: Hodder and Stoughton, 1875. C20.6. A respectful criticism, on religious grounds, of N's claims for the Catholic Church and the papacy in the Letter to the Duke of Norfolk. Pearson was a Congregational minister.

2082. Pugin, Augustus Welby. Church and state; or Christian liberty; an earnest address on the establishment of the hierarchy. London: Longman, Green, 1875. C20.4. I. A republication of A. W. Pugin's 1850 tract by his son, E. Welby Pugin, who thought it would provide an answer to Gladstone's Expostulation.

2083. Roman Catholic Church, Province of Westminster. Pastoral letter of the Cardinal Archbishop and Bishops of the Province of Westminster. London: n.p., 1875. NL14.14.

2084. Sandys, Richard Hill. In the beginning; remarks on certain modern views of the creation. London: Basil Montagu Pickering, 1875. NL26.12. I. See 2095.

2085. Seccombe, John T. Science, theism, and revelation, considered in relation to Mr. Mill's essays on nature, religion, & theism. London: Simpkin, Marshall, 1875. C18.2.

2086. Société Scientifique de Bruxelles. Séance inaugurale du 18 novembre 1875; (extrait du compte-rendu). Brussels: Alfred Vromant, 1875. C17.2.

2087. Tondini de Quarenghi, Cesare. Anglicanism, Old Catholicism, and the union of the Christian episcopal Churches; an essay on the religious questions of Russia. London: Basil Montagu Pickering, 1875. NL26.25. I.

2088. Tondini de Quarenghi, Cesare. Some documents concerning the association of prayers in honour of Mary Immaculate for the return of the Greek-Russian Church to Catholic unity; forming an appendix to "The Pope of Rome and the Popes of the Oriental Orthodox Church." London: R. Washbourne, 1875. NL26.25A. I.

2089. Ullathorne, William Bernard. Mr. Gladstone's Expostulation unravelled. London: Burns and Oates, 1875. C12.4. See also Ullathorne's earlier pastoral letter, 2046.

2090. Walsh, William Joseph. Evidence given in the case of O'Keeffe v. M'Donald at the Wicklow Summer Assizes, 1875. Dublin: McGlashan & Gill, 1875. C17.13. I. See 2035.

WORK BY UNIDENTIFIED AUTHOR

2091. Anon. An exposition of the Church in view of recent difficulties and controversies and the present needs of the age. London: Basil Montagu Pickering, 1875. C18.8. Argues that the
"Latin-Celtic" races are in apostasy, and that the future of
the Roman Catholic Church lies with the Saxon races and the
"mixed Saxons"--Germany, England, and the United States.

1876

2092. De Lisle, Ambrose Phillipps. On the perpetual belief of the
Catholic Church of Christ concerning the office and authority
of S. Peter. N.l., n.p., n.d. C20.8. I. From the Union
Review (1876). A Catholic review of Gladstone's Vaticanism
(London: Murray, 1875). Cf. 2063.

2093. Fottrell, George. The Irish judges and the Irish chairmen.
Dublin: M'Glashan and Gill, 1876. NL80.5. On judicial reform in Ireland; reprinted from the Fortnightly Review (March
1875).

2094. Harper, Thomas. Evidence and certainty, in their relation to
conceptual truth; a lecture delivered before the Catholic
Academia, in Manchester, on Tuesday, February 29th, 1876. Manchester: J. Roberts, n.d. NL22.4. I.

2095. Sandys, Richard Hill. In the beginning, remarks on certain
modern views of the creation; part II. London: Basil Montagu
Pickering, 1876. NL26.13. I. A sequel to 2084.

2096. Tondini de Quarenghi, Cesare. Études sur la question religieuse de Russie; la prière et l'appui du Saint-Siége et de
l'episcopat dans l'oeuvre de la réunion des Églises; notice
historique sur l'association de prières en l'honneur de Marie
Immaculée pour le retour de l'Église Gréco-Russe a l'unité
Catholique par le P. Cæsarius Tondini de Quarenghi. Paris:
E. Plon, 1876. NL82.17. I. Pages uncut. The French version
of 2088.

WORK BY UNIDENTIFIED AUTHOR

2097. C., R. The infallible Church; a full reply. London: Lane &
Son, 1876. C10.2. A defense of Manning's The Temporal Mission
of the Holy Ghost and a response to the exchange of correspondence between Lord Redesdale and Manning in the Daily Telegraph.

1877

2098. Barnes, Lavinia Fairfax. Mes premières et dernières impressions de Bruxelles, écrites dans une lettre improvisée dès
mon retour en Angleterre. N.l., n.p., 1877. NL79.7.
Corrections in ink.

2099. Breen, J. D. Anglican orders: are they valid? A letter to a
friend. London: Burns, Oates, 1877. NL18.21. Breen was a

Benedictine.

2100. [Brittain, H.] One of the Working Classes, pseud. Thoughts concerning education: by one of the working classes. Birmingham: W. Downing, n.d. NL18.15. D? I.

2101. Brownlow, W. R. Bernard. Slavery in the Roman empire and its gradual abolition; a lecture. N.l., n.p., n.d. NL18.26. I.

2102. Neate, Charles. Besika Bay: a dialogue after the manner of Lucian, in Latin elegiacs. Oxford: James Parker, 1877. NL24.5. I.

2103. Newman, Francis William. Etruscan interpretation. N.l., n.p., n.d. NL81.3. "Reprinted from 'Fraser's Magazine,' for March 1877."

2104. Plummer, Alfred. Intemperate criticism; some remarks on an article in the Saturday Review on Mr. Plummer's edition of Dr. Döllinger's Hippolytus and Callistus. Durham: Andrews n.d. NL25.21. A reply to a review critical of Plummer's translation of Döllinger's Hippolytus and Kallistus in the Saturday Review, 18 Aug. 1877.

2105. Sandys, Richard Hill. In the beginning, remarks on certain modern views of the creation; part III. London: Basil Montagu Pickering, 1877. NL26.14. I. Pages uncut. Sequel to 2084. 2095.

1878

2106. Conestabile, Carlo, Count. Opere religiose e sociali in Italia; memoria del Conte Carlo Conestabile; traduzione dal testo francese. Padua: Tipografia del Seminario, 1878. NL79.18.

2107. Connolly, James. Catholic education; a sermon preached in the Church of the Passionist Fathers, St. Joseph's Retreat, Highgate, in aid of the poor schools of the Mission, on Sunday, November 13, 1870. London: Burns, Oates, 1870. NL19.16. I.

2108. Jenkins, Robert Charles. Harvey: and his claims as a discoverer; a lecture, delivered at Folkstone on the three-hundredth anniversary of his birth (April 1st, 1578). London: T. Richards, 1878. NL22.20. I.

2109. Jenkins, Robert Charles. St. Mary's Minster in Thanet, and St. Mildred. London: Mitchell and Hughes, 1878. NL22.19. I. Reprinted from Archæologia Cantiana, 12 (1878).

2110. Parker, James. Did Queen Elizabeth take "other order" in the "Advertisements" of 1566? A letter to Lord Selborne, in reply to His Lordship's criticisms on the "Introduction to the Revisions of the Book of Common Prayer." Oxford: James Parker, 1878. NL25.15. I. A reply to Roundell Palmer, Lord Selborne's remarks in Notes on the Liturgy of the English Church.

2111. Pusey, Edward Bouverie. The rule of faith as maintained by the Fathers, and the Church of England; a sermon preached before the University on the fifth Sunday after Epiphany 1851; with a preface on papal infallibility from Bossuet. Oxford: James Parker and Co., 1878. NL11.12.

2112. Pusey, Edward Bouverie. Un-science, not science, adverse to faith; a sermon preached before the University of Oxford on the twentieth Sunday after Trinity, 1878. Oxford: James Parker & Co., 1878. NL11.11. I.

2113. Ullathorne, William Bernard. The discourse at the solemn Requiem for His Holiness Pius IX., at St. Chad's Cathedral, Birmingham. Birmingham: E. M. & E. Canning, 1878. NL12.19.

2114. The Whitehall Review. "Rome's recruits": a list of Protestants who have become Catholics since the Tractarian Movement; re-printed, with numerous additions and corrections, from "The Whitehall Review" of September 28th, October 5th, 12th, and 19th, 1878. London: "The Whitehall Review," 1878. NL99.4.

WORK BY UNIDENTIFIED AUTHOR

2115. Historicus, pseud. Leo XIII. and the Jesuits: the complicated vexed, and chaotic situation! N.l., n.p., n.d. NL22.10. In-cludes criticisms of Cardinal Manning.

1879

2116. A[llnatt], C. F. Which is the true Church? London: Burns and Oates, 1879. NL19.3.

2117. Collette, Charles Hastings. Cardinal Newman; a chapter in the history of Dr. J. H. Newman's religious opinions. London: McGowan's Steam Printing Company, 1879. NL4.2. Violently anti-Newman.

2118. Harington, John. A short view of the state of Ireland, writ-ten in 1605 by Sir John Harington, Knt., and now first edited by Rev. W. Dunn Macray, M.A., F.S.A. Oxford and London: James Parker, 1879. NL80.11. No. 1 of the series, Anecdota Bodleiana: Gleanings from Bodleian MSS.

2119. Malais, Armand Jean Edouard. Des couleurs liturgiques. Dieppe: Paul Leprêtre, 1879. NL23.6.

2120. Parker, John Henry. Early history of Rome; remarks on the article in the "Edinburgh Review," No. 306, April, 1879; and another in the "Jahresbericht über die Fortschritte der classichen Alterthumswissenschaft, herausgegeben," von C. Bursian, 1878. N.l., n.p., n.d. NL25.12.

2121. Parker, John Henry. Notes on the dates of the paintings in the Roman catacombs. N.l., n.p., n.d. NL25.13. I. A reply to criticisms by J. S. Northcote in The Month and Catholic Review, 17, No. 68 (Aug. 1879), 597-99, where Parker is called "the pet archeologist of the Anglicanism of the present day."

2122. [Sing, Thomas.] The Shilling Fund; or a new and ready means of providing for several and pressing wants of the Catholic

Church in England. London: Washbourne, 1879. NL82.8. I.

1880

2123. Bellasis, Edward. On the laws of arms, chiefly in connection
with changes of name; a lecture. N.l., n.p., 1880. NL18.5.
On heraldry.

2124. Capecelatro, Alfonso. Epistola pastoralis ad clerum et
populum Campanum. N.l., n.p., 1880. NL25.11. I.

2125. King, Francis. The royal supremacy with reference to Convocation, the Court of Appeal, and the appointment of bishops,
historically examined in a letter to the Rt. Hon. W. E. Gladstone, M.P. London: Parker and Co., n.d. NL10.15. I.

2126. Meyrick, Thomas. My imprisonings; or, an apology for leaving
the Jesuits. N.l., n.p., n.d. NL23.24. "Privately printed."
Incomplete copy.

2127. Newman, Francis William. Royal Asiatic Society of Great Britain and Ireland; notes on the Libyan languages, in a letter
addressed to Robert N. Cust, Esq., Hon. Secretary R. A. S.
[London: Trübner,] 1880. NL81.10. I.

2128. Pieruzzini, Pirro. Alcune favole. Livorno: Gius. Meucci,
1880. NL81.16. Contains a letter to N from Pieruzzini, the
Nicaraguan consul.

2129. Ullathorne, William Bernard. Church music: a discourse given
in St. Chad's Cathedral on the half jubilee of its choir. London: Burns and Oates, 1880. NL12.20.

1881

2130. Broglie, Auguste Théodore Paul de, abbé. Le positivisme et
la science expérimentale; conférence faite au Salon des Œuvres
de Paris. Paris: Imprimerie de la Société des Publications
Périodiques, 1881. NL18.17. "Extrait des Annales de Philosophie Chrétienne."

2131. Goldie, Francis. A bygone Oxford. London: Burns and Oates,
1881. NL28.32.

2132. Morris, William Bullen. The apostle of Ireland and his modern
critics; by W. B. Morris, priest of the Oratory, with an introductory letter by Aubrey De Vere. London: Burns & Oates,
1881. NL23.31. I.

2133. Pusey, Edward Bouverie. Unlaw in judgements of the Judicial
Committee and its remedies; a letter to the Rev. H. P. Liddon,
D.D., Canon of S. Paul's. 2nd ed. London: Parker & Co.,
1881. NL11.13.

2134. Reilly, Robert. Lectures by Professor Cryan, F.K.Q.C.P.I.,
M.R.I.A.; edited with memoir, etc. Dublin: M. H. Gill and

Son, 1881. NL26.2.

2135. Russell, Edward Richard Russell, Baron. The independent prerogative of the understanding in the domain of moral judgement,
being the inaugural address delivered at the commencement of
the seventeenth session of the Literary and Philosophical
Society of Liverpool. N.l., n.p., n.d. NL26.9. I.

2136. Ward, William George. The extent of free will. London: Wyman
& Sons, 1881. NL8.5. Sent by Ward. From the Dublin Review
(July 1881).

1882

2137. Perraud, Adolphe Louis. Les défenseurs de la Cité de Dieu;
discours prononcé le 11 août 1882, dans la cérémonie de
cloture du Congrès des Œuvres Ouvrières. Autun: Dejussieu
Père et Fils, 1882. NL25.18. Perraud was Bishop of Autun.

2138. Pusey, Edward Bouverie. "Blessed are the meek"; a sermon
preached at the opening of the chapel of Keble College, on S.
Mark's Day, 1876. 2nd ed. Oxford: Parker, 1882. NL99.19.
I.

2139. Soderini, Edoardo. La quistione [sic] egiziana e l'Inghilterra. Rome: Editrice Romana, 1882. NL82.10. I.

WORK BY UNIDENTIFIED AUTHOR

2140. A Lady, pseud. Our journey to the Chapel of Our Lady of Knock.
Dublin: M. H. Gill & Son, 1882. NL80.16.

1883

2141. Blunt, Wilfred Scawen. The wind and the whirlwind. London:
Kegan Paul, Trench, 1883. NL79.9. A religious poem.

2142. Carreras, Luis. Los Duques de la Torre y el casamiento de
su hijo. Paris: Galvez y Bardaji, 1883. NL79.13. Most
pages uncut.

2143. Hillier, W. Should Christians support Mr. Bradlaugh, the
avowed atheist, in his attempt to get into Parliament?
Report of a lecture delivered by the Rev. W. Hillier, minis-
ter of the Baptist Chapel, Bartholomew St., Exeter, in the
Royal Public Rooms, Exeter, March 2nd, 1883. 2nd ed. Exeter:
Exeter "Gazette and Telegram," n.d. NL99.30.

2144. Jenkins, Robert Charles. A few thoughts on the report of the
Ecclesiastical Courts' Commission, in a letter addressed to
Sir Walter James, Bart., of Betteshanger. Folkstone: R.
Goulden, n.d. NL99.31. I.

2145. Jenkins, Robert Charles. From the death of St. Athanasius to
the death of St. Basil and the Council of Constantinople

(A.D. 373-381); a chapter of ecclesiastical history. London: Kegan Paul, Trench, 1883. NL80.15.

1246. Lindsay, Colin. Mary Queen of Scots and her marriage with Bothwell; seven letters to the "Tablet." London: Burns and Oates, 1883. NL80.21. Sent to N.

2147. Newman, Francis William. A Christian commonwealth. London: Trübner, 1883. NL24.8.

2148. Rambouillet, abbé. La consubstantialité et le dogme de la Trinité. Amiens: Rousseau-Leroy, 1883. NL26.1. I. Pages uncut. "Extrait de la Revue des Sciences Ecclésiastiques."

2149. Soderini, Edoardo. Leone XIII, l'Irlanda e l'Inghilterra. Rome: Editrice Romana, 1883. NL82.9. I.

1884

WORK BY UNIDENTIFIED AUTHOR

2150. An Irish Catholic Layman, pseud. Letters of an Irish Catholic layman; being an examination of the present state of Irish affairs in relation to the Irish Church and the Holy See, (1883-4). 7th ed. Dublin: J. J. Lalor, n.d. NL22.18. D?

1885

2151. Domenichetti, Richard Hippisley. The Thames; Newdigate Prize poem, 1885. Oxford: A. Thomas Shrimpton and Son, 1885. NL20.8. I.

2152. King, F. Wilson. Adelbert of Bremen; a sketch of his life. Birmingham: Herald Press, n.d. NL22.30. I. Corrections in ink. "Reprinted from the Proceedings of the Birmingham Philosophical Society. Vol. IV., Part II., Page 355."

2153. Menet, John. Rest in the tabernacle of God; a sermon preached in Farnham Church, on the thirteenth Sunday after Trinity, August 30th, 1885, being the day after the funeral of the Rev. William John Copeland, B.D., Rector of Farnham. Bishop's Stortford: Arthur Boardman, 1885. NL23.21.

1886

2154. Broglie, Auguste Théodore Paul de, abbé. Les progrès de l'apologétique; leur nécessité et leurs conditions. Paris: Annales de Philosophie Chrétienne, 1886. NL18.16. I. Pages uncut. "Extrait des Annales de Philosophie Chrétienne."

2155. Broglie, Auguste Théodore Paul de, abbé. L'histoire religieuse d'Israël et la nouvelle exégèse rationaliste. Paris: Annales de Philosophie Chrétienne, 1886. NL18.18. Sent by de Broglie.

2156. Joanne Chrysostomo, abbot. *Vita metrica Sancti Patris Nor-*
berti. Naumur: Viduæ F. J. Dounfils, 1886. NL26.28.

2157. Newman, Francis William. The new crusades; or, duty of the
Church to the world; addressed especially to ministers of
religion. Nottingham: Stevenson, Bailey, and Smith, 1886.
NL81.9.

2158. [Salmon, John.] S. J., pseud. The round towers of Ireland;
their origin and uses. Belfast: D. T. Doherty, 1886. NL22.26.

2159. Thomas, Léon Benoît Charles. *L'Église et la société moderne*
d'après l'encyclique de Léon XIII, suivi d'un discours sur
Jeanne d'Arc. Paris: Douniol, 1886. NL26.6. I. Pages uncut.

1887

2160. Broglie, Auguste Théodore Paul de, abbé. *L'histoire reli-*
gieuse d'Israël et la nouvelle exégèse rationaliste, II.
Paris: Annales de Philosophie Chrétienne, 1887. NL18.19. Sent
by de Broglie. Sequel to 2155.

2161. Bryce, James, ed. La Vita Justiniani di Teofilo Abate (nel
Codice Barberiniano XXXVII, 49). Rome: R. Società Romana di
Storia Patria, 1887. NL79.10. I. Most pages uncut.

2162. Hurter, Hugh. The Catholic doctrine about Hell, from the
Compendium of Dogmatic Theology by H. Hurter, S. J.; trans-
lated by Kenelm Digby Best, Congr. Orat. London: Burns and
Oates, 1887. NL22.9.

2163. Parker, John. The authority of the apostolic traditions as
expounded by the Council of Trent. London: Church Printing
Company, n.d. NL81.14. I.

2164. Parker, John. The Holy Scriptures in the Church of Rome.
London: Church Printing Company, n.d. NL81.15.

2165. Reade, Compton. The bridge of souls. Hereford: Jakeman and
Carver, n.d. NL82.20. I.

2166. Robert, Charles. Encore la non-universalité du Déluge. Paris:
Berche & Tralin, 1887. NL81.18. Offprint from the Revue des
Questions Scientifiques (Oct. 1887). Robert was an Oratorian
from Rennes.

2167. Vacant, J. M. A. Le magistère ordinaire de l'Église et ses
organes. Paris: Delhomme et Briguet, 1887. NL82.19. I.
Pages uncut.

2168. Vennekens, F. Necessité d'une restauration du pouvoir temporel des Papes, par l'abbé F. Vennekens, docteur en Philosophie,
bachelier en Théologie; quatrième édition revue et augmentée
précédee de la lettre de S. S. le Pape Léon XIII à S. Ém. le
Cardinal Rampolla, Secrétaire d'État (15 Juin 1887). 4th ed.
Brussels: A. Vandenbroeck, 1887. NL82.21.

1888

2169. Brownlow, William Robert. Christmas with Bishop Grandisson; or, the services in Exeter Cathedral, A.D. 1368. Plymouth: W. Brendon and Son, 1888. NL18.23. I.

2170. Kelly, Thomas. The rival claims of Catholicism & Protestantism. Dublin: M. H. Gill & Son, 1888. NL22.28.

1889

2171. Axon, William E. A. On General Gordon's copy of Newman's "Dream of Gerontius," a paper read before the Manchester Literary Club on Monday, November 12th, 1888. N.l., n.p., 1889. NL79.6. "Not published."

2172. Broglie, Auguste Théodore Paul de, abbé. La vraie religion; sa définition, les conditions de son existence, ses caractères distinctifs. Paris: Annales de Philosophie Chrétienne, 1889. NL18.20.

2173. Winthrop, Augusta Clinton. "The bugle-call" and others. Boston: W. B. Clarke, 1889. NL27.19. Inscribed with some annotation by the author.

1890

2174. [Catholic Truth Society.] Manchester dialogues; first series; I: the pilgrimage. N.l., n.p., n.d. NL23.1. I. Lacks title-page. This and the following three pamphlets came out of the Catholic Truth Society's Conference at Manchester, 14-15 October 1889. All four "dialogues" concern Catholic teaching on miracles.

2175. [Catholic Truth Society.] Manchester dialogues; first series; II: are miracles going on still? N.l., n.p., n.d. NL23.2.

2176. [Catholic Truth Society.] Manchester dialogues; first series; III: Popish miracles tested by the Bible. N.l., n.p. n.d. NL23.3.

2177. [Catholic Truth Society.] Manchester dialogues; first series; IV: Popish miracles. N.l., n.p., n.d. NL23.4.

2178. Pallen, Condé B. The Catholic Church and socialism; a solution of the social problem. St. Louis: B. Herder, n.d. NL25.10. I.

Author Index
and
Subject Index

AUTHOR INDEX

Anonyms and pseudonyms are
listed at the end of the author index.